"*Reading the Gospels* is written in clear and engaging prose. The preliminary discussion of method, historical background, the historical Jesus, and the formation of the Gospel tradition are clear and concise and open up access to the Gospels rather than being dry material that distracts from the larger goal. It walks the fine line between opening the Gospels to the reader and supplanting or competing with them. McMahon discusses the historical backgrounds, theological themes, and summaries of the narrative flow for each Gospel.

"The overall tone of the work is inviting. It does not talk down to students or make biblical study seem like an arcane province of specialists, but invites readers into the activity of reading and thinking about the Gospels in conversation with others. The text articulates a Christian and Catholic understanding of the Gospels in ways that allow both Christians and non-Christians to participate in the conversation."

—David A. Bosworth, assistant professor of old testament, The Catholic University of America

"The opening chapters of *Reading the Gospels* provide students with the foundational material they will need in their encounter with the Gospel text. McMahon's explanation of the origins of the historical-critical method and the ways that contemporary scholars use it in their work with the Gospels is clear and concise. Similarly, his treatment of the historical Jesus gives students a connection to the world in which Jesus and the evangelists lived so that they can understand the text as it is written and interpret it for our own times. An abundance of sidebars and summary boxes provide students with essential tools for their study without cluttering the main text. *Reading the Gospels* is an excellent introduction to the study of the Gospels for undergraduate students."

—Linda S. Harrington, assistant professor of theology, Briar Cliff University

Reading the Gospels

Biblical Interpretation in the Catholic Tradition

Christopher McMahon

ANSELM
ACADEMIC

Created by the publishing team of Anselm Academic.

Cover images:
Main image from National Trust Photo Library I Art Resource, l\Ty
Batoni, Pompeo (1708-1787). Saint Matthew. Credit Line: Basildon Park; The I1iffe Collection (The National Trust).
Photo: John Hammond.
Basildon Park, Berkshire, Great Britain

Background Image royalty free from iStock

Printed in the United States of America

7038

ISBN 978-1-59982-007-1

To
Kelly, Katrina, Liv, and Em
For teaching me how to read the Gospels

Author Acknowledgments

At the outset, I would like to express my gratitude to the colleagues and friends to whom I have dedicated this book. They, among many others, have each taught me how to read the good news of Jesus, not through exegetical seminars or pious reflection, but through the dramatic, yet subtle and often quiet ways the gospel permeates each of their lives. The good news of Jesus has gently but powerfully illuminated my world through their example, and while the critical approach taken in this text might not find consensus among them, I hope they will discern, perhaps each in a different way, the impact of their witness on my attempt to provide not only a critical or academic reading of the Gospels but one that is also theological and life-forming. I pray that readers of this book will find friends and models such as those I have mentioned above, for without such people, the Gospels will at best remain mere curiosities regardless of the reading strategies or critical tools one might employ.

The publishing team at Anselm Academic, especially Jerry Ruff, Brad Harmon, Paul Peterson, and Jackie Captain, as well as other readers, worked tirelessly to improve the manuscript at every turn. Paul, in particular, caught several errors along the way and made suggestions that helped sharpen my presentation on several topics. The Christian Brothers, through the ministry of Saint Mary's Press and Anselm Academic, continue to leave their mark on the church in the United States, and all bishops, priests, religious, and laity owe the Christian Brothers a debt of gratitude for their tireless energy and selfless dedication in service of the gospel.

My colleagues at Saint Vincent College, particularly Patricia Sharbaugh and Rabbi Jason Edelstein, provided me with valuable feedback along the way and guided me to many useful sources. Rene Kollar, OSB, the dean of the School of Humanities and Fine Arts, and Jason King, the chair of the Department of Theology, supported a course reduction during one semester and, as with all of my endeavors, provided constant friendship and encouragement along the way. Kimberly Baker, Nathan Munsch, OSB, Campion Gavaler, OSB, Tom Hart, OSB, Jack Aupperle, and Elliott Maloney, OSB, also provided me with fellowship and encouragement throughout the course of this project. Additionally, Ashley Myers worked as a research assistant for one semester and helped track down several articles as I began work on the book.

The community of Scottdale Mennonite Church, my wife's church community and mine by marriage and fellowship, afforded me the opportunity to teach an adult Sunday school class and to preach during the months of writing the book, and they provided valuable feedback on my presentation of the material. The benefit of being part of two church communities, one Catholic and the other Mennonite, has made me doubly blessed over the years.

Finally, my wife, Debra Faszer-McMahon, has supplied the supreme and most consistent example of the gospel in my life. Moreover, her pedagogical acumen, her attention to detail, and her patient endurance have improved every aspect of this book and my life. As always, the efforts of those mentioned here do not diminish my responsibility for this text, and any errors or oversights are my own.

Publisher Acknowledgments

Thank you to the following individuals who reviewed this work in progress:

Micah D. Kiel
Saint Ambrose University, Davenport, Iowa

Paul Peterson
Religious editor, Wilmington, Delaware

Contents

In his classic essay "Fern-seed and Elephants," C. S. Lewis (1898–1963) decried the state of modern New Testament studies. He criticized its preoccupation with the history behind the biblical text as well as its general neglect of claims made by Scripture itself.[1] Lewis, admittedly only an amateur theologian, felt compelled to address the thoroughgoing skepticism of exegetes like Rudolf Bultmann (1884–1976) and others, who in the early part of the twentieth century insisted on reading the New Testament in a way that seemed to completely divide the life and ministry of Jesus from the proclamation of the early church. For Lewis, that way of reading seemed to neglect the realities to which the text bore witness. Lewis thought modern biblical interpretation had become preoccupied with generating complex hypotheses about the prehistory of the text and then baptizing those hypotheses with the certainty of empirical science. While Lewis admitted in his essay that the history behind the biblical text deserved attention, he also argued that such attention must be chastened and subordinated to the text itself.

Yet given both Lewis's critique of the method and his affirmation of the importance of the history behind the text, the question of exactly how to proceed remained unanswered. In the material that follows, a few of the basic insights and questions of modern Catholic biblical scholarship will provide a map of the issues at stake in the interpretation of the Bible in general and the Gospels in particular. This map will, in turn, help readers make sense of the structure and methodology used throughout the subsequent chapters of this book.

Modern Catholic Biblical Studies and the Historical-Critical Method

One cannot adequately explore the story of modern Catholic biblical interpretation here, but a few issues and episodes might help readers understand why reading the Bible is not nearly as straightforward as it might seem at first. In fact, the story of modern Catholic biblical interpretation intersects with the development of major philosophical and political movements, and it forms the center of important battles within the Catholic Church itself. In this section, a brief and functional description of the historical-critical method will set the stage for an overview of the method's controversial history and its vindication in the official teaching of the Catholic Church. Finally, this section briefly considers how the historical-critical method has emerged as a major point of contention within the Catholic Church and beyond.

The Historical-Critical Method (Loosely) Defined

The term *historical criticism* often leaves students understandably perplexed. The history of the term, its many meanings, and the variety of methodologies it embraces can almost rob or void the term of any concrete significance.[2] For the purposes of this work, one may define historical criticism or the historical-critical method as the disciplined attempt to place a given text into its appropriate historical, theological, and literary context. This disciplined activity centers on one basic question: What did the author(s) intend to convey when a given text was composed? Notice that the method does not begin with a question as to what meaning God may have intended to convey to the community of believers, to Israel or the church; instead, the question posed is straightforwardly historical and, therefore, quite limited. The task of the exegete, the interpreter of Scripture, is certainly theological in the end, but it begins simply as a historical question, for the interpreter wants to discern what an author intended to say to a particular audience—and neither the author nor the intended audience are available for direct questioning. One is simply left with the text itself, and from the text one must discover the answers to the question of context. That is, these answers must be "drawn out" of the text (this is the meaning of the word *exegesis*), though other texts may be available to help round out the picture of the history in question.

The phrase *the historical-critical method* has many layers. First, it refers to the study of a text in order to determine its historical accuracy. In fact, the word *critical* should be construed carefully. At its root, *critical* (from the Greek word *kriticos*, meaning "able to discern or judge") simply refers to the act of judging. So a historical-critical approach to the Gospels asks the interpreter to make a judgment about the text's relationship to historical events. For example, when Matthew and Luke each narrate the birth of Jesus in the opening chapters of their respective Gospels, they make certain claims about when and how that birth took place. Historical-critical exegesis

attempts to make judgments about how well these narratives reflect actual historical events. After all, the two narratives are, in several places, incompatible, and judging which narrative stands closer to the historical event becomes important for interpreting the material. To the extent that one argues that either Matthew or Luke presents a more historically accurate account of Jesus in one respect or another, one is practicing historical-critical exegesis. Depending on how the method is practiced, it can tend to separate historical events from the biblical narrative—hence Lewis's complaint: the judgments of historical-critical exegetes seemed to be consistently running against the historicity of the biblical narratives.

Second, the historical-critical method also makes judgments about how various historical factors helped shape the biblical text. For example, historical-critical exegetes will ask questions about the sources used to compose a given biblical passage. Sometimes these sources can come from the broader culture, or sometimes the source can be another biblical text. How those sources have been edited or redacted also deserves serious consideration. Historical-critical exegetes may also ask questions about the "form" of a biblical passage. For example, one might ask if a given text is poetry as opposed to prose. If so, what would the identification of poetry as the genre of a biblical text mean for its interpretation?

Third, the historical-critical method attempts to examine the identity of the author of a text and the intended audience insofar as the text holds clues for the interpreter. Obviously, some texts better lend themselves to concrete and specific contextualization than other texts. For example, the book of Job in the Old Testament contains no concrete historical markers, and scholars have assigned dates as early as the eighth century BCE and as late as the second century BCE; the concrete historical circumstances of

Job remain extremely vague. In contrast, Paul's First Letter to the Corinthians contains enough historical referents and markers to allow scholars to place it at a very particular time and place: it was addressed to the fledgling Christian community in Corinth around the year 54 CE, and the context of the audience can be inferred from the specific references Paul makes to reports and earlier letters sent to him by members of the Corinthian community.

In sum, the historical-critical method attempts to paint a picture of the world behind the text, including the intentions and processes involved in the creation of the text. One cannot overestimate the importance of this world behind the text, for it is the conviction of Christians everywhere that God's revelation, God's self-disclosure, occurs in the concrete circumstances of history. This conviction is at the heart of the Christian understanding of God's word, God's self-communication for the salvation of the world. Yet historical-critical exegesis can present the Christian tradition with some problems, and even dangers, as well.

THE WORD OF GOD AS A SYMPHONY

The expression *word of God* has several senses. What follows comes from the Roman Catholic synod of bishops (a representative gathering of bishops every few years), which set forth the document *The Word of God in the Life and Mission of the Church* to highlight the multiple meanings that the expression *word of God* has within the Christian tradition. In the adapted excerpts below, one will notice that the word of God is not exclusively or even primarily understood as a text.

a. In Revelation, the Word of God is the Eternal Word of God, the Second Person of the Most Blessed Trinity, the Son of the Father, the basis for intra- and extra-communication of the Trinity.

b. Therefore, the created world *"tells of the glory of God"* (Ps 19:1); everything is his voice (cf. Sir 46:17; Ps 68:34).

c. *"The Word became flesh"* (Jn 1:14): The Word of God par excellence, the ultimate and definitive Word, is Jesus Christ.

d. In view of the Word who is the Son-Incarnate, the Father spoke in ancient times to the fathers through the prophets (cf. Heb 1:1). Through the power of the Holy Spirit, the apostles continue to proclaim Jesus and his gospel.

e. Sacred Scripture, under divine inspiration, unites Jesus-the-Word to the words of the prophets and apostles. . . . Through the charism of divine inspiration, the books of Sacred Scripture have a direct, concrete power of appeal not possessed by other texts or holy writings.

f. But the Word of God is not locked away in writing. Even though Revelation ended with the death of the last apostle, the Word-Revealed continues to be proclaimed and heard throughout church history.

The Word of God displays all the qualities of true communication between persons. For example, it is informative, because God communicates his truth; expressive, because God makes plain his manner of thinking, loving and acting; and finally, it is an appeal addressed by God to a person to be heard and given a response in faith.

—THE TWELFTH ORDINARY GENERAL ASSEMBLY OF THE SYNOD OF BISHOPS, *THE WORD OF GOD IN THE LIFE AND MISSION OF THE CHURCH*

Problems with the Historical-Critical Method

For a variety of reasons, historical-critical exegesis has endured a troubled history within Roman Catholic circles. In fact, the advent of historical-critical exegesis roughly coincides with the period known as the Enlightenment, a movement that extended from the late seventeenth to the early nineteenth centuries and sought to emancipate human beings from structures of authority in order to facilitate a more open and dynamic society.[3] This movement generally viewed Christianity and its claim to ultimate authority with great suspicion, especially since both Catholic and Protestant churches still tended to subordinate human reason to the demands of revelation as it was articulated through religious authorities (e.g., individual pastors, church hierarchy, doctrine, the Bible). Moreover, Christian leaders seemed to be invested in the status quo, the established order of society that tended to guard

THE FOUR SENSES OF SCRIPTURE

Although John Cassian (360–453) originated the concept of the *four senses of Scripture* (*Conferences*, 14. 8), his insights built upon the work of Alexandrian theologians like Origen (c. 250), who emphasized the manifold spiritual dimensions of the biblical texts. For his part, Cassian distinguished three distinct spiritual senses of the text along with its literal or historical meaning. The four senses of Scripture became the hallmark of medieval Christian exegesis (see also Thomas Aquinas, *Summa Theologica* Ia, q. 1, a. 100).

The Historical or Literal Sense

The historical or literal interpretation of the text stands in sharp contrast to its spiritual meaning. The historical or literal sense of the text should not be confused with a naïve biblical fundamentalism or literalism. Rather, the literal meaning of the text was simply the meaning of the text that could be gained by looking at the text in its literary context. This was considered the most banal sense of the text because it could be accessed without the "eyes of faith."

The Allegorical Sense

The first of the three spiritual senses of the text is the allegorical. For the ancients, the literal or historical sense of Scripture was the least important. The allegorical sense functioned as a doorway to the exploration of some mystery or doctrine of the faith. A prominent example of this approach to Scripture can be found in Scripture itself: in Galatians 4:21–31 the Apostle Paul offers an allegorical reading of the story of Sarah and Hagar from Genesis 16 and 21. In this example, the two women are not considered as individuals, but instead represent contrasting approaches to the relevance of the Mosaic Law for Gentile Christians (see also Midrash within Judaism).

The Anagogical Sense

The anagogical sense bolsters the allegorical by offering a "deeper" spiritual sense whereby Scripture discloses the object of Christian hope: heaven and union with God.

The Moral or Tropological Sense

The tropological or moral sense of Scripture provides the reader with instruction on how to improve one's life and how to live practically. Cassian used the city of Jerusalem to exemplify how one word in Scripture could have four

continued

THE FOUR SENSES OF SCRIPTURE *continued*

different senses: (1) historically, it is "the city of the Jews"; (2) allegorically, it is the church of Christ; (3) anagogically, it is the heavenly city of God; (4) tropologically (i.e., morally), it refers to the human soul. Each biblical text, therefore, carries multiple meanings, all held together in dynamic tension. This fourfold approach to biblical interpretation became so widespread that a medieval Latin maxim, attributed to the thirteenth-century writer Augustine of Dacia, became a definitive hermeneutic for Scripture:

Littera gesta docet; quid credas allegoria;
Moralis quid agas; quo tendas anagogia.

[The literal sense teaches deeds; allegory what you are to believe; the moral sense what you are to do; the anagogical sense where you are going.]

the privileged role of the church. Quite understandably, church authorities saw the Enlightenment and its approach to the Bible, the central authority in the Christian tradition, as hostile and dangerous.

Many scholars of the modern era pursued the practice of historical-critical exegesis as a way of unmasking traditional Christianity as a fraud, or at least a mistake. By means of this sort of open hostility, the Enlightenment helped to provoke two extreme positions on the relationship between faith and reason within the Christian community. On the one hand, many Christians began to assert that human beings could only come to know who God was and what God wanted through the use of human reason. All intermediaries like Scripture, church doctrine, theology, bishops, and popes were obstacles to the true knowledge of God. This position became known as Rationalism, and the rationalists held the conviction that any claim about God that did not conform to demands of human reason was dubious at best. When rationalists approached the Bible, they tended to dismiss the miraculous elements and reduced the biblical material to a set of timeless truths couched in primitive mythological or symbolic language—these primitive elements were dispensable and the timeless truths became accessible and affirmable by human reason.

Predictably, the rise of the Enlightenment and Rationalism created a backlash in many quarters, and in the Christian churches this backlash was evident in the emergence of Pietism and its corresponding suspicion of human reason. For Pietist Christians, the only way one could know God and God's will was through faith and a corresponding *sacrificium intellectus* ("sacrifice of the intellect"). Also later known as Fideism, this outlook was shared across confessional lines. In fact, even the phrase *sacrificium intellectus* is a paraphrase of the Jesuit obligation to subordinate one's mind to become obedient to the gospel (Jesuits are an order of priests in the Catholic Church). Among many subgroups within various Christian communities (e.g., Catholic Jansenists, Lutheran Pietists, Anglican Methodists) various shades of Fideism became part of their life and theology, and the echoes of this movement still permeate contemporary Christianity. Pietism sowed the seeds that would eventually become biblical fundamentalism in the late-nineteenth century, with its suspicion of any attempt to attenuate the biblical text and thereby the demands of Christian faith.

The Catholic Church was certainly not immune from these debates, and as in the case of the scientist Galileo Galilei in the seventeenth century and the modernist controversy in the nineteenth and twentieth centuries, it did not always steer a middle course in the debates either. It must be said, however, that the Catholic Church had long asserted that there was a close relationship between faith and reason, a position emphasized in the work of great theologians like Anselm of Canterbury and Thomas Aquinas in the Middle Ages. In the nineteenth century, the Catholic Church found it necessary to address and clarify the issue once again, and at the First Vatican Council (Vatican I, 1869–1870), it declared the inadequacy of both Rationalism and Fideism and clearly reaffirmed the inherent goodness and health of human reason and the manner in which both reason and faith direct human beings toward God. This reaffirmation, which might seem far removed from the questions of biblical interpretation, actually helped to set the stage for a positive assessment of the historical-critical method and its potential as a tool for biblical interpretation in the twentieth century. In 1943, Pius XII issued *Divino afflante spiritu* ("Inspired by the Divine Spirit"), an encyclical letter that promoted the limited use of the historical-critical method within the Catholic Church. In the years following this encyclical, however, there was a heated debate within the Catholic Church concerning how far one could pursue historical-critical exegesis and still remain faithful to Christian doctrine. It was not until the Second Vatican Council (Vatican II, 1962–1965), which issued *Dei verbum* (*The Dogmatic Constitution on Divine Revelation*), that the historical-critical method was officially adopted as a necessary means by which one should interpret the Bible. The determination of the necessity of the method and its connection to a doctrine of divine revelation demands attention.

Historical Criticism and Divine Revelation in *Dei Verbum*

The doctrine of revelation quickly became one of the most controversial issues confronted by the bishops gathered at Vatican II. In the period leading up to the council, the commission responsible for drafting texts for the bishops to discuss devised a document that reflected the concerns of the counter-Reformation; that is, it reflected the theology that grew out of Roman Catholic reactions to the doctrines of the Protestant reformers. So whereas many Protestant theologians tended to emphasize the sole authority of the Bible for Christian living, Roman Catholics had emphasized the dual roles of Scripture and tradition. The document drafted by the commission prior to the council actually characterized the economy of revelation as comprising two distinct "fonts," or sources, of divine revelation. The bishops at the council rejected this approach as theologically inadequate and set about the long and arduous task of reformulating the document. At the end of the council's last session, the final document was approved, *Dei verbum*. The approach to revelation expressed in that document broadly reflects the doctrine of revelation as understood by Christian theologians today.

Dei verbum begins with a discussion of the nature and purpose of divine relation by focusing on the deep connection between revelation and salvation. According to the document, the ultimate purpose of revelation is that human beings might "come to share in the divine nature" (see 2 Peter 1:4).[4] As described in *Dei verbum*, revelation does not center on the disclosure of information, though it does include information (knowledge is always constitutive of any relationship). Rather, divine revelation constitutes a personal communication in which God shares all that God is. In revelation, God creates communion or fellowship with human beings, and it is in this fellowship that human beings come to know and share in who God is. The realization of this purpose, therefore, cannot be reduced to information or tactics. The communication of the divine plan, and the plan itself for that matter, is relational and, therefore, necessarily historical for human beings. Revelation unfolds through an economy of word and deed.

> [T]he deeds wrought by God in the history of salvation manifest and confirm the teaching and realities signified by the words, while the words proclaim the deeds and clarify the mystery contained in them. By this revelation then, the deepest truth about God and the salvation of man shines out for our sake in Christ, who is both the mediator and the fullness of all revelation. (*Dei verbum*, 2)

Human experience itself teaches that relationships are constituted through both word and deed. In much the same manner the words of Scripture and the deeds of history illuminate each other so that event and text stand together in the context of the church's relationship with God. For Christians, revelation culminates, or finds its fullest expression, in the person of Jesus. Jesus is the supreme Word and deed of God, and the life of Jesus is the definitive revelation of God. In Jesus, Christians come to know God and are drawn into a divine fellowship or communion, and it is this communion that forms the heart of the church's teaching on revelation.

The doctrine of revelation, as articulated in *Dei verbum*, locates Scripture within the context of the communion that represents the goal of God's revelation, emphasizing Scripture as relational rather than simply informational. The texts that make up the canon of Scripture uniquely express the preaching of the apostles and bear witness to the unrepeatable events of Christ's saving work. Yet the life of the church is inseparable from the texts of Scripture; this

is what Catholics mean when they speak of the relationship between Scripture and tradition.

> The Church, in her teaching, life and worship, perpetuates and hands on to all generations all that she herself is, all that she believes. . . . The words of the holy fathers witness to the presence of this living tradition, whose wealth is poured into the practice and life of the believing and praying Church. Through the same tradition the Church's full canon of the sacred books is known, and the sacred writings themselves are more profoundly understood and unceasingly made active in her. (*Dei verbum*, 8)

This entire second chapter of *Dei verbum* is dedicated to exploring the way the lives of the faithful, in conjunction with pastors (i.e., bishops), impact the understanding of the faith and the understanding of Scripture. Tradition, therefore, is not something separate from Scripture; rather, it is part of the process of reading Scripture, reflecting on Scripture, and reflecting on the experience of faith that is personal, but also more than personal. It is a reflection on a faith that belongs to a people that God has called together from throughout the world and from across history. It is through this historical and communal process of formation that "the believing and praying Church" comes to understand and live more fully the gospel.

Biblical interpretation itself is also concrete and historical, because human living and the human experience of God's revelation are equally concrete and historical. Although the church always affirms that God is the ultimate author of the Bible, the following excerpts demonstrate that a careful balance must be achieved when describing the relationship and agency between God as author and the historical human authors in the creation of the biblical texts.

> In composing the sacred books, God chose [human beings] and while employed by [God]

they made use of their powers and abilities, so that with [God] acting in them and through them, they, as true authors, consigned to writing everything and only those things which [God] wanted.

. . . It follows that the books of Scripture must be acknowledged as teaching solidly, faithfully and without error that truth which God wanted put into the sacred writings for the sake of salvation. . . .

However, since God speaks in Sacred Scripture through [human beings] in human fashion, the interpreter of Sacred Scripture, in order to see clearly what God wanted to communicate to us, should carefully investigate what meaning the sacred writers really intended, and what God wanted to manifest by means of their words. (*Dei verbum*, 11, 12)

The exegete must attempt to discern the meaning the ancient writers intended to express given their circumstances and their culture. The document even suggests that there is a rough analogy between the manner in which the Word became flesh in Christ and how the Holy Spirit works through human authors in the production of Scripture. While God remains the ultimate author of Scripture, human beings are nonetheless "true authors," and it is incumbent upon anyone who interprets Scripture to ascertain the intention of the historical human author. This is a cumbersome task and an elusive goal, but it is a necessary part of biblical interpretation. The necessity of the method was reaffirmed in the 1993 document "On the Interpretation of the Bible in the Church," issued by the Pontifical Biblical Commission (PBC) in response to growing dissatisfaction with the historical-critical method. The PBC left no doubt about the place of the method in Catholic exegesis: "The historical-critical method is the indispensable method for the scientific study of the meaning of ancient texts."[5]

A Few Theological Points on Inspiration and Interpretation

According to the doctrine of inspiration noted in *Dei verbum* and generally articulated across the Christian tradition, God must be recognized as the true author of the Bible. While all Christians affirm the inspired character of the sacred books (that is, the divine authorship of the books), they disagree on precisely *how* to understand God's authorship and the corresponding role of the human authors. Most approaches to the problem have focused on the individual human author in what is often called an "author-centered approach."

Author-centered approaches to an understanding of inspiration focus on the relationship between God and the individual human author. According to some ancient approaches to the question of inspiration, the biblical author sat at a table with pen in hand while an angel dictated the text. God remained the undisputed author of the text and the human being had an instrumental role.

According to one interpretation of the idea of the human author as instrumental cause, the human being is simply the pen by which God inscribes the biblical text. This idea of instrumental causality leads to the claim that the words of Scripture themselves are preserved from all error because they are quite simply the words of God. The human author was as insignificant to the process by which the books were written as a pen is to a student taking notes in class. The pen may frustrate the student's efforts to some extent, but it makes no positive contribution to the process of writing. The text is therefore removed from the human context of both its composition and its canonization.

This understanding of instrumental causality often yields a doctrine of plenary (i.e., full) verbal inerrancy wherein God is really the sole author of the biblical text so that the text can contain no errors whatsoever. The following

ALLEGORY, SENSUS PLENIOR, AND EXCESS MEANING

In medieval theology, scholastics developed what was called "the fuller sense" (*sensus plenior*) of a biblical text. This fuller sense went beyond the intention of the author. Raymond Brown defines the *sensus plenior* as "the deeper meaning [of the text], intended by God but not clearly intended by the human author, that is seen to exist in the words of Scripture when they are studied in the light of further revelation or of development in the understanding of revelation."[6] This approach to the fuller meaning of the text developed out of the scholastic understanding of instrumental causality, whereby God used the words of human beings to communicate meaning beyond the intent of the human author. In some ways, it is similar to the allegorical approach championed in Alexandrian theology in the early centuries of the church. While the *sensus plenior* has not played a significant role in contemporary discussions, the insights of Paul Ricoeur and his emphasis on the excess or surplus meaning of a text resonates strongly with the concerns articulated as *sensus plenior*.

espoused the doctrine of plenary verbal inerrancy. Rather, they have adopted an understanding of inspiration that emphasizes both the limiting and the creative roles of the human author. The human being is still the instrument by which God authors the text, but in this interpretation of instrumental causality there is an emphasis on the creativity and limitations of the instrument, the human author. This approach to inspiration yields a doctrine of limited verbal inerrancy. Limited inerrancy suggests that the text of Scripture is infallible with regard to its teaching on matters of faith and salvation. On matters of history and science the Bible may in fact be erroneous because while God is the ultimate author of Scripture, human beings, as instruments of the author, make choices in the creative expression of God's word and may be limited by a variety of factors like the lack of adequate scientific or historical knowledge. This is precisely the point made in *Dei verbum*, number 12, when reference is made to the culture of the human authors and "customary forms of speech." In order to interpret the Bible, one must develop a sense of the biblical author's historical, literary, and theological context.

Author-centered approaches to inspiration, however, ignore one fundamental element in any doctrine of inspiration: the role of the believing community, the people of God. The Catholic Church approaches the doctrine of inspiration not only from the perspective of the human author but also from the perspective of the human community. In fact, most of the biblical books are the result of multiple sources and the subsequent work of editors and scribes. For

quote helps explain how such instrumental versions of inspiration can lead to distorted and expansive claims of biblical inerrancy:

> Inerrancy follows from divine authority, period. For whatever God utters is without error. And the Bible is the Word of God. Therefore, the Bible is without error. But if this is so, then the inerrancy of the Bible cannot be lost by simply adding the human dimension. As long as it is God's word, then it is thereby inerrant, whether or not it is also the words of men.[7]

The authority and sovereignty of God, staples of Calvinist and much evangelical theology, control the reading of Scripture and discount any meaningful role played by the human and historical aspects of the biblical text.

The Catholic Church, and most other Christian churches, have often taken an author-centered approach to inspiration but have not example, modern theories about the origin of the Pentateuch emphasize the emergence of different traditions over the course of centuries (J, E, D, and P), and these sources were subsequently forged into five books rather late in time. Moreover, what is one to make of the various additions to already completed biblical texts made by scribes responsible for making copies of these texts over the course of centuries? For example, the story of the woman caught in adultery in John, chapter 8, was added by a scribe long after the Gospel had been written. Yet Christians still read this story as part of Scripture.

The Catholic Church teaches that Scripture is to be read and interpreted as part of a community of believers, because it is this community in which the Holy Spirit dwells. According to Karl Rahner (1904–1984) and other Catholic theologians, any understanding of the inspired character of Scripture must include an account of its composition, its canonization, and its continuing value within the dynamic Christian communities of different eras. In the following quote from his major work *Hearers of the Word*, Rahner dismisses the older notions of inspiration and instead offers an account of inspiration that places an emphasis on the relationship between revelation, the church, and Scripture.

> In the familiar interpretation of inspiration, God's intention would be achieved even more perfectly if man's function were but a secretary's. In our interpretation, the opposite is the case. A man [*sic*] intends to write a book, and he is to want to do this precisely according to God's ultimate intention. God's will is a supernatural and historical community of redemption, which finds its objective and self-realizing ultimate end in the book. And as he wills that community effectively and absolutely, historically and eschatologically, and in an historical process beginning anew in himself, God *eo ipso* is, in a real sense, an author.[8]

For Rahner and so many theologians today, the image of the biblical authors as God's secretaries fails to do justice to the complexities behind the formation of the biblical material and the process of canonization. Any adequate account of inspiration must account for God as the ultimate author while at the same time accounting for the historical and human character of the inspired texts. For Rahner, as seen in the quote above, God "of its (i.e., God's) very nature" (this is what the Latin phrase *eo ipso* means) is the author of the books because God wills the believing community into existence and guides it in history.

Biblical Interpretation in Crisis

Many theologians would agree that the past several decades have witnessed a crisis in biblical interpretation. This crisis is expressed by theologians from two distinct ends of the theological and political spectrum, even though their concerns are fairly similar. On the one side, the historical-critical method has suffered attacks from those who characterize it as vain and "modern" insofar as it seeks to establish singularity of meaning. The French philosopher Jacques Derrida (1930–2004) amplified this critique in a famous essay on the biblical story of the Tower of Babel (Genesis 11:1–9) in which he suggested that the imposition of diverse languages, which compromised the building of the tower, was no punishment; rather, it was a gift. For Derrida and other so-called post-modernists, the danger of the historical-critical method rests in its concern to define and limit the meaning of a text, thereby doing violence to the way the text and the reader play or interact.[9] At the other end of the spectrum, however, more "conservative" voices have assailed the historical-critical method precisely for its inability to bring the biblical text together with the living tradition of the believing community, the church. They argue that the method reduces the biblical text to a historical artifact while it downplays the notion that the text bears witness to God's revelation to human beings.

Although these critiques come from two ends of the political spectrum within the church, one must observe that the major critiques of the method made by both "sides" tend to focus on the power of the historical-critical method to limit and confine a text. In other words, a wide range of theologians agree that the historical-critical method is problematic insofar as it attempts to limit or to singularly "fix" the meaning of the biblical text. In what follows, a discussion of the criticism leveled from both ends of the spectrum will help readers begin to appreciate the difficulties and complexities involved in reading and interpreting the biblical text.

A Philosophical Critique of the Historical-Critical Method

The twentieth-century French philosopher and literary critic Roland Barthes (1915–1980) offered one of the most decisive critiques of historical-critical methods in his 1967 essay, "The Death of the Author."[10] In that essay, Barthes attacks any interpretive method that relies on an account of the author's identity, circumstances, views, and so on. In short, for Barthes, any attempt to reconstruct "the world behind the text" in an effort to distill the meaning of the text is dangerous. Barthes alleges that such an approach to the text, far from being technical and sophisticated, is actually ragged and even violent. In short, "to give a text an Author" is to assign a single interpretation to it and "to impose a limit on that text." Instead, Barthes argues, readers must recognize that in

the act of reading, of engaging the text, one separates the text from the author. To do this self-consciously is to liberate the text, to free it so that it might speak in all of its dimensions. Barthes capitalizes the word *Author* in the essay to emphasize the hegemonic power given to the author in relation to the text, and he uses the image of the text as a "tissue of quotations" assembled from a variety of sources, and not just the mind of an individual author. In fact, Barthes wants to avoid even assigning an "Author" to a text, believing that the connection between "author" and "authority" threatens to limit the power of the text. Rather, Barthes prefers to speak of the "scriptor," who may physically produce the text in some sense, but who is merely functional and stands at a distance from the text. The work is actually produced as a text, Barthes would argue, in the act of reading. So, in a sense, the text is rewritten with every reading:

> Once the Author is removed, the claim to decipher a text becomes quite futile. To give a text an Author is to impose a limit on that text, to furnish it with a final signified, to close the writing. Such a conception suits criticism very well, the latter then allotting itself the important task of discovering the Author (or its hypostases: society, history, psyche, liberty) beneath the work: when the Author has been found, the text is "explained"—victory to the critic. (Barthes, "The Death of the Author," 147)

The task of the interpreter is the discovery of "a multi-dimensional space." It is the job of the reader, the interpreter, to refuse all claims to ultimate meaning, to singular interpretations, and thereby refuse closure.

Certainly Barthes owes a debt to a number of predecessors who had earlier articulated concerns about assigning ultimate meaning to texts, but Barthes does stand at the head of the line when it comes to contemporary discussions about the interpretation of texts, along with other notables like Paul Ricoeur, Hans Georg Gadamer, Jacques Derrida, Michel Foucault, and numerous other critics. But for the purposes of this introduction, perhaps the most important voices have come from liberationist theologies. Feminist, Latin American, Asian, Womanist, Mujerista, and Black theologies all, to some extent, share the critical concerns of Barthes (or perhaps Barthes has articulated, from a philosophical perspective, what these movements, in their longer pre-histories, have been saying).

Now many have noted that one can take Barthes's position out of context and use it in a destructive and absurd spirit. After all, the context of any "scriptor's" activity plays a role in interpretation, but Barthes's point concerns the hegemonic role that the contextual approach has come to assume in modern interpretation. Particularly within the Christian tradition, history and historical claims are unavoidable and even a principal aspect of the traditional understanding of revelation. Such is the case, in particular, with feminist biblical hermeneutics as articulated by such luminaries as Elisabeth Schüssler Fiorenza and Rebecca Chopp.[11]

Within feminist theology and liberationist theologies in general, the interpretation of Scripture has been a point of contention. In some circles, there has been a distinct movement away from the historical-critical method as the means of getting to "the world behind the text." Like Barthes and others, these critics allege that an ideological concern guiding historical-critical approaches to the text seeks to fix a text and its interpretation in some objectified past. Such a concern stands in sharp contrast to those who emphasize the liberating power of the biblical material and its capacity to subvert all attempts to fix or stabilize meaning. Yet these critics are countered by many Christian theologians of various stripes who steer a middle course between the historical-critical method and the more radically post-modern and liberationist concerns articulated by others.

Schüssler Fiorenza, for example, recounts an anecdote about her encounter with a graduate student who decried the way her professors were introducing students to the interpretation of the Bible.[12] The student was concerned with the professors' interest in the history behind the text whereas, to her mind, the only important issue was the world "in front of the text"—that is, how the text proposes to transform the world. After all, the student reasoned, dead white men have been behind the emergence of the historical-critical method, and their ideological commitments seem to control its outcome. Schüssler Fiorenza, while sympathetic to the student's concerns, nonetheless cautioned the student against a full demonization of the historical-critical method. After all, Christian feminist theology and feminist hermeneutics, she argued, are invested in historical claims about the place of women in the ministry of Jesus and in the early Christian communities. For Schüssler Fiorenza and others, the problem with the historical-critical method is the ideologies associated with it and embedded in its approaches, but the concern to research, interpret, and write history more accurately, more fully, and more dynamically and with an eye to the creation of a more grace-filled future remains a central concern for all Christian theology. The Christian tradition has always maintained that God works in history, and, in particular, in the person of Jesus, to defeat the powers of violence and evil, and a refusal to deal adequately with historical questions has remained a heretical temptation since the first century (e.g., Docetism, Gnosticism, and so on).

THE DIFFERENT "WORLDS" OF THE BIBLICAL TEXT

The World behind the Text

This world is the object of historical-critical investigation. In this world, the questions the interpreter asks include: What was the author's intention? What were the historical, cultural, theological, and sociological factors that shaped the author's approach? What sources or traditions did the author use? How did the text get edited or redacted over time? Since the Christian tradition claims that God's revelation is realized in history through certain non-repeatable events, questions about "the world behind the text" are indispensable.

The World of the Text

The text itself provides a world for the interpreter. This world is not concerned about history or the world beyond the reader's own horizon. As the reader is attentive to the text, its structure, its "play," and its world, the reader becomes vexed and provoked. Biblical interpretation prizes the power of the text to engage readers apart from historical questions. Like a piece of music one encounters on the radio, one does not need to know the artist, the composer, or the original purpose of the music to be provoked by its musicality, its arrangement, and its character. So too it is with the biblical text.

The World in front of the Text

The Bible envisions a world that is not yet. It seeks to engage readers and hearers so that they may become agents of change and participate, in some anticipatory way, in the world that is not yet.

An Example

If one reads the Beatitudes in Matthew (5:3–10), there are at least three "worlds" into which one could group the questions that arise in the wake of that reading. First, one might ask about the ancient parallels between the *makarisms* or "happy sayings" of nonbiblical literature and find that Jesus (or Matthew) is imitating an ancient literary form, or one might compare the Beatitudes found in Matthew with those found in Luke in an effort to understand Matthew's sources and his editorial tendencies. In these cases, one is inquiring about "the world behind the text." Alternatively, as a reader notices the structure and flow of the passage, the careful balance between the present and future tenses in each verse, and the subtle word choices made by the evangelist, the reader is being attentive to "the world of the text." Finally, as one asks about how one might become a "peacemaker," or "pure of heart," or "poor in spirit" in one's life as an individual, or how these blessings might be visited on a community of people, then one seeks after "the world in front of the text." These three "worlds" are not totally separate one from the other. In fact, how one responds to questions or issues raised in one "world" will impact how one engages the other "worlds" of the text as well.

Cardinal Ratzinger (Benedict XVI) and the Historical-Critical Method

As the prefect for the Congregation for the Doctrine of the Faith (CDF), Joseph Cardinal Ratzinger (later to become Pope Benedict XVI) also served as the head of the Pontifical Biblical Commission (PBC) and the International Theological Commission (ITC), two advisory bodies composed of theologians from across the globe. Over more than two decades as the cardinal prefect for that most important congregation,

Ratzinger exercised considerable influence on theological matters, including the interpretation of Scripture. Ratzinger's prowess as a theologian made him an interesting, if controversial, choice to head the CDF. Critics worried that he would bring a commitment to a particular school of thought to his job as "watchdog." In doing so, he would not simply intervene where orthodoxy, or right teaching, was an issue; rather, his interventions would tend to reflect his own theological predilections more than any limited concern for orthodoxy. Many still disagree about how well Ratzinger did his job, but there is little debate about the influence he exerted on Roman Catholic theology at the end of the twentieth century, and his approach to biblical interpretation provides an interesting example of this influence.

In 1988, Ratzinger was invited to New York by the Erasmus Institute, an ecumenical think tank headed by Richard John Neuhaus, then a Lutheran minister, to deliver an address on biblical interpretation. The title of his talk was indicative of his concerns: "Biblical Interpretation in Crisis: On the Question of the Foundations and Approaches of Exegesis Today."[13] In that address, Ratzinger laments the way the historical-critical method had been freighted with philosophical and ideological presuppositions that tend to compromise its validity and orient it against the church. Of particular concern was the method's natural scientific tendency to reduce Scripture to a mere set of historical facts.

Ratzinger views the historical-critical method as an example of the hubris, or excessive pride, of modernity. Contemporary exegetes often seek a level of methodological precision that would yield conclusions of the same certainty as in the field of the natural sciences. Yet Ratzinger notes that within the realm of the natural sciences, there exists the so-called uncertainty principle, which should be applied to the historical-critical method. The uncertainty principle was developed by the German physicist Werner Heisenberg (it is often called the Heisenberg principle), who demonstrated that the outcome of a given experiment or measurement is inevitably influenced by the observer.[14] In the field of historical inquiry, the uncertainty principle suggests that there can be no simple reproduction of history *wie es eigentlich gewesen*—"as it actually was"—to borrow a famous phrase from Leopold von Ranke, the father of modern historical science. The historian or the interpreter, for that matter, always stands between the data and the account he or she renders, so that the subjectivity of the interpreter becomes decisive for the outcome. In other words, the subjectivity of the historian or the interpreter is the condition for the possibility of objectivity.

Ratzinger's constructive proposal for contemporary exegesis includes historical-critical exegesis, but it is to be disentangled from the Enlightenment philosophical presuppositions that have governed much of its implementation. Biblical interpretation must not operate on the analogy of the natural sciences; rather, attentive to the power and depth of the biblical text, the exegete must acknowledge the power of the word. Only with a developed openness to and sympathy with the text can the exegete engage the text with the possibility of encountering God. To exclude the encounter with God as a possibility from the outset is to fundamentally distort Scripture. Moreover, in line with *Dei verbum's* account of the economy of revelation, the inner connection between the event in history and the words of Scripture (as well as the tradition of the believing community) provides an important hermeneutical principle: the biblical text must be placed in its appropriate historical context, but the text must also be read in light of the total movement of history, with the centrality of God's revelation in Christ always playing the key role.

Although Ratzinger and liberationist critics come from opposite sides of the political spectrum within the church, they nonetheless share a common concern regarding the ideological baggage of historical-critical approaches to Scripture. At the same time, they also share a commitment to history and the claim that God works in and through history to reveal the plan by which all creation may be saved from sin and death. It stands to reason, therefore, that historical inquiry, or historical-critical exegesis, remains an indispensible tool in the interpretation of Scripture, yet a tool that must be used with humility and in conjunction with the church's tradition and the *sensus fidelium* (i.e., the sense of the faithful) in order to understand and live up to the demands of the gospel more adequately.

The Plan for What Follows

The historical-critical method is indispensible for any interpretation of the Gospels. Yet, given the issues described above, interpreters must apply the method without succumbing to the totalizing interpretations it might seem to yield. There is always more to the text, more to the story than simply what historical criticism has to offer, but historical criticism will always provide a doorway into the material that cannot be neglected. This book tries to strike a somewhat uneven balance insofar as the vast majority of the material in the following chapters will address what we have been calling "the world behind the text." Whether the issues are theological, literary, or sociological, the primary emphasis will be historical, but this emphasis should serve as one movement within a broader context of biblical interpretation that seeks to enact the Gospels in the world. For whether or not the reader self-identifies with the Christian tradition, the tradition claims significance for the Gospels precisely insofar as they have the capacity to transform and to redeem the world,

and the texts should be read and assessed with this claim in mind.

Background Material

Prior to any treatment of the Gospels themselves, this book attempts to clear some ground by providing background on the history and culture of first-century Palestine and the religious, political, and theological developments that shaped the world of Jesus and the New Testament authors in general. The presentation remains limited and selective and instructors will, no doubt, choose to supplement the presentation made here.

Chapter 2 treats the complex issue of historical Jesus research. It sets forth an account of the various attempts or "quests" for the historical Jesus, and provides a skeletal outline of the life and ministry of Jesus as it is understood by contemporary historians and exegetes. Although far from complete, the text steers a middle course in the minefield that is contemporary historical Jesus research and attempts to acknowledge the controversies among scholars where they are readily apparent. The chapter aims to provide students with a basic overview of the life and ministry of Jesus so as to establish a baseline for measuring and understanding the creative activity of the evangelists (i.e., the authors of the four Gospels).

The presentation of background material concludes in chapter 3 with an overview of the basic process by which the Gospels came into existence. In addition to treating issues like the Synoptic Problem (the question of chronology and influence among the three most strikingly similar Gospels: Mark, Matthew, and Luke) and the traditions behind the Fourth Gospel, the chapter also addresses the development of Christology and its impact on the New Testament. This chapter will assist students as they begin to grasp the basic evolutionary dynamics operative in the first century and come to distinguish the life and ministry of Jesus from the proclamation of the early church. Such a distinction will inevitably promote a better perspective on the dynamics of the Christian tradition and a better sense of the power and the historical perspective of the Gospels themselves.

Chapters on the Gospels Themselves

One of the primary goals of this text is to provide enough information and sufficient tools to assist students and teachers adequately to bring the study of the Gospels to life, but to do so without supplanting the text of the Gospels with a textbook—a thin line indeed. The first three chapters on the background of the Gospels naturally take students away from the biblical text in an effort to help them subsequently engage the text more fruitfully. The next four chapters, however, direct students' attention to the Gospels themselves. Each of these four chapters provides historical background on the author, the historical circumstances of the intended audience of the Gospel, a detailed overview of the structure and flow of the narrative, and a discussion of the major and distinctive theological themes developed in each Gospel. The chapters, however, do not provide a full-blown commentary; rather, each chapter provides interpretive and pedagogical aids for students and instructors as they engage in an ongoing conversation about the meaning(s) of the Gospels. Naturally, summaries of the biblical material give the reader a sense of the larger "flow" of each Gospel, but these summaries are not meant to be exhaustive or even fully inclusive. Rather, they will provide appropriate prerequisite reading activities for students, enabling them to engage the biblical text itself more thoughtfully and constructively prior to class meetings.

The presentation of the Gospels will not follow the canonical order; rather, the Synoptic Problem will dictate the order of presentation. Mark will be treated first, providing a kind of base from which to pursue the other Gospels. This presentation will allow for the creativity and ingenuity of Mark to shine forth and will appropriately highlight the manner in which Matthew and Luke follow and then depart from the Markan tradition, which they inherit. The subsequent chapter will focus on Matthew's creative and subtle redaction of Mark. Of course, Matthew is more than just an editor of Mark, but his creativity and theological concerns come into bold relief when contrasted with the Markan prototype. Luke's Gospel will take the reader beyond the Markan tradition and explore the ways Luke exploits his unique source material, as well as the sources he has in common with Matthew, to provide a richly unique narrative, one that often surprises and challenges readers. Finally, the Fourth Gospel, John, provides a fascinating contrast with the synoptic tradition. Yet points of overlap with the Synoptic Gospels help to ground John as a consistent witness to the saving work of God in Jesus Christ.

Each chapter contains numerous sidebars that provide supplemental information and discussions, as well as charts and illustrations. Also, each chapter will contain units titled "Scripture in Detail" that treat in some depth a select passage from the Gospel. In addition, brief units titled "Alternative Approaches" will offer novel interpretations, that is, interpretations that do not necessarily focus on or presuppose the "author's original intention," but help convey the power of the biblical material always "to say something more." These two devices will provide approachable examples of biblical exegesis that readers can emulate, and along with ample endnotes and brief bibliographies, they will help to provide an initial orientation for further research into the Gospels.

The author and editors of this text hope to help students read the Gospels and, regardless of personal faith convictions, begin to grasp the fundamental importance of the Gospels in the Christian tradition in general, and from the Catholic perspective in particular. The book is meant to develop an appreciation for the demands the Gospels place on those who would seek to enact the good news of Jesus in the world. The text may be judged a success or a failure against this modest claim. As always, textbooks offer themselves as mere tools that require the insight and experience of able educators and their students in order to be enacted. Yet, for the fullest understanding of the Gospels themselves, one requires a community of disciples, and this conviction forms the basic presupposition of the approach to the Gospels presented here.

| FOR FURTHER READING

Collins, John J. *The Bible after Babel: Historical Criticism in a Postmodern Age*. Grand Rapids, MI: Eerdmans, 2005.

Fitzmyer, Joseph A. *The Biblical Commission's Document "On the Interpretation of the Bible in the Church": Text and Commentary*. Subsidia Biblica no. 18. Rome: Pontifical Biblical Institute, 1995.

Witherup, Ronald D. *Scripture: Dei Verbum. Rediscovering Vatican II*. New York: Paulist, 2006.

| ENDNOTES

1. C. S. Lewis, "Modern Theology and Biblical Criticism," in *Christian Reflections* (Grand Rapids, MI: Eerdmans, 1995), 152–166. (The essay appears in various collections under two different titles, "Fernseed and Elephants" and "Modern Theology and Biblical Criticism.")

2. See James Barr, *History and Ideology in the Old Testament* (Oxford: Clarendon, 2000), 32–58.

3. Joseph Fitzmyer argues that the historical-critical method has been around in some form since ancient times, beginning with the practice of textual criticism on classic Greek texts like Homer. These methods were applied by Origen and others to the Bible. During the Middle Ages, while allegorical interpretation held sway in the church, many strong voices argued for a more literal interpretation. Fitzmyer does admit that with the Enlightenment biblical exegesis underwent some major developments. See Joseph A. Fitzmyer, *The Biblical Commission's Document "On the Interpretation of the Bible in the Church": Text and Commentary*, Subsidia Biblica no. 18 (Rome: Pontifical Biblical Institute, 1995), 26–36.

4. *Dei verbum*, 2.

5. See Fitzmyer, *The Biblical Commission's Document*, 26.

6. Raymond E. Brown, "Hermeneutics," in *The New Jerome Biblical Commentary*, ed. Raymond E. Brown, Joseph A. Fitzmyer, and Roland E. Murphy (Englewood Cliffs, NJ: Prentice Hall, 1990), 1157.

7. N. L. Geisler, "Inerrancy and Free Will," *Evangelical Quarterly* 57 [1985]: 350–51, quoted in R. F. Collins, "Inspiration," *The New Jerome Biblical Commentary*, eds. R. E. Brown, et al. (Englewood Cliffs, NJ: Prentice Hall, 1990), 1031.

8. Karl Rahner, *Hearers of the Word: Laying the Foundation for a Philosophy of Religion*, rev. ed., trans. Michael Richards (New York: Herder and Herder, 1969), 60.

9. See Jacques Derrida, "Des Tours de Babel," in *Poststructuralism as Exegesis*, ed. David Jobling and Stephen D. Moore, *Semeia* 54 (1992): 3–34. The essay was originally published in English and French in 1985 and has appeared in various volumes over the years.

10. Roland Barthes, "The Death of the Author," in *Image, Music, Text*, trans. Stephen Heath (New York: Hill and Wang, 1977), 142–148.

11. See especially Elisabeth Schüssler Fiorenza, *Bread Not Stone: The Challenge of Feminist Biblical Interpretation*, tenth anniversary ed. (Boston, MA: Beacon, 1995) and Rebecca S. Chopp, *The Power to Speak: Feminism, Language, and God* (New York: Crossroad, 1989).

12. Schüssler Fiorenza, *Bread Not Stone*, 93–94.

13. Joseph Cardinal Ratzinger, "Biblical Interpretation in Crisis: On the Question of the Foundations and Approaches of Exegesis Today," in *Biblical Interpretation in Crisis: The Ratzinger Conference on Bible and Church*, Encounter Series, ed. Richard J. Neuhaus (Grand Rapids, MI: Eerdmans, 1989), 1–24.

14. Werner Heisenberg, "Über den anschaulichen Inhalt der quantentheoretischen Kinematik und Mechanik," *Zeitschrift für Physik* 33 (1927): 879–893.

CHAPTER 1

THE HISTORICAL BACKGROUND OF FIRST-CENTURY PALESTINE

Anyone who has even casually read the New Testament will notice that the world that stands behind the text is vastly different from our own. Palestine in the first century of the Common Era (CE; what used to be called *Anno Domini* [AD] or "The Year of Our Lord") was certainly a complicated scene. It had served over the centuries as a crossroads of several major cultures, including Greek, Persian, Egyptian, and Babylonian. Moreover, the governing authority of this diverse but remote outpost stood more than one thousand miles away, across the vast Mediterranean Sea, in Rome. These and other factors contributed to the complex social, cultural, and political situation that is the background of the New Testament and the story of Jesus. References to the histories and cultures of these ancient lands abound in the pages of the Gospels and other New Testament books, and the modern exegete needs to become familiar with these histories and cultures to understand the text. This chapter will outline some of the most important factors shaping the background of the New Testament.

Greek Influences on First-Century Judaism

Any adequate understanding of the New Testament presupposes familiarity with the story of Israel and its covenant with God. Yet many readers succumb to the temptation to simplify the background of the New Testament by referring only to the Old Testament, as if knowing the stories of the Jewish people as narrated in Scripture was sufficient for understanding the context of the New Testament. Giving in to such a temptation, however, creates a distorted picture of first-century Judaism; for Judaism, even as it was expressed within the relatively limited orbit of Jesus' ministry (i.e., in Jerusalem and Galilee), was neither a parochial nor a monolithic faith. Rather, following the close of the Old Testament period (c. 150 BCE), Judaism continued to be influenced by new cultures, such as those produced by the Greek and Roman empires, so that even in the most remote corners of the Mediterranean world, Judaism had a rich and complex background. Even Aramaic, the everyday language of Palestinian Jews such as Jesus and his disciples, comes from the Babylonian language that dominated the region during the Babylonian and Persian periods (c. 600 BCE–300 BCE). Subsequently, as the Greek armies of Alexander (the Great) of Macedonia took control of Palestine in the fourth century BCE, they imported a vibrant culture that exerted influence in the region for the next several centuries during what has become known as the Greek period (c. 330 BCE–100 BCE).

IMPORTANT DEVELOPMENTS IN THE HISTORY OF PALESTINIAN JUDAISM

587–539 BCE The Babylonian Exile

The Babylonian exile marks the end of the monarchy in Judah. Judah is forever marked by the destruction of the Temple and the years its leaders spent in exile in Babylon.

532–333 BCE The Dominance of the Persian Empire in Palestine

The Persians, having conquered the Babylonians, establish their own extensive empire. The Jewish exiles in Babylon are sent home to rebuild the Temple. The Jews are now a people but no longer a sovereign nation.

333–164 BCE The Greek Period

Alexander [the Great] of Macedonia conquers the Persian Empire and establishes a Greek empire that devolves to his generals after his early death. Two of those kingdoms, the Ptolemaic Kingdom and the Seleucid Kingdom, vie for control of Jerusalem and Palestine.

332 BCE–200 BCE The Greek Period I: The Ptolemeys

The Ptolemaic Empire: the part of Alexander's Empire that was centered in Egypt (ruled by the Ptolemy family) controls Palestine for more than a century after Alexander's death.

200 BCE–164 BCE The Greek Period II: The Seleucids

The Seleucid Empire: the part of Alexander's Empire that was centered in Asia (ruled by the Seleucid family) takes control of Palestine from the Ptolemaic Kingdom around 200 BCE.

164–63 BCE The Maccabean Kingdom

Following the atrocities of the Seleucid king, Antiochus IV Epiphanes, Jewish rebels ally themselves with Rome to throw off the yoke of the Seleucids.

63 BCE The Beginning of Roman Dominance

Under the leadership of the Roman general Pompey, the relative autonomy of the Maccabean Kingdom comes to an end, and Rome begins to control and dominate Palestine.

66 CE–70 CE The First Major Jewish Revolt against Rome

Jewish rebels lead a revolt against Rome that is initially successful but eventually suppressed by Roman legions under Vespasian (and then under his son, Titus); Jerusalem and the Temple are destroyed in 70 CE.

c. 132 CE The Second Major Jewish Revolt

The Roman emperor Hadrian plans to rebuild Jerusalem as a Greco-Roman city (*Colonia Aelia Capitolina*) dedicated to the Roman god Jupiter. When news of these plans reaches pious Jews, they revolt under the leadership of Simon bar Kosibah. The Romans put down the revolt and ban Jews from entering the city.

While readers of the New Testament cannot help but notice that the Roman Empire dominated the politics of first-century Palestine, if one looks a little deeper, one can discern that the culture of the region was, in some ways, more heavily influenced by Greece than by Rome. To note the most obvious example of the cultural hegemony of the Greeks in the first century, the language of the New Testament is Greek, not Latin. The zeal with which Alexander and his successors imparted (or imposed) Greek culture was remarkable, and the long-term effects of the Greek presence in the eastern Mediterranean can still be appreciated today. Perhaps of greatest importance for the purposes of reading the Gospels are the intellectual achievements of Greece, particularly evidenced in its philosophical schools of thought.

Readers can discern the hallmarks of Greek philosophy embedded within the language and outlook of the New Testament. Even though the Greek philosopher Plato lived almost four hundred years before Jesus, his thought remained a powerful force within Judaism and early Christianity as well. The basic contours of Plato's thought may be summarized as a form of "idealism" in which what is most real tends to be beyond the physical world. For Plato, the forms (*idea* in Greek), and ultimately, the transcendentals (i.e., the One, the True, the Good, the Beautiful) are the ultimate ground of reality. Those who are caught up in the world of the senses will miss out on what is truly real, Plato believed, so one must cultivate a sense, a habit, for discerning that which is beyond the material world. A strong sense of morality permeates Plato's metaphysics (i.e., an account of what is real); it involves living in the world reflectively and in accordance with the transcendentals.

Many followers of Plato sought to expand his philosophy, and over the centuries several schools of platonic thought emerged. Within Judaism, Plato probably had no stronger ally

than a philosopher and statesman named Philo (c. 20 BCE–50 CE). Philo was part of the large Greek-speaking Jewish community in Alexandria, Egypt, where Greek culture had long been integrated into the beliefs and customs of the local Jewish population. For Philo and many Greek-speaking or Hellenistic Jews, the banalities and materialism of the Old Testament (e.g., animal sacrifice, the polygamy of the patriarchs, anthropomorphic descriptions of God) were troubling in light of the claims made by Greek philosophers. The stories and theology of the Old Testament seemed rather primitive and did not align well with the claims made by philosophy, which tended to be more theoretical and systematic than the narratives and legal codes of the Old Testament.

The Old Testament became increasingly subject to allegorizing interpretations, that sought to go beyond the merely literal level of the text to uncover its transcendent meaning. For example, Philo's allegorical interpretation of Genesis made the stories of Israel's ancestors, the patriarchs, into stories about how the soul progresses in its journey toward God. Thus the stories had no historical currency; they merely had symbolic significance as a description of a universal journey of the soul.[1] Similarly, Philo offered an allegorical interpretation of Jacob's dream about the ladder to heaven that appears in Genesis 28:12–15. For Philo, Jacob's journey from Beer-sheba to Haran underscored the soul's mystical journey toward perfection and the consecutive steps necessary for this journey. Philo saw Jacob's journey from Beer-sheba to Haran as a journey of self-discovery where Beer-sheba represents natural knowledge and Haran represents the self. In other words, Jacob's journey represents the first step in the journey into God, and it begins by moving away from the knowledge of things to the knowledge of self. Rather than asking questions about the events in the narrative, Philo related this journey of Jacob to the contemplation of God. Such allegorizing tendencies played a large role in the development of early Christian doctrine and early Christian approaches to the interpretation of Scripture.

Platonism was not the only philosophical school to influence early Judaism. In fact, Stoicism was a major influence in the region and continued to supply both Judaism and early Christianity with many of their basic concepts and much of Christianity's early technical language. The founders of Stoicism, Zeno (333 BCE–264 BCE) and Epictetus (first-century CE), envisioned a universe dominated by reason. For the Stoics, *logos* (the Greek term for "word") was the organizing principle of the universe, and human living was directed by conformity to the *logos*. Resignation to fate and total detachment from joy and grief were common ideals within Stoicism (hence the use of the term *stoic* in modern English to describe someone who seems remarkably unaffected by extreme circumstances). Yet Stoic ideas did not exclude compassion, a key component of developing Christian moral tradition. Rather, Epictetus and other Stoic philosophers emphasized the moral virtue of respecting and caring for all people, regardless of their social status, making compassion part of a Stoic moral vision (though not part of the common modern assumptions about Stoicism). Stoicism, Platonism, and several other Greek religious and philosophical traditions exerted significant influence on the early Christian movement, and elements of their thought and practice permeate early Christian writings and remain a factor in any understanding of the emergence of the Christian tradition.

HEALING AND MEDICINE IN THE FIRST CENTURY

Greek philosophy as well as Greek religious practices left their mark on the culture of first-century Palestine, including the worldview of the earliest Christians. These influences included belief in miraculous healing, as evident in the healing stories found in the Gospels. For example, in the healing of the man with the withered hand (Mark 3:1–6), the opponents of Jesus watch him carefully to see if he will heal the man on the Sabbath. When he does heal the man, the opponents begin to plot against Jesus. What many readers may find strange is the fact that the opponents of Jesus do not question whether Jesus actually has the power to heal: the opponents acknowledge Jesus' power to heal, and thus focus their critique entirely on whether Jesus will heal on the Sabbath, an act that violates the sanctity of the day according to their reading of the Torah.

This acceptance of Jesus' power to heal is less surprising given that throughout the eastern Mediterranean various healing cults had proliferated, among them the healing cult of Asclepius, the Greek god of medicine. From the time of Alexander, the cult of Asclepius had become increasingly popular. While the cult of Asclepius was predominant in Asia Minor, in Egypt, the healing cult of Serapis was immensely popular. In both of these cults, a sacred shrine was the locale for the healing event, which was usually accompanied by ritual and followed by an offering or sacrifice. Although these cults sound very strange to modern readers, it is useful to recall that real knowledge of the human body and the means to remedy illness remained a dark mystery until the end of the nineteenth

continued

HEALING AND MEDICINE IN THE FIRST CENTURY *continued*

century. Even so, Greek philosophy (particularly the Stoics) held room for the practice of healing arts and in Sirach 38:9–15 one finds support for such practices.

Itinerant healers and wonder workers complemented the healing cults, and prominent among these itinerants was Apollonius of Tyana, a contemporary of Jesus. Some ancients regarded Apollonius as a "divine man" (*theios anēr*), and a century after his death they even had a popular narrative of his life and healings commissioned by the Roman imperial household, within which were several admirers, including the wife of the emperor (Philostratus, *Life of Apollonius*). Many contemporary scholars believe that the healing cults of the ancient world as well as the tradition of itinerant healers such as Apollonius help to explain the ancient mindset around the miracles recorded in the New Testament.

In addition to the philosophical outlooks of Platonism and Stoicism, language itself represents perhaps the most important contribution the Greeks made to the background of the New Testament. Throughout the eastern Mediterranean, including many parts of Palestine, Greek had been the language of commerce, diplomacy, and politics. But the Greek that was spoken was not the classical Greek of Athens or the great schools of the day; rather, *koinē* ("common") Greek was the language of commerce and the language of the educated classes. Among Palestinian Jews, the language of the home and the synagogue was Aramaic, as it had been for several centuries. As the Greek language came to take on a prominent role in the marketplace, many people simply adapted to this development as best they could. For example, consider the way many native English-speaking students speak Spanish. Inevitably, even with command of an expansive Spanish vocabulary and grammar, these speakers will nonetheless speak Spanish like an English-speaker. English grammar and syntax will serve as the default template in the brain, and even as one learns to adopt different linguistic structures and new vocabulary, it is difficult if not impossible to move away from this default tendency. In Palestine and the eastern Mediterranean in general, local languages (usually Semitic languages) tended to exercise a lot of influence over how Greek was used. Scholars often call this "Semitic interference," and this interference affects how the language of the New Testament is both understood and translated. For example, the disturbing command to "hate" one's parents in Luke 14:26 can be attributed to the Semitic idiom where the word *hate* is used to express preference ("I like this more than that" would be rendered "I hate this and love that"; see Matthew 10:37 for an improved rendering of the verse.

Greek culture exerted influence on first-century Judaism in only a few areas, and any remotely adequate account of its influence is well beyond the scope of this chapter and this text. Readers should be aware, however, that some New Testament scholars will go so far as to argue that Greek culture and thought were more decisive in the formation of early Christianity than was Judaism.[2] These scholars remain in the minority, however, and their position is not adopted in this text.

The Roman Presence in Palestine

Greek cultural and political dominance continued for more than two centuries, abating only with the emergence of the Roman Empire, which came to control Palestine in the first century BCE. In fact, the Roman presence in Palestine initially resulted from an invitation from Jewish revolutionaries in the second century BCE. During the Maccabean revolt against the last Greek ruler of Palestine (the Seleucid king Antiochus IV Epiphanes), leaders of the revolt solicited support from Rome, and Rome was only too happy to oblige given that it shared a common enemy (i.e., the Seleucids) with the Jewish revolutionaries. Eventually the Romans began to assert control over the region, and with Pompey's arrival in 63 BCE, Romans occupied Palestine and controlled its affairs for the next several centuries.

The lifetime of Jesus spanned the reigns of two emperors: Octavian (Caesar Augustus; 27 BCE–14 CE) and Tiberius (14 CE–37 CE). While neither emperor ever came in direct contact with Jesus or even traveled to Palestine, they both decisively influenced the circumstances of Jesus' life and that of the early Christian community. Octavian, for his part, was viewed as the author of the great *Pax romana augusta*: "The Roman Peace of Augustus." This period of time marked the end of the civil wars that had dominated the empire for years, and decisive victories effectively brought an end to open competition for control of Rome and the incessant desire for further expansion of the empire through military victories (though in reality, both struggles continued). This peace of Rome proved to be a propaganda tool introduced by Octavian, and it was used to give the Roman populace a sense of prosperity and contentment. The British historian Edward Gibbon, who first coined the phrase *Pax Romana*, alleged that this "Roman peace" lasted until the death of Marcus Aurelius (c. 180 CE),[3]

but this peace was significantly disturbed on several occasions. For example, a time of struggle followed the death of the last emperor from the household of Julius Caesar, a man named Nero (c. 67 CE). While the *Pax Romana* was a powerful propaganda tool, the subjugated people of Palestine could only see such a "peace" as ironic if not oxymoronic. The evangelist Luke makes use of this notion of a *Pax Romana* by contrasting the birth of Jesus, the real prince of peace (Luke 2:14; 19:38), with the violent "peace" of Rome. The "peace" the inhabitants of Palestine enjoyed came at the edge of a Roman sword wielded by one of Rome's client kings—a dubious peace indeed.

One of these client kings casts a particularly long and ominous shadow over the New Testament—Herod the Great. Herod was the heir to the Maccabean family's claim on Palestine, but throughout the decades following the revolt, the religious character of the Maccabean revolution deteriorated significantly. The descendants of the Maccabees had controlled the office of high priest and had considerably expanded their power as virtual kings of Palestine. These descendants were often called the Hasmonean family after the name of one of their ancestors, a certain Asamōnaios, the great grandfather of Mattathias, the patriarch of the Maccabee family. Herod was actually not a direct descendant of the Maccabees. In fact, he was from the neighboring country of Edom, but he was from a closely allied family and had secured the hand of one of the Hasmonean daughters as his wife. Herod ingratiated himself with the Roman emperor, Octavian, even after he had supported one of Octavian's rivals, Marc Antony, prior to the Battle of Actium (c. 31 CE). Such maneuvering is no doubt a testimony to Herod's skill as a politician and ruler. In fact, Rome had such confidence in Herod that they granted him the power to rule his subjects directly so that only the emperor himself could hold Herod accountable.

Even though the opening chapters of Matthew and Luke only mention Herod the Great in conjunction with the birth of Jesus (Herod had died around 6–4 BCE), one can discern Herod's presence in the life and ministry of Jesus. Herod expanded and embellished the Jerusalem Temple, and he also helped to entrench his allies in the Sanhedrin and in the office of high priest. Herod's son, Herod Antipas, became the ruler of Galilee after the death of his father, and it was the ineptitude of another son, Herod Archelaeus, that had the latter recalled to Rome and that required the installation of a prefect who could govern Jerusalem and the surrounding area directly.

Responsibility for collecting taxes, administering Roman law, and keeping order fell to the *praefecti* (or prefects; after c. 40 CE they were called *procuratores*), Roman administrators drawn from the lower Roman nobility (the so-called equestrian order, analogous, in some sense, to the cavalry or the knights of medieval Europe). While their resources were rather sparse compared to those of the legate in nearby Damascus, the Roman prefects in Palestine did have the authority to execute criminals and could call upon the Roman legate in Damascus for assistance should the need arise (Roman legions were stationed there).

The prefects were equipped with local troops, sometimes mercenaries or even conscripts, who were always available, but these soldiers were not the elite legionnaires. The low quality of these forces and perhaps their lack of what today might be called "professionalism" paved the way

for abuse and corresponding resentment in Judea and Jerusalem. And yet these forces were crucial to the maintenance of Roman authority and the authority of the religious establishment; leaders tolerated these troops because their own power and indeed their well-being rested on the protection the troops could afford.

Although the center of Roman administration in the region was Caesarea Maritima, a seaside-port city northwest of Jerusalem, control of Jerusalem, especially during the great pilgrimage feasts, became a priority for the Roman prefects as they worked to bolster their allies within the religious leadership of Jerusalem and thereby maintain their own power. The arrest and execution of Jesus recorded in all four canonical Gospels supports this picture of the relationship between Roman prefects and the religious establishment. Jesus' provocative speech

ROMAN PREFECTS AND JEWISH HIGH PRIESTS IN THE EARLY FIRST CENTURY

ROMAN PREFECTS	HIGH PRIESTS
Coponius (6 CE–9 CE)	Annas, son of Seth (6 CE–15 CE)
M. Ambivius (9 CE–13 CE)	
Annius Rufus (12 CE–15 CE)	
	Ishmael, son of Phiabi (15 CE)
Valerius Gratus (15 CE–26 CE)	Eleazar, son of Annas (16 CE–17 CE)
	Caiaphas, son of Annas (18 CE–36 CE)
Pontius Pilatus (26 CE–36 CE)	
Marcellus (36 CE–37 CE)	
Marullus (37 CE–41 CE)	Jonathan, son of Annas (37 CE–41 CE)

and actions during a pilgrimage feast would have been quite dangerous from the standpoint of the Roman administrators.

The Roman authorities managed to integrate themselves with the religious establishment in Jerusalem because Rome appointed the high priest, just as the Persian governors and the Greek kings did before them. Of course, imperial administrators needed support among the local leadership, and they always sought to establish a symbiotic relationship with local leaders. Among the families eligible for the office of high priest, one emerged that seemed to be uniquely able to sustain an agreeable relationship with Roman prefects. As prefects moved in and out of power, Annas and his son-in-law, Caiaphas, were able to maintain power for a long time, probably because they had established a working rapport with the Roman prefects.[4] Notice that the longest serving perfects coincide with the long terms of both Annas and Caiaphas, the two high priests mentioned in connection with the trial and execution of Jesus in the Gospels.

The Social System of First-Century Palestine

Much like the world today, obscene disparities between the wealthy and the poor deeply marked the Roman world. The vast majority of the population was poor and barely survived on their meager earnings. Some segments of the peasantry, however, were more fortunate insofar as they learned a trade and were thus able to withstand the effects of natural disasters and political upheavals that often cost others their lives.

Patriarchy characterized all of the social systems of first-century Palestine; in other words, the social system generally revolved around men. Yet, one must be cautious in characterizing the place of women within this society.

Facile assumptions about the marginalization of women leave little room for the complexity of the historical data on this question. No doubt, in many places the status of women reflected the worst stereotypes: women were treated as property with no real freedom and were constantly subject to the wishes and plans of their husbands and other male relatives. While there is evidence that such attitudes toward women existed in first-century Palestine, historians also find many examples of strong, powerful, and relatively independent women in the New Testament. These examples should come as no surprise since within Greco-Roman society women often enjoyed greater power and a measure of independence in comparison to conservative urban Jewish society.[5] Given that first-century Palestine was a crossroads of both Jewish and Greco-Roman cultures, the status of women cannot be easily fixed, and readers should be prepared to find disturbing examples of radically marginalized women as well as positive examples of powerful, influential, and relatively independent women.

Slavery was a universal social institution in the empire and neighboring territories. Unlike the chattel slavery found in the Americas in the early modern period, in which race was the decisive factor, slavery in the Roman world was based on social status and fortune or circumstances. Particularly in the border regions of the empire, raiding parties would abduct people and enslave them. The recovery of a lost loved one, therefore, required either a counterraid or some form of payment whereby the slave might be "redeemed." Individuals from the peasant class were often tempted to sell themselves into slavery to avoid the very real possibility of starvation. The majority of the population in Roman Palestine lived on the edge of ruin and disaster, conditions that made slavery an appealing option. Slaves (*douloi*, often translated as "servants" in modern New Testament translations) were the property of their master and had no rights whatsoever—not even the right to a family (a slave's children were the property of the slave's master). Moreover, slaves (both male and female) were subject to the sexual demands of their masters and had no recourse in Greco-Roman society. The lot of a slave in the first century was dreadful, yet the notion of freedom or autonomy as modern North Americans understand it was surely a distant fantasy for most of those who lived in first-century Palestine, whether Jew or Gentile, slave or free.

Social status in the Roman Empire, and especially in the eastern Mediterranean, revolved around the values of honor and shame. These values are understood differently today and are even somewhat alien to the sensibilities of modern North American readers. In the world of the New Testament, one's honor centered on how one was understood and valued by others. As such, relationships in an honor-shame culture were dyadic; identity came through relationship to others and not through introspection, unlike in contemporary American culture where it is often said that "you know in your heart" who you really are.

A slave, for example, had little honor in Roman society because his or her relationships were quite limited and unidirectional (i.e., the master directed the slave at all times), while the wife of a Roman senator, for example, could enjoy great honor. Factors beyond one's control—like age, gender, health, and wealth—played a major role in allowing one to accrue honor and, conversely, to lose it. Additionally, physical space and appearance were often crucial in maintaining honor, and any attempt to challenge one's honor often came in the form of compromised space: physical proximity, a touch or bump, striking someone, or even wearing inappropriate clothing. Exactly how or to what extent one's honor was compromised depended on the audience

that witnessed such actions. Affronts to one's honor in private could be handled in one manner, while public affronts had to be handled differently. Moreover, the connection between physical boundaries and honor was more pronounced when women were involved, for a woman's honor was connected to her discretion and her avoidance of even the remotest possibility that her sexual exclusivity or purity could be compromised.

Throughout the Roman Empire, the wealthy dominated and determined the social order. A system of patronage came to define politics, economics, and social life in general. In the patronage system, the wealthy became the benefactors of those without financial or political resources. At the simplest level, there existed a prefeudal system of tenant farming and other agricultural operations where the landowner would allow peasants to work the land. Benefactors, or patrons as they are sometimes called, did not receive payment for their deeds. Rather, their clients, or those who benefitted from the good graces of the patron, were expected to show loyalty and gratitude to their patrons, to speak well of them and to proclaim their good character. While these relationships were not legal agreements, they were the stuff upon which Roman society was built, and the New Testament bears the marks of the patron-client system in several areas. For example, the New Testament language of faith and grace comes from the system of patronage. *Faith* (*pistis* in Greek) at a basic level simply means "to trust." The client was supposed to trust the goodwill of the patron (in the context of Christian theology, faith is more complex than "trust"). Additionally, *grace* (*charis* in Greek) was often used to describe the benefits that the patron would give to clients. These parallels are notable, and the New Testament writings seem to make use of the patronage system as an analog for the relationship between God and humanity.

PURITY AND DEFILEMENT IN JUDAISM

Purity was a major issue for first-century Jews. Purity and cleanliness require a world of order, everything in its place and a place for everything. The ultimate place was Yahweh's dwelling with Israel, the holy of holies, or the inner sanctuary of the Temple. The purity of human beings and animals can be measured in relation to the Temple.

People

Gentiles, or non-Jews, were unclean. While contact with Gentiles was often unavoidable, it was actively discouraged. Israelite males were more "clean" than were females in general, and they could access the inner Temple precincts. Only priests and Levites, a selective subset of Israelite men, were authorized to make sacrifice and perform rituals in the Temple, and only the high priest could enter the inner sanctuary of the Temple.

Animals

Some animals were considered innately unclean when it came to the scale of purity. For example, any land animal that swarmed was an abomination. Other animals were always unclean and could not be eaten because they were perceived to be disordered, especially animals without cloven hoofs and those that did not chew the cud (i.e., regurgitate their food in the process of digesting it), such as carrion eaters, dogs, bears, and foxes. Animals that were suitable for the meal table had cloven hoofs and chewed the cud. Within this last category of animals were those suitable for sacrifice, namely domesticated animals without blemish.

Mary Douglas has noted a parallel between people, animals, and purity in Judaism illustrated in the following diagram.[6]

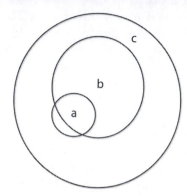

c– all who are under the covenant, both clean and unclean

b– the clean without blemish, (i.e., those fit for Temple use)

a– the firstborn without blemish and therefore consecrated to the Temple; some of those consecrated to the Temple *may subsequently become unclean*, however, making them ineligible to work in or approach the Temple

Things

Corpses, blood, and other items that come into contact with unclean individuals or animals were also unclean. Stone, however, never transmitted uncleanness, so one did not need to worry about whom or what had been traveling on a particular road or leaned against a certain rock. In other words, while purity was a big concern among first-century Jews, such concerns did not paralyze the community. One simply tried to avoid that which was unclean, and when one encountered that which was unclean, one did what was necessary to remove the impurity (e.g., one could find a purification pool, or *mikveh*, just about anywhere there was a Jewish population in the first century).

Theological Developments within Judaism

Students of the Old Testament quickly learn to recognize that Scripture reflects significant developments in Israelite religion over the course of centuries. The religious outlook of the patriarchs, that of Moses, of the eighth-century prophets, and the religious concerns of priestly traditions of the postexilic period, all mark significant changes in the religious worldview of Judaism and its corresponding practices. The centuries between the close of the Old Testament and the writing of the New Testament texts, often called the intertestamental period, witnessed ongoing developments in the Jewish religion, developments that form the backdrop for the ministry of Jesus and the theology of the early Christian church.

The intertestamental period saw the culmination of trends that had defined Second Temple Judaism for almost five hundred years. Following the Babylonian exile, the Jewish religion began to take on a different hue. Scholars have identified certain distinctive features of Judaism in this period:

- The Temple and its cult assumed major importance for all forms of Judaism in the Second Temple period. Yet there was also a growing awareness that a life of prayer and study must accompany the cultic activity of the Temple. As a result, synagogues began to appear. In synagogues people would gather, usually on the Sabbath, to pray and study the Torah. No cultic activity (i.e., sacrifices) took place in synagogues.
- The Torah, along with the Prophets, became central to Israel's understanding of itself and its covenantal relationship with Yahweh. In the Second Temple period there was a growing emphasis on the observance of the statutes found in the Torah. The emergence of Scripture coincided with the so-called end of prophecy after the Babylonian exile, where over several centuries, the figure of the prophet slowly diminished as a lived reality in Jewish society and became instead merely a literary figure within the authoritative texts (i.e., biblical texts).
- Israel became more concerned with itself (exclusivism) and less connected to the outside world. Israel was no longer an autonomous political entity, and so it did not have to deal with the great questions of international relations (i.e., war and peace, national policies, etc.). In conjunction with this development, however, Judaism was still conscious of its universalistic vocation to be a "light to the nations" so that all people would be brought together to worship Yahweh, the true God.
- The exclusivism of the Second Temple period also coincided with the emergence of apocalyptic eschatology as a major theological factor.

Each of these features helped to contribute to the distinctive theology and practice of Judaism in the first century. As such, they also became decisive in the story of Jesus and the emergence of the Christian community.

The Temple, Torah, and Exclusivism

The destruction of the Jewish Temple in 587 BCE brought the era of the first Temple, Solomon's Temple, to a close. The Second Temple was initially completed around 515 BCE amid great controversy. Some Israelites from the northern kingdom of Israel had stayed on in the region south of Galilee and north of Jerusalem following the Babylonian conquest and had intermarried with other nationalities that had been settled there after the destruction of the northern kingdom of Israel by the Assyrians in 722 BCE.[7] Known as the Samaritans, they developed their own worship on Mount Gerazim and opposed the rebuilding of the Temple in Jerusalem following the return of exiles from Babylon (see Ezra 4:4–24). Their opposition created animosity that persisted for centuries, as is evident in the pages of the Gospels. The rebuilding and embellishment of the Temple was not finally completed until the time of Herod the Great, who died around 6 BCE.

In the two centuries that followed the initial rebuilding of the Jerusalem Temple (c. 515 BCE–330 BCE), there was a great push toward consolidation, and a form of Judaism began to emerge that was far more normative than it had been in the period before the exile. Except for the relatively small number of Samaritans, the new Temple was the center of worship and the focal point of Yahweh's presence with Israel, even for the thousands of Jews who now lived in other lands in what is called the Diaspora. Even during the Babylonian exile one can see in the work of the prophet Ezekiel an emerging priestly and cultic focus in the theology of Israel. In fact, Ezekiel spends several chapters outlining the dimensions of a future rebuilt Temple and emphasizes its importance in the life of Israel (see Ezekiel, chapters 40–48). With the rebuilding of the Temple, the priestly class, and not the warrior-king, would dictate how the religious life of Israel would unfold. It was at this time that the high priest emerged as the ruler of Jerusalem, the theocrat to govern the Jewish people in Jerusalem under the watchful eye of the foreign government that controlled the region.

Around the year 400 BCE, two men emerged to lead Israel in its religious reformation: Nehemiah and Ezra.[8] There is some confusion over where to place Ezra in relation to Nehemiah (scholars dispute whether the two were contemporaries or whether Ezra was active several decades after Nehemiah), but both men exerted a strong influence over the shape of Second Temple Judaism. First, a kind of covenantal exclusivism began to emerge within Judaism. Prior to the exile, one reads of alliances and intermarriages between Israelites and various foreigners. With the reforms of Nehemiah and Ezra, Jews were forbidden from intermarrying with non-Jews (i.e., Gentiles), and the whole tenor of the faith seems to have moved sharply in the direction of purity and exclusivism, a movement that is exacerbated or furthered by the emergence of Scripture at this time (Nehemiah 13:23–30).

Before Nehemiah and Ezra, there was no such thing as "scripture" per se. In other words, although certainly ancient texts generally were regarded as important, those texts had not been enumerated, separated, and canonized until approximately 400 BCE when the "book of the Law," or the Torah, began to be recognized as the definitive collection of narratives and statutes for Israel. With the emergence of canonical texts that enumerated quite specifically the parameters of the covenantal relationship between Yahweh and Israel, there was a corresponding attentiveness to the specific demands of legal observance. In other words, now that a definitive set of texts could tell one how to live the covenant faithfully, people generally became more attentive to those demands. In the Second Temple period, one begins to find an emphasis on purity and defilement in Jewish life that does not appear to have been as evident in the preexilic period. To be sure, Israel had its cult prior to the exile, and it clearly had a developed sense of purity and defilement. Yet with the emergence of the Torah, the demands of covenantal observance could be more scrupulously observed, and an entire class of people emerged at this time—the scribes—to help discern these demands.

THE GREAT JEWISH FEASTS

The Jewish calendar is based on the phases of the moon. The day begins at sunset and concludes with the following sunset. The following list includes the months of the Jewish calendar with the corresponding months in the common modern-day calendar in parentheses:

Nisan (March–April)

Iyyar (April–May)

Sivan (May–June)

Tammuz (June–July)

Ab (July–August)

Elul (August–September)

Tishri (September–October)

Marheshvan (October–November)

Kislev (November–December)

Tebeth (December–January)

Shebat (January–February)

Adar (February–March)

The older calendar in the preexilic period (i.e., prior to the Babylonian exile) used the Canaanite names for the months. Additionally, the New Year is reckoned in the spring in some Old Testament passages whereas autumn is held as the beginning of the New Year in other Old Testament texts. In the Mishnah, the early rabbis designated four New Year's observances: (1) the first of *Nisan* was the New Year for kings and feasts; (2) the first of *Elul* was the New Year for tithes on cattle; (3) the first of *Tishri* was the New Year for foreign kings; (4) the first of *Shebat* was the New Year for fruit trees.[9] To complicate matters even further, the solar year (i.e., twelve lunar months) is approximately eleven days longer than the twelve lunar months that comprise the Jewish calendar. To keep the feasts within their appropriate seasons, every three years is a leap year in which an extra month is added to the end of the calendar year. During these leap years, there are two months named *Adar*: *Adar Aleph* and *Adar Beth*. The first *Adar* serves as a "spacer" month and no major feasts are celebrated during this month. With the second *Adar*, the feasts of the calendar are observed.

Sabbath—The seventh day of the week, corresponding to Saturday in the modern calendar, was set apart as a day of rest and prayer. The Sabbath observance emerged early in Israel's history, but the theological rationale for the observance is ambiguous. In Exodus 20:8–11, the six-day creation of the world followed by Yahweh's rest (see Genesis, chapter 1) is the reason for observing the Sabbath: "In six days the Lord made the heavens and the earth, the sea and all that is in them; but on the seventh day he rested. That is why the Lord has blessed the sabbath day and made it holy" (Exodus 20:11). In Deuteronomy 5:12–15, the Israelites are reminded of their former status as slaves in Egypt. The Israelites must not work nor may any of their slaves or animals, because it all belongs to God, and the Sabbath is the ritual whereby Israel acknowledges this basic tenet. The Sabbath was an enduring symbol of Yahweh's covenant with Israel, and violations of the Sabbath rest were punishable with death (Exodus 31:15–17). Yet later rabbinic literature makes it clear that exactly what kind of work was prohibited on the Sabbath was a matter of great debate. Additionally, it was acknowledged that in matters of life and death one might technically violate the Sabbath without incurring guilt or blame. In the Mishnah there are thirty-nine examples of work that may not be done on the Sabbath, but there are also numerous documents that describe work that may be done on the Sabbath as well as exceptions to the rules regarding work.[10]

continued

THE GREAT JEWISH FEASTS *continued*

Passover (*Pesach*—14 of *Nisan*)—Many scholars believe that this first great pilgrimage feast originated from the blending of two ancient feasts: one commemorating the Exodus from Egypt and another celebrating a new cycle of planting and harvesting—Unleavened Bread (15 of *Nisan*).

Pentecost (*Shavuot*; also called "the Festival of Weeks"—6 of *Sivan*)—This feast has its origins as the conclusion of the grain season, but it took on greater significance as it was tied to the events of the Exodus and more specifically to the giving of the Law on Mount Sinai. Pentecost is one of the great pilgrimage feasts in Second Temple Judaism.

Day of Atonement (*Yom Kippur*—10 of *Tishri*)—This is a late feast, even though the scapegoat ritual and the pouring of the blood over the mercy seat (*kapporet* in Hebrew) are both prescribed rituals in Leviticus, chapter 16. The feast became extremely important in the Second Temple period as it was the principal celebration of Israel's purification and cleansing from sin.

Booths (*Succoth*—15 of *Tishri*)—The third of the great pilgrimage feasts in Second Temple Judaism marked the fall harvest as well as the time of the wilderness wandering. As a commemoration of Israel's time of wandering after the Exodus, Jewish families would erect tents and spend the week living in them as an act of recollection, as a memorial.

Dedication (*Hanukkah*—25 of *Kislev*)—This feast developed late in Israel's history, though it has great significance in the context of Jewish nationalism. The feast celebrates the purification and rededication of the Jerusalem Temple following the defeat of the Seleucid king Antiochus IV Epiphanes. Antiochus had erected a statue of Zeus in the Temple precincts and had Greek sacrifices offered there while observance of Jewish Law and the cult of Yahweh were prohibited under pain of death (see 1 and 2 Maccabees). During the rededication of the Temple, legend says that despite insufficient oil to keep the menorah lit for the eight-day celebration, the menorah did not go out.

Apocalyptic Eschatology

Following the Babylonian exile (587–539 BCE), the Persians incorporated Palestine into one of their imperial subdivisions known as Satrapies, bringing to an end Israel's (or more precisely, Judah's) status as an independent nation. This development had a decisive impact on the shape of Second Temple Judaism because without the ability or the need to conduct foreign affairs, establish trade policies, and form alliances, the Jewish people were left in a position to develop what might be called a subculture or a counterculture within the larger Persian Empire. As an empire of diverse peoples and beliefs, the Persians were relatively content to allow this development, so long as it did not compromise the power and integrity of the empire itself.

When Alexander (the Great) of Macedonia launched his campaign to spread the influence of Hellenistic culture throughout the world (c. 335 BCE), his brand of cultural imperialism eventually led to significant changes in the political and religious situation of the Jewish people. While the immediate aftermath of Alexander's conquests did little to change the status quo, the rise of the Seleucid Empire (one of the empires to emerge from the breakup of Alexander's short-lived empire) and its control of Jerusalem beginning in c. 200 BCE posed one of the most serious challenges to Jewish identity and practice. The Seleucid King Antiochus IV Epiphanes (215–164 BCE) wanted to homogenize and hellenize his empire, and this meant the obliteration of all distinctively Jewish practices and customs. Antiochus plundered the Temple to finance his military exploits, and he outlawed the observance of the Mosaic Law under pain of death (see 2 Maccabees 6:1—7:42). Yet Antiochus was still able to garnish support from some sectors of Jewish society, including some important aristocratic families. These families and their allies actively supported the hellenization of the region, and this development created deep divisions within Judaism that lasted up to the first century.

In response to the outrageous behavior and policies of Antiochus, a group of Jewish nationalists who were zealous for the Mosaic Law launched a revolt. They were led by a family eventually known as the Maccabees. Judas, the eldest of several brothers, initially led the revolt, and he was able to win a level of independence for the Jewish people after defeating the Seleucid armies. This hard-won independence, however, would be relatively short lived given that the Maccabean victories were the result of, among other factors, an alliance with Rome against the Seleucids. Yet the political victories and compromises also contributed to important theological developments, not the least of which was the emergence of a form of apocalyptic Judaism.

Apocalyptic Judaism, or more generically, apocalyptic eschatology (*apokalypsis* means "revelation"; *eschatos* means "last" or "end"), refers to a theological movement that exercised considerable influence within Judaism in the years before and after the time of Jesus. Apocalyptic theology

APOCALYPTIC

Apocalyptic is defined as a genre of revelatory literature with a narrative framework in which a revelation from God is given to a human being, usually through an intermediary. The revelation makes known a transcendent reality that envisages eschatological salvation and the existence of another, supernatural world, and it is usually intended for a group in crisis with the purpose of exhortation or consolation by means of divine authority.[11]

had its roots in the eschatology of the prophets. They had long looked to a future when Yahweh would enter history in an act of salvation and establish a new covenant that would enable the world to be drawn to Yahweh through the witness of Israel. A righteous king would rise up to rule the people, ushering in peace, prosperity, and security. This event was thought to be imminent; hence the term *eschatology*, meaning the current age is the last age before Yahweh's decisive intervention in history. While such hope may have dimmed early in the Second Temple period, the persecution of the Seleucids and prophetic eschatology provided the foundation for a new, urgent, and dramatic eschatology.

Conservative voices in the prophetic and Deuteronomistic traditions had long contended that covenantal fidelity would be rewarded with long life and prosperity for the nation (e.g., Deuteronomy, chapter 30). While there were various attempts to qualify that position, the fundamental outlook of the tradition permeated a large swath of Second Temple Judaism. Yet with the Seleucid persecution, the inadequacies of the Deuteronomistic position became increasingly apparent. During the persecution, those Jews who chose to remain faithful to the covenant were made to suffer or were killed, and the Deuteronomistic tradition could not adequately address this situation. Thus, the tradition began to shift emphasis toward the nearness of Yahweh's future vindication of Israel. Special concern to defend Yahweh's righteousness and *chesed* (covenantal love and fidelity) became necessary, particularly when understood in light of the righteous suffering of the Maccabean martyrs and others.

At this time, a more fully developed understanding of an afterlife, articulated in terms of a general resurrection of the dead, emerged within Second Temple Judaism. This move afforded theologians the opportunity to, among other things, make sense of righteous suffering. Evil forces, led by the devil and his allies on earth, were trying to destroy the righteous, but in the near future, Yahweh would intervene and bring an end to the evil designs of demonic forces and the human empires they controlled. Given all of this emphasis on suffering and future vindication, it is no wonder that apocalyptic literature always addressed people in crisis and those suffering persecution. After all, if one were invested in the established social and political orders, there would be no need to hope and pray for an immediate (or imminent) end to that order.

Jewish apocalyptic theology provides the New Testament and the message of Jesus with its basic footing. Readers should be aware of the novelty of Jewish apocalyptic theology in the context of the Old Testament canon. In fact, with the exception of the book of Daniel (written in the second century BCE), there are no apocalyptic works per se in the Old Testament, and some of the most basic notions Christians take for granted in the New Testament are nowhere to be found in the Old (e.g., the devil, demonic possession, exorcisms, and resurrection). Some New Testament scholars, however, are somewhat uneasy with an interpretation of Jewish apocalyptic theology that emphasizes the ultimate "end of the world." Rather, they interpret apocalyptic theology and its corresponding worldview much more as a struggle between political and cultural forces. For example, N. T. Wright, the eminent Anglican bishop and New Testament scholar, summarizes first-century Jewish apocalyptic theology this way: Israel's election by Yahweh has come under threat, first by Israel's own infidelities and second by the corresponding domination from foreign powers allied with a Jewish leadership that has been compromised by those powers. The remedy to this situation will only come about when Yahweh intervenes and establishes his kingly rule.[12]

For Wright, the unfolding of the apocalyptic drama made Israel more keenly aware of Yahweh's identity and set the stage for the theological developments that took place as the early Christian community began to reflect on the identity of Jesus (i.e., New Testament Christology). According to Wright, the monotheism expressed in texts like the Shema (Deuteronomy 6:4–9) were not compromised or threatened, since some Jews of the late Second Temple period had begun to read texts such as Daniel, chapter 7 and its description of "one like a son of man," as suggesting that Yahweh encompassed a plurality of divine beings. In fact, the first-century Hellenistic Jewish philosopher Philo understood that God's word in Genesis, chapter 1 was "another God," yet such a statement did not violate the first commandment or the Shema.[13] In fact, Wright argues that following the Babylonian exile, there had emerged within Jewish thought significant speculation about God's wisdom and God's word, speculation that moved between two poles: (1) God must be understood as separate from the world where evil and sin reign, and (2) God is not remote but is active in the history of Israel and the world to combat and defeat the power of evil. Apocalyptic theology, then, revolves around the working out of these two convictions. Insofar as God had elected Israel, made a covenant with Israel, and continued to bless Israel in the course of history, God was now, in apocalyptic thought, entering

THE MAJOR SECTS WITHIN PALESTINIAN JUDAISM

SECT OR GROUP	DESCRIPTION	TORAH	POLITICS	APOCALYPTIC
Herodians	What many would today call secular Jews who had made significant compromises in their religious observances and who were invested in an alliance with Rome	Were very comfortable with playing down or ignoring many of the demands of the Torah, particularly if the demands conflicted with the dominant culture	Were allied with Rome and viewed devout Jews as potential revolutionaries	Were invested in the political and social status quo and therefore had no interest in apocalyptic theology
Sadducees	Priests associated with the Temple in Jerusalem	Strict adherence to the letter of the Torah, particularly as it applied to the Temple service; all theology was to be measured against the demands of the Torah; if it was not in the Torah, it was not theologically significant	Content with any alliance, including one with Rome or the Herodians, so long as it guaranteed the proper functioning of the Temple	Apocalyptic theology was not found in the Torah and did not pertain to the Temple; moreover, the Sadducees were heavily invested in the status quo and had no interest in apocalyptic theology
Pharisees	Laypeople who were regarded as teachers, they focused on extending the standards of Temple purity to the home and to daily life	In addition to the demands of the written Torah, Pharisees emphasized the role of an oral torah, or oral tradition, which was given to Moses on Mount Sinai	Longed for release from foreign oppression, and thus were anti-Rome and opposed to the Herodians, but were also willing to make some compromises and adopt a realpolitik when necessary	Not militaristic but generally embraced apocalyptic theology and its hopes and expectations for the overthrow of Roman rule and the advent of God's kingly reign

continued

THE MAJOR SECTS WITHIN PALESTINIAN JUDAISM *continued*

Essenes	Priests and their supporters who had become disenchanted with the high priests in Jerusalem and who retreated from public life to await the coming of a new Temple with a new priesthood	Shared Sadducees' concern for Torah instructions regarding the Temple, but sectarian literature (Dead Sea Scrolls) demonstrates their need to move beyond strict and exclusive adherence to Torah	Oppression was the result of an improper priesthood serving in the Temple; political forces allied in this profanation of the Temple must be judged by Yahweh	Highly invested in apocalyptic theology; a war between the forces of Yahweh and the forces of evil (sons of light vs. sons of darkness in the *War Scroll* [1QM]) will inaugurate God's kingly reign
Zealots	Militant revolutionaries who actively sought to overthrow Roman rule; they emerged after the lifetime of Jesus but had their roots in the Galilean countryside	Unknown	Violently opposed the Roman government of the region and all who were allied with it; sought to build an insurrection against Rome; active in the Jewish revolt of 66 CE	Unknown

into history at the *eschaton* as word (wisdom) or as "the son of man."

God's decisive entry into human history would not constitute the "end of the world," according to Wright. Rather, everything about Israel's beliefs and practices suggests that the *eschaton* should be seen an earthy, political event—similar in many ways to the prophetic eschatology that had emerged in the preexilic era. For many Jews of the first century, hope for resurrection was constitutive of the *eschaton*, but this hope did not represent a desire to flee from the world or to escape into some distant place. Resurrection was instead an important symbol of God's transformation of the world. Wright understands Jewish hope for resurrection as the indispensible way of expressing the hope of future vindication of the righteous amid the suffering that Israel had been undergoing since the time of the Babylonian exile.[14] Jewish apocalyptic theology, according to Wright, envisions a renewal of the created order established by God. This new order would supplant the existing order in which pagans dominated, and the true Israel would fulfill its vocation to bring Gentiles to the knowledge and worship of Yahweh. Hope for the resurrection became the primary means by which Israel expressed its hope for a "return from exile," the forgiveness of sins (the cause of its continuing exile), and the reestablishment of the true Israel, the symbol of the true humanity intended by God in creation.[15]

Quite naturally, little agreement exists within first-century Judaism on these matters, and who or what constituted the true Israel often became a matter of heated debate. After all, there was substantial room within first-century Judaism for great differences at the level of what one might call secondary beliefs, and these differences would create rival descriptions of who could be counted as part of the true Israel and, therefore, who would be saved from destruction.[16] The Pharisees, for example, saw the true Israel as those Jews who embraced a concern for purity and holiness in all aspects of daily life. For the Essenes, a group of somewhat reclusive priests and their supporters, the true Israel would be defined by those who followed "the teacher of righteousness" and abided by the rules of the community. For others, the true Israel was defined simply as those who were under the covenant and who participated faithfully in the Temple ceremonies. Throughout the first century, various movements sought to redefine the boundaries between the true Israel (those who would see resurrection) and God's enemies (those who would be destroyed), and the literature produced by these movements proves that this tendency was ubiquitous if not universal. The New Testament itself is rife with examples of redefining boundaries. Faithfulness to the covenant in the present, amid the persecutions and violence of foreign oppressors, would be rewarded in the future with resurrection and participation in a new world that God would soon inaugurate in the *eschaton*.

Conclusion

The world of Jesus and the early Christian writers was far more complex than this chapter might seem to suggest. While one must not get bogged down in the "world behind the text," failure to take this background into account also threatens to distort the text. When readers of the Gospels take the time to become familiar, even in a cursory way, with the complex world of the New Testament, their ability to appreciate the nuances and difficulties presented in the writings of the evangelists increases substantially. Moreover, when the biblical text is appropriately contextualized, the theological importance of the Christian understanding of revelation in history comes into bolder relief.

| QUESTIONS FOR UNDERSTANDING

1. What was the impact of Greek philosophy on the world of the New Testament?

2. What was the patronage system, and how did it operate?

3. How did the values of honor and shame function in the world of the New Testament?

4. List and describe four distinctive features of Second Temple Judaism.

5. What were the specific historical circumstances that gave birth to Jewish apocalyptic eschatology?

6. Why should readers be cautious about characterizing the place of women in first-century Palestine?

| QUESTIONS FOR REFLECTION

1. Given the discussion of the historical, cultural, and theological background of the New Testament in this chapter, how might this information aid the interpretation of the Gospels? Can this information hinder the interpretation of the Gospels? Explain.

2. The hellenization of Palestine deeply divided Judaism, with some advocating accommodation to the dominant culture and others embracing an apocalyptic theology and resisting that culture even to the point of death. How does one's stance on accommodation to the dominant culture affect one's attitude toward apocalyptic theology? If one is rewarded or punished by the dominant culture, how does that relate to one's own approach to apocalyptic eschatology?

3. How do the values of honor and shame pertain to contemporary Western culture? Explain.

| FOR FURTHER READING

Getty-Sullivan, Mary Ann. *Women in the New Testament*. Collegeville, MN: Liturgical, 2001.

Malina, Bruce J. *The New Testament World: Insights from Cultural Anthropology*. Rev. and enl. ed. Louisville: Westminster John Knox, 2001.

Wright, N. T. *The New Testament and the People of God. Christian Origins and the Question of God*, vol. 1. Minneapolis, MN: Fortress, 1992.

| ENDNOTES

1. Philo, *On Dreams*, 1.

2. John Dominic Crossan and Burton Mack are two prominent proponents of this thesis. Together with other scholars they argue that the life and ministry of Jesus were essentially that of a peripatetic Cynic philosopher. Only the imposition of Jewish apocalyptic thought by subsequent generations of early Christian writers moved the account of Jesus' life and ministry away from its original focus.

3. Edward Gibbon, *The History of the Decline and Fall of the Roman Empire*, Penguin Classics abridged edition (New York: Penguin), 9–14.

4. See Joachim Gnilka, *Jesus of Nazareth* (Peabody, MA: Hendrickson, 1997), 34–41.

5. See Bonnie Thurston, *Women in the New Testament: Questions and Commentary* (New York: Crossroad, 1998), 8–28, for a brief but helpful overview.

6. See Mary Douglas, *Purity and Danger: An Analysis of Concepts of Pollution and Taboo* (London: Rutledge, 1966), 51–71, and Bruce J. Malina, *The New Testament World: Insights from Cultural Anthropology*, revised edition (Louisville, KY: Westminster John Knox, 1993), 165.

7. See the inscriptions of Sargon II related to the fall of Samaria in *Ancient Near Eastern Texts Relating to the Old Testament*, ed. James B. Pritchard (Princeton, NJ: Princeton University Press, 1955), 284–287.

8. The dating of both Ezra's and Nehemiah's careers is notoriously difficult. No clear consensus has emerged in the literature, but most of the proposed solutions concur that the careers of these two figures unfold at the close of the fifth century or perhaps at the start of the fourth. See Robert North, "The Chronicler: 1–2 Chronicles, Ezra, Nehemiah," in *The New Jerome Biblical Commentary* 23:82–83.

9. *m. Rosh. Hash.*, 1.1.

10. See *m. Sabb.* 7.2 for examples of the thirty-nine prohibited tasks. For examples of relaxed rules regarding the Sabbath rest, see *Jubilees*, 50:8–12, and the *Damascus Document*, 10–11.

11. This is the definition adopted by the Society of Biblical Literature, as emended by David Hellholm, "The Problem of Apocalyptic Genre and the Apocalypse of John," in A. Y. Collins, ed., *Early Christian Apocalypticism: Genre and Social Setting*, Semeia 36 (Decatur, GA: Scholars Press, 1986), 27.

12. N. T. Wright, *The New Testament and the People of God* (Minneapolis: Fortress, 1992), 243.

13. Philo, *On Dreams*, 1:229.

14. Wright, *People of God*, 332.

15. Ibid.

16. Ibid., 336.

CHAPTER 2

THE HISTORICAL JESUS

The previous chapter sketched the contours of the first-century Palestinian world from which the Gospels emerged. The present chapter shifts attention from a presentation of background generalities to the heart of the Gospel message: the life, ministry, and death of Jesus of Nazareth. Of course, some readers might rightly ask whether this is "jumping the gun" a bit. After all, there has been no direct presentation of the Gospels themselves, and how can there be a presentation of the life and ministry of Jesus prior to a presentation of the Gospels?

Although such hesitation is appropriate, the rationale for treating the life and ministry of Jesus at this point in the text will become increasingly apparent over the course of the next chapters. But two points ought to be made here. First, as mentioned in the introduction, the Christian tradition understands God's revelation as realized in an economy of deeds (i.e., events in history) and words (i.e., text and tradition). In an effort to understand the interplay between event and text, it will prove helpful to gain an understanding of the life and ministry of Jesus in its historical context so that the presentation of the Gospels may, in turn, focus attention on the manner in which the evangelists, the human authors and editors of the Gospels, supplemented, ordered, and created their own proclamations of the gospel. Second, readers who are engaged in their first serious academic study of the Gospels

often become preoccupied with historical questions or issues. For example, when reading the accounts of the parable of the Great Feast or the Beatitudes in Matthew and Luke, students might rightly ask, given the differences in the accounts, "What did Jesus actually say?" Did Jesus give two different versions of the Beatitudes, or did he offer variations on the same parable on occasion? The question, "What did Jesus actually say or do?" admits that each of the evangelists was selective in his respective account of the gospel. Even if one were to adopt a consistent harmonization or blending of the Gospels (such an attempt breaks down quickly), that harmonization reaffirms the distinction between the gospel proclamation contained in the biblical texts and the events behind the text. By treating the question of the historical Jesus and outlining the limitations of our historical knowledge, this chapter hopes to relativize historical questions so that the full power of the evangelists' proclamation may come to the fore.[1]

Questing for the Historical Jesus

An account of how the quest for historical knowledge of Jesus came about will help to identify some of the perplexing philosophical, theological, and practical questions involved in any reconstruction of Jesus' life and ministry. A cursory summary of the three quests for the historical Jesus will serve as a caution for readers as they begin to formulate questions about the history of Jesus behind the Gospels.

The Old Quest for the Historical Jesus

Concern for reconstructing the historical Jesus emerged with the advent of the Enlightenment, though some would argue it is as old as Christianity itself.[2] In the eighteenth and early nineteenth centuries, hostility toward Christianity and its institutions came to a head in the revolutions that swept Europe, and this hostility did not begin to abate until the end of the nineteenth century. The philosophical and political insights of the Enlightenment fostered a wholesale rejection of the old order of Europe in which the Christian church held considerable cultural and political influence. Attacks on the Christian church were not limited to its political and social position in Europe; rather, the fundamental tenets of the Christian faith came under assault. The Enlightenment took special care to reassess the status and content of the Bible, particularly by shredding its historicity.

Hermann Samuel Reimarus (1694–1768), the first to assail the historical reliability of the Gospels, helped to inaugurate what has come to be known as the old quest for the historical Jesus. He argued that the aims of Jesus were different than the aims or goals of his disciples who, after the crucifixion, attempted to spiritualize his teachings and thereby transform what had originally been a nationalist revival movement into a religious one. Reimarus thus concluded that traditional Christianity was, to put it bluntly, a fraud. Historical research, he argued, unmasked this fraud and helped to put Jesus front and center while the dogmas of the Christian tradition

were forced to the margins. The contrast between the so-called Jesus of history, or the historical Jesus, and the Christ of faith can be traced to the work of Reimarus.

Throughout the nineteenth century other scholars attempted to offer portraits of the historical Jesus behind the canonical Gospels, including philosophers like David Friedrich Strauss (1808–1874). Strauss set forth his position in his major work entitled *The Life of Jesus Critically Examined* (1836), which went through several editions during Strauss's own lifetime. A student of the great German philosopher Georg Wilhelm Friedrich Hegel (1770–1831), Strauss argued that the Gospels were myths that attempted to communicate a reality that Hegel designated as the ideal of "God-manhood."[3] This somewhat complicated ideal may be described as a human life that actualizes the great spiritual orientation of human existence: union with God. For Strauss, Jesus was not *the* incarnation of God, but he was a sign and an example of what human beings might become if awakened to the spiritual foundations of their existence. So the disciples structured their accounts of Jesus so as to evoke the experience of a personal encounter with Jesus, the quintessential God-man or Spirit-person. This account or proclamation required evocative language to be effective, that is, it needed to go beyond simply reporting the events of Jesus' life if it was to get people to respond or react in a certain way. Straus suggested that myth was the means by which the disciples framed their proclamation, but they did so unconsciously. For Strauss, Christianity was not a fraud but a mistake or a misunderstanding of this basic dynamic; a mistake that could be corrected. This correction, however, required the demise of traditional Christianity, but at the same time would allow for the emergence of a new, more authentic and nondogmatic religion that understood the role and function of the ancient Christian myth.

What scholars have called the old quest, that is, the nineteenth-century quest for an account of Jesus behind the Gospels, ended in 1906 when Albert Schweitzer (1875–1965), a notable composer, physician, Nobel Peace Prize winner, and theologian, published his book, *The Quest of the Historical Jesus: A Critical Study of Its Progress from Reimarus to Wrede*. In this book, Schweitzer basically substantiated George Tyrrell's famous image of historical Jesus research at the time: Tyrrell (1861–1909) had remarked that such research was like looking down a dark well, seeing one's own dim reflection at the bottom of the well and mistaking it for the historical Jesus.[4] Schweitzer argued that Reimarus, the deist philosopher looking for political and social revolution, saw Jesus as a revolutionary; Strauss, the Hegelian philosopher, portrayed Jesus within the parameters of Hegelian philosophy; and the list went on. Schweitzer suggested that any responsible quest for the historical life and ministry of Jesus must take into account two important factors. First, sources for the quest are sparse, and those sources are not really concerned about relating the history of Jesus' life. Rather, the Gospels primarily reflect the cares and concerns of the earliest Christians and only secondarily reflect Jesus' actual life and ministry. Second, the appropriate historical and theological context for Jesus was first-century Jewish apocalyptic eschatology. Thus any portrait of Jesus must place him squarely in that context, as a consequence making him much less intelligible and attractive to contemporary audiences.

Schweitzer's thesis built upon the work of William Wrede (1859–1906; *The Messianic Secret*, 1901), who went so far as to take on the nature of the Gospels as sources for a history of Jesus. While Schweitzer believed that Wrede's skepticism went too far, the latter's work served as a warning against any facile assumptions about the historicity of the Gospels. Additionally, Johannes Weiss (1863–1914; *Jesus' Proclamation*

of the Kingdom of God, 1892) provided Schweitzer with important insights on the apocalyptic character of Jesus' message and ministry. In the end, Schweitzer sided with Weiss in characterizing Jesus and his ministry as an expression of Jewish apocalyptic theology. As such, the historical Jesus resists any attempt to make him immediately relevant to modern audiences.

The event that perhaps best concluded the old quest was the publication of Martin Kähler's book *The So-Called Historical Jesus and the Historic Biblical Christ* (actually published before Schweitzer's book).[5] For Kähler (1835–1912), the "historical" (*geschichtliche* in German) Jesus cannot be identified as the object of faith. Christians profess a faith in the risen Christ, and it is this "historic" (or *historische* in German) Jesus that makes a difference in history. Kähler's distinction between the historically reconstructed Jesus and the Christ of faith proclaimed within the community continues to influence theological circles today.

Bultmann and the Emergence of a New Quest

Rudolf Bultmann (1884–1976), a Lutheran pastor and theologian, helped Christian theology move beyond the seemingly intractable situation created by the demise of liberal theology and the old quest by articulating the Christian tradition in contemporary terms, precisely as an authentic expression of religious faith within a modern context. Bultmann argued that historical Jesus research rightly had no bearing on Christian faith. Only the mere fact of Jesus' existence was sufficient as the precondition for the proclamation of the early church. Yet, Bultmann was not unconcerned with historical issues. In fact, he pioneered an account of the history behind the development of the gospel tradition in terms of form criticism: the prehistory of the individual Gospel stories as oral tradition. This historical work, however, was meant to describe how the early church came to understand and communicate its faith in Christ. Equipped with this historical understanding (mostly through the reconstruction of the oral and literary forms through which the tradition passed), theologians could more effectively identify the historical and cultural factors that shaped the Gospels so as to liberate the real religious and transformative power of the early Christian proclamation (the kerygma). For Bultmann, and for Martin Kähler before him, only the kerygma of the risen Jesus has significance for believers, not a historically reconstructed figure of the past.[6] This kerygma was recoverable only when the mythical worldview of the New Testament, which encased the kerygma, could be stripped away.

For Bultmann and his supporters, a largely non-Christian symbolic and mythical worldview permeates the pages of the New Testament: heaven is up in the sky and hell and the abode of demons is deep within the earth. A battle between the forces of heaven and hell dictate the ebb and flow of human history, and the final consummation of that battle is breaking upon the writers of the biblical books. The corresponding view of salvation within that mythical worldview consists of rescue from diabolical forces through the intervention of the God-man's atoning sacrifice by which victory over the powers of evil is secured. For Bultmann, such a worldview must be demythologized since this mythical narrative cannot be the hope of Christians, and it is especially repugnant to the sensibilities of modern Christians.

The modern scientific worldview demands that contemporary Christians abandon ancient non-Christian mythologies so that the New Testament's understanding of the human condition will remain decisive for the modern believer and not its mythical worldview. In the Christian kerygma, embedded within the New Testament, the existence of the human person with and

without faith remains the indispensible core of Christian faith. The human being outside faith, or one who lives "according to the flesh," is subject to the impermanence and decay associated with the world. In faith, however, human beings live "according to the Spirit," that is, a life based on what cannot be seen and what is not disposable. For Bultmann, the eschatology usually associated with Jewish apocalyptic theology must now be read as an account of the new life of the believer, a new creation, free from the trouble of this transitory and disposable world. Bultmann asserts that this discovery is dependent on the New Testament. The revelation that takes place in Christ is the revelation of the love of God; this love frees one from oneself and opens one up to the freedom and possibility of the future. Christian faith knows the act of God in Christ as the condition for the possibility of human loving and authenticity. That is why, for Bultmann, the significance of the Christ occurrence rests not in historical questions but in discerning what God wants to say to humanity in the proclamation of Christ. The cross of Christ is to be understood not as an occurrence outside of oneself and one's world; rather, the meaning of the cross is found in the lives of believers who commit to the suffering that authentic freedom demands.

Many refused to accept Bultmann's radical rejection of the historical Jesus from the scope of Christian theology, including some theologians who were supportive of Bultmann's overall project. Ernst Käsemann (1906–1998), one of Bultmann's former students, in particular, took exception to Bultmann's position on the historical Jesus. In a paper delivered at a meeting of Bultmann's former students, Käsemann framed his criticism of Bultmann's position around three points: (1) there was a danger of Docetism (i.e., a belief that Jesus only appeared to be human and enter into history) in Bultmann's approach to the kerygma; (2) the evangelists composed the Gospels because they were in fact concerned with the earthly Jesus; (3) the Christian tradition has always identified the risen Christ of the kerygma with the earthly Jesus. Together, these three points convincingly argue that, contrary to Bultmann's assertion, the quest for the historical Jesus was theologically necessary and that the biblical sources would yield historical fruit. While the new quest insisted on the integrity and fruitfulness of historical Jesus research as an integral part of contemporary Christian faith, the precise methodology for such research as well as its precise place within contemporary theology remain a matter of considerable debate in what scholars have now come to call the third quest.

In the mid-1980s, N. T. Wright identified a distinct movement in historical Jesus research as the third quest. This new wave of Jesus research has several distinctive features that differentiate it from the earlier quests, but in any given author one can also trace various concerns back to previous scholarship. For example, the Jesus Seminar, a group of scholars and other interested individuals, have produced a series of works that seem, in many ways, to evoke the old quest and the new quest by using historical Jesus research to attack traditional forms of Christianity. John P. Meier, a prominent figure in historical Jesus research, has argued that the third quest represents a significant departure from both the old and the new quests. The following list represents the distinctive features of the third quest as identified by Meier:

1. The third quest is characterized by its diversity; it has an ecumenical and international character (whereas earlier quests were almost exclusively male, German, and Protestant).

2. It clarifies the question of reliable sources (i.e., the New Testament is viewed as the primary source for research and other texts and artifacts like the apocryphal gospels or the Dead Sea Scrolls are only secondary sources).

3. It presents a more accurate and nuanced picture of first-century Judaism.

4. It employs new insights from archaeology, philology, and sociology.

5. It clarifies the application of criteria of historicity (i.e., unlike previous quests it consistently and carefully applies certain criteria for sifting the New Testament and other sources for historically reliable material).

6. It gives proper attention to the miracle tradition (as opposed to the previous quests that relegated the miracle tradition to the status of legend or myth).

7. It takes the Jewishness of Jesus with utter seriousness and portrays Jesus within the context of first-century Judaism.[7]

Two of these listed features of the third quest stand out as particularly significant. The third quest's placement of the historical Jesus squarely within the context of first-century Palestinian Judaism stands in sharp contrast to the tendency of previous quests to contrast Jesus with his Jewish context. While it is difficult to overestimate the value of this shift, perhaps more distinctive of the third quest is its emphasis on the rigorous application of criteria in any historical assessment of New Testament material on Jesus.

The Criteria for Historical Jesus Research

John Meier, in his magisterial treatment of the historical Jesus (*A Marginal Jew*), repeatedly argues that whether one affirms or denies the historicity of a particular story from the Gospels, one must articulate the principle on which that judgment is based.[8] Meier's allegiance to the criteria of historicity comes out clearly in the following quote:

It is only in the light of this rigorous application of historical standards that one comes to see what was wrong with so much of the first and second quests. All too often, the first and second quests were theological projects masquerading as historical projects. Now, there is nothing wrong with a historically informed theology or Christology; indeed, they are to be welcomed and fostered. But a Christology that seeks to profit from historical research into Jesus is not the same thing and must be carefully distinguished from a purely empirical, historical quest for Jesus that prescinds from or brackets what is known by faith. This is not to betray faith. . . . Let the *historical* Jesus be a truly and solely *historical* reconstruction, with all the lacunae and truncations of the total reality that a purely historical inquiry into a marginal figure of ancient history will inevitably involve. After the purely historical project is finished, there will be more than enough time to ask about correlations with Christian faith and academic Christology.[9]

Now one might rightly argue that such "bracketing" of faith in favor of historical rigor amounts to a *sacrificium fides* (i.e., "sacrifice of faith"), a compartmentalization of faith and critical reason that scholars such as Bultmann had decried in the twentieth century. But on the other hand, Meier wants to confine historical Jesus research to the discipline of history so as to avoid the pitfalls of the earlier quests in which historical rigor was feigned in favor of self-serving theological portraits of Jesus based on conjecture rather than evidence.

This emphasis on methodology in the third quest stands out as one of the great merits of this stage in the quest for the historical Jesus. Yet, at the same time, many scholars wonder whether the appeal to a consistent methodology really just masks the positivism of so much historical Jesus research: one can really know for sure what happened in the past simply by looking at the data available. But Meier's emphasis on methodology at least supplies scholars with some measure of common ground on which to base

their disagreements, so long as one truly abandons the hope of producing an objective account of the historical Jesus upon which there can be universal consensus.

Recognizing that consensus among historians remains an elusive goal, Meier has suggested that historical Jesus research ought to be compared to a committee meeting. While such a comparison will make many cringe, the analogy appears to be quite apt. As on any committee, there are a wide range of positions and backgrounds represented. For the purposes of reconstructing the historical Jesus, Meier envisions a committee of experts on the first century, early Judaism and early Christianity. This committee is composed of intelligent and honest Catholics, Jews, Protestants, agnostics, atheists, and so on.

In this imaginative scenario, Meier sequesters the committee in the basement of the Harvard Divinity School library (or any library in which one has access to all the best historical resources) until they produce a consensus document on the historical Jesus. This scenario is meant as a kind of humorous parable about historical Jesus research and the nature of committee work. Although some suggest that in his fantastic scenario Meier surrenders control of the historical Jesus project to the veto power of the atheist, Meier simply wants to emphasize the nature and the importance of consensus building in historical Jesus research, and the role of the nonbeliever cannot be ignored here. If one of the committee members wants to argue in favor of the historicity of a given story from the New Testament, he or she must make a case, using accepted methodologies, and convince others that he or she is correct. In the end, according to Meier, the document that will emerge from that library basement will be fairly thin and will reflect a relatively pale portrait of Jesus, but such is the nature of historical Jesus research.

Meier's emphasis on methodological rigor makes the articulation of criteria central to his project. He has outlined five major primary criteria for historical Jesus research.[10] These criteria represent the principles by which one makes judgments about whether a given biblical story, or part of a story, is historical, and the criteria necessarily presuppose an understanding of how the Gospels developed. This basic understanding of the gospel tradition reflects the general consensus of New Testament scholars and affirms that Jesus of Nazareth, his life and ministry, form the basis of the tradition.

This first stage in the development of the tradition came to an end with the crucifixion and death of Jesus, and a new stage emerged with the experience of the Resurrection. At this point the tradition took a major turn; the one who had made a proclamation about the kingdom of God now became the object of that proclamation: "Jesus is risen! Jesus is Lord." The early Christian kerygma represents the second stage in the development of the gospel tradition. Finally, the Gospels combined elements of stage one, in the form of the memory tradition of the earliest Christian communities, with the experience of the risen Jesus and the proclamation of the kerygma.

Of course, there can be no clean or neat separation between stages one and two. Rather, in addition to preserving the memory tradition of Jesus' life and ministry, the evangelists created faith proclamations for various communities of believers enduring various problems or issues. As such, one would expect to find a large amount of material in the Gospels that, in fact, does not come from stage one. The five criteria discussed below are meant to help distinguish what material comes from stage one and what material is the product of the early church's concerns and therefore represent developments from stages two or three.

STAGES IN THE FORMATION OF THE GOSPEL TRADITION

STAGE	STAGE ONE (PRIOR TO 30 CE)	STAGE TWO (30 CE–68 CE)	STAGE THREE (69 CE–100 CE)
Description	This is the stage during which Jesus lived and taught about the coming of the kingdom of God. The stage comes to a close with the death of Jesus.	Following the death of Jesus, his followers begin to proclaim his Resurrection from the dead and his living presence within the church. This proclamation (kerygma) focuses on Christ's Resurrection and the abiding presence of Christ and not on the details of his ministry.	The kerygma begins to incorporate the memory tradition of Jesus' life and ministry, thus transforming the Christian proclamation so that it takes on the form of a narrative of Jesus' life and ministry.
Material	There is no written material from this stage, but historians have devised criteria to help sift out that material that can be traced back to stage one.	Paul's Authentic Letters and portions of Acts and the Gospels contain examples of the primitive apostolic kerygma.	The Gospels

One basic indicator of historicity is the so-called criterion of embarrassment. This criterion presupposes that the New Testament, and the Gospels in particular, were written to propagate or to promote faith in Jesus and that the earliest Christians, therefore, naturally tried to portray Jesus in the best possible light, making creative and theologically insightful additions to the memory tradition of Jesus' life and ministry. These creative additions would necessarily move in the direction of enhancing the appeal of Jesus. The criterion of embarrassment seeks to identify a story or saying of Jesus in the New Testament that might compromise or embarrass the early church and its proclamation. It follows that any material in the Gospels that actually hurts the church's credibility is probably not an embellishment or fabrication of the early church. Rather, the material in question should be attributed to a memory about what Jesus said or did: stage one material.

One example of material that would satisfy the criterion of embarrassment is Jesus' trial and execution by public authorities. It is hard for modern Christians to imagine how horribly shameful such a public execution would be. Moreover, to suggest that the one who underwent such a horrific and shameful death was Israel's savior, the one who would throw off the oppressors and act as God's eschatological judge was no doubt a hard sell for those earliest apostles and missionaries trying to promote the Christian faith (see 1 Corinthians 1:23–24). The criterion

THE GOSPELS AND THE TWO-SOURCE HYPOTHESIS

The Gospels of Matthew, Mark, and Luke are called the Synoptic Gospels (*synoptic* means to see together) because of their obvious similarities. Yet the obvious differences demand a nuanced account of their interrelationship. Most scholars accept what has come to be called "the two-source hypothesis" as the appropriate way of explaining the relationship among the three Synoptic Gospels (this theory will be presented in greater detail in the next chapter). Mark represents the most basic form of the gospel story, but Mark was not the origin of all the material in Matthew and Luke. In fact, Matthew and Luke had material in common, and the origin of this material came from a document that contained many sayings of Jesus, often abbreviated with the letter Q, and thus was born the two-source hypothesis: two sources, Mark and Q, account for the differences and similarities among the three Synoptic Gospels along with special source material that accounts for material unique to Matthew and Luke (abbreviated M and L respectively). When applying the criterion of multiple attestation of sources, scholars will often appeal to the two-source hypothesis as justification.

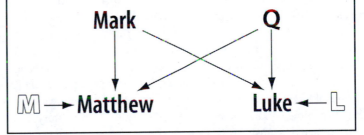

of embarrassment argues that the earliest Christians would not likely have gone out of their way to weaken their own tenuous position, and if one can identify those stories that are difficult or embarrassing, then these stories may be attributed to stage one (i.e., Jesus' life and ministry).

The criterion of multiple attestation of forms and sources is perhaps the most objective of the criteria because it simply focuses on the principle that material found in more than one independent source or in several different literary forms is more likely to be rooted in stage one. Decisive in the application of this criterion is the recognition that many New Testament sources are actually dependent on one another (e.g., Matthew and Luke are both dependant on Mark; see the chart on page 47 and chapter 3 for a full discussion) so that what looks like multiple witnesses to a certain saying or deed of Jesus might only be singular attestation. Equally important for the application of the criterion is the accurate identification of literary forms; if one finds two different literary forms (e.g., a healing story and a controversy story), agreeing on a mode of behavior or a pattern of speech, then that also may be judged to go back to stage one. For example, Jesus' reputation as a healer is confirmed in both healing stories and conflict stories, and this evidence suggests that this reputation goes back to stage one.

The criterion of rejection and execution operates on the conviction that no one would dispute that Jesus died on a Roman cross (late Islamic traditions not withstanding). In other words, those in power executed Jesus. It stands to reason, therefore, that Jesus had come to be viewed as a threat by those in power; why else would they have carried out a trial and a public execution? This criterion operates by isolating material in the New Testament that might help to explain how Jesus could have threatened the established order (e.g., he claimed a kind of sweeping authority, he spoke or acted against the Temple, he questioned social norms that carried political overtones).

The criterion of discontinuity or dissimilarity is the oldest of the criteria, employed in a de facto manner by Reimarus and made the explicit centerpiece of any historical claims by Bultmann. In contemporary historical Jesus research, however, it has come under fire, and scholars like Morna Hooker and others have worked to temper the use of the criterion.[11] The criterion originally sought to isolate sayings and deeds of Jesus that could not be derived from either first-century Judaism or the practice of the early church. The

place of women in Jesus' ministry provides an apt example of the criterion's application. Jesus is portrayed in the Gospels as including unaccompanied women (i.e., women without husbands or male relatives around) among his closest friends and associates, and this was unusual for a first-century Jew. Moreover, the earliest Christians were well on their way to enshrining gender distinctions in their theology (cf. the Pastoral Epistles). Jesus' practice of having women among his closest friends and disciples stood in sharp contrast, or was dissimilar, to the practices of both early Judaism and the early Christian church.

The criterion of coherence rounds out Meier's five primary criteria. While the other criteria seem to exclude so much material from stage one, this criterion looks to recover discarded passages by examining how those passages resonate with material that has already satisfied other criteria. For example, if the application of the other criteria established that Jesus exercised special concern for the poor and other marginalized figures in his ministry (e.g., the poor, the sick, women), and we also had a passage that otherwise satisfied none of the criteria but depicted Jesus reacting favorably when he was approached by a woman with a public reputation as a sinner (e.g., Luke 7:36–50), then one may call the story historical. While this story does not, strictly speaking, satisfy any of the other criteria, it does cohere well with the pattern of behavior exercised by Jesus during his lifetime, and it is "the kind of thing Jesus said and did" during his ministry. This is particularly the case where we have identified both sayings and corresponding actions that were characteristic of Jesus.

While some scholars raise questions about the use of specific criteria, and not all scholars would agree on the use or importance of individual criteria, the development of methodological rigor in historical Jesus research stands as an important advance in the field. As Meier has

PRIMARY CRITERIA FOR HISTORICAL JESUS RESEARCH

CRITERION	DESCRIPTION	EXAMPLES
Embarrassment	The criterion of embarrassment focuses on the sayings or deeds of Jesus that would have created difficulty for the early church's efforts to promote faith in Christ. The criterion points to sayings or deeds of Jesus that were inconvenient or embarrassing but nonetheless part of the memory tradition of the church and thus a part of the Gospels.	Jesus' baptism by John and his execution by the authorities as a criminal.
Multiple Attestation of Forms and Sources	The criterion looks for sayings or deeds of Jesus that are reported in more than one independent source (e.g., Paul and Mark but not necessarily Matthew and Mark) as well as more than one form (i.e., parable and miracle story).	The Last Supper reported in Mark 14:22–25 and in 1 Corinthians 11:23–26.
Rejection and Execution	The criterion seeks to isolate those sayings and deeds of Jesus that would help explain why some people in power found Jesus to be worthy of public execution.	Jesus' triumphant or messianic entry into Jerusalem and his cleansing of the Temple.
Discontinuity or Dissimilarity	This criterion seeks to isolate sayings and deeds of Jesus that cannot be derived from first-century Judaism or from the practice of the early church.	Jesus' status as an unmarried adult male.
Coherence	This criterion, in some ways, supplements the rest. It operates by examining material that otherwise would not enjoy historical credibility (i.e., material that does not satisfy the other criteria listed above and suggests that such material may be admitted as historically plausible if the material coheres well with other material that has been judged historical.	The parable of the Good Samaritan does not satisfy any other criterion of historicity, but may be admitted as historical, albeit in a loose sense, since it coheres well with what we already know about Jesus.

consistently pointed out, whether one affirms or denies the historicity of a particular piece of data, one must make an argument based on a set of criteria. Although the use of criteria will not solve the problem of "gazing down a dark well," it nonetheless represents an important move forward in the quest to understand the limitations of historical Jesus research and its place within the study of the Gospels.

Applying the Criteria: A Tentative Sketch of the Historical Jesus

The application of the criteria mentioned above is no simple matter. In fact, the criteria are simply tools, and like all tools, they require intelligence, character, and sophistication on the part of those who would use the tools for them to work effectively. In other words, the criteria cannot work by themselves, apart from people.[12] What follows below represents a generalized overview of what contemporary historians claim to know about Jesus of Nazareth, the historical human being. Readers should recognize two important points regarding the following sketch: (1) what follows is not a full-scale treatment of historical Jesus research; and (2) this sketch is limited by the data available and by the limitations of historical investigation (Christians believe that there was a lot more to Jesus than what "history" can say). The results of historical Jesus research, and even the sketch provided here, are substantiated by rigorous research and argumentation, but that does not mean that new evidence and new insight cannot alter the overview that has been offered here. It is all very tentative. This sketch is offered with the hope that the creativity and theological insight of the evangelists, as well as their fidelity to the memory of Jesus, might be better appreciated by readers.

Birth, Family, and Ancestry

The story of the birth of Jesus by a virgin through the powerful intervention of the Holy Spirit remains a staple of Christian faith, yet as a piece of the historical Jesus, it fails to find consensus among historians (recall the image of the committee meeting mentioned above). Yet the Gospels themselves do indicate that some of Jesus' opponents seem to have questioned his parentage (John 8:41–42), and Jesus' own attitude toward his family seems rather unusual (e.g., Mark 3:21; John 7:5). Jesus' contemporaries regarded him as the son of Mary and Joseph, and that is about as much as historians can say about the parents of Jesus. Yet even as early as the second century, opponents of the Christian movement mocked Christian beliefs by circulating a story about the mother of Jesus and her rape by a Roman soldier.[13] Needless to say, it appears that there were issues around the circumstances of Jesus' birth from a very early time, but few historical conclusions emerge clearly. Mark, for his part, remains remarkably silent about Jesus' origins, and Matthew and Luke supply readers with strikingly incompatible accounts of Jesus' birth. In the end, historians are left with little evidence upon which to base a solid judgment about Jesus' family, but the criteria mentioned in the previous section can help pull out a few items worthy of note.

The name of Jesus, *Yeshu* (an abbreviated form of the name Joshua or *Yehoshua*), as well as the names of Jesus' parents and siblings in the Synoptic Gospels (i.e., Joseph, Mary, James, Joses, Simon) suggest to some scholars that the family of Jesus was, perhaps, part of the reawakening of Jewish nationalism occurring in Galilee in the first century. John Meier believes these names indicate that like most of their Galilean neighbors, Jesus' family was frustrated with Roman occupation, and the act of naming children after the great heroes of the Bible pointed

SKETCHES OF THE HISTORICAL JESUS

As George Tyrell's parable of looking down a dark well reminds us, every account of the historical Jesus is subject to the criticism that it is self-serving. In the chart below, four prominent scholars are listed along with a brief description of their background and a summary of their approach to the historical Jesus. All are well-respected scholars, yet they embrace different methodologies and come to different conclusions about Jesus.

SCHOLAR	BACKGROUND	SKETCH OF JESUS
Burton Mack	An academic trained in Germany and teaching at Claremont University, Mack is committed to the sociological reconstruction of early Christianity.	Relying on sociology in order to reconstruct the early Christian movement, Mack sees the Gospels as myth—documents that construct a new worldview and social order. He also seeks to uncover the earliest traditions about Jesus through a reconstruction of the hypothetical document Q. He sees Jesus as the founder of a new social movement.
E. P. Sanders	This progressive mainline Protestant scholar is most noted for his work on early Judaism and Christianity; he offered a portrait of Judaism as a religion of grace and redemption rather than a religion of "works-righteousness."	Jesus was a reform-minded Jew, interested in recovering and affirming Judaism in his ministry.
E. Schüssler Fiorenza	A Harvard professor and perhaps the preeminent Catholic feminist scholar of Jesus, she has challenged the presuppositions of historical-critical methodologies.	Jesus was an egalitarian preacher who cut through distinctions of gender and religious difference to institute a new kind of community.
John Meier	A Roman Catholic priest, Meier has taught at Catholic University and Notre Dame.	Jesus proclaimed the advent of God's kingdom, gathered disciples into a new community of faith, performed miracles, and embraced his own death as a religiously significant event.

to a hope that simmered just beneath the surface—a hope for God's decisive intervention in Israel's history to bring about deliverance from Gentile oppression and the restoration of Israel. Additionally, the early Christian tradition of explicitly tying Jesus to the Davidic family tree (e.g., Romans 1:3–4), itself evidence of a certain eschatological hope, needs to be taken seriously as part of an early tradition about Jesus. While no historian can establish the genetic relationship between Jesus and David, the criteria (specifically that of multiple attestation) suggest that

Davidic descent was clearly a staple within the Christology of the earliest community of Christians, and perhaps as far back as Jesus' own ministry.

The circumstances around the upbringing of Jesus remain hopelessly opaque, though a few generalities emerge from the Gospels. First, it seems probable, given the archeological evidence at hand, that Jesus spoke Aramaic as his primary language and had some knowledge of Hebrew and maybe even a little Greek (as a craftsman living among Gentile towns, knowing Greek would have been an asset for doing business). While Jesus and his family cannot be counted among those who were well off, his status as a *tektōn*, or "craftsman" (Mark 6:3), suggests that they were not among the utterly destitute.

The identification of Jesus' brothers and sisters in the Gospels touches on significant theological issues in the history of the Christian tradition, usually dividing Catholics and Protestants. For their part, Catholics will take the position that Jesus had no true brothers or sisters (i.e., no brothers and sisters who shared the same set of biological parents) because Catholic doctrine holds that Mary remained always a virgin. Protestants, on the other hand, generally not holding the doctrine of Mary's perpetual virginity, will often argue that the plain sense of the Gospels points to the fact that Jesus did have brothers and sisters, and they would suggest that these siblings were the offspring of Mary and Joseph following the birth of Jesus (often called the Helvidian position). Jerome, in his controversial fourth-century work, *Against Helvidius*, argued against such a position, positing instead that "the brothers and sisters" of Jesus mentioned in the Gospels were really only cousins. But such an argument ignores the fact that the New Testament often uses the word *cousin* (*anepsios*) to distinguish those relatives who were not brothers and sisters (*adelphoi / adelphai*, the term found in Mark 6:3 and Matthew 13:55–56). Not until the second

century, well after the Gospels were written, did widespread concern over the "brothers and sisters of Jesus" emerge. The *Protoevangelium of James* (a nonbiblical book) describes Joseph as having had children by a previous wife, thus accounting for the "brothers and sisters" of Jesus as stepbrothers and stepsisters. The linguistic evidence and the text of the New Testament both seem to favor the so-called Helvidian position, (i.e., the brothers and sisters of Jesus mentioned in the Gospels were his true brothers and sisters born after Jesus), but this evidence does not necessarily exclude the position that the brothers and sisters mentioned in the New Testament were the halfbrothers and halfsisters of Jesus from a previous marriage by Joseph (the so-called Epiphanian solution), an understanding that reflects the doctrinal position of the Catholic Church.[14]

Modern books like Dan Brown's popular *Da Vinci Code* have quite naturally moved the question of Jesus' family away from his mother and siblings to Jesus himself: Did Jesus have his own family? Some have argued that since marriage was the standard and practically universal practice within first-century Palestinian Judaism, the silence of the New Testament on the issue of Jesus' marital status should lead one to conclude that Jesus in fact was married. Arguments from silence are notoriously shaky, however. Given that the New Testament regularly records the names of women with whom Jesus had been associated, omission of the name of Jesus' wife would seem inexplicable. Moreover, celibacy was not unheard of in the first century. Both Josephus (see *Jewish War* 2.8.2) and Philo (*That Every Good Person Is Free* 12–13) suggest that at least some of the Essenes were celibate, and even the Old Testament provides the example of the prophet Jeremiah's celibacy. It is possible that Jesus, like the Essenes, John the Baptist, and even Jeremiah, chose celibacy as an eschatological symbol—the time is short, and it is not the time to invest in this world and in the things of this world.

Jesus, John the Baptist, and the Shape of Jesus' Ministry

Contrary to the Gospels, the first-century Jewish historian Josephus (*Jewish Antiquities* 18.3.3) does not describe John the Baptist in relationship to Jesus and portrays John not as an eschatological prophet but as a moralizing philosopher. While Josephus's characterization of the Baptist should not be allowed to trump the biblical material, it does supply an interesting perspective on the Baptist. Historians must account for the ministry and message of John within the context of first-century Judaism and recognize that the New Testament portrayals of him represent early Christian interests.

As historians look at John's ministry, particularly at his practice of baptizing, they interpret it in light of the water purification rituals shared by other "desert groups" (specifically the Essenes of Qumran) in first-century Judaism. In this context, three important convictions emerge: (1) the belief that Israel had gone astray; (2) purification was offered to those who seek it through repentance; (3) this repentance offered hope for salvation on the day of judgment. These convictions provide the interpretive matrix for John's message and his baptism. Thus John's baptism was a one-time action that accentuated his role in the unfolding eschatological drama; it did not signal entry into a new group or sect as was the case in Jewish proselyte baptism or early Christian baptism. John's baptism symbolized the final pouring out of the Spirit on those who would repent at this last hour. John understood his baptism as a dramatic acting out of the candidate's repentance while anticipating and announcing the definitive action of God in the outpouring of the Holy Spirit by "the one mightier than I" (e.g., Mark 1:7).

The question of the relationship between Jesus and John forces historians to deal with the biblical account of baptism of the former by the latter (e.g., Mark 1:9–11). The criterion of embarrassment suggests that this episode goes back to stage one. After all, why would Christians create a story where Jesus submitted to John's baptism, thereby creating unnecessary problems, unless there was a pervasive memory tradition of Jesus' baptism by John? Additionally, there are multiple attestations (Mark and Q) for the baptism as well as significant discontinuity between early Jewish and Christian baptism. Specifically, while first-century Jewish baptism generally inaugurated one into the Jewish community as did early Christian baptism, the latter also united one to Christ's death and Resurrection (Romans 6:3–11). Jesus' baptism provides something of a window into the religious mind-set of Jesus and, according to Meier, historians may infer the following conclusions regarding the religious mind-set of Jesus at the start of his ministry:

- He believed that the end of Israel's history was approaching.
- He believed Israel had gone astray and was in need of repentance.
- The only way to escape the coming wrath was not to claim descent from Abraham, but to undergo conversion of mind and heart.
- His baptism was a way for him to acknowledge John's role as an eschatological prophet.[15]

Meier concludes that Jesus submitted to John's charismatic ritual because he believed that it was necessary for salvation from God's judgment. As Meier points out, however, Jesus' consciousness of sin does not equal "personal sin" in first-century Judaism.[16] One may cite passages in Ezra and Nehemiah as examples of how Jews of the Second Temple period could identify themselves as sinners without necessarily identifying sin with personal transgressions (Ezra 9:6–7; Nehemiah 9:16–37; see also 1QS 1:18–2:2). In the example both Ezra and Nehemiah associate themselves and their unrepentant contemporaries with the generations that brought about the destruction of the nation two hundred years earlier. So perhaps Jesus envisioned his own baptism "for the remission of sins" as part of a corporate act of penance for the sins of the entire nation, or even the entire world.

Moving beyond the baptism scene and asking the question of the relationship between Jesus and John the Baptist takes one to the Fourth Gospel (i.e., John) where we find the only direct evidence regarding Jesus' direct association with John the Baptist beyond the baptism scene. In John 1:28–45 (see also 3:22–30) Jesus appears with the Baptist in the desert near the area by the Jordan where John was engaged in a ministry of baptism. Jesus spends some time with his disciples baptizing, while John continues to baptize nearby.[17] The criterion of embarrassment helps to substantiate that Jesus and his first disciples came from John's circle since there is a tendency within the Fourth Gospel to suppress any direct connection between the ministry of John and the ministry of Jesus. In the Synoptic Gospels we find some evidence of what Jesus thought of John. In Matthew 11:2–6 John sends disciples to ask if Jesus is "the one who is to come." Moreover, Jesus also uses Old Testament images (Isaiah 35:5–6; 29:18–19; 61:1) to tell John that the *eschaton*, or "end," has arrived. The lack of any response of faith or acknowledgment on the part of the Baptist argues, through the criterion of embarrassment, in favor of the historicity of the episode. The absence of that affirmation of faith on John's part does nothing to underwrite the Christian cause, particularly given that the followers of John the Baptist were still an independent force in the first century.

The popularization of contemporary speculation about Jesus' background and formative years stand in sharp contrast with the material presented here. For example, historians have no real evidence that Jesus went to India, or Britain, to study and prepare for his ministry, and there is no evidence that he had a family of his own. In fact, what historians can affirm about Jesus' formative years fits remarkably well with what one finds in the Gospels. Jesus' entire life seemed to be directed toward the ministry he undertook and the message he proclaimed. All of this unfolded in the fertile soil of first-century Palestine and among the people it produced—especially John the Baptist.

The Advent of God's Kingdom

Scholars agree that the advent of the kingdom of God formed a central symbol in the ministry of Jesus. This unanimity, however, belies the complexity of the symbol and the different ways scholars have interpreted the Greek expression *hē basileia tou theou* (the kingdom of God; Matthew's use of the expression "kingdom of heaven" represents a pious Jewish attempt to avoid using "God" in a frequently cited formula). The expression generally ought to be read and translated in a way that minimizes spatial or temporal notions—that is it should not be understood as implying that the kingdom of God has delineated boundaries or is simply a circumlocution for heaven. New Testament translations often render the phrase as "reign of God" in an attempt to articulate the interpersonal or relational aspects inherent in the symbol. In other words, the symbol is meant to capture the fact that "kingdom" expresses a relationship between God and human beings, even an experience, in which God reigns as king over the world.[18] Other scholars, however, have moved in the opposite direction, emphasizing the political aspects of the symbol and insisting that the image of a kingdom was meant to challenge the empire of Rome, which was oppressing the region. They assert the spatial-temporal aspects of the symbol and argue for translating *basileia* as "empire," thereby unmistakably emphasizing the politically and socially subversive character of Jesus' ministry.[19] In the end, the caveats issued by both sides should be noted when approaching this central symbol of Jesus' ministry.

Among New Testament scholars, debates have long raged as to how Jesus understood and used the expression *kingdom of God*. Some suggest that the symbol ought to be interpreted against the backdrop of first-century Jewish apocalyptic theology, but even that suggestion opens up more difficulties. As noted in the previous chapter, N. T. Wright has provocatively suggested that end-of-the-world language in first-century Judaism addresses that radical transformation of this world by the decisive intervention of God. Moreover, there are passages in which the kingdom of God is obviously a present reality, and such a realized eschatology stands in tension with an emphasis on a future apocalyptic judgment.

In Luke 11:20, Jesus provides perhaps the clearest example of a realized kingdom of God when he says, "If it is by the finger of God that [I] drive out demons, then the kingdom of God has come upon you." Yet, in both Matthew and Luke, Jesus also instructs his disciples to pray for the advent of God's kingdom in the near future (the Lord's Prayer in Matthew 6:10 and Luke 11:2). Additionally, the hope for a future arrival of God's kingdom permeates many parables and several sayings of Jesus regarding the future judgment of humanity (e.g., Mark 9:42–48). Although many elements in Jesus' preaching and ministry signal the expectation of a future yet imminent arrival of the kingdom, any Schweitzer-like dismissal of Jesus as an apocalyptic "freak" is unwarranted given the realized eschatology evidenced in at least some of these passages. But rather than argue extensively over how precisely to understand apocalyptic symbols in general, or specifically as it pertains to Jesus' use of the expression *kingdom of God*, it might be wise to follow a lead from William Loewe, who has offered a more functional and theological approach to this elusive symbol.

By asking the simple question, "What does the kingdom accomplish?" or, "What is it for?" Loewe has been able to synthesize the various temporal and political approaches to the kingdom mentioned above. The kingdom of God is meant to bring human and cosmic fulfillment and an answer to the problem of evil.[20] The solution to the problem of evil is not a mythical battle between angelic and demonic forces; rather, it involves a response to God's love and mercy uniquely present in Jesus. Jesus' proclamation of the kingdom in word and deed provoked a response from those whom Jesus encountered—either a response of rejection or of faith and conversion. The response of faith and conversion occurs at a fundamental level of one's being, at the level of one's knowing and valuing, something theologians often call a *horizon*. The horizon of human experience is defined by mistrust, abuse, and exploitation, and Jesus' proclamation of the kingdom offers a shake-up of that horizon that has been skewed by violence, fear, and sin. By making the unrestricted love of God available as the source of acceptance, healing, and liberation, Jesus provokes and enables a transformation of one's horizon of meaning and value at both an individual and cultural and social levels. While these claims stretch the boundaries of historical inquiry, Loewe's theological take on the central symbol of Jesus' ministry helps to make intelligible other elements of that ministry.

The Kingdom Inaugurated in Words and Deeds

While scholars like John Meier find it difficult to trace any given parable back to stage one, most scholars would argue that parables were nonetheless central to Jesus' ministry.[21] Yet, the precise nature of parabolic discourse in the context of Jesus' ministry remains a matter of dispute, as competing approaches vacillate between two extremes. At one end of the spectrum, parables are often interpreted allegorically. In other words, they are interpreted in such a way that each and every element in the story stands for something else. Although parables themselves often permit such interpretations, the thoroughgoing allegorization of parables can make their meaning hopelessly obscure and leave the reader looking for authoritative guides for the proper interpretation. The opposite end of the spectrum focuses instead on the moral bottom line. In other words, the interpreter's task is to move beyond the particulars of the parable to distill some universal moral truth behind the passage. The effect of such a moralizing tendency is to make the parable itself rather inconsequential; reducing it to a mere means for delivering a moral command that otherwise could have been given directly if the audience had only been brighter.

Dichotomies such as the one just presented are rhetorical devices that are often used to clear a path for a third way, an alternative that will eschew the two extremes in favor of some compromise. Such a third way defines much of contemporary scholarship on the parables. But for the purpose of introducing students to the dynamics of Jesus' parables, a rather antiquated definition of parables will be employed. In the middle of the twentieth century, the British biblical scholar C. H. Dodd constructed a helpful definition that steers a middle course between allegory and simple morality lesson. He describes a parable as "a metaphor or simile drawn from nature or common life, arresting the hearer with its vividness or strangeness in order to leave the mind in sufficient doubt about its precise application to tease it into active thought."[22] For Dodd, the hearers are provoked by the parable in such a way as to leave them pondering and even playing with the text and their own relationship to it. In the parable, bottom line moralizing is frustrated as meaning is both revealed and concealed at the same time. By destabilizing the audience's assumptions, the parable provokes a dynamic response.

Luke's parable of the Dishonest Steward provides a good model of the dynamics just discussed (Luke 16:1–9). It is doubtful that this parable goes back to stage one (it satisfies none of the primary criteria mentioned above), but it may be considered the kind of thing Jesus might have said—a loose appeal to the criterion of coherence. This parable tells the story of a corrupt steward, a servant responsible for running the business affairs of a large estate, whose misdeeds have been exposed. He is notified that his master will perform an audit, and knowing that the audit will fully document his corruption, the steward decides to take preemptive action. The steward goes to his master's creditors and falsifies their statements so that each of them is recorded as owing far less than they actually owe. In effect, the steward is ingratiating himself with these creditors prior to his own dismissal; he hopes that this action will secure employment or at least goodwill in the future. Upon discovering the steward's actions, the master surprisingly lauds the unjust steward for his cunning. Then Jesus says to his audience, "For the children of this world are more prudent in dealing with their own generation than are the children of light" (Luke 16:8).

This stunning turn of events no doubt shocks the audience—it still shocks many preachers today. After all, how could such an unjust man be held up as a positive example? In many ways, the parable emphasizes the cunning and the zeal behind the steward's actions, all in the name of self-preservation. Those who are committed to "this world," the world of temporal affairs, the world of money or mammon, are ruthless and amazingly persistent in their pursuits. Those committed to the gospel, however, are comparably less zealous and less committed, according to the parable; in other words, where are the Gordon Geckos and Donald Trumps of the gospel? Through the parable, Jesus shocks and provokes the audience to reconsider their outlook and to become more devoted in their commitment to the gospel. They are being summoned to a new level of conversion and repentance, seeing the world anew and discovering joy and passion in a God who loves them and who desires to be all in all. Moreover, the response to the parable thus subverts the health and wealth theology Jesus derides throughout this section of Luke.

Like the parables, the miracles of Jesus did more than just "fix" what was broken. Not only did the miracles benefit those who were infirm or possessed, they also provoked onlookers to acknowledge God's love and mercy in the lives of those who were on the margins of society. The sick, the possessed, and the dying were marginalized for a variety of reasons. They would be declared ritually impure or unclean, they became signs of malignant forces, or they were seen as suffering the punishment due to sin. All of these interpretations forced them to the margins, and it was precisely at the margins of first-century society where Jesus met them. In their encounter with Jesus, the sick, the possessed, and the dying became the focal point and the prime exemplars of "kingdom living" in the ministry of Jesus. As Jesus healed them, expelled their demons, or raised their dead, he redefined clean and unclean and redefined the boundaries of Israel in the eyes of many onlookers. Such was the kingdom of God, a kingdom inaugurated in the person and ministry of Jesus and in the response of conversion he makes possible.

MAGIC OR MIRACLE?

The ancient world is replete with examples of magic. In fact, some reputable scholars have identified Jesus as a practitioner of magic and have classified his miracles as a form of magic. Other scholars, however, contrast the powerful actions of Jesus and the magic known to the ancient world. Magic, they would argue, involves the manipulation of a deity or natural forces to bring about a particular outcome so that the magician usually agrees to perform his or her magic for a fee—the magician actually "works" for a client. The miracles of Jesus, on the other hand, involve a different dynamic, and John Meier has identified seven general characteristics that distinguish them from magic (*A Marginal Jew*, 2:535–616):

1. There is a relationship of faith and love between the human and the deity or divine agent.
2. The person in need is a disciple, worshiper.
3. The miracle is performed with a terse but intelligible set of words.
4. There is no reason to think that the deity is coerced into acting on behalf of the human.
5. Miracles are done in obedience to Jesus' Father and in the context of his "mission."
6. Miracles are understood as symbolic representations of the kingdom.
7. Miracles do not directly punish or hurt anyone.

To identify Jesus as a magician ignores the evidence, according to Meier, especially the absence of any charge of magic leveled against him during his lifetime (only in the second century do we find Justin Martyr reporting the charge of "magic" against Jesus; see *Dialogue with Trypho* 69.7 and *First Apology* 30.1). When one becomes attentive to the subtleties of the miracle tradition, one gains greater appreciation of their religious significance, particularly the manner in which miracles emphasize a personal relationship of faith, the importance of community, and conversion.

Moreover, Jesus' practice of open table fellowship functioned in a similar way. His custom of eating and drinking with public sinners caused no small amount of dissention, but these actions were, like his miracles, dramatic parables in action. He empowered onlookers by enacting a kind of love that is possible when people understand and experience themselves as loved unconditionally. As one experiences this unrestricted love of God, one becomes more deeply converted in a way that casts out fear, and it is fear that rests at the heart of all attempts at perfunctory exclusion. While this conversion is never quite complete (people are always looking for ways to exclude others), Jesus uniquely provokes a response to his enactment of the kingdom in word and deed and thus not only announces God's in-breaking kingdom, but also inaugurates it.

Crowds, Disciples, and the Twelve

For many years, Christian theologians, particularly Roman Catholic theologians, have asserted that Christ did not explicitly establish a church, per se. While these assertions are understandable as warnings against those who would retroject modern ecclesiology into the life and ministry of Jesus, the evidence is much more complex than such assertions suggest. In fact, John Meier and others have suggested that during his lifetime Jesus gave structure to a community around him, and while there is a measure of spontaneity involved, that community also had a distinct form and purpose.[23]

Among those who followed Jesus, one may distinguish at least three distinct but concentric circles around Jesus (and probably more than just three). First, there were the crowds. The crowds were composed of those who had heard of Jesus and who, as occasion warranted, showed up at any given moment to hear Jesus and witness his

wondrous deeds. Many were undoubtedly transformed by their encounter with Jesus, while others remained confused and unsure about the man from Galilee. From these crowds, Jesus drew some to become his disciples.

The term *disciple* (*mathētai* in Greek) is actually used in a surprisingly restrictive manner in the New Testament; only those who met specific criteria could be called disciples:

- Disciples were called and designated as such by Jesus; the initiative always rested with Jesus.
- Discipleship required a subversion of the values of honor and shame as they were traditionally understood; disciples needed to make a radical break from personal and social ties that defined one's place in society, family, friends, and profession.
- Disciples had to accept hostility, suffering, and even death.
- Disciples were defined by their embrace of several specific practices: baptism, simplicity in prayer, and feasting rather than fasting.

These marks, along with the modeling of Jesus, helped to form a new community, a kinship among Jesus' followers. Scholars often use the expression *fictive kinship* to describe this new set of relationships; the term refers to the process of granting someone who is not a member of a family the title, rights, and obligations normally given to family members.[24] This family, the obligations it engendered, and the social order it seemed to threaten, made the situation of the earliest followers of Jesus rather tenuous. Jesus' call to discipleship threatened to subvert the norms that governed first-century Palestine. The fact that Jesus could include both public sinners and the impoverished in a community with pious and more respectable members of society suggests that this was part of his intention. While the Gospels do not use the word *disciple* to describe the women who followed Jesus (probably because there was no feminine form of the word in Aramaic), there is little doubt that they were in fact disciples.[25]

The criterion of dissimilarity suggests that the group known simply as the Twelve existed during Jesus' lifetime and ceased to exist shortly after his death; notice that the phrase figures prominently in the Gospels, but in all other New Testament texts it appears only once in the Pauline letters (1 Corinthians 15:5) and once in Acts (6:2), and the phrase appears to fade after the close of the New Testament period. It seems that Jesus used this designation of the Twelve as a means of symbolizing Israel's renewal or its reconstitution. This group embodied the positive response to Jesus and stood out as the symbol for the fulfillment of Israel's hope for God's kingly rule, his reign. While Jesus and his followers radically redefined the content of these hopes, these hopes remained intelligible only as an expression of Israel's history and its Scriptures.

Jesus' practice of table fellowship, as mentioned above, is more than just an example of Jesus keeping dangerous company or his propensity to trouble the religious establishment. The parabolic character of this action must be affirmed while at the same time acknowledging the subversive community Jesus was inaugurating with such an act. Eating with others creates fellowship or community; through his practice of open table fellowship, Jesus was offering to create a community that included those most on the margins in the first century, prior to any act of repentance on their part. The free offer of fellowship stood in sharp contrast to the

WOMEN, DISCIPLESHIP, AND MARY MAGDALENE

The assertion that the New Testament does not call any women in the company of Jesus "disciples" strikes many as problematic. It appears as though several women who traveled with and supported Jesus and the others seem to fit the requirements of disciples. In fact, recent scholarship has focused much attention on one of the most interesting and important figures in the early church, Mary of Magdala. Although she is never explicitly designated a disciple in the Gospels, she nonetheless stood by Jesus at his crucifixion (Mark 15:40) and was among the women who found the empty tomb (Mark 16:1–8). After the Resurrection, Christ speaks to her (Matthew 28:1–10; John 20:11–18) and sends her as "the apostle to the apostles" in John 20:18. The distortion of her legacy (e.g., portraying her as a prostitute) by subsequent tradition has no basis in Scripture but rather bears witness to the misogyny of the time. With her reputation besmirched, her importance as a disciple and exemplar diminished rapidly even as the mother of Jesus was increasingly portrayed as the model of discipleship.

exclusivism that had come to define many sectors of first-century Palestinian Judaism. Jesus' practice of table fellowship anticipated the arrival of God's reign in ways that many first-century Jews would find perfectly intelligible but also scandalous.

Jesus, the Authorities, and Conflict

Interpreters of the New Testament must always understand the ministry of Jesus within the context of the religious renewal and reform of first-century Judaism, not as a movement against Judaism. After all, Jesus and all of his closest disciples were Jews, and they understood themselves within the context of God's covenant with Israel, although some have suggested that portraying Jesus as a reformer of Judaism somehow diminishes Jesus' claim to authority, or implies something was fundamentally wrong with first-century Judaism. Concerns over Christian distortions of Judaism are well-founded, given the history of anti-Semitism in Christian theology, but understanding Jesus as a religious reformer does not imply anti-Semitism. Neither does it diminish Jesus' claim to authority. Rather, Jesus' claim to authority is only intelligible within the context of first-century Judaism (see the following chapter on the development of New Testament Christology). Moreover, religious traditions are vital only to the extent that they can give birth to reform movements, and the leaders of these movements must be located within the traditions they reform. Most historians agree that Jesus worked to redefine Israel's identity and mission in light of his own sense of authority and mission within the context of the covenant.

The observance of Torah (the Jewish Law) was central to the life of first-century Jews and therefore central to Jesus and his disciples. The Torah contained the foundational stories of Israel, the commandments of God as well as the statutes and decrees to which Israel was bound in covenant. Often overlooked in the characterization of Torah observance is the interconnection between the narratives in Torah (*haggadah*) and the commandments in Torah (*halakhah*). Take, for example, the first commandment: "I, the Lord, am your God, who brought you out of the land of Egypt, that place of slavery. You shall not have other gods besides me" (Exodus 20:2–3). Notice how the commandment itself

ANTI-SEMITISM IN NEW TESTAMENT STUDIES

The New Testament often seems to present the practices of first-century Judaism in a negative light. In fact, the Gospels themselves paint the opponents of Jesus in a negative light, making expressions like *the scribes and Pharisees*—or *the Jews* in John's Gospel—evoke a thoroughly negative response from readers. In the New Testament, first-century Judaism often gets portrayed as narrow-minded, vain, loveless, and merciless. In Paul's letters the observance of Mosaic Law, a staple within first-century Judaism, is denounced as illicit for Gentile Christians, giving rise to a persistent yet invalid contrast of Judaism as a religion of "works-righteousness" (i.e., a religion where one tries to "earn" God's favor) and Christianity as a religion of grace. So pervasive has this characterization of Judaism been that many of the great theologians of the Christian tradition wrote obscenely anti-Semitic works (e.g., John Chrysostom and Martin Luther to name only two). It wasn't until the work of G. F. Moore, who identified the anti-Semitic bias of Christian theology and New Testament studies that this trend began to change. After the Holocaust, a full-blown reassessment of Christian theology began to take hold. By the 1970s scholars like Krister Stendahl, Jacob Neusner, and E. P. Sanders inaugurated a new era in New Testament studies, one in which a more balanced and historically accurate picture of first-century Judaism began to emerge. Moreover, scholars began to recognize the polemical dimensions of New Testament writings and began to distinguish material that reflected Jesus' own interactions with his contemporaries (i.e., stage one material) and material that reflected the controversies that enveloped early Christian and early Jewish communities (see the chapters on Matthew and John).

presupposes the narrative of covenant and exodus. If the commandments were to be torn from the narratives, the commandments would have the potential to become violent and capricious (even nonsensical). With this caveat in mind, many of the disputes between Jesus and the religious authorities of his day can be put into perspective: Jesus, like other rabbis of the period, argued about how best to understand and apply the commandments within the narrative context of Israel's history and within the context of its lived experience. A principle concern for Jesus (and others) was keeping the Torah powerfully connected to the narratives of Israel's gracious election by God.

Sabbath observance provides an apt example of how Jesus' attitude toward Torah observance encompasses both the letter of the commandment as well as the broader narrative in which it was embedded. In Mark 3:1–6, for example, religious authorities prepare to confront Jesus when he approaches a man with a deformed hand on the Sabbath. Mark tells readers that they wonder whether he will heal on the Sabbath and thereby, at least according to one strand of Torah interpretation, violate the Sabbath rest. In response to the onlookers Jesus asks, "Is it lawful to do good on the sabbath rather than to do evil, to save a life rather than to destroy it?" By asking this question, Jesus invokes a basic rabbinic principle regarding Sabbath observance: observance of the Sabbath cannot be used to justify the loss of life that otherwise might be saved. A passage from the Mishnah, a collection of rabbinic teachings from the first and second centuries, clearly articulates this principle, "Whenever there is doubt whether life is in danger this overrides the Sabbath."[26] The central issue of Jesus' confrontation with the authorities was not the abrogation or rejection of Torah; rather, the issue was the right observance of Torah. Jesus, acting in concert with the prophetic tradition

of the Old Testament and in conjunction with then-current rabbinic teachings, stresses God's love for humanity as the decisive factor in the application of Torah.

Jesus' attitude to Torah and his interpretation of it went beyond questions about Sabbath observance, but the episode mentioned above provides ample evidence of just how Jesus and his followers could provoke the conservative religious establishment. But however provocative Jesus' interpretation of Torah could be, it appears that he still stood within the tradition established by the rabbis regarding how best to live out the demands of the Torah, and so Jesus was well within the boundaries of first-century Judaism in this regard. The cause of Jesus' arrest and execution involves many factors, not the least of which was the manner in which Jesus could draw attention to himself and away from the political and religious authority structures of the day. Perhaps the most provocative incident in Jesus' ministry was his messianic entry into Jerusalem and the accompanying demonstration in the Temple. Historians are by no means in agreement as to the time frame of these events: The Synoptic Gospels directly link the two events and put them side by side, while John has the Temple incident at the start of Jesus' ministry. But most agree that these events crystallized the opposition to Jesus among the Jerusalem elite. The accusation related to the Temple and claims of messianic identity recorded in all of the Gospels tend to support these events as central to Jesus' arrest and execution. Both of these actions were at the heart of Jesus' proclamation, and the decision to arrest and execute Jesus sent a clear message: this man subverts Israel's identity and the established order, stay away from him. But Jesus' threat to the established order only emerged from his conviction that the demands of the covenant could only be properly understood against the backdrop of God's love for Israel.

Death, Discipleship, and the Kingdom

The death of Jesus was neither an accident nor a random event. Jesus died because of the way he lived. During his ministry Jesus could foresee how his life was working to seal the judgment against him, and he warned those who followed him of a similar outcome. In the Synoptic Gospels, there is a threefold prediction of Jesus' suffering and a threefold prediction of the disciples' suffering. But to characterize this prediction as fatalism or as a form of despair is to take it out of context, for Jesus' proclamation included some important claims, claims that, as N. T. Wright has correctly observed, focus on the way Jesus understood himself as the embodiment and realization of Israel's hope that God would visit them and redeem them from violence, oppression, and sin.

Throughout his ministry, Jesus eschewed the title of *Messiah* and all of the nationalistic and militaristic connotations it carried in first-century Palestine.[27] Jesus preferred the self-designation, "Son of Man," a figure that stood out in apocalyptic Judaism as exercising God's judgment on the nations (see Daniel, chapter 7). So inflammatory was this self-designation that when Jesus used it at his trial before the high priest Caiaphas, it caused outrage among those present. Almost no one in the Sanhedrin or in any other position of power was ready to acknowledge the claim of Jesus (Nicodemus and Joseph of Arimathea are two possible exceptions mentioned in the Gospels), and thus the near universal rejection of Jesus by those in power seemed to be the obvious outcome.

The canonical Gospels all report that Jesus anticipated his death and even offered to interpret it for his closest followers. The account of Jesus' last meal with his disciples records an event that symbolically blended elements of the table fellowship Jesus practiced throughout his ministry along with elements of Jewish ritual meals, including the imminent celebration of the Passover Seder.[28] It is within this context that Jesus' attitude toward his death is best grasped. N. T. Wright sees in this last supper of Jesus a provocative blending of Jesus' own story with that of Israel: Jesus proclaims a new covenant made in his blood, a covenant that establishes the forgiveness of sin. In this meal, Jesus interprets his life as the climax or *eschaton* of Israel's entire story.[29] While historians cannot search the mind of Jesus to discover his intentions at that moment, Wright nonetheless argues that Jesus went so far as to see his death as vicarious substitution: Jesus would embody the suffering of Israel and even suffer in place of the people of Israel in the tradition of the Maccabean martyrs and even the Suffering Servant of Isaiah, though other scholars remain understandably skeptical about attributing such interpretations to Jesus himself.[30]

Although the trial scenes in the Gospels must be viewed with some caution from the perspective of the historian, they also contain important and insightful details. First, as was noted in chapter 1, there seems to have been a close working alliance between the high priest, Caiaphas, and the Roman prefect, Pontius Pilate. The story of the Jewish and Roman trials may not be entirely accurate from the point of view of contemporary history, but they do accurately portray a level of collusion in the arrest and execution of Jesus. In fact, most historians note that the Jewish Sanhedrin could not execute people; that power was reserved for the Roman prefect.[31] So the Jewish authorities could not have put Jesus to death on their own. Moreover, the crimes that brought Jesus before the authorities blend political and religious issues, and Jesus did nothing to dissuade the authorities that this proclamation carried with it political and religious implications. His triumphant demonstration upon entering the holy city of Jerusalem at

Passover would have definitely caught the eye of the Romans and the Sadducees. Additionally, his actions in the Temple would have caused concern from both the Romans and the Sadducees. As such, while the means and exact extent of the collaboration between the Jewish and Roman authorities may never be known, the Gospels nonetheless point historians in the right direction by emphasizing this connection.

Jesus died as thousands of others had died in the eastern part of the empire. He was splayed out on a cross and left to die of shock, exhaustion, dehydration, or asphyxiation. As long as he hung outside the city walls, he stood as a reminder to all who passed by of the manner in which dissidents were treated in Jerusalem. The cross was certainly meant to shame the crucified and to terrorize passersby. Jesus' death was not marked by exceptional cruelty; tragically, it was the all too common means of sending a message to the general populace.[32]

Conclusion

The quest for the historical Jesus remains one of the most contested subjects in the field of New Testament studies, and the present chapter does not pretend to have settled any of the seemingly intractable debates involved in some of the most important areas of research. In fact, all that has been offered here is an overview—an outline or pale sketch of what historians think they know about the historical Jesus. In some ways, Bultmann is correct: the historical Jesus is not and cannot be the object of Christian faith. But as all teachers of the New Testament know, students are always interested in historical questions, and rightly so. From the perspective of the Christian tradition, a tradition in which historical claims play a crucial role in the articulation of faith, historical Jesus research functions as an important resource in the ongoing attempts to understand what the evangelists were up to as they created their Gospels. Questions concerning "the world behind the text" (or perhaps "the man behind the Gospels") continue to intrigue readers, and the Christian tradition has generally determined that it is better off for wrestling with these questions on their own terms. In the next chapter, a discussion of the development of the New Testament, and particularly its Christology, will help to set off historical questions from the theological and Christological questions the evangelists raise in their Gospel narratives.

| QUESTIONS FOR UNDERSTANDING

1. What role did the Enlightenment play in the emergence of historical Jesus research?

2. How did Albert Schweitzer bring the old quest to a halt?

3. Describe Rudolf Bultmann's approach to the historical Jesus.

4. Compare and contrast the new quest and the third quest.

5. How do the parables and miracles of Jesus function in relationship to his proclamation of God's kingdom?

6. Who were the followers of Jesus? How did this group represent a challenge to some of Jesus' contemporaries?

7. How did Jesus understand his own death? What evidence do we have?

QUESTIONS FOR REFLECTION

1. Should historical Jesus research overrule or exercise authority over Christian doctrine or practice? In other words, if historians can reasonably demonstrate, for example, that Jesus taught "x," should this teaching become normative for Christians? Explain.

2. In his ministry, Jesus practiced open table fellowship and reached out to the most marginalized in his society. Do you think that this practice of Jesus influences contemporary Christian practices? Explain and provide examples.

3. The last part of this chapter connects the death of Jesus to the fate of his disciples. Does such an emphasis on dying seem appropriate? Fanatical? Dangerous? Explain.

FOR FURTHER READING

Gnilka, Joachim. *Jesus of Nazareth: Message and History*. Trans. by S. Schatzmann. Peabody, MA: Hendrickson, 1997.

Johnson, Luke Timothy. *The Real Jesus: The Misguided Quest for the Historical Jesus and the Truth of the Traditional Gospels*. San Francisco: Harper, 1996.

Wright, N. T. *Jesus and the Victory of God*. Christian Origins and the Doctrine of God, vol. 2. Minneapolis, MN: Fortress, 2006.

ENDNOTES

1. Much of the material in this chapter has been revised from the presentation found in Christopher McMahon, *Jesus Our Salvation: An Introduction to Christology* (Winona, MN: Anselm Academic, 2007), chapters 1 and 2.

2. See Anthony J. Godzieba, "From '*Vita Christi*' to 'Marginal Jew': The Life of Jesus as Criterion of Reform in Pre-Critical and Post-Critical Quests," *Louvain Studies* 32 (2007): 111–133.

3. See David F. Strauss, *The Life of Christ Critically Examined* (Philadelphia: Fortress, 1972), 777–778.

4. George Tyrrell, *Christianity at the Crossroads* (London: Longmans, 1913), 47.

5. Martin Kähler, *The So-Called Historical Jesus and the Historic Biblical Christ* (Philadelphia: Fortress, 1964).

6. Rudolf Bultmann, "New Testament and Mythology: The Problem of Demythologizing the New Testament Proclamation," in *New Testament and Mythology and Other Basic Writings*, ed. Schubert Ogden (Philadelphia: Fortress, 1984; German original published in 1941).

7. John P. Meier, "The Present State of the 'Third Quest' for the Historical Jesus: Loss and Gain," *Biblica* 80 (1999): 459–487.

8. John P. Meier, *A Marginal Jew: Rethinking the Historical Jesus*, 4 vols., Anchor Bible Reference Library (Garden City, NJ: Doubleday, 1991–2009).

9. Ibid., 1:463.

10. Ibid., vol. 1, chap. 6.

11. Morna Hooker, "On Using the Wrong Tool," *Theology* 75 (1972): 570–581.

12. For a good discussion of this issue in relation to John Meier's work, see the following essays: Tony Kelly, "The Historical Jesus and Human Subjectivity: A Response to John Meier," *Pacifica* 4 (1991): 202–228; Ben Meyer, "The Relevance of 'Horizon,'" *Downside Review* 386 (1994): 1–15.

13. See Origen, *Against Celsus*, 1.32.

14. See Meier, *Marginal Jew*, 1:318–319; *idem.*, "The Brothers and Sisters of Jesus in Ecumenical Perspective," *Catholic Biblical Quarterly* 54 (1992): 1–28; *idem.*, "On Retrojecting Later Questions from Later Texts: A Reply to Richard Bauckham," *Catholic Biblical Quarterly* 59 (1997): 511–527; see also *CCC*, nos. 499–500.

15. Meier, *Marginal Jew*, 1:109.

16. Ibid., 113.

17. See also John 4:1, where the Pharisees hear that Jesus and his disciples are baptizing more followers than John the Baptist.

18. See Norman Perrin, *Jesus and the Language of the Kingdom: Symbol and Metaphor in New Testament Interpretation* (New York: Harper, 1976), 196.

19. See, e.g., Stephen J. Patterson, *The God of Jesus: The Historical Jesus and the Search for Meaning* (Harrisburg, PA: Trinity, 1998).

20. William P. Loewe, *A College Student's Introduction to Christology* (Collegeville, MN: Liturgical, 1996), 47–48.

21. Meier, *Marginal Jew*, 2:145–146, 290–291.

22. C. H. Dodd, *Parables of the Kingdom* (New York: Scribner, 1936), 16.

23. Most of the material in this section is derived from John Meier, *A Marginal Jew: Rethinking the Historical Jesus*, vol. 3, *Companions and Competitors* (New York: Doubleday, 2001), 19–252.

24. N. T. Wright, *Jesus and the Victory of God* (Minneapolis, MN: Fortress, 1996), 430–432.

25. The discussion of female disciples does not touch directly upon the Catholic Church's argument against the ordination of women. Part of that argument, however, does involve the contention that women were not numbered among the Twelve or the contention they were not apostles (cf. Romans 16:7, which some see as a reference to women apostles in the early church). See John Paul II, *Ordinatio Sacerdotalis* and The Congregation for the Doctrine of the Faith, *Inter Insigniores* for the arguments against women's ordination.

26. *Mishnah Yoma* 8.6, from H. Danby, *The Mishnah* (Oxford: Oxford University Press, 1933).

27. Wright, *Victory of God*, 487–489; Wright cites Wrede and Bultmann as two influential figures who advocated the identification of Jesus as the Messiah as a postresurrection event.

28. The meal could not have been the actual Passover Seder, which was celebrated on the evening that began the feast. If it was the Passover Seder, then the trial and execution of Jesus would have taken place on Passover. Readers will recall that in the Jewish calendar, the day begins at sunset and the evening meal was the first meal of the day.

29. Wright, *Victory of God*, 553–563.

30. Ibid., 576–592. In early Judaism, there were stories that envisioned salvation from the present evil age through the sufferings of certain figures that embodied the sufferings of Israel.

31. See Josephus, *Jewish War*, 22.8.1.

32. For a brief but gruesome account of crucifixion in the Roman world, including a discussion of who was crucified by the Romans and why, see Gerard Sloyan, *The Crucifixion of Jesus* (Minneapolis, MN: Fortress, 2004), 14–20.

CHAPTER 3

THE FORMATION OF THE GOSPEL TRADITION

The previous chapter set forth a cursory overview of what contemporary historians think Jesus actually said or did. One more bit of groundwork deserves attention prior to the study of the Gospels themselves: How did the memory traditions about Jesus develop over the course of decades to yield the narratives found in the Gospels? In other words, how does one move from Jesus' oral proclamation of the advent of God's kingdom to a written proclamation about what God has accomplished in Christ, in his life, death, and Resurrection and in the life of the believing community? The dynamics of this movement and two issues in particular will be the subject of the present chapter. First, following a brief overview of the three-stage development of the gospel tradition, the chapter will discuss the trajectory of christological development in the New Testament—how the early Christian community came to articulate the religious significance of Jesus in relation to God. Second, the chapter will explore how the material in the Gospels grew and developed. More specifically, it will focus on the development of the synoptic tradition (i.e., the tradition that stands behind the three Synoptic Gospels: Mark, Matthew, and Luke).

The Gospel Tradition in Broad Terms

The term *gospel* in English (*godspel* in Old and Middle English) translates the Greek word *euangelion*, meaning "good news" or "glad tidings." In the ancient world prior to the rise of Christianity, the Greek word had cultural currency within a secular context: *euangelion* was associated with the announcement of a marriage, a birth, or some other public achievement. The cognate verb (*euangelizesthai*) was used in the Septuagint (commonly abbreviated LXX), the Greek translation of the Old Testament used by early Greek-speaking Jews as well as the early Christians, to translate an important passage in Isaiah 61:1:

> The spirit of the Lord God is upon me,
>> because the Lord has anointed me;
> He has sent me to bring glad tidings to
>> the lowly,
>> to heal the brokenhearted,
> To proclaim liberty to the captives
>> and release to the prisoners.

In Luke chapter 4, this passage becomes decisive for understanding Jesus' identity and mission. For the Essenes at Qumran, this text, along with another "good news text" in Isaiah 52:7, took on an apocalyptic tone: God was sending his anointed one to release the true Israel from the powers of the demonic.[1]

Proclaiming the gospel originally entailed an oral event: a spoken word was delivered to an audience. The content of the initial oral proclamation of the gospel, the kerygma, or "faith proclamation," is a matter of some conjecture. In the writings of Paul, for example, it is not clear to what extent the faith proclamation, or the gospel, amounted to a narrative of Jesus' life. Rather, for Paul, and perhaps for the early church in general, it appears that the initial proclamation of the gospel focused on the death and Resurrection of Jesus: Jesus has conquered sin and death; he reigns in glory and is alive and present transforming the lives of believers. Surely the memory tradition about what Jesus said and did in his lifetime, preserved in oral form, continued to sustain the believing community, but how much of these stories were part of the proclamation? It is apparent that over time the kerygma began to take the form of a narrative of Jesus' life and ministry, and that narrative has become synonymous with "the gospel." Precisely how or when this development occurred remains a matter of speculation, but Mark's Gospel represents the first attempt at writing such an account of the gospel, and it, therefore, represents an important milestone in the history of Christian theology.

THE DEVELOPMENT OF THE GOSPEL TRADITION

The introductory chapter in this text explored, in part, the Roman Catholic Church's understanding of divine Revelation and its relationship to Scripture. Embedded within that discussion was a presentation of the Second Vatican Council's *Dogmatic Constitution on Divine Revelation* (*Dei verbum*) and its approach to the connection between historical event and the emergence of the sacred text: Scripture. As part of the council's deliberation, the council fathers took into account the insights of critical biblical scholarship on the development of the gospel tradition. The Pontifical Biblical Commission (a commission set up to advise the main doctrinal office at the Vatican about biblical matters) outlined the development of the material in the Gospels.[2] This account states that the Gospels developed in three distinct yet interdependent stages, stages discussed briefly in the previous chapter.

Stage I: The gospel tradition began with the career of Jesus and his proclamation of the advent of God's kingdom. Throughout his public ministry, Jesus provoked those who encountered him to experience the advent of this kingdom in his ministry, indeed in him. Throughout his ministry, Jesus challenged the boundaries of first-century Judaism, including prohibitions against table fellowship with the unclean, public sinners, and other outcasts. After he called into question the function of the Temple, thereby confronting the political and religious establishment, Jesus was arrested, tried, and executed as a criminal by Roman authorities.

Stage II: The death of Jesus brought stage one to an end. At that point, those closest to Jesus had abandoned him, except for the women among his disciples. Subsequently, however, these same disciples began to proclaim the Resurrection of Jesus, even at the cost of their lives. Needless to say, something dramatic happened to the disciples in order to change their outlook and even their understanding of Jesus. Christians believe that the decisive event was the Resurrection and the outpouring of the Holy Spirit. The early followers of Jesus now proclaimed him (not the advent of God's kingdom) as "Lord" and "Savior" in their liturgy and in their preaching.

continued

THE DEVELOPMENT OF THE GOSPEL TRADITION *continued*

Stage III: The proclamation (*kērygma* in Greek) began to take on a new form as it incorporated the memory tradition of Jesus' ministry. As such, the kerygma became more of a narrative. Mark's Gospel is the earliest example of this new form of the kerygma—it is not simply a report of Jesus' actions in stage one. Rather, the insights born of the Resurrection are incorporated into the memory tradition of Jesus' ministry so that the Gospels produce a more comprehensive account of the gospel: the life and ministry of Jesus point to the Resurrection, and the Resurrection becomes the means by which the opaque ministry of Jesus can be illuminated and rightly understood.

These three stages illustrate the movement of the gospel from the disciples' experience of Jesus to an oral proclamation of the kerygma to a literary proclamation. This process was accompanied by the development of a theology that sought to integrate more closely the life of Jesus with the proclamation of his Resurrection. This latter dynamic is evidenced in the complex development of New Testament Christology.

The transition from a spoken proclamation—in which pastors, evangelists, apostles, and prophets, usually direct witnesses of the events they proclaim, are the authoritative sources of the good news—to the written proclamation presents the interpreter of the Gospels with some important and complex issues.[3] The dynamism and relational nature of an orally proclaimed story differs significantly from the more static nature of an authoritative text. For example, when Paul presented the gospel in Corinth, he was surely questioned about it. In fact, his witness created a special relationship between himself and the churches he established there so that they would expect to receive corrections and encouragement from him when necessary. Paul, a living man and witness to the Resurrection (see 1 Corinthians, chapter 15), was available as the authoritative source of the gospel he presented.

On the other hand, a text makes another claim to authenticity. Like the oral proclamation, the text makes a claim to authority that rests on a connection to a witness, even an eyewitness. This connection underscores the "apostolic" character of the Gospels, even when those Gospels are not directly attributable to a member of the close circle of disciples around Jesus (e.g., Luke). However, delving into the question of authorship would take the discussion too far afield at this point. For now, the issue at hand concerns the transformation of the apostolic kerygma from an oral proclamation to an authoritative text. As a text, however, the story becomes fixed and, to some extent, immovable. Of course, one must take into account the work of scribes and their editorial activity—adding, deleting, and putting the text in the form made available to later generations. But clearly the text becomes distanced from the events and people (witnesses) that gave it birth. This distancing underscores the nature of biblical language and the power of its witness. While the text remains irrefutably connected to the events of history witnessed within the community, the text does not remain simply a report or exposition of events. Instead, the text and the story it proclaims act as a summons to a relationship with God, with Christ, and with the community of believers. A community has handed on the story, first in oral form and then as authoritative text. While the text is stable in a sense, that stability belies an invitation to interpret and apply the text in the life of the believing community. The gospel genre is thus unique in the ancient world inasmuch as it calls for a unique response and creates a unique set of relationships for the reader.

Although the Gospels are unique in the ancient world, this does not mean that they are entirely without precedent. First, the Gospels have a connection to the story of Israel, and in particular to the stories of the prophets in Israel. Willard Swartley cites the story of Jeremiah as one example.[4] The book of Jeremiah narrates the story of the prophet's birth, followed by an account of his call and commission by God, and then an account of the prophet's words and actions. The central conflict in the story finds resolution in the suffering and rejection of Jeremiah by the religious authorities of the day. While the oracles of Jeremiah are comparatively disproportionate to those of Jesus in the eyes of the Christian tradition, the structure of Jeremiah's story roughly mirrors that of Jesus, and both stories include many similar elements.

Second, within the Greco-Roman world a kind of biography emerged that provides some parallels to the gospels as well. In some instances in Greco-Roman biographies, a "divine man" (*theois anēr*) would work miracles and act as a divine messenger and intermediary among human beings. The subjects of these Greco-Roman biographies were usually philosophers or other persons who exercised noble virtue (*aretē*), and the biographies (often called "areteologies") became the means by which readers were called upon to imitate these noble heroes. While many scholars have trumpeted the similarities between Greco-Roman, or Hellenistic, biographies and the Gospels, the dissimilarities are also evident, especially when it comes to Mark. Hellenistic biographies invariably contain infancy narratives and place a high priority on the wondrous works of a child prodigy, elements present in Matthew

and Luke but absent in Mark. More importantly, Hellenistic biographies show little concern with God or with the community of believers, whereas in Mark and the other Gospels these concerns are central. Thus, while there are some similarities with Hellenistic biography and even with the stories of Old Testament prophets, Mark's Gospel stands out as unique, or *sui generis*, in relation to other ancient literature.

New Testament Christology: Titles, Roles, and Patterns

Christology is the study of how Christians have understood and articulated the religious significance of Jesus in relation to God. As one reads the New Testament, it is apparent that the early believers' experience of Jesus and of his Resurrection in particular, both confirmed and challenged the earliest Christians' understanding of God. To appreciate this dynamic of confirmation and challenge, one ought to recall that Jesus and all of his earliest followers were first-century Palestinian Jews. As such, they were profoundly committed to the monotheism of Israel, particularly as it was expressed in texts like the Shema from Deuteronomy 6:4–9: "Hear O Israel! The Lord is our God, the Lord alone!"

The Shema was a fundamental affirmation of Israel's fidelity to Yahweh and a repudiation of the worship of any alternative gods. Every day, Jewish men (and perhaps many women) recited the prayer as they tied small leather boxes called phylacteries (*tefillin* in Hebrew) to their foreheads and left arms. In these phylacteries were placed small scrolls with the text of the Shema as well as other texts. On the doorposts of Jewish households one would find small cylinders (*mezuzah* in Hebrew) that also contained a copy of the text from Deuteronomy. These rituals powerfully symbolized how this commitment to the monotheism of Israel's covenant was to guard one's thinking, one's actions, and one's comings and goings. The earliest Christians had to deal with Israel's profound monotheism, even while they had experienced God's presence in the power of Christ's Resurrection. In short, the earliest followers of Jesus looked for ways to push the envelope of first-century Jewish monotheism as they gave voice to the powerful and transformative presence of God in Christ. While simple declarations like "Jesus is God" (i.e., Yahweh) would have been difficult for first-century Jews to either understand or to affirm, the material in the Old Testament and the intertestamental literature supplied ample resources for early Christians as they constructed the earliest Christologies.

The Christology of the New Testament makes use of a variety of titles or roles that had been circulating within first-century Judaism to make sense of Jesus. This variety of titles and the tension it creates within the New Testament should not come as a surprise given the novelty of the earliest Christians' experience and the difficulties presented by the monotheism of the Jewish tradition. Within this variety, however, one may discern distinct uses of language, and the present discussion will utilize three categories to explore the christological language of the New Testament: title, role, and pattern. These categories overlap in the sense that just because a christological term or image is classified as a title does not mean that it does not also function with a particular pattern or that it does not also point to a particular function or role. The taxonomy of title, role, and pattern will merely act as a useful tool for making sense of the variety of terminology presented in the New Testament.

In what follows, the category "title" embraces those terms that function like proper names. In some sense, they are like the names of "characters" taken from the Old Testament who became important vehicles for the early Christian confession of faith. Two of the most prevalent and obvious examples of such titles include "Lord" (e.g., Philippians 2:11), when it designates the divine name (Yahweh), and "Messiah," or its Greek translation, *christos* or "Christ" (e.g., Matthew 16:16). Titles are singled out because they played an important role in the kerygma and in early Christian liturgy. With a title one can say, for instance, "Jesus, you are the Messiah," or, "Jesus is Lord."

A role, on the other hand, is more descriptive and functional than a title (though a title can also be a role). The example of Jesus as the "great high priest" in the Letter to the Hebrews stands out as an example of a role (Hebrews 4:14). In this image, Jesus is connected to the Temple ritual in which the sins of the people are forgiven. Jesus acts as the great high priest who makes sacrifice to remove the sins of the people permanently. As a role (but not a title), the image of the high priest is a means of describing how Jesus *functions* in relationship to God and to humanity. However, since there is no evidence of Jesus being declared "high priest" in the kerygma, nor do we have evidence of its use as a title in a liturgical context, it is simply a role and not a title. Alternatively, the terms *messiah* and *Son of David* are clearly both used as titles used in Scripture, but they are also roles. They are roles because both point to an individual who will work to bring about the fulfillment of the promises made to Israel about the restoration of the monarchy, the purification of the Temple, and the defeat of Israel's enemies (more on these functions below). So titles can also be roles, but not all roles (e.g., the great high priest) are also titles.

These titles and roles do not function apart from the story of Judaism. The titles and roles that the New Testament uses to understand and proclaim Jesus are thus necessarily plotted within a narrative so that different chronological moments in Jewish history or the life of Christ become the focal point for understanding Jesus' identity and his relationship to God. Readers should take note, however, that there is no clear delineation of roles, titles, and patterns in the New Testament. In fact, titles and roles often overlap (e.g., "Son of David" functions as both role and title) and christological patterns are not always stable, making use of a variety of titles or roles and plotting them differently. The presentation that follows will attempt to summarize and categorize in general terms the major christological titles, roles, and patterns in the New Testament in an effort to provide readers with some way of dealing with the wide range of Christologies found in the Gospels.

Although most Christians assume that the title *Christ* or *Messiah* ought to be the focus of any presentation of New Testament Christology, the title and role of *Son of Man* may provide a more suitable starting point, at least from the historian's point of view. As indicated in the previous chapter, Jesus himself generally eschewed any simplistic self-description and took particular care to avoid the nationalism and violence associated with titles like *messiah*. His preferred self-description or self-interpretation revolved around the title and role of the Son of Man.[5] Exegetes and historians have long puzzled over the precise origin and meaning of the phrase *son of man* (*bar nasha* in Aramaic). At least three distinct alternatives are present in the literature on the subject.

1. The phrase may be understood in an indefinite sense meaning "a human being" or "mortal." The prophet Ezekiel appears to use a similar phrase this way throughout his writings to contrast himself (as a mere mortal) with the glory of the transcendent God.

2. The phrase may also be understood in a generic sense, with a viable translation something like, "a person in my position."

3. Lastly, the phrase may be a direct reference to an eschatological figure found in Daniel 7:13 but also in other apocryphal literature like *1 Enoch*.

Most scholars believe that Jesus used the phrase in the eschatological sense and in conjunction with his role as Suffering Servant of Yahweh. The Suffering Servant (Isaiah 49:3) was understood as a corporate figure who, representing the righteous in Israel, would redeem Israel through righteous suffering. The Son of Man, on the other hand, was God's agent of eschatological judgment, the one who would punish the wicked and reward the righteous. Jesus' appropriation of both of these roles strikes many scholars as unique.

The christological pattern presupposed by both the Suffering Servant and the Son of Man points to the near future, and Jesus' use of the title is a key indicator of this fact. Whenever Jesus employs the title *Son of Man* in the Gospels it is almost always in conjunction with some future event: his impending suffering, his future glorification, or judgment. For example, in Mark's trial scene, Jesus alludes to his coming vindication by God: "you will see the Son of Man seated at the right hand of the Power and coming with the clouds of heaven" (Mark 14:62). By virtue of his Resurrection, Jesus will be placed at God's right hand (see also Psalms 110:1). To be seated at the right hand is to receive happiness and power; it is a position signifying intimacy with royal or divine power. In the future, Jesus will come on the clouds as the vindicated Son of Man and execute judgment against the faithless and the unjust and vindicate the righteous faithful.

The title *messiah* provides an appropriate point of transition from a Christology of Jesus to a Christology of the early church. It is apparent that Jesus himself had an ambivalent attitude toward the messianic expectations of first-century Judaism, and a little background information on this title may help to explain the reasons for his ambivalence. The Aramaic word *messiah* simply means "anointed one," and is translated into Greek with the word *christos*, or Christ. In the Old Testament and even

THE SON OF MAN IN 1 ENOCH

In the apocryphal book of Enoch, one section, often called "The Similitudes of Enoch," contains numerous references to the Son of Man in conjunction with the Last Judgment. Selected excerpts from *1 Enoch* 48 are provided below. The first excerpt clearly demonstrates dependence on Daniel 7:14, but the rest of the material is more unique, though always with an emphasis on the Son of Man's role in the final judgment of the nations.

> And in that place I saw the fountain
>   of righteousness
> Which was inexhaustible:
> And around it were many fountains
>   of wisdom:
> And all the thirsty drank of them,
> And were filled with wisdom,
> And their dwellings were with the righteous
>   and holy and elect.
> And at that hour that Son of Man was named
>   in the presence of the Lord of Spirits,
> And his name before the Head of Days.
>
> Yea, before the sun and the signs
>   were created,
> Before the stars of the heavens were made,
> His name was named before the Lord
>   of Spirits.
> He shall be a staff to the righteous whereon
>   to stay themselves and not fall,
> And he shall be the light of the Gentiles,
> And the hope of those who are troubled
>   of heart.
> All who dwell on earth shall fall down and
>   worship before him,
> And will praise and bless and celebrate with
>   song the Lord of Spirits.
> And for this reason hath he been chosen and
>   hidden before Him,

> Before the creation of the world and
>   for evermore.
> And the wisdom of the Lord of Spirits hath
>   revealed him to the holy and righteous;
> For he hath preserved the lot of the
>   righteous,
> Because they have hated and despised this
>   world of unrighteousness,
> And have hated all its works and ways in the
>   name of the Lord of Spirits:
> For in his name they are saved,
> And according to his good pleasure hath it
>   been in regard to their life.
>
> In these days downcast in countenance
>   shall the kings of the earth have
>   become,
> And the strong who possess the land
>   because of the works of their hands,
> For on the day of their anguish and
>   affliction they shall not (be able to)
>   save themselves.
> And I will give them over into the hands of
>   Mine elect:
> As straw in the fire so shall they burn before
>   the face of the holy:
> As lead in the water shall they sink before the
>   face of the righteous,
> And no trace of them shall any more be
>   found.
> And on the day of their affliction there shall
>   be rest on the earth,
> And before them they shall fall and not
>   rise again:
> And there shall be no one to take them with
>   his hands and raise them:
> For they have denied the Lord of Spirits and
>   His Anointed.
> The name of the Lord of Spirits be blessed.[6]

throughout much of the ancient Near East, anointings were customarily performed on individuals who were assuming new positions in the community (i.e., a king, a priest, or a prophet). The symbolic meaning of anointing was generally derived from its origins as a practical matter. Anointing with oil often occurred prior to battle or a contest since oil could deflect an oblique blow (notice that contemporary fighters use oils or jellies on their face for the same reason). Additionally, oils were used for their medicinal or healing properties. Thus, anointing came to signal divine protection and mission. The title *messiah*, or anointed one, gradually became associated chiefly with the kings of Judah and with the office of high priest. During the Second Temple period the term began to be used in conjunction with Israel's hope of future deliverance from foreign oppression and purification of the Temple. While there was no uniform set of expectations concerning a messianic figure in first-century Judaism, the role of messiah generally included some combination of the following achievements:

- inauguration of a new age
- punishment of the wicked (resurrection of the dead?)
- defeat of Gentile (i.e., non-Jewish) oppressors
- purification of the Temple
- reestablishment of the Davidic monarchy

On the one hand, it seems apparent from the pages of the Gospels that Jesus did not envision himself as the one who would bring defeat to Israel's political enemies or vindicate the violent nationalism that was so rampant in Galilee and in other parts of first-century Palestine. On the other hand, however, Jesus does not miss an opportunity to identify himself with messianic hopes of the crowds (e.g., his entry into Jerusalem, his cleansing of the Temple). Through a variety of symbolic actions and provocative pronouncements, Jesus encouraged these hopes even as he sought to redefine what it meant for him to be the Messiah. The earliest Christians identified Jesus as the Messiah and oriented themselves toward a future Parousia (second coming) when Jesus would be publically vindicated as God's anointed one by fulfilling the basic functions of the Messiah outlined above.

The Greek word *parousia* was often used to describe the visit of the emperor, and the word easily came to be used to refer to the coming of Christ in judgment. The word thus became an effective image for the apocalyptic expectations that played an important role in early Christianity—Jesus would become Lord of all at the Parousia and execute judgment against those who oppressed God's people. This hope for Christ's coming in judgment and glory helped to bridge (1) the early Christian experience of Jesus as decisive for Israel's future and (2) the expectation within apocalyptic Judaism of resurrection and final judgment. At the Parousia, God would definitively inaugurate the kingdom that Jesus had proclaimed and thereby bring about the defeat of Israel's enemies and the resurrection of the dead. This future vindication is contrasted with the ministry of Jesus, in which he is depicted as a lowly servant. The christological pattern that shifts between these two stages, one lowly and one exalted, is often called "two-step Christology."

In stage two, during the decades immediately after the death and Resurrection of Jesus, the early kerygma seems to envision the Resurrection and exaltation of Jesus as elevating him to a new status. The life of Jesus in which he went around the countryside unrecognized by even his closest friends becomes contrasted with his glorification after his death. Yet, even at this early stage in the development of New Testament Christology, there is an urgency behind the integration of this exalted Christ with the life and ministry of Jesus that so many of his

SOME IMPORTANT TITLES AND ROLES IN NEW TESTAMENT CHRISTOLOGY

TERM	DESCRIPTION
New Adam	**Role** Jesus recapitulates humanity by overcoming Adam's disobedience with his obedience.
Christ / Messiah	**Title and Role** Jesus vindicates Israel over and against the forces of evil and oppression; he fulfills the promises Yahweh made to Israel through David and to the prophets.
High Priest	**Role** Jesus is able to offer the definitive sacrifice of himself; this sacrifice removes the sin of the faithful so that there is no further need of sacrifice.
Lord	**Title** Jesus has affected a union between Yahweh and Israel; sin is destroyed.
Savior-Redeemer	**Title and Role** The Greek word *sōtēr* or "savior" was used by Greek kings as a self-designation signifying their success in saving the nation from destruction and decline. Jesus is regarded as the true savior, the one who actually conquers death and grants life eternal. Like *savior*, the title or role of *redeemer* comes from a social context. Those who were enslaved could be purchased and given their freedom. The one who paid the price was then the slave's redeemer. By way of analogy, Jesus redeems humanity from their enslavement to sin and evil.
Son of David	**Title and Role** Like *messiah* this title signifies the continuity of Jesus with the promises made by Yahweh through the prophets; Jesus is viewed as a figure of national hope for restoration and a sign of divine protection against oppression.
Son of God	**Title and Role** Jesus is given the task of bringing about the redemption of Israel from its period of oppression and servitude. In this role, Jesus' identity unfolds and his intimacy—his union—with God becomes increasingly apparent.
Son of Man	**Role** Jesus, through his suffering, will vindicate Yahweh and act as cosmic judge, condemning the wicked and blessing the righteous.
Suffering Servant	**Role** Through his suffering, Jesus brings to a close the era of Israel's sinfulness and separation from Yahweh; the nation can find peace and union with God.
Word-Wisdom	**Role** God's word creates, destroys, judges, and preserves the universe, yet God's word also dwells in the Torah, and now, through the teaching and person of Jesus.

followers clearly recall. As stage two gives way to stage three in the development of the gospel tradition, one can begin to see the integration of postresurrectional Christologies and the memory tradition of Jesus' life and ministry so that Jesus begins to be depicted as the Messiah and Lord at earlier and earlier points in the narrative of the Gospel.

Raymond Brown, the great pioneer in American Catholic biblical studies, coined the term *christological moment* to refer to scenes taken from the life and ministry of Jesus that became the vehicle for the expression of a postresurrectional Christology.[7] In other words, the identity of Jesus, made known through the power of the Resurrection, began to be read back into the narrative of Jesus' life and ministry. The evangelists (and the early church) expressed the identity of Jesus, through a variety of literary and theological devices, by selecting key moments from the story of Jesus. Interestingly, the selection of these moments seems to reflect a trajectory in which

CHRISTOLOGICAL PATTERNS IN NEW TESTAMENT CHRISTOLOGY

PATTERNS	TITLES AND ROLES ASSOCIATED WITH THIS PATTERN	EXAMPLES	DESCRIPTION
Parousia Christology	Lord, Christ, Son of Man	Acts 3:19–21; 1 Corinthians 16:22	At a point in the near future, Jesus will come in glory and power to judge the living and the dead and definitively inaugurate God's rule on earth.
Resurrection-Exaltation Christology	Lord, Christ, Son of God	Philippians 2:5–11; Acts 13:33	By passing through suffering, humiliation, and death Jesus is exalted at his Resurrection.
Ministry Christology	Christ, Son of God, Son of Man, Suffering Servant, Son of David	Mark 1:11, 9:2–8	Moments in the life and ministry of Jesus provide glimpses of Jesus' true identity as he serves the marginalized and encounters resistance and hatred, until he finally suffers to bring about the victory for God and God's people over sin and death.
Preexistent Christology	Lord, Word, Wisdom, Son (New Adam or Divine Man?)	1 Corinthians 10:4; Colossians 1:15–20; John 1:1–14; (Philippians 2:5–11)	From the origins of the universe and throughout the history of Israel, God's wisdom, or God's word, dwelt in the world and guided Israel; in Jesus, the word of God has come to instruct and guide Israel to union with God.

the decisive christological moment emerged earlier and earlier in the story. The earliest Gospel, Mark, for example, uses Jesus' baptism as the decisive scene in which to disclose Jesus' identity. In other words, Jesus' baptism is Mark's inaugural christological moment; the sky opens, God's voice is heard, and so on. For both Matthew and Luke, however, the birth of Jesus is the key early christological moment. Brown identified this rearward developmental pattern as characteristic of New Testament Christology, but he also cautioned against a simplistic characterization of the evidence; after all, some of the material in Paul's letters indicates that this rearward development is not perfectly linear.

Son of God, a title often used to signify important christological moments (e.g., Mark 15:39), often confuses students of the New Testament given its close association with later Trinitarian theology. The title provides a basis for those developments that will eventually lead to the articulation of the Trinitarian doctrine of God, but in the pages of the New Testament, one must be cautious about reading the insights of later theology into early Christian texts. In the Old Testament, the "son of God" is a role rather than a title, and it tended to categorize both angels and human beings who were selected to accomplish divinely ordained tasks. For example, in the book of Job, "the Adversary" (*ha satan* in Hebrew) is described as a "son of God" (Job 1:6) as he is commissioned by God to test Job's righteousness. Additionally, the people of Israel are designated as "God's son," either collectively or as individuals, particularly the king of Judah, the descendent and heir of David (see Psalm 2, a coronation psalm, and Psalm 110, a royal enthronement psalm). Moreover, since the king is seen as God's son, it would be tempting to make a connection between the messiah and the son of God, yet there is no explicit textual evidence to support this connection in first-century Judaism; it is a connection made in the Gospels.

By way of summary, then, a *son of God*, prior to its use in the New Testament, was someone who was commissioned by God with a particular task or mission, and the application of this title to Jesus certainly points to his intimacy with God (especially in Matthew), but perhaps it primarily expresses the role of Jesus. The title *Son of God* is thus applied to Jesus to signify his unique God-given task of accomplishing the redemption that God had promised to Israel in the covenant. The sonship of Jesus takes on a special dimension in John, where the uniqueness of Jesus' task is coupled with the uniqueness of his identity in relationship to God. In the Fourth Gospel and elsewhere in the early Christian tradition, Jesus is called "the only begotten Son." The image of Jesus as God's only begotten Son not only reflects his unique intimacy with his Father but this intimacy is also made available to those united with Christ in faith. In that union, believers enjoy an adopted sonship and cry out to God, "Abba, Father!" (Galatians 4:4–6).

The intimacy of Jesus as God's Son naturally leads to the question of Christ's preexistence, and this question is addressed in various ways throughout the New Testament. First-century Judaism was not without resources for developing titles and roles connected with a preexistence pattern of Christology, and even as early as Paul's Letters, one can find examples of a preexistent Christology. Two well-known passages from the Pauline corpus provide powerful examples of this christological pattern. The first of these is the hymn in Philippians 2:6–11. In this passage, Christ is held up as an example to be emulated.

> [Christ], though he was in the form of God,
> did not regard equality with God some-
>   thing to be grasped.
> Rather, he emptied himself,
> taking the form of a slave,
> coming in human likeness;

and found human in appearance,
   he humbled himself,
becoming obedient to death,
   even death on a cross.
Because of this, God greatly exalted him
and bestowed on him the name
that is above every name,
that at the name of Jesus
every knee should bend,
of those in heaven and on earth and under
   the earth,
and every tongue confess that
Jesus Christ is Lord,
to the glory of God the Father.

In this hymn, the dynamics of self-emptying (*kenōsis* in Greek) and glorification center on humble obedience and death on the cross. The basic pattern of descent (self-emptying) and ascent (exaltation) is obvious, but questions have long circulated about what it means for Christ to be described as existing "in the form of God" (*en morphē theou*). Moreover, what does it mean to say he "did not regard equality with God *something to be grasped*" (emphasis added—the Greek noun used here [*harpagmon*] is related to the verb *harpazō*, meaning "to steal")? While some have suggested that the hymn clearly makes Jesus divine in his preexistence, others contend that, like Adam, the preexistent Christ was made in

DOES THE NEW TESTAMENT CALL JESUS GOD?

New Testament scholars have long debated whether the New Testament actually calls Jesus God. While the Son's relationship to the Father does not find explicit formulation until the Council of Nicea in 325 CE ("God from God, light from light, true God from true God, begotten not made, consubstantial with the Father . . ."), there are several passages in the New Testament that appear to identify Jesus as God. In each of the following texts, *theos* appears to be predicated of Jesus. In each of these passages, however, there remains a difficulty in that apparently a distinction between *theos* and *ho theos* is maintained in the first two passages but not in the second two passages in the chart below.

JOHANNINE PASSAGES

PASSAGE	GREEK TEXT	ENGLISH TRANSLATION
John 1:1	*kai theos ēn ho Logos*	. . . and the Word was God.
John 1:18	*monogenēs theos*	. . . the only Son, God . . .
John 20:28	*ho kurios mou kai ho theos mou*	My Lord and my God!
1 John 5:20	*en tō hiō autou Iēsou Christō, houtos estin ho alēthinos theos*	. . . in his Son Jesus Christ. He is the true God . . .

continued

DOES THE NEW TESTAMENT CALL JESUS GOD? *continued*

In addition to these texts from the Johannine tradition, several letters in the New Testament contain passages where Jesus appears to be identified as God (*ho theos*).

PASSAGE	GREEK TEXT	ENGLISH TRANSLATION
Romans 9:5	*kai ex hōn ho christos to kata sarka ho ōn epi pantōn theos*	and through them according to the flesh is Christ, God who is above all (author's translation)
Titus 2:13	*tou megalou theou kai sōtēros hēmōn Iēsou Christou*	our great God and savior Jesus Christ (author's translation)
Hebrews 1:8	*pros de ton huion· ho thronos sou ho theos*	. . . but of the Son [he says]: "Your throne, O God . . ."
2 Peter 1:1	*en dikaiosunē tou theou hēmōn kai sōtēros Iēsou Christou*	. . . through the righteousness of our God and savior Jesus Christ . . .

While each of these texts presents strong evidence of the early Christian identification of Jesus and God, the broader context of each of these passages, as well as other evidence found throughout the New Testament, provides ample evidence of the ambiguities inherent in New Testament Christology. There is clear tension between the movement to identify God and Jesus in the passages above and the need to differentiate the two (e.g., the instances in which Jesus prays to his Father). It is precisely this tension that gives momentum to the trajectory of New Testament Christology, leading to the articulation of the Trinitarian doctrine of God in the Christian tradition. That doctrine, while very much rooted in Scripture (both Old and New Testaments), does not find formal articulation until several centuries after the close of the New Testament (Council of Constantinople in 381 CE).

---

the image of God but refused, unlike Adam, to "steal" equality with God. In the latter perspective, Christ is the preexistent heavenly man who empties himself out of humility but is rewarded with the divine name ("Lord") because of his obedience to God. In other words, he is rewarded with the divine prerogatives that Adam and Eve sought on their own (Genesis 3:5). It is noteworthy that Paul uses this hymn in a context where he reminds the Philippians that they ought to have the mind of Christ, a humble mind (Philippians 2:1–5). There are many other issues and a wide variety of opinions on the interpretation of the Philippians hymn, but suffice it to say that it raises as many christological issues as it solves.

Another key text in the Pauline literature comes from the letter to the Colossians 1:15–20.

> He is the image of the invisible God,
> the firstborn of all creation.
> For in him were created all things in heaven and on earth,
> the visible and the invisible,
> whether thrones or dominions or principalities or powers;

all things were created through him
and for him.

He is before all things,
and in him all things hold together.
He is the head of the body, the church.
He is the beginning, the firstborn from
the dead,
that in all things he himself might
be preeminent.

For in him all the fullness was pleased
to dwell,
and through him to reconcile all things
for him,
making peace by the blood of his cross
[through him], whether those on earth
or those in heaven.

As in the Philippians hymn, this passage raises the question: what does "image of . . . God" mean here? Once again, it is obvious that the hymn regards Christ as present at the creation of the universe and understands all creation as sustained through him. This thematic connection of Christ with creation will prove fruitful for further elaboration on the precise relationship between the Son and God as the first century comes to a close, particularly in the Fourth Gospel.

The first three verses of John's prologue (1:1–3) give readers ample evidence of the growth of New Testament Christology, particularly in the emphasis on Christ's identification with God and Christ's preexistence.

In the beginning was the Word,
and the Word was with God,
and the Word was God.
He was in the beginning with God.
All things came to be through him,
and without him nothing came to be.

The identification of Jesus with the preexistent word of God (*Logos* in Greek) marks an important move in New Testament Christology, a move that will provide the Christian tradition with its most fertile language for expressing the relationship of Jesus and God, his Father, in a manner that overcomes the subordination and differentiation implied in images of father and son.

The word of God and its personification has its roots in the Old Testament, particularly in what has come to be identified as the wisdom tradition. Both Wisdom and Word signify the active presence of God in the world—creating, communicating, sustaining, and guiding. Examples are numerous, but the following selection highlights the roles performed by the hypostasized Word and Wisdom.

Creation stands out as an apt point of departure. While Genesis 1:1—2:4 provides a dramatic example of the creative power of the word (*dabar* in Hebrew), the creative work of the word also finds expression in the wisdom tradition in the Psalms. In Psalms 33:6, for example, one finds a strong affirmation of the word's role in creation: "By the Lord's word the heavens were made; by the breath of his mouth all their host." Additionally, Psalms 107:20 envisions God's word healing the dead in their graves, and in Psalm 147 the word of God changes the course of nature. But perhaps the most dramatic account of the word's dynamic power comes to us from Isaiah (55:10–11):

For just as from the heavens
the rain and snow come down
And do not return there
till they have watered the earth,
making it fertile and fruitful,
Giving seed to him who sows
and bread to him who eats,
So shall my word be
that goes forth from my mouth;
It shall not return to me void,
but shall do my will,
achieving the end for which I sent it.

The Old Testament envisions the word of God as both the means by which the world was created and the mode through which God continues to engage the world and works to redeem it. For the first-century Jewish philosopher Philo, the biblical understanding of God's word provided the key by which he could integrate the insights of Greek philosophy and Scripture. Greek philosophy emphasized the utter perfection of God and God's remoteness and separation from the created world. Such a picture of God hardly resonates with the God of creation, with Yahweh and the Exodus, or the God of the prophets. To reconcile the insights of Greek philosophy with the God of the Old Testament, there had to be some way for God to be connected with the created order. It had long been affirmed among the Greeks that reason, or the *Logos*, provided human beings with their connection to the realm of the divine. This point is reflected in the following passage from Philo:

> And the Father who created the universe has given to his archangelic and most ancient Word a pre-eminent gift, to stand on the confines of both, and separated that which had been created from the Creator. And this same Word is continually a suppliant to the immortal God on behalf of the mortal race, which is exposed to affliction and misery; and is also the ambassador, sent by the Ruler of all, to the subject race. And the Word rejoices in the gift and, exulting in it, announces it and boasts of it, saying, "And I stood in the midst, between the Lord and You."[8]

The word thus stands at the height of the development of New Testament Christology, though without explicitly settling the issue of the precise relationship between Jesus and God. One should not be surprised to find in the texts of the New Testament a variety of Christologies, all of which point to one fundamental reality: "God was reconciling the world to himself in Christ" (2 Corinthians 5:19). The Christologies of the New Testament bear witness to the early Christian attempts to state this article of faith within the context of first-century Judaism without violating the Shema and the first commandment.

The Synoptic Tradition

The development of the gospel tradition and the development of Christology in the first century are certainly complex problems, but perhaps no single issue in the study of the New Testament generates as much heat and consternation as that of the relationships among the three Synoptic Gospels. At least from a Roman Catholic perspective, no dogmatic or doctrinal issues are associated with the answer to the Synoptic Problem, but the manner in which some scholars engage the debate belies that fact. The politics around the issue are striking, and the hypotheses that attempt to explain the interdependence of the Synoptic Gospels seem to be freighted with extraneous ideological baggage.

The three Synoptic Gospels (Matthew, Mark, and Luke) have for a long time posed a problem for the student of the New Testament. It is obvious, even to the most casual reader, that Matthew, Mark, and Luke are closely related to one another. Evidence of verbatim readings (i.e., passages that are recounted almost word for word in more than one Gospel), closely paralleled readings, as well as wide disparity in parts has invited speculation and argument since the second century. The problem of the relationships of the Synoptic Gospels—the Synoptic Problem—can be phrased as follows: How does one account for both the similarities and the differences among these Gospels? Any attempt to articulate a responsible answer to this question requires some understanding of the evidence.

In their magisterial analysis of the Synoptic Gospels, E. P. Sanders and Margaret Davies list eight important points on the synoptic material.[9] The percentages they identify, they acknowledge, are not exact, given the fact statistics used in the study of the New Testament are often based on the number of verses, but the length of those verses varies greatly. The same holds true when one bases a statistical analysis on words. The statistics Sanders and Davies employ are thus merely illustrative of the Synoptic Problem.

STATISTICS ON THE SYNOPTIC GOSPELS

	MARK	MATTHEW	LUKE
Verses of Markan Material	661	529	396
Verses Unique to Mark	111	—	—
Verses Unique to Matthew and Luke (Q)	—	220	220
Verses Unique to Matthew (M)	—	319	—
Verses Unique to Luke (L)	—	—	533
Total Verses	661	1,068	1,149

1. The same passages often appear in all three Synoptic Gospels.

2. Usually all three Synoptic Gospels agree on the placement and order of material. Where they do not agree, Mark is almost always supported by either Matthew or Luke.

3. Matthew includes about 85 percent of Mark's Gospel while Luke includes about 65 percent of Mark.

4. The wording of material common to all three Synoptic Gospels is often verbatim. Where there are differences Mark is almost always supported either by Matthew or by Luke.

5. The agreements between Matthew and Luke begin where Mark begins the story of Jesus and end where Mark ends the story (note that the infancy material and the Easter material are unique to Matthew and Luke).

6. The material in Mark is closer to both Matthew and Luke than Matthew and Luke are to each other. In other words, Mark is the bridge between the other two.

7. Matthew and Luke have about 220 verses in common that do not have a parallel in Mark. In this material there is sometimes almost verbatim agreement and sometimes loose agreement.

8. The material Matthew and Luke share but that is not found in Mark is often arranged in different order.

Any proposed solution to the Synoptic Problem must take into account the above points. Any solution to the Synoptic Problem must exceed the standard of possibility and ascend to the heights of probability. This is a high bar for any hypothesis, and there are always temptations either to take short cuts or to ignore Ockham's razor: "the simplest solution is usually the best solution."

The canonical order of the Synoptic Gospels can be attributed to the early Christian church and its conviction that Matthew was the oldest Gospel. Papias, a second-century writer whose works have been lost in the course of history but whose position on the matter was recorded by other writers like Eusebius, alleged that Matthew wrote his Gospel first and in Hebrew (Aramaic?). Augustine and other church fathers addressed the Synoptic Problem by suggesting that Matthew's was the first Gospel written,[10] then Mark wrote a condensed version of Matthew, and Luke later expanded Mark. The following quote is taken from Augustine's discussion of the evangelists and their work in *The Harmony of the Gospels.*

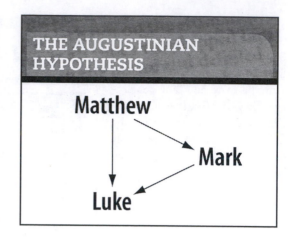

THE AUGUSTINIAN HYPOTHESIS

> Now, those four evangelists . . . are believed to have written in the order which follows: first Matthew, then Mark, thirdly Luke, lastly John. Hence, too, [it would appear that] these had one order determined among them with regard to the matters of their personal knowledge and their preaching [of the gospel], but a different order in reference to the task of giving the written narrative. As far, indeed, as concerns the acquisition of their own knowledge and the charge of preaching, those unquestionably came first in order who were actually followers of the Lord when He was present in the flesh, and who heard Him speak and saw Him act. . . .
>
> Of these four, it is true, only Matthew is reckoned to have written in the Hebrew language; the others in Greek. And however they may appear to have kept each of them a certain order of narration proper to himself, this certainly is not to be taken as if each individual writer chose to write in ignorance of what his predecessor had done, or left out as matters about which there was no information things which another nevertheless is discovered to have recorded. But the fact is, that just as they received each of them the gift of inspiration, they abstained from adding to their several labors any superfluous conjoint compositions. For Matthew is understood to have taken it in hand to construct the record of the incarnation of the Lord according to the royal lineage, and to give an account of the most part of His deeds and words as they stood in relation to this present life of men. Mark follows him closely, and looks like his attendant and epitomizer [*pedissequus et breviator*]. For in his narrative he gives nothing in concert with John apart from the others: by himself separately, he has little to record; in conjunction with Luke, as distinguished from the rest, he has still less; but in concord with Matthew, he has a very large number of passages. Much, too, he narrates in words almost numerically and identically the same as those used by Matthew, where the agreement is either with that evangelist alone, or with him in connection with the rest.[11]

This hypothesis, however, rested on unstable ground. The fact is that both Matthew and Luke share material in common with each other that is not found in Mark—around 220 verses—and this material usually does not follow the same order. If Luke were borrowing from both Matthew and Mark, why does he regularly retain the same order as Mark, when dealing with material shared by Matthew and Mark, but not the same order as Matthew, when dealing with material found only in Matthew?

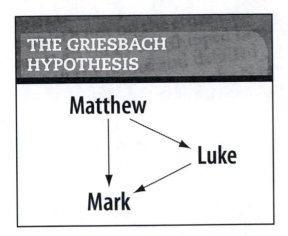

THE GRIESBACH HYPOTHESIS

Matthew

Luke

Mark

Subsequent to Augustine, J. J. Griesbach (1745–1812) offered the first serious attempt to wrestle with the Synoptic Problem anew and modified Augustine's approach.[12] Like Augustine, he followed the testimony of Papias and other early fathers of the church in accepting Matthean priority, but he contended that Luke then used Matthew as a source for his work. According to Griesbach, Mark was the last Gospel written. Mark made use of both Matthew and Luke, and he generally followed Matthew, though he occasionally favored Luke while always keeping both of these sources in mind. Like Augustine, Griesbach saw Mark as a condenser and abbreviator who summarized his sources and eliminated what was superfluous or repetitious, including the citation of Old Testament passages. On only the rarest occasion, Mark inserted verses in order to smooth out transitions.

General dissatisfaction with the premise of Matthean priority grew in the nineteenth century until Karl Lachmann (c. 1835) and others posited the priority of Mark. Several important factors contributed to the assertion of Markan priority, none of which were conclusive in themselves, but when taken together were seen to explain the data more adequately than either Augustine or Griesbach. Among the most important arguments for Markan priority were the following: (1) Mark's use of Aramaic, (2) his primitive theology, (3) his omission of important material that is common to both Luke and Matthew (e.g., the birth of Jesus, the Lord's Prayer, and the postresurrection appearances), and (4) the manner in which Matthew and Luke preserved the Markan order of stories in material they all shared, but diverged in their order otherwise. While most scholars would not take points one and two as convincing, the last two points have taken root in contemporary debate. To most scholars, it makes little sense for Mark to have removed passages like the infancy narrative or the Lord's Prayer from his account of the Gospel. In fact, there is some evidence that the Lord's Prayer was in use in Christian liturgy early in the first century. Why would Mark exclude this important material but carefully preserve the parable of the Sower and the Seed (Mark, chapter 4)? Perhaps even more compelling for many New Testament scholars today is the argument from order. Both Matthew and Luke tend to follow Mark in their ordering of the material (i.e., episodes are ordered in the same sequence in all three Gospels), but where Matthew and Luke diverge from Mark, they also diverge from one another. Most scholars suggest that this fact indicates that Mark functioned as a template or an outline for both Matthew and Luke, who then worked independently of each other to modify and supplement Mark with other material.

The order of the material common to all three Synoptic Gospels makes it likely that Matthew and Luke both copied from Mark. The points at which Matthew and Luke diverge from Mark can be explained more readily when Markan priority is affirmed rather than Matthean priority. For example, the miracles recorded in the first half of Mark are grouped together in Matthew, chapters 8–9. This small section of miracles in Matthew smartly parallels a similar teaching section in Matthew, chapters 5–7. It makes better sense for Matthew to have gathered and organized the Markan material than it does for Mark to have scattered the Matthean material. Similar examples can be found in Luke and Mark. Additionally, when one reads material common to all three Synoptic Gospels, the discrepancies between Mark on the one hand and Matthew and Luke on the other make sense as attempts by the latter two evangelists to improve or to make more suitable Mark's style or his presentation.

One basic problem associated with the hypothesis of Markan priority was the fact that Matthew and Luke shared more than 220 verses not found in Mark. The Augustinian and Griesbachian approaches both solved the problem by suggesting that Luke made use of Matthew. But if Mark's Gospel was written first, and Matthew and Luke used Mark independent of one another (a necessarily staple of argument for Markan priority), then how does one account for these verses found in both Matthew and Luke but absent

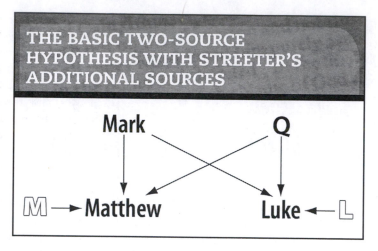

THE BASIC TWO-SOURCE HYPOTHESIS WITH STREETER'S ADDITIONAL SOURCES

from Mark? Matthew and Luke never insert these 220 verses in the same place within the basic (Markan) narrative, though it is often ordered similarly in Matthew and Luke. Moreover, this common material (e.g., the Lord's Prayer, the Beatitudes, the parable of the Great Feast) seems to have a general theological consistency, suggesting that it came from the same source. In 1838, Christian Weisse posited the existence of a second source common to Matthew and Luke but not used by Mark. Some twenty-five years later Julius Holtzmann (c. 1863) offered further proof that this source was a written document (now

A MINOR AGREEMENT

MARK 1:40	MATTHEW 8:2	LUKE 5:12
A leper came to him [and kneeling down] begged him and said, "If you wish, you can make me clean."	And then a leper approached, did him homage, and said, "Lord, if you wish, you can make me clean."	Now there was a man full of leprosy in one of the towns where he was; and when he saw Jesus, he fell prostrate, pleaded with him, and said, "Lord, if you wish, you can make me clean."

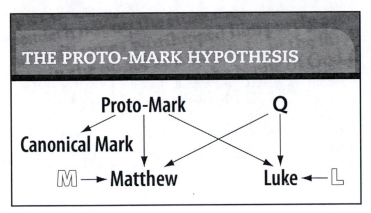

THE PROTO-MARK HYPOTHESIS

is the so-called minor agreements. In several places in the triple tradition, Matthew and Luke seem to make identical changes to the Markan material (e.g., Mark 1:40; Matthew 8:2; Luke 5:12).

These minor agreements have led some scholars to modify the two-source hypothesis. Two important variations include (1) the idea that Matthew and Luke both used a different form of Mark, sometimes called "Ur Markus" or "Proto-Mark." Thus the canonical Gospel of Mark would have been a later version than the one used by both Matthew and Luke.

simply called Q after the German word *quelle* meaning "source"), and the theory was expanded in the early twentieth century by B. F. Streeter (c. 1924), who included sources for the special material found only in Matthew (M) and Luke (L) respectively. While Streeter envisioned these sources as written documents, most scholars today regard this material as part of an oral tradition that contributed to the evangelists' creative theological interests. These oral traditions may find confirmation in the reports of Eusebius, who as late as the fourth century could still testify to the authority of the oral traditions behind the Gospels.[13] This theory represents the most satisfactory explanation of the Synoptic Problem to date.

Several problems challenge a strict understanding of the diagram offered above. First, there is evidence that today's version of Mark is dependent on earlier sources. For instance, there is at least one doublet in Mark (Mark 6:30—8:26) and evidence of an overlap between Mark and Q (e.g., Mark 1:12–13) that suggest that Mark relied on several sources to help compile his Gospel. Another problem the two-source hypothesis does not solve

Others suggest that the minor agreements are the result of an improvement on what would become the canonical version of Mark (today's version of Mark). This revision is called Deutero-Mark ("Second-Mark"). If Matthew and Luke used Deutero-Mark as their source, this fact explains the minor agreements. According to both modification theories, neither Proto-Mark nor Deutero-Mark survived, so both remain, as Q does, hypothetical reconstructions.

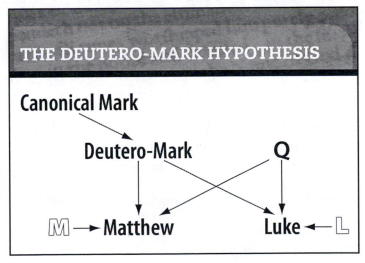

THE DEUTERO-MARK HYPOTHESIS

Conclusion

The development of the gospel tradition, its Christology, and the narrative material in the Synoptic Gospels, stands as a challenge for any-one who wants to read the New Testament seri-ously. Earlier assumptions about the relationship between the Gospels and the history of Jesus or even the history of the early church are frustrated by the evidence in the Gospels, and as readers struggle to make sense of that evidence, available theories or hypotheses about the development of the gospel tradition raise new questions even while they solve others. At this point, it should be evident that reading the New Testament in gen-eral and the Gospels in particular is a demanding discipline, and the presentation provided here is merely cursory. As the reader moves forward, the present text should fade into the background as the actual text of the Gospels takes center stage.

I QUESTIONS FOR UNDERSTANDING

1. What is the kerygma, and why is it impor-tant for understanding the development of the gospel tradition?

2. Do the Gospels simply report what Jesus said and did in his ministry? Explain.

3. Compare and contrast the approaches to the Synoptic Problem taken by Augustine and Griesbach.

4. What are the reasons for positing Markan priority?

5. What is Q? Who first postulated its existence, and what problem or issue does it solve?

6. What are so-called minor agreements, and why are they important for understanding and solving the Synoptic Problem?

I QUESTIONS FOR REFLECTION

1. Take a moment to consider the relationship between "event" and "proclamation." How are the two related? Can proclamation, in turn, become an event? How might this relationship be understood in light of the Fourth Gospel's characterization of the word (Logos) incarnate as Jesus?

2. Look at the sidebar titled, "Does the New Testament Call Jesus God?" and select one of the passages mentioned there. In your library, locate a commentary on your passage (biblical commentaries are shelved in the section of your library labeled BS in the LOC cataloging system). Be sure to select an academic commentary devoted to the specific biblical book in which your passage occurs (e.g., make sure you find a commen-tary dedicated to Romans if you are looking at that passage rather than a commentary on the entire Bible). Summarize the material on the verse. Does the commentator think that this passage calls Jesus God? Explain the issues involved.

3. Read through the Q material in Matthew and Luke. How would you characterize the genre of material in Q? Can you begin to construct a theology of Q?

FOR FURTHER READING

Brown, Raymond E. *An Introduction to New Testament Christology*. New York: Paulist, 1994.

Schneiders, Sandra. *The Revelatory Text: Interpreting the New Testament as Sacred Scripture*. Collegeville, MN: Liturgical, 1999.

Stein, Robert H. *The Synoptic Problem: An Introduction*. Grand Rapids, MI: Baker, 198

ENDNOTES

1. See 11Q13.

2. See *Dei verbum*, no. 19.

3. For a robust discussion of the issues involved here as well as an excellent presentation of the nature of biblical language in light of contemporary thought, see Sandra Schneiders, *The Revelatory Text: Interpreting the New Testament as Sacred Scripture* (Collegeville, MN: Liturgical, 1999).

4. Willard M. Swartley, *Israel's Scripture Traditions and the Synoptic Gospels: Story Shaping Story* (Peabody, MA: Hendrickson, 1994).

5. For a good summary of the major points in the discussion of the "Son of Man," see John R. Donahue, "Recent Studies on the Origin of 'Son of Man' in the Gospels," *Catholic Biblical Quarterly* 48 (1986): 484–498, and John Collins, "The Son of Man in First-Century Judaism," *New Testament Studies* 38 (1992): 448–466. For a discussion of the use of the word *nationalism* in this context, see N. T. Wright, *Jesus and the Victory of God*, 398–403 and 594–597.

6. R. H. Charles, ed., *The Apocrypha and Pseudepigrapha of the Old Testament* (Oxford: Clarendon, 1917), 216–217.

7. Raymond Brown, "Aspects of New Testament Thought," in *The New Jerome Biblical Commentary*, ed. R. Brown, J. Fitzmyer, and R. Murphy (Englewood Cliffs, NJ: Prentice Hall, 1990), 1357.

8. Philo, *Who Is the Heir of Divine Things?* in Philo Volume IV: Loeb Classic Library, no. 261, F. H. Colson, trans. (Cambridge, MA: Harvard University Press, 1932), n. 205–206, p. 385.

9. E. P. Sanders and Margaret Davies, *Studying the Synoptic Gospels* (London: SCM, 1989), 53–65.

10. Eusebius, *Ecclesiastical History* 3.39.

11. Augustine, *Harmony of the Gospels*, 2.3–4, trans. Philip Schaff, Nicene and Post Nicene Fathers.

12. J. J. Griesbach, *Symbolae criticae ad supplendas et corrigendas variarum N. T. lectionum collections* (Halle, 1793). For an English translation of Griesbach's works, see B. Orchard, *J. J. Griesbach: Synoptic and Text-Critical Studies 1776–1976*, SNTSMS (Cambridge: Cambridge University Press, 1978).

13. Eusebius, *Ecclesiastical History*, 3. 39. 3–15.

THE GOSPEL ACCORDING TO MARK

Introduction: Historical and Theological Background

The Second Gospel has long struck readers with its brevity and starkness, particularly when read against the color and character of the other canonical Gospels. For example, one finds no heartwarming depiction of the infant Jesus in Mark, nor is there an image of Jesus as the gentle and serene teacher spinning great discourses or parables. Rather, Mark gives readers both an abrupt beginning and a highly enigmatic conclusion, framing a fast-paced narrative with only relatively brief didactic sections, and often leaving modern readers overwhelmed and unsettled. Its exploration of dark themes such as doubt, failure, and suffering has even led some to call Mark "the scariest Gospel."[1] A brief exploration of the background issues associated with Mark's Gospel will help readers to make sense of Mark's unique approach to the proclamation of God's good news in Jesus Christ by giving readers a sense of the historical and theological context in which Mark operated.

Authorship and Lived Context

In his fourth-century work *Ecclesiastical History*, the historian Eusebius of Caesarea records the tradition, going as far back as the second-century church writer, Papias, that attributes the second of the canonical Gospels to Mark, the interpreter or secretary (*hermeneutēs*) of Simon Peter (see 1 Peter 5:13).[2] Other traditional commentators identify the author of the Gospel with John Mark, or more precisely, "John, who is called Mark" (Acts 12:25), the one-time traveling companion of both Paul and Barnabas (see Colossians 4:10, 2 Timothy 4:11, and Philemon 24). The identification of the author of the Gospel with a figure from early Christian literature might seem like a pious legend to some, but the traditional attribution actually has the ring of historical plausibility: If the early Christians were going to attribute the Gospel to a great authority (a common practice in the ancient world called "pseudepigraphy"), why not choose Peter himself instead of his interpreter? The fact that the Gospel is attributed to such a minor figure (instead of Peter) suggests that the traditional attribution of the Gospel remains plausible. A reading of the Gospel itself suggests, however, that the author is not simply a reporter or secretary as the tradition seems to suggest, but a creative agent who appears to draw from several sources. Further complicating the issue of the authorship of the Second Gospel is the fairly negative portrayal of Peter in the narrative and that the theology of Mark seems to be somewhat more Pauline than Petrine.[3] In the end, the identity of the author of the Second Gospel remains unresolved.

The great second-century bishop and theologian Irenaeus suggests that Mark wrote his

Gospel after the deaths of Peter and Paul, who are said to have died during Nero's persecution of the Christians in Rome (c. 64 CE).[4] Other internal evidence from the Gospel seems to support Irenaeus' dating of the text.[5] After all, Mark places a strong emphasis on the suffering of Jesus and his followers, and such an emphasis makes sense in the face of Nero's fierce persecution; most commentators generally concur with Irenaeus and therefore date the Gospel to around 70–73 CE. While the traditional location of Rome as the site for authorship is still popular among scholars today, some scholars have suggested a Palestinian or Syrian setting for the Gospel, using the evidence that is normally taken to support a Roman provenance for Mark. These scholars associate Mark with the Jewish Revolt and the sporadic persecution of Jews and Christians in the area (i.e., Syria or Palestine) at this time rather than the persecution in Rome.[6] Complicating matters further is the presence of numerous Latin words and expressions in the Greek text of Mark (e.g., 4:21; 5:9, 5:15; 6:27, 6:37; 7:4; 12:14; 12:42; 15:16, 15:39). For many scholars, the presence of these Latin words in an otherwise Greek text suggests an area in which Roman culture predominated, which could be Rome or several Roman cities in and around Syria. Although some scholars in the past had wrongly supposed that Latin words in a Greek text could only have occurred in the western part of the Roman Empire, evidence from the Talmud (the ancient Hebrew commentary of Mosaic Law) suggests that the influence of Latin was felt anywhere Roman imperial power predominated.

Although historians can know with certainty only a few things about the author and the specific historical context of Mark, Francis Moloney identifies four facts that readers should acknowledge when considering the author and the lived context of Mark's Gospel.[7] First, Mark demonstrates a familiarity with the Roman world, Roman government, and the Roman language (i.e., Latin).

Second, Mark and the community for which he writes are invested in the mission to the Gentiles. Third, the community of Mark has, or is undergoing, an experience of persecution and suffering that has created tension and failure within the community. Fourth, the destruction of Jerusalem during the Jewish Revolt (70 CE) is near to the experience of Mark and his community. While the traditional association with the aftermath of the Neronian persecutions makes good sense of these facts (and this context will provide the basic framework for what follows), other contexts are certainly plausible, provided they can account for the obvious suffering, betrayal, and guilt experienced by Mark's community that is so prevalent in the text. Many scholars continue, however, to argue for a Syrian setting for Mark.

The Structure and Flow of the Gospel

In the nineteenth and even into the twentieth century, many scholars considered Mark to stand as a basic historical account of Jesus' life and ministry. They tended to view Mark as a mere collection of Jesus material: snippets of sayings and deeds of Jesus loosely strung together "like a strand of pearls."[8] When one reads the Gospel more closely, however, one begins to understand that such a characterization of Mark is fundamentally mistaken. Mark is no mere collector of stories, simply preserving the traditions of Jesus' words and deeds; rather, Mark is a creative and capable theologian who carefully constructs his presentation of the good news, weaving together a narrative and a theology that is at once faithful to the memory tradition of Jesus and one that speaks to the lived context of his contemporary audience.

The Gospel of Mark omits any account of the birth of Jesus, and it is not clear whether Mark had access to the traditions about Jesus' birth, traditions that found their way into both Matthew and Luke. Rather, Mark begins his proclamation with the cry of John the Baptist. The baptism scene seems almost abrupt when compared to the way the other Synoptic Gospels develop the scene. Immediately following his baptism by John, Jesus utters his definitive proclamation: "This is the time of fulfillment. The kingdom of God is at hand. Repent, and believe in the gospel" (1:15). In the seven chapters that follow, Mark takes readers on a fast-paced journey as the narrative reports healing after exorcism after healing. There is little time for the characters to reflect or readers to catch their breath, as each scene further discloses the nature of the coming kingdom and Jesus' role in inaugurating it. Tension in the narrative grows as initially only the reader and the demons in the narrative recognize Jesus' true identity (1:24; 5:7). Throughout the first half of the narrative, Jesus puts the forces of evil on notice and causes conflict and division wherever he goes, providing dramatic evidence that indeed the kingdom is at hand.

The entire Gospel turns on the episode in which Simon Peter confesses Jesus as Messiah (8:27–31). Following Peter's confession, Mark's narrative becomes much more focused on didactic material and less and less focused on Jesus' miracles and exorcisms. Each of three large units of teaching begins with a "passion prediction" in which Jesus subverts the expectations of his followers by defining his messianic status through his anticipated rejection and execution (8:31–33; 9:30–32; 10:32–34). Following his passion predictions, Jesus calls his disciples to a radically new way of living, emphasizing alternative attitudes toward wealth and privilege, and even embracing the possibility of death.

The narrative culminates in Jerusalem where Jesus confronts the authorities in the city, forecasts the demise of Jerusalem and its Temple in apocalyptic language (chapter 13), and is arrested, abandoned by his disciples (esp. 14:50–52), put on trial, and executed. These climactic scenes are suffused with tension. Jesus is left, in the end, dying on the cross, abandoned by his friends and the crowds. Ultimately he cries out to God: "My God, my God, why have you forsaken me?" (15:34; see also Psalms 22:2). This dark scene provokes simultaneous responses of fear and hope in the reader since the psalm of an innocent person that Jesus is quoting begins with a cry of abandonment but ends with an abiding hope in Yahweh. This dynamic of graphic fear and underlying hope permeates the Gospel, especially its conclusion.

The conclusion to the Markan account troubles many readers: where one might expect to find a bold narrative relating the Resurrection and appearance of Jesus, Mark's Gospel ends with the three women fearfully leaving the empty tomb and disobeying the angelic figure by telling no one of what they have seen. Problems associated with the ending of Mark will be discussed later in the chapter.

Mark's use of intercalation uniquely delineates his narrative style. Throughout the Gospel, Mark has inserted, or intercalated, one story into another, so that each story might help to interpret or accentuate the other. One of the most commonly cited examples of this technique is the story of Jesus cursing the fig tree in 11:12–14, 20–21. In this strange and remarkable story, Jesus approaches a fig tree out of season, finds no fruit on it, and curses it, saying, "May no one ever eat of your fruit again!" In verses 20–21, Jesus and his disciples return to the vicinity of the tree to find it withered and dead, a direct result of Jesus' powerful words. The story is broken up, however, by verses 15–19 in which Jesus goes to the Temple and chases out the vendors and the moneychangers. The story culminates with Jesus denouncing the practices he witnesses in the Temple: "Is it not written: 'My house shall be called a house of prayer for all peoples?' But you have made it a den of thieves." In combining the two stories, Mark signals his readers that the two are linked and interpret one another. The fig tree represents the religious leadership of Jerusalem, epitomized by the religious leaders associated with the Temple (the Sadducees). The absence of fruit on the tree in the presence of Israel's messiah (trees were to bear fruit out of season in the messianic age) symbolizes the absence of righteousness among Jerusalem's ruling class. The forecast of the Temple's destruction finds its symbolic counterpart in the cursed fig tree. Mark employs this technique throughout his Gospel, as he does more than merely record the traditions of Jesus.

The use of intercalation to weave together episodes (or "pericopes") represents only one aspect of Mark's rich narrative texture. Ched Myers discerns five narrative elements that structure the plot of Mark's Gospel: (1) giving a mandate; (2) acceptance or rejection of the mandate; (3) confrontation; (4) success or failure; (5) consequence.[9] The main plot is the advent of Jesus as the Son of God. Jesus is given and accepts the mandate to proclaim the in-breaking kingdom of God, thus leading to confrontation and ultimately to the cross. The reader is left to evaluate the success or failure of Jesus' proclamation: If the reader or hearer responds with faith in the risen Christ, then the cross of Christ is overcome and the proclamation will be a success; without the response of faith, the cross will mark the failure of Jesus' proclamation.

Myers detects three subplots as well:

- Jesus mandates the building of a new community of believers or disciples. His disciples reject that mandate once they realize that it is the way of the cross. This rejection is followed by a series of confrontations and the failure of the disciples. Yet their failure is not the last word, for through the Resurrection, the disciples have another opportunity to live out Jesus' mandate.

- A second subplot involves the crowds, especially as they are represented as the beneficiaries of Jesus' miracles of healing and exorcism. The crowds receive the mandate that Jesus' authority surpasses that of the scribes and Pharisees. But as the crowds begin to realize that Jesus' authority calls them to go beyond their own nationalistic assumptions, they, like the disciples, reject Jesus and at his trial, they call for the release of Barabbas.

- The third subplot involves the mandate for a new social and political order, evident in Jesus' challenge to the legal system, the tax system, the cult, and the purity system. The established leaders of Israel—the Herodians, Sadducees, Pharisees, and scribes—immediately reject this mandate, and the Jerusalem narrative reports the confrontation between Jesus and the ruling elite, climaxing in his condemnation and execution. Yet, as the reader knows, the established social and political order in Jerusalem is doomed, as Jesus predicts in chapter 13.

PHYSICAL SETTINGS IN MARK

Structural and narrative aspects of Mark are complemented by the use of a variety of settings. Bonnie Thurston has explored the significance of some of these settings in Mark, correlating the Gospel's theological themes and the locale in which they are explored.[10] The following represents a rough summary of her insights.

The Wilderness (Mark 1:1–39; 6:31, 6:35)
Mark sees the wilderness as an opportunity for intimacy with God, while at the same time also representing an opportunity for diabolical forces to pull one away from God. The wilderness is a lonely place, and therefore at once

continued

both comforting and threatening. The devil lurks there, but it is also a place of great intimacy with God. This intimacy was the focal point of many of the prophets of the northern kingdom of Israel. For them, the wandering in the wilderness was a time of intimacy with God, when God pitched his tent among his people.

House and the Sea (Mark chapters 2–7)

Jesus may have had a house or a home base in Capernaum. Several passages indicate that Jesus stayed regularly in [his own?] house (2:15; 3:20). We also see Jesus staying in the houses of those close to him (1:29, 1:33; 5:21–24, 5:35–43; 7:24–30). Throughout the early ministry of Jesus, we find him teaching and healing in homes. It appears that this is where Jesus is most comfortable and it is where others are most comfortable listening and responding to him. The home is a sign of intimacy and stability.

The sea, on the other hand, represents change, chaos, and danger. The stilling of the storm (4:35–41) evokes the Old Testament image of God creating the world out of watery chaos (Genesis, chapter 1, and Psalm 33:6). By evoking this image, Mark places Jesus in the position of God in the act of creation: Jesus, asleep in the back of the boat, serenely calms the storm that so terrifies the others. As violence and death begin to announce themselves in the ministry of Jesus (3:6), the identity and power of Jesus sets all things in perspective.

The Valley (Mark 8:22—10:52)

In chapters 8–10 we see Jesus and the disciples as a traveling band: a peripatetic teacher with his disciples. The torturous route from Tiberias to Jerusalem through the Jordan Valley (also called, the Rift Valley), and in particular, the way from Jericho to Jerusalem, is barren and threatening. It is no mistake that the teaching that Jesus delivers in this area is equally demanding. In order to make it to Jerusalem, there are costs involved.

The Mountain (Mark 9:2–13)

The teachings Jesus delivers in the Jordan Valley are initially interrupted by the mountaintop narrative of Jesus' transfiguration. In the Old Testament as well as throughout many religious traditions and the story of Jesus, mountains are places of manifestation, of heavenly vision, of otherworldly experiences. The confirming and consoling epiphany and metamorphosis of Jesus in chapter 9 helps to confirm and support the difficult teachings Jesus is delivering. On the mountaintop, the connection between suffering and glorification is made and the decisive insight into the life and ministry of Jesus is confirmed. But humans do not dwell on mountains, and so the journey to Jerusalem continues.

The City (Mark chapters 11–15)

The journey to Jerusalem ends with the story of the healing of the blind man, Bartimaeus (10:46–52). This healing story functions as the transition between the teaching that has gradually opened the eyes (or will continue to open the eyes) of the disciples and the actualization of that teaching in the events of Jesus' suffering and death. The city, Jerusalem, is where God uniquely dwells with his people in the Temple. As such, it should be a place of great joy and celebration. Yet the reader has known since chapter 8 that for Jesus and his disciples, Jerusalem is the place where Jesus will encounter cynicism, hardness of heart, and ultimate rejection and death.

Thurston argues that Jerusalem serves as a general symbol of religious institutions. She notes that in 1:5, "all the inhabitants of Jerusalem" went out to receive the baptism of repentance from John the Baptist. She provocatively asks, what was it about the religious establishment that led so many to confess their sins outside that establishment? In the end, the city is a symbol of life together—a life with God. But it is also the symbol of corruption and rejection of God.

PHYSICAL SETTINGS IN MARK *continued*

The Cross (Mark chapters 14–15)

Mark's Gospel centers on the cross. On this point there is no real debate. The cross is a unique place and a unique event. Even though untold numbers were brutally executed on Roman crosses, "the cross" of Christ is singular. On the one hand, Christ is utterly alone—apart from God in his suffering and apart from the rest of humanity in his innocence. On the other hand, as Thurston points out, Jesus experiences radical solidarity with all human beings who suffer and feel abandoned by God. When Jesus cries out, "My God, my God, why have you forsaken me?" he quotes Psalm 22, which concludes on a note of confidence in God. In quoting this psalm, Jesus also looks forward to vindication from God.

The Garden (14:32–42 and 16:1–8)

Creation begins with a garden (Genesis, chapter 2), and salvation history unfolds with God planting Israel as a garden (Isaiah, chapter 5). It makes perfect sense, then, that the story of Jesus should conclude with a garden. First, the decisive moment in God's saving plan has Jesus in the garden making the decision to do the will of his Father. Second, the new life that this decision makes possible is made known with the discovery of the empty tomb, which John's Gospel tells us is located in a garden.

Theological Themes

The proclamation of the kingdom of God provides the framework for Mark's presentation of both his Christology and his account of discipleship. The phrase *kingdom of God* gives voice to Israel's hope for God to break through and rule the world definitively, and Jesus' own life anticipated the realization of the kingdom. The climax of Jesus' life is his suffering and death, which also provides the interpretive key for understanding his ministry of healing, exorcism, and teaching. Only at his death do human beings recognize Jesus' identity as Son of God (15:39), an identity stated in the prologue (1:1) and now declared by a Gentile soldier.

Jesus' self-designation "Son of Man" grounds Mark's Christology, and the role this figure plays within writings in the contemporary literature adds depth to the Markan portrayal. For example, in Daniel, chapter 7 (written in the second century BCE), and the Enoch literature (written in the first century CE), the son of man is an angelic figure (possibly messianic) that plays a key role in judging the world and defeating the forces opposed to God. As the Son of Man, Jesus is also identified by Mark as fully human, subject to suffering and death. In order to fulfill his role as apocalyptic judge, Jesus must undergo rejection as God's anointed (*christos*) and suffer. Brendan Byrne has suggested that the entire Gospel revolves around three stories that focus on Jesus as God's Son.[11] The first story is Jesus' baptism (1:9–11), where the reader witnesses God's definitive declaration of Jesus' divine sonship. In what follows, the disciples, the Jewish authorities (usually scribes, Pharisees, and occasionally Herodians or Sadducees), and the crowds try to piece together this identity, with varying degrees of success. In the second such story, Simon Peter proclaims Jesus as "messiah," an identity confirmed by the voice from heaven in the subsequent transfiguration narrative (8:27—9:8). The third story unfolds at the foot of the cross where the Roman centurion declares, "Truly, this man was the Son of God" (15:39). Through this emphasis on suffering and rejection, Mark ties together Jesus' identity as Son of God, Messiah, and Son of Man.

Mark links his Christology and his account of discipleship through the theme of suffering. At the outset of the narrative Mark portrays the disciples as examples to be emulated, for they abandon everything to follow him (1:16–20; 2:13–14). But they have difficulty understanding Jesus (6:30–44; 8:1–10) and dealing with their fears (4:35–41). At the climactic point in the narratives, all of the disciples abandon Jesus and leave him to die alone on the cross. For Mark, the real disciple must imitate Jesus in both his ministry and in his suffering; failure to do so is the moral equivalent of rejecting him.

For more than a century, the so-called messianic secret has played a significant role in the interpretation of Mark's Gospel. William Wrede first promoted this reading, beginning in the middle of the nineteenth century, in response to those who characterized Mark as a historian and a collector of the early Jesus tradition.[12] Wrede insisted that Mark's Gospel is thoroughly theological as well, citing as evidence the way Mark portrays Jesus' identity in his ministry. Mark's Jesus repeatedly warns his disciples to tell no one about what they have seen, admonishes even unclean spirits and demons to keep quiet (1:25, 1:34; 3:11–12), and only permits the revelation of his identity after his Resurrection from the dead (9:9).

For Wrede, the secrecy motif seemed to serve an apologetic purpose: it is the means by which Mark explains why no one openly embraced or proclaimed the messianic identity of Jesus until after his death. Wrede believed that Jesus had no messianic notions about himself and that the early Christian community developed its own interpretation of him as the Messiah after his Resurrection. Many modern scholars find this last point somewhat troublesome; they argue that the ministry of Jesus is

suffused with messianic ideas and associations. In fact, the arrest of Jesus and the charges leveled against him involve these messianic ideas; note in particular Pilate's question, asked in each of the canonical Gospels, "Are you the king of the Jews?" (Mark 15:2, Matthew 27:11; Luke 23:3; John 18:33).

The secrecy motif, however, also corresponds to the difficulties Jesus himself had with the title *messiah*. The title itself was freighted with nationalistic, violent, and even political revolutionary overtones, ideas not characteristic of Jesus' ministry. For Mark, the only way to apply the title meaningfully and accurately to Jesus is to do it in light of the cross, for only when *messiah* is disassociated from violent nationalism can one apply it to Jesus.

Mark's Account of the Gospel

The Advent of the Strong One (Mark 1:1—3:6)

The first half of Mark's Gospel centers on the inauguration of Jesus' ministry and the reaction of those to whom he is sent (Mark 1:1—8:26). As readers make their way through this portion of the Gospel, they notice Mark's emphasis on the power of Jesus to overcome evil in its various forms. The theme of Jesus' identity as "the strong one" unfolds dramatically throughout this section as Jesus serves notice that the kingdom of God is at hand and the powers of evil are being destroyed.

Mark's Gospel begins with a prologue that sets up the rest of the Gospel. M. Eugene Boring suggests that the opening verse of the Gospel, "The beginning of the gospel of Jesus Christ [the Son of God]," actually describes the entirety of the narrative that follows and not just the next few lines.[13] According to Boring, the Gospel is realized in the life of discipleship, in the lives of those who follow Jesus, and as such, the narrative is only the beginning. The actualization of the narrative in the lives of believers as they follow after Jesus truly constitutes the good news, and this conviction on the part of the author helps the reader to better appreciate the ending of Mark.

The narrative itself unfolds with an opening and preparatory contrast between John the Baptist and Jesus. The opening fulfillment passage (i.e., a passage that fulfills a prophecy from the Old Testament) calls the reader's attention to the Old Testament and the role of John the Baptist in relation to Jesus' ministry. The quote is interesting because, contrary to Mark's assertion that the passage comes from Isaiah ("As it is written in Isaiah the prophet" [1:2]), it is not from Isaiah. Rather, pieces, or ideas, from Exodus and Malachi are combined with a passage from Isaiah to produce the final quotation.[14]

A messenger or forerunner will prepare "the way" (1:3) and readers should note the manner in which the word *way* functions in Jesus' ministry (e.g., the way of the exodus, the way of salvation, the way to conduct one's life). Of the sixteen times *way* (*hodos*) occurs in Mark, all but two of these occurrences carry a deep theological meaning. The description of "the one who is to come" envelops or encloses John's characterization of himself. This structural device, called a "chiasm" (the Greek letter *chi* [X] is a perfect mirror of itself), commonly occurs in both oral and written form. Represented graphically as a chiasm, the passage (1:7–8) would take the following shape:

a. One mightier than I is coming after me.

> b. I am not worthy to stoop and loosen the thongs of his sandals.

> b¹. I have baptized you with water;

a¹. he will baptize you with the holy Spirit.

The coming one is Jesus, described by John as "one mightier than I." The notion of strength and, more importantly, of one who is "mightier," will be important for understanding the first part of Mark. In the material that unfolds in Mark chapters 1–3, and really throughout the first eight chapters of Mark, Jesus confronts the power of evil and dramatically inaugurates its eschatological conquest. This dynamic of confrontation and victory substantiates Jesus' claim in 1:14–15, "the kingdom of God is at hand," and with the advent of this kingdom, the appropriate response encompasses repentance-conversion (*metanoeō*) and faith (*pisteuō*). The entire first half of Mark revolves around the strength of Jesus in demonstrating the in-breaking of the kingdom, and the invitation to respond appropriately, that is, with repentance and faith. On the other hand, there is confusion, doubt, and hostility, all of which result in the opposite response to Jesus and his proclamation: disbelief and murderous hostility (3:6).

Yet the truth of Jesus' identity is confirmed by the voice from heaven at Jesus' baptism: "You are my beloved Son" (1:11). By the end of 1:28, the central issues in the plot become defined: Jesus is sent as God's Son to confront the powers of evil, especially as they are represented in the social and political status quo, to announce the kingdom as the replacement of the status quo, and to call for the response of repentance and faith. Yet only a few are willing to cross over and respond appropriately, for the cost is great, as Mark's audience knows all too well in its own experience of suffering.

Mark 2:1—3:6 contains a collection of stories that center on a series of controversies culminating in an alliance among the Pharisees and the Herodians and the unfolding plot to kill Jesus. This sequence of stories begins with the intercalation of a healing and conflict story in 2:1–12, typical of Mark, where the basic elements of a healing story are interrupted by a controversy-pronouncement story about the power to forgive sins. The healing story includes verses 2–5 and 11–12. The story has all the characteristics of a healing story.

- seriousness of sickness: "carried by four men"

- word: "rise, pick up your mat and walk"

- cure and demonstration: "he rose, picked up his mat"

- reaction of onlookers: "they were all astounded"

The controversy story in 2:6–10 similarly has the basic elements one would expect in such a story:

- action or saying: "your sins are forgiven"

- reaction or questioning: "He is blaspheming. Who but God alone can forgive sins?"

- counter question: "Which is easier . . . ?" (Notice that when Jesus engages in a controversy, his initial response to his adversaries is not an answer but a counter question.)

- teaching or a pronouncement: "the Son of Man has authority"

The stories have been brought together by Mark to illustrate more effectively the kind of worldview Jesus' proclamation and actions are meant to subvert. The old Deuteronomistic ideology suggested that there was more or less a direct correspondence between suffering and sin: as one sinned, so one suffered. Such an outlook would have been particularly attractive to the elites in Jerusalem, who did not necessarily buy into the apocalyptic outlook shared by the Pharisees and others. This initial confrontation over Jesus' power and authority is

THE BASIC ELEMENTS OF AN EXORCISM STORY AND A HEALING STORY

The structure of passages has long interested biblical scholars, and with the advent of form criticism in the early twentieth century, there was a growing emphasis on the distinctive form a story took when it was transmitted orally. That form remained in the written version of the passage. While scholars are still interested in a story's oral form, they are not willing to confine the form or structure of a passage to the question of its oral transmission, or its *Sitz im Leiben* (i.e., its "setting in life"). Rather, they insist that all biblical texts possess a structure, and some of these structures reflect a certain consistency. For example, form critics identified the following elements in the form of an exorcism story (see, e.g., Mark 5:1–20):

- meeting the demon (Mark 5:2)
- dangers posed by demonic possession (Mark 5:3–5)
- recognition of the exorcist (Mark 5:6–7)
- an exorcism (Mark 5:8, 13)
- demonstration of success (Mark 5:13–15)
- amazement and fame (Mark 5:14, 16–17)

Similarly, certain basic elements appear in most healing stories (see, e.g., Mark 2:1–12):

- seriousness of sickness (Mark 2:3–4)
- contact or word (Mark 2:5, 11)
- a cure (Mark 2:11)
- demonstration of cure (Mark 2:12)
- reaction of onlookers (Mark 2:12)

All accounts of exorcism and healing do not necessarily follow these patterns precisely. Yet these are the common recurring elements in these types of stories. As readers encounter these story forms, it may be helpful to refer to their common structure.

telling. If he has the power to heal (and even his opponents seem to admit that he has this power), and thereby overcome the power of sin, does he also have the power to pronounce the forgiveness of sin? The power to forgive

SUFFERING AND THE DEUTERONOMISTIC TRADITION

The Deuteronomistic tradition is a unique strand of Old Testament theology that is reflected in parts of the Pentateuch, the Former Prophets (i.e., Joshua, Judges, 1 and 2 Samuel, 1 and 2 Kings), and some of the Latter Prophets (especially Jeremiah). The theological emphasis of this tradition centers on the free election of Israel by God and the importance of Mosaic Law as the means by which Jews are to respond to God's act of election. This response had to be made by everyone and had to be constantly renewed. The scene in Deuteronomy 30:15–20 is characteristic of the Deuteronomist's outlook—covenantal fidelity brings with it rewards, and transgressions bring suffering.

> Here, then, I have today set before you life and prosperity, death and doom. If you obey the commandments of the Lord, your God, which I enjoin on you today, loving him, and walking in his ways, and keeping his commandments, statutes and decrees, you will live and grow numerous, and the Lord, your God, will bless you in the land you are entering to occupy. If, however, you turn away your hearts and will not listen, but are led astray and adore and serve other gods, I tell you now that you will certainly perish; you will not have a long life on the land which you are crossing the Jordan to enter and occupy. I call heaven and earth today to witness against you: I have set before you life and death, the blessing and the curse. Choose life, then, that you and your descendants may live, by loving the Lord, your God, heeding his voice, and holding fast to him. For that will mean life for you, a long life for you to live on the land which the Lord swore he would give to your fathers Abraham, Isaac and Jacob.

The passage from Deuteronomy expresses the outlook that sees suffering as punishment for wickedness or transgression of divine commandments. The wisdom tradition in Israel, embodied in books like Proverbs, the Psalms, and Wisdom, challenged this outlook, and the book of Job stands as a provocative confrontation, with suffering as a theological mystery. This appears to be the tradition within which Jesus stands in the Gospels. These critiques notwithstanding, many in first-century Palestine intuitively held this view even if it was also open to challenges and reassessment.

---

sins is considered God's alone. In first-century Judaism, that power was realized through the divinely sanctioned work of the Temple in Jerusalem. Through the Temple cult, particularly on the Day of Atonement (Yom Kippur), the high priest pronounced the forgiveness of sins for the Jewish people. The fact that Jesus was not only healing people but also making explicit the implicit claim that he had the power to overcome evil apart from the prescribed rituals of the Temple, completed his thoroughgoing critique of the religious, social, and political establishment.

The series of controversies that follow serve to illustrate the basic dynamics of Jesus' ministry. Though none of the issues at stake, nor Jesus' stance on those issues, places him outside the confines of rabbinic Judaism, the consistent pattern that he adopts, along with his claim to authority, make him remarkable and dangerous in the eyes of his enemies. In Mark 2:15–17, the question of Jesus' table fellowship emerges for the first time, followed by the question of Jesus, and his disciples' willingness to eat and drink "with tax collectors and sinners." These controversies tend to depict Jesus as something of a libertine with respect to Torah observance, but readers should take note of the eschatological dimension of Jesus' proclamation and his rationale for "stretching" Torah observance the way he does: the kingdom is at hand, and it is breaking in here and now in the person and proclamation of Jesus. The response of conversion and faith (1:14–15) now becomes decisive, and the religious politics of Torah observance must give way to God's bounty, God's offer of mercy and fellowship in Christ. The rejection of this offer by the Pharisees and Herodians in Mark becomes telling. Jesus is a divisive figure: he provokes conversion and faith but also violent and even murderous intentions. The tensions established in the first chapters become heightened throughout the Gospel, leading to the climax of the narrative tension in chapters 15 and 16.

The Initial Training of the Disciples (Mark 3:7—6:6)

The next section of Mark mirrors the first in some ways. The first section began with the call of the disciples and ended with a note of unbelief or rejection, and this second section on Jesus' ministry in Galilee also begins with the disciples and ends with Jesus' rejection. In the meantime, readers will notice the development of Jesus' ministry in the second section (e.g., the inclusion of the parables in chapter 4) and, in particular, the failures of the disciples become increasingly apparent.

While the opponents of Jesus have just gone off to plot his death in 3:6, the reader's attention is directed to the positive response Jesus has provoked and the widespread and growing popularity he now enjoys among the people of Galilee (3:7–10). Mark, however, also includes the corresponding reaction of the demonic world to Jesus' authority and power: the demons scream, cower, and obey in Jesus' presence (3:11–12). Although the demons know Jesus' identity, its disclosure is not to be entrusted to the demonic world, and they are commanded to keep silent: only the response of conversion and faith will make known the identity of Jesus in the world of human beings.

The next episode (3:20–35) provides another example of intercalation in Mark, this time connecting the dialog about Jesus' true family with the opposition of the scribes and Pharisees. The episode begins with the family of Jesus, coming from Jerusalem (the center of religious and political authority), alleging that Jesus has gone mad ("he is out of his mind"). Immediately following the episode with Jesus' family, the opponents of Jesus misconstrue his power over demons, alleging it comes from associating with demons. This opposition provides Jesus with the opportunity to respond with a more accurate account of his exorcisms. Jesus is the "stronger one" who has bound the devil and now plunders his house. Moreover, Jesus launches a counteraccusation against his opponents, namely, that those who deny the power of God's spirit (i.e., blaspheme the Holy Spirit) are guilty of an unforgiveable sin. The reader is then brought back to the question of Jesus' family. Like Jesus' opponents, his family represents an obstacle to his mission. Their misunderstanding can only be remedied through conversion and faith, and to the extent that they are unable or unwilling, they remain obstacles. Such a position contrasts with the depiction of Jesus' relationship with his mother in Luke and John, and amplified in the later Christian tradition. Mark seems to draw from a tradition that placed little or no emphasis on this relationship.

Chapter 4 moves the reader into an engagement with the parabolic teachings of Jesus, which

Mark groups here. Readers are often surprised to find so few parables in Mark (most of the great parables come from Q and Luke's special material). The parable of the Sower (4:1–9) inaugurates this section, and its vivid narrative is remarkable, with the parable's application to the ministry of Jesus readily apparent. The confusion of the disciples thus becomes important in this section, for it sets up the enigmatic interpretation of parables within the ministry of Jesus. Mark's use of Isaiah 6:9 in 4:11–12 proves central to his presentation of Jesus, his message, and the response it generates: "The mystery of the kingdom of God has been granted to you. But to those outside everything comes in parables, so that 'they may look and see but not perceive, and hear and listen but not understand.'" In the context of Isaiah, the prophet has just been commissioned by God to speak the prophetic message to Judah. God warns Isaiah that his message requires conversion and repentance, and that such a response will not be forthcoming.

Similarly, in Mark, Jesus predicts that his proclamation of the kingdom's advent will not meet with the necessary response of conversion and faith. The parable of the Seed Grows of Itself (4:26–29), unique to Mark's Gospel, reinforces the characterization of the response Jesus has received and that the disciples will receive: even if nothing appears to be growing (i.e., audiences appear to be rejecting you), take heart, for the kingdom may be at work even if it is not visible. In 4:33–34, the parable section closes with a contrast between the implied confusion within the larger crowds and the disciples of Jesus to whom he explains the parables.

The Calming of a Storm at Sea (4:35–41) accentuates Mark's presentation of the disciples, who appear to be just as confused here as they are by the parables Jesus just delivered. Although Jesus supplies the disciples with interpretations of the parables, this move serves to accentuate the overall negative portrayal of the disciples, who still don't really understand Jesus even with his assistance. In a quintessentially Markan passage (which Matthew and Luke repeat), the storm on the Sea of Galilee throws the disciples into a panic while Jesus sleeps in the stern of the boat. When the disciples wake Jesus, he calms the storm, evoking the divine power in creation (Psalms 29; 65:8; 89:10). Then he asks, "Why are you terrified? Do you not yet have faith?" Mark develops a contrast with the themes of fear and faith throughout his Gospel; the disciples are given every opportunity to receive the gift of faith and to see their circumstances, however trying, with the eyes of faith. Yet, they repeatedly fail. Additionally, the story of calming the storm serves as an illustration of Mark's Christian church in Rome as it suffers through the torments of persecution under Nero. The church is composed of people "in the boat" and "out at sea"; Jesus is indeed present with them, but the storms of persecution batter the boat nonetheless.

The failure of the disciples to apprehend and cultivate the gift of faith and conversion finds contrast in the powerful stories of healing in chapter 5, where those from outside the circle of Jesus' disciples respond with faith and confidence in Jesus. First, the story of the Gerasene demoniac (5:1–20) is one of the most remarkable in the New Testament. The basic features of an exorcism story were outlined earlier in this chapter as meeting the demon, the dangers of demonic possession, recognition of the exorcist, the exorcism itself, demonstration of the exorcism's success, the amazement of the onlookers, and the consequent fame of the exorcist.

The man possessed by a demon is forced to live among the tombs, among the dead; his possession is so extreme (characterized as a "legion" of demons) it requires more than the strongest fetters to contain the man. Such dramatic scenes highlight Jesus' ministry as an eschatological confrontation with the forces of evil, and the use of the word *legion* to describe the demons suggests to some commentators that the forces of evil have a powerful ally in the Roman Empire.

An intercalation of two healing stories involving Israelites follows the story of the Gerasene demoniac. The stories are joined because each demonstrates how, in the face of opposition and scorn, these two individuals persist in their faith and find healing. The ruler of the synagogue and the woman with the hemorrhage both seek out Jesus with an almost blind confidence and trust. Their faith is implicitly contrasted with that of the disciples who have been "spoon fed," so to speak, by Jesus, and yet their faith is

ARAMAIC IN THE GOSPELS

In Mark 5:41, we read Jesus commanding the daughter of Jairus with the words *"Talitha koum"*—an Aramaic phrase transliterated into the Greek alphabet by the evangelist. The presence of Aramaic in Mark (cf. 7:34) raises a number of questions for the reader, including: (1) What is Aramaic? (2) Were the Gospels originally written in Aramaic? (3) Why do Aramaic phrases occur in some parts of the New Testament?

1. Aramaic is a Semitic language that came to prominence as the lingua franca of the Neo-Assyrian Empire in the eighth century BCE and was subsequently used administratively by both the Neo-Babylonian Empire and the Persian Empire. In fact, the Aramaic language was so influential that its alphabet replaced the paleo-Hebraic alphabet that had been used in Israel prior to the Babylonian exile. The later Second Temple period witnessed the rapid decline of Hebrew as a spoken language, and Aramaic began to predominate as the first language of many Jews. While Greek increasingly became the language of commerce for many people in the eastern Mediterranean, Aramaic remained popular. Many eastern rite Christians use a form of Aramaic as a liturgical language (e.g., Chaldean Rite Christians in Iraq).

2. While early Christian writers like Papias seem to suggest that Matthew was originally written in Aramaic, most scholars believe that the Greek of the Gospels displays stylistic features that preclude the notion that they are translations of other texts. Rather, almost all New Testament scholars believe that the Gospels were composed in Greek, even if they make use of some traditional material that had been preserved in Aramaic. Joachim Jeremias (1900–1979) made a career of reconstructing the "very voice" (*ipsissima vox*) of Jesus by offering conjectures about the Aramaic substrata of the Gospels.[15] Joseph Fitzmyer and others, however, have long pointed out the phenomenon of Semitic interference in "common" or Koine Greek used in the first century and have adopted a cautious approach to the reconstruction of the so-called Aramaic substratum of Jesus' sayings.[16]

3. Some scholars have argued that the preservation of Aramaic in the Gospels provides a sure sign of a passage's antiquity, making it more probable that it goes back to stage one. Moreover, the fact that Mark preserves the Aramaic of this passage over and against Matthew and Luke suggests the primitive character of Mark in relation to the other Gospels.[17] Others suggest that the preservation of Aramaic in this passage owes itself to the notion of a magical formula whereby Jesus was able to affect the healing and raising of the girl.[18]

weak and waffling. The demoniac, the synagogue ruler, and the woman with a hemorrhage, in their faith and persistence in pursuing Jesus, collectively act as foils to the disciples (i.e., they are portrayed so as to accentuate the disciples lack of faith and lack of courage). The fact that Jesus himself called the disciples does not make them immune from failure, and no disciple can rest on this status or office; only the disciple who follows through, in spite of fear and adverse consequences, can really be called a disciple.

The story of the anonymous woman with the hemorrhage (5:25–34) holds special significance in the gospel tradition for many reasons, not least because the story demonstrates the basic characteristics of Jesus' miracles within the context of his ministry. At first glance, she appears to receive an almost magical dispensation of healing power from Jesus. After all, there is no personal contact or connection, merely the touching of his cloak. But Jesus refuses to let the interaction remain on a purely mechanical level—he demands, "Who touched my garments?" The woman comes forth, and at great risk, tells Jesus (and presumably the entire crowd) what had transpired. Jesus addresses her as "Daughter" (*thaugatēr*), thereby signifying the new family that she has now joined as she receives new life after twelve years of uncleanness and marginalization. This story is intercalated with the raising of Jairus's twelve-year-old daughter and draws attention to the symbolic value of the number twelve (Israel) and the power of Jesus to transform that which is unclean, even the dead—which will cause controversy with the Pharisees in the next section (7:1–23).

Mark concludes the section on the initial instruction of the disciples with the account of Jesus' rejection in his hometown (6:1–6). The example of Jesus serves as a reminder to the disciples that rejection and derision accompany the proclamation of the gospel. What Jesus endures, those who follow him will also endure.

The instruction provides a brief foretaste of the teaching on suffering and discipleship that will unfold in chapters 8–10.

Sending, Feeding, and Transition (6:7—8:26)

The next major section of the narrative revolves around a Markan doublet, the two feeding stories in 6:34–44 and 8:1–10. Doublets in Mark often intrigue scholars inasmuch as these seem to suggest that Mark's Gospel was dependant on some written source material. Yet whatever sources Mark may have had at his disposal, he nonetheless makes the material his own here. The first part of this section (6:6–33) centers on the sending and the return of the disciples. They are initially sent out to go and do what Jesus has done: drive out demons, summon people to conversion, and heal the sick.[19] The sending and the returning of the Twelve envelops the story of Herod Antipas and his execution of John the Baptist. Herod's casual and cruel indifference toward the Baptist (he is easily moved by others to execute John) portends the attitude of the authorities toward Jesus (compare Pilate in 15:2–15), and Mark ties together these stories to indicate that the sending of the disciples will inaugurate rejection and persecution for Jesus and for his followers.

Both feeding stories (chapters 6 and 8) form part of a narrative sequence involving both a boat and a dispute. Both feeding stories develop eucharistic themes, and the importance of these stories for understanding the Eucharist in the early church is evidenced by the image of loaves and fishes in early Christian representation of the Eucharist in the Roman catacombs.[20] The strong eucharistic themes should not preclude a reading of Old Testament imagery here as well. Both Moses (Exodus, chapter 16) and Elisha (2 Kings 4:42–44) are said to have fed multitudes, and the parallel with Jesus' feeding in chapters 6 and 8 is certainly drawn intentionally by the author. Moreover, both the walking on water (6:45–52) and the dispute about purity (7:1–23) evoke the story of the Exodus and Israel's wandering in the wilderness. Jesus is positioned in the narrative to minister in this context, but also to play the role of Yahweh.

Jesus is the one who walks on water (the crossing of the Red Sea), defines what is clean and unclean (Leviticus), and feeds the hungry (Exodus, chapter 16). As the scribes and Pharisees give voice to their unbelief and resist Jesus, just as Korah and others murmured against Moses in the wilderness (e.g., Numbers, chapter 16), tension builds around Jesus and the disciples. The double telling of the feeding story in chapters 6 and 8 helps to reinforce the messianic bounty supplied by Jesus in his teaching and in his very person. Moreover, the allusion to Psalm 23 in Mark, chapter 6 (e.g., characterization of the crowd as "sheep without a shepherd," the need or "want" of the crowds,

AN ALTERNATIVE EXEGESIS: THE SYROPHOENECIAN WOMAN IN MARK 7:24–30

As mentioned in the introduction, the "alternative exegesis" sidebars explore interpretations of passages that move beyond the framework taken in this introduction, which focuses (though not exclusively) on an interpretation of the Gospels within their historical context. The power of the text "to say something more," to have meaning beyond one particular context, always needs confirmation, lest one render a single interpretation as definitive or hegemonic and thus attenuate the revelatory power of the sacred text.

In the story of Jesus' encounter with the Syrophoenecian woman, readers are often stunned by the interaction. Jesus' treatment of the woman seems uncharacteristically harsh, but the resolution serves to tone down the story's subversive potential. Ranjini Wickramarante Rebera has offered a powerful rereading of this encounter, one that provocatively emphasizes the empowerment of the woman in securing her liberation.[22]

Rebera's exegesis centers on the manner in which the woman challenges her place as an unclean person within the worldview of Israel. At this point in Mark's presentation, Jesus has already confronted the Pharisees over their excessive and oppressive concern for purity, but now Mark draws the reader's attention to a woman who is doubly impure or unclean. As a Greek and, by implication, a pagan, she is neither religiously nor ethnically and racially clean. Yet, she cries out and asserts herself before Jesus even as he tries to hide from the crowds. As she asserts herself, the reader is made aware that her trespassing, her crossing over from the unclean state, is not for her own sake but for that of her possessed daughter; like so many women in the developing world, she uses whatever power she can muster to act on behalf of another. She acknowledges Jesus' power ("Lord") and thereby acknowledges her status as unclean. Yet, in beseeching Jesus on behalf of her daughter, she also gives Jesus power to express his ministry among the Gentiles.

In sum, the Syrophoenecian woman claims inclusion for her "unclean" child and for herself. By doing so, she enables Jesus to put into radical practice the politics of the kingdom, a politics that counters the politics of purity, cleanliness, and exclusion. The Syrophoenecian woman stands as the agent of the story, as one who is herself empowered, and who empowers others, even Jesus.

mention of sitting in "verdant" pastures) helps to accentuate the role of Jesus as Yahweh tending his lost people.[21]

The key transition between the first half of Mark and the second half is provided by the story of the Blind Man of Bethsaida in 8:22–26. This is one of the few stories recounted in Mark but not in either Matthew or Luke. The story unfolds similarly to the healing of the deaf man in 7:31–37, with the strange manner of touching and the use of spittle in healing (contrast this with the mere touch of Jesus' garment in 5:27). Yet, the unique feature of this passage is the two-stage process in which the man receives his sight, pointing toward the two-stage enlightenment of the disciples as their faith grows and unfolds in multiple phases.[23] The metaphor of blindness and sight seems apt for the transition that begins to unfold in the next section. As the disciples receive the proclamation of Jesus and witness his mighty works (e.g., healings, exorcisms), they come to a certain faith in Jesus as the Christ. Yet, this faith, affirmed in the proclamation of Simon Peter, stands in need of further development, as exemplified by the response of Jesus to Simon Peter's hesitation to accept the predicted suffering and rejection of the Messiah.

Jesus' Instruction on Christology and Discipleship (Mark 8:27—10:52)

The second half of Mark moves beyond the fast-paced action of the Gospel's first half, with fewer exorcisms and healings and more didactic material in chapters 8–10, where Jesus sets forth a teaching on his own status and destiny as the Messiah and also the destiny of those who would be his followers. In chapter 11, the action will move to Jerusalem, where the confrontation with the religious and political authorities comes to a head even as Jesus forecasts the destruction of Jerusalem and the final eschatological battle (chapter 13). Finally, Jesus' trial, death, and the announcement of his Resurrection punctuate the stark, urgent, and somewhat dark and anxious tone of the entire Gospel.

Peter's confession provides the narrative's turning point, as the tone and direction of the Gospel change considerably from this point forward: Jesus is destined to be confronted and executed by the authorities in Jerusalem. The scene begins with the questioning of the disciples about the reputation of Jesus among the crowds, and the response echoes that of Herod in chapter 6. The way the crowds understand Jesus is honorific but inadequate. Simon Peter responds to the more personal prompt from Jesus by identifying him as the Messiah. The disciples finally demonstrate insight into the identity of Jesus and seem to be prepared for the next step.

Then Jesus begins to redefine what it means for him to be the Messiah, subverting all of the most basic expectations about messianic figures in first-century Judaism. Simon Peter in particular takes exception and is severely rebuked by Jesus. Readers should take note that in his prediction of rejection and suffering Jesus speaks in terms of the Son of Man and not the Messiah, the title Simon Peter has just confessed. As discussed in an earlier chapter, the title *Son of Man* overlaps, to some degree, with the title *Messiah* as the decisive figure who inaugurates the *eschaton* and acts as judge. In Mark's depiction of Jesus, the Son of Man is almost always connected to the rejection and suffering of Jesus and so also incorporates the image of the Suffering Servant in Isaiah. The identification of Simon Peter as "Satan" connects Peter's rejection of suffering with the temptations of Satan in chapter 1 and made explicit in the Q tradition (see Matthew 4:1–11 and Luke 4:1–13). This parallel is especially notable in Matthew 4:10, where Jesus rebukes Satan with the same expression used against Simon Peter in Mark 8:33.[24]

Jesus' instruction on discipleship emphasizes the need of the disciples to accept, as he does, rejection by the religious and political establishment, and even to accept the same manner of execution he will suffer: "Whoever wishes to come after me must deny himself, take up his cross, and follow me" (Mark 8:34). While many have spiritualized this aspect of the instruction, including Luke with his modification of the passage to include carrying a cross "daily" (Luke 9:23), the image of the cross and the demand to lose one's life for Christ and the gospel were no doubt concrete references for the Markan community, which had undergone severe persecution at the hands of Roman authorities (true whether one places Mark in Rome or in Palestine during the Jewish Revolt). The cross was, for them, a scandal, a stumbling block, and a terrifyingly real possibility for those who lived and proclaimed their faith in Christ. Yet the instruction and admonition to real discipleship is not simply a matter of personal response to Christ; it is the cause of the gospel, the ongoing proclamation of the in-breaking kingdom in the person and work of Christ.[25]

SCRIPTURE IN DETAIL: THE TRANSFIGURATION (MARK 9:2–8)

The story of the transfiguration follows on the heels of Simon Peter's confession and Jesus' teaching on Christology, suffering, and discipleship. A detailed reading of the passage will help to illuminate the connection between it and the material that surrounds it.

Attempting to discern the basic elements and structure of a pericope provides the interpreter with the initial means of engaging a biblical passage. In examining a passage for structure, generally there are no right or wrong outlines per se. Rather, an outline of a biblical passage is meant to highlight the essential features and promote an insightful reading of the passage. One looks for a certain elegance and balance in an outline.

I. Introductory Formula (9:2)

  A. Temporal clause ("six days")

  B. The witnesses (Peter, James, John)

  C. Location ("a high mountain, apart by themselves")

II. The Appearance of Jesus Changes (9:2–3)

  A. "he was transfigured"

  B. his clothes become dazzling white "such as no fuller on earth could bleach them"

III. Appearance of Moses and Elijah (9:4)

IV. Peter's Response (9:5–6)

  A. "It is good that we are here"

  B. Suggestion to make three tents

  C. Description of a psychological state of awe and terror

V. The Cloud (9:7)

  A. Description of cloud "casting a shadow over them"

  B. The voice from the cloud speaks and instructs the disciples

VI. Concluding Formula (9:8)

The outline above structures the commentary that follows. In the introductory formula there are several items of note. First, the events that take place occur after six days, or on the seventh day, after the confession of Peter and Jesus' initial teaching on his role as suffering

continued

SCRIPTURE IN DETAIL: THE TRANSFIGURATION *continued*

Son of Man and Messiah. Accompanying Jesus are Peter, James, and John, the three disciples with whom Jesus is closest in the synoptic tradition, who will also exercise leading roles in the early church. The four move to the top of a mountain, the place of divine and human interaction (see Exodus, chapters 3, 19).

The description of Jesus' transformation resonates with the kind of transformation found in the Resurrection accounts in the other Gospels. Jesus' transformation recalls the physical transformation of Moses on Mount Sinai in Exodus. The appearance of Moses and Elijah are decisive for interpreting the passage. In many cases, exegetes have identified the two as representing the Law and the Prophets, understood as the two parts of the Jewish Scriptures at the time of Jesus. Yet it is remarkable that the appearance of Moses and Elijah do not measure up to that of Jesus, for they appear normal while only Jesus is transformed or transfigured. Moses and Elijah thus present a contrast to Jesus in this scene.

Peter's reaction embodies the misunderstanding of the disciples. Surely it is good to witness this remarkable event, but his suggestion to make tents for Moses, Elijah, and Jesus misses the mark on at least two points. First, by making three tents Peter places all three on the same level, and from the opening line of the Gospel the reader knows that this is a misunderstanding of Jesus' identity and his role. Second, Peter's request evokes the Jewish Feast of Sukkoth or Booths, a celebration commemorating Israel's wandering in the wilderness during the Exodus. At that time, Yahweh dwelt with his people in a tent or a booth. In effect, Peter wants to capture the mountaintop moment and preserve it. Peter has taken this time of intimacy with Jesus and with his Father, as well as Moses and Elijah, as a kind of end point, a concluding event. The reader knows, however,

that the message and mission of Jesus does not have its end point in a mountaintop experience; rather, the way of Jesus and the way of discipleship lead to suffering, rejection, and the cross.

As the cloud overshadows the observers—and presumably Moses and Elijah—they hear the voice from heaven. It is God's own voice, last heard in a similar scene at the baptism of Jesus (1:11). This time Jesus is identified as "my beloved Son," and the onlookers are told to "listen to him." Of course, what Jesus has been saying and what he will continue to stress in the next chapter centers on the necessity of his own suffering and on the suffering of those who would follow him. In other words, the transfiguration is a confirmation of Jesus' teaching on Christology and discipleship. Moreover, the fact that neither Moses nor Elijah is transformed or transfigured suggests that their stories represent a contrast to Jesus' story. In particular, both Moses and Elijah are rescued or preserved from suffering and rejection by God. In the case of Elijah, he is rescued from Ahab and Jezebel when a fiery chariot carries him off to the heavenly abode. Moses, for his part, lives a long life (one hundred and twenty years—the limit of the human life span after the flood) before he dies in the Transjordan. Neither of the two most prominent agents of God's saving plan undergoes rejection and suffering like that of Jesus, and therefore neither of them shares in the glorification Jesus will undergo at his Resurrection and exaltation. The voice from the cloud, then, calls the disciples to recognize this fact and to accept Jesus' teaching on his destiny and the destiny of his disciples.

In the end, the mountaintop experience disappears, and Jesus is with his disciples as before. The journey to Jerusalem continues as Jesus sets forth the demands of discipleship during the next chapter.

The question of Elijah's return, an event highly characteristic of first-century Jewish expectations about the *eschaton* (see Malachi 3:22–24), follows the transfiguration story. The connection between Elijah and John the Baptist helps to accentuate the eschatological tension in Jesus' ministry while also serving to heighten the expectation of suffering and rejection for Jesus and his disciples. In the unfolding eschatological struggle, strong faith will be essential. A negative example of faith unfolds even as Jesus, Peter, James, and John are "on the mountain" of the transfiguration: when they return, they find the other disciples have been unable to heal a demon-possessed boy (9:14–29) even though, as Jesus points out, "everything is possible to one who has faith" (9:23). The inadequacy of this "faithless generation" troubles Jesus (9:19), particularly as it

GEHENNA

The word *Gehenna* is often translated as "hell" in the New Testament (the NAB preserves *Gehenna* while the NRSV and other versions translate the word as "hell"). Gehenna is the Greek transliteration of the Hebrew *ge-hinnom*, or "Valley of Hinnom" (in some places it is *ge ben-hinnom*, "Valley of the son of Hinnom"). The valley was located outside the southwest walls of Jerusalem. In the century or so prior to the Babylonian exile, residents of Jerusalem reportedly offered children as sacrifices to Molech, a deity commonly associated with the Phoenicians. See, for example, Jeremiah 7:30–34:

> The people of Judah have done what is evil in my eyes, says the Lord. They have defiled the house which bears my name by setting up in it their abominable idols. In the Valley of Ben-hinnom they have built the high place of Topheth to immolate in fire their sons and their daughters, such a thing as I never commanded or had in mind. Therefore, beware! days will come, says the Lord, when Topheth and the Valley of Ben-hinnom will no longer be called such, but rather the Valley of Slaughter. For lack of space, Topheth will be a burial place. The corpses of this people will be food for the birds of the sky and for the beasts of the field, which no one will drive away. In the cities of Judah and in the streets of Jerusalem I will silence the cry of joy, the cry of gladness, the voice of the bridegroom and the voice of the bride; for the land will be turned to rubble.

And Jeremiah 32:35:

> They built high places to Baal in the Valley of Ben-hinnom, and immolated their sons and daughters to Molech, bringing sin upon Judah; this I never commanded them, nor did it even enter my mind that they should practice such abominations.

There has been some disagreement about the identity of the god Molech and the frequency of child sacrifices, but the historical arguments are not important for understanding how the image of Gehenna developed. With the advent of apocalyptic eschatology and visions of eschatological judgment beginning in the second century BCE, images of fire and demons became part of the envisioned punishment for evildoers. Gehenna's connection with fire and demonic foreign deities made it an apt image for the place of eschatological punishment. It appears, however, that Mark provides the first example of the symbolic use of Gehenna as the place of punishment.

seems to include his disciples. When confronted with the need to have faith, the boy's father cries out, "I do believe; help my unbelief!" (9:24). This cry seems to reflect the anguish of the struggling, suffering Markan community, strongly tempted to abandon their faith in the face of persecution.

The block of material surrounding the second instruction on Christology and discipleship (9:30—10:31) begins with the disciples' struggle to accept the truth of Jesus' teaching as they discuss the implications among themselves but avoid addressing Jesus directly. The quick segue to the nonsensical dispute about the greatest in the kingdom (9:33–37) serves, once again, to highlight the inadequacy of the disciples and their failure to grasp the teaching of Jesus. Everything Jesus has been saying runs counter to the spirit of the disciples' argument, and to reinforce his point, Jesus brings a small child into the discussion. Readers should immediately disabuse themselves of contemporary notions about the innocence and social importance of children. In the first century, children were nobodies; they had no social standing or social value.[26] Jesus tells his disciples that they must welcome the child—welcome nobodies—and put themselves in the service of nobodies. In other words, any conversation about "greatness" must begin with service to the least. Conversely, anyone who leads even the least important person into sin will be judged and will suffer the pains of Gehenna (9:45).

In this section of Mark's Gospel (9:38–50), Jesus continues to correct his disciples on various matters. This collection of material might seem, at first glance, to be rather haphazard, but Vincent Taylor convincingly argues for the material's coherence.[27] The material appears to coalesce around verses 43–48 and the words "to sin" (literally "to stumble" in Greek). Those who stumble or cause others to stumble need to take heed and adopt the life of discipleship, learn to practice the gospel, and embrace the name of Jesus, the name of a Christian. The images of salt and fire

are connected to perseverance, purification, and testing, and indicate that this material was once part of early Christian catechesis or instruction, catechesis particularly relevant for Mark's community.[28] Yet, the demands of discipleship transcend any set of commandments, as evidenced in 10:1–31. Many distractions threaten real discipleship, including the desire for a different spouse or for riches, but the disciple is called to a more perfect obedience, a complete surrender to the gospel. Disciples are to live in fellowship with one another and avoid the kinds of disputes about greatness that initiated this section of Mark.

The third instruction on suffering, Christology, and discipleship closes this section and brings the reader to Jerusalem (10:32–52). The disciples once again fail to grasp or to live out the instruction of Jesus. He once again must intervene in a dispute about greatness (10:35–45), urging his followers to embrace the instruction he has given. In a savage piece of irony, in response to their questions about their place in the kingdom, Jesus tells James and John that they can only find greatness if they will drink the cup of suffering and death. When they agree to "drink," Jesus promises them suffering but refuses to grant them authority in the messianic kingdom. The healing of blind Bartimaeus frames the teaching Jesus has been giving since Simon Peter's confession in 8:29. Like the two-stage healing of the blind man that provided the transition to Jesus' instruction (8:22–26), the Bartimaeus healing provides a transition to the Jerusalem narrative and the climax of Mark's narrative.

Jesus' Ministry in Jerusalem (Mark 11:1—13:37)

The final movement in Mark's dramatic proclamation of the gospel unfolds in the passion and death of Jesus. The failure of the disciples and their lack of understanding are mirrored by the lack of understanding and overt hostility of the authorities in Jerusalem. The so-called apocalyptic discourse in chapter 13 highlights the eschatological dimension of this conflict and provides an appropriate transition to the account of Jesus' arrest, trial, and execution.

Jesus' triumphal entry into Jerusalem provides readers with an example of a political-religious demonstration. At the great pilgrimage feast of Passover, Jesus waits on the Mount of Olives, just to the east of Jerusalem, across the Kidron Valley, while his disciples stage his entrance to the city. The scene is meant to evoke two passages from Zechariah. The prophet describes the day when Yahweh will become king over the earth: "That day his [Yahweh's] feet shall rest upon the Mount of Olives, which is opposite Jerusalem to the east. The Mount of Olives shall be cleft in two from east to west by a deep valley, and half of the mountain shall move to the north and half of it to the south" (Zechariah 14:4). Additionally, Zechariah 9:9 describes the Messiah (the king) coming to Jerusalem:

> Rejoice heartily, O daughter Zion,
>   shout for joy, O daughter Jerusalem!
> See, your king shall come to you;
>   a just savior is he,
> Meek, and riding on an ass,
>   on a colt, the foal of an ass.

While Jesus has cautioned his disciples about using the title *Messiah*, he also misses no opportunity to identify with the hopes and expectations of his fellow Jews. He is the Messiah, just not the messiah they expect. Rather than a warrior who will conquer and rule with a sword or with divine power against the Gentiles, the Messiah is instead the one who wages battle against demonic forces within both Israel and in the world of the Gentiles. He identifies himself as son of David, and he is lauded upon his entry to the city (Mark 11:9–10):

> Hosanna! (i.e., "grant salvation!" from
>   Psalms 118:25)
> Blessed is he who comes in the name of
>   the Lord!
> Blessed is the kingdom of our father
>   David that is to come!
> Hosanna in the highest!"

Jesus comes to save God's people, yet they are not prepared to accept the shape that salvation will take.

As the promised one, Jesus performs the prophetic and messianic act of cleansing the Temple from defilement (11:15–19). The intercalation of the Temple incident and the withered fig tree has already been discussed in the introductory material above. The barren fig tree is meant to represent the Jewish authorities, whose failures are echoed in the indictment of the Temple abuses. Jesus' criticism ("Is it not written, 'My house shall be called a house of prayer for all nations? But you have made it a den of thieves.'") concentrates on economic exploitation by means of a conflated quotation from Jeremiah 7:11 and Isaiah 56:7. Describing Jesus' chasing the moneychangers and the pigeon vendors out of the Temple precincts, the episode seems to emphasize the manner in which the poor, in particular, were manipulated and victimized by the economics of the Temple system. Moneychangers exploited the requirement that people pay the Temple tax, not in the Roman currency commonly used in the marketplace, but with religiously acceptable coins (i.e., Jewish coins without the image of the emperor; see Exodus 30:13–15). Anyone who has dealt with currency exchange at international airports knows about the slice taken by those providing this sort of exchange service. For their Temple sacrifices the poor commonly bought pigeons, as they had no animals of their own to bring as offerings (for the various uses of pigeons in the Temple cult see Leviticus 12:6; 14:22; 15:14, 15:29). The quotation from the prophets—and obvious parallels in the Old

Testament—interprets Jesus' action as a prophetic critique of the Temple. But it was also a messianic action, for the renewal and purification of the Temple was a common aspect of Jewish messianic expectation (see *1 Enoch* 90:28–42; Wisdom of Solomon 17:30). Coupled with the fig tree episode, Mark sets the stage for the final conflict between Jesus and the authorities in Jerusalem.

In Mark 11:27—12:44 Jesus and the religious elite of Jerusalem engage in an argument about authority; notice how Jesus answers the chief priest, scribes, and elders with a counterquestion in 11:29–30. The section is punctuated by the parable of the Tenants (12:1–12). The image of Israel as a vineyard planted by God is borrowed from Isaiah, chapter 5, where the symbolism is used as a parable of judgment. Jesus uses the parable in the same way here, threatening the leaders with divine judgment for their lack of justice and lack of faith. In the controversy that follows (12:13–17), opponents try to trick Jesus into speaking against the Romans, but Jesus, using a counterquestion, turns the tables on them. The section closes with opponents of Jesus, the Sadducees in this case, mocking Jesus' proclamation of the Resurrection. Jesus laments such hardness of heart and the unwillingness to believe. The fruit of God's covenantal love and mercy, the practice of protecting the marginalized and loving God (see Mark 12:28–34), is absent among Jesus' opponents, and the hour has grown late. The lack of faithful response among the elite of Jerusalem marks the Temple as well as the entire city, but the poor, the little ones, provide the way forward in the time of trial and tribulation (12:41–44).

The so-called apocalyptic discourse in chapter 13 has piqued the imagination of modern exegetes, particularly with regard to dating the Gospel in relation to the events surrounding the Roman destruction of Jerusalem in 70 CE. Rather than becoming preoccupied with the historical background of the material in this chapter, Brendan Byrne has offered a reading of the discourse that emphasizes the oscillating structure of the material and its rhetorical function within Mark's community of readers and hearers.[29] The discourse is quite obviously an example of apocalyptic eschatology as it contains apocalyptic themes and code words throughout, including: tribulation, handing over, patient endurance, and the elect. Yet the discourse moves subtly between the present and the future, between hope and threat. In the present, believers should maintain their hope even in times of turmoil and tribulation. While these events unfold, readers should not be dismayed that the end has not come yet. But the end is coming, and the Son of Man will come in judgment against the wicked. Prior to that judgment, there will be great pain and tribulation, conflict, and apostasy (i.e., abandoning or turning away from the faith). Byrne describes the following structure of the discourse:

PRESENT: WARNING AND EXHORTATION	FUTURE: APOCALYPTIC PROGRAM
(1) 13:5–6 False prophets	
	(2) 13:7–8 Prelude to affliction
(3) 13:9–13 "Watch out . . . " (trials)	
	(4) 13:14–20 Great affliction
(5) 13:21–23 "Be watchful . . . " (false messiahs)	
	(6) 13:24–28 Coming of the Son of Man (example of fig tree)
(7) 13:33–37 Be watchful!	

"THE DESOLATING ABOMINATION" (MARK 13:14)

The phrase "the desolating abomination" (Mark 13:14) is borrowed from Daniel 9:27; 11:31; 12:11; and 1 Maccabees 1:54, where it refers to the altar of the Greek god Zeus erected by the Seleucid emperor Antiochus IV Epiphanes in the Jerusalem Temple around 168 BCE. The altar to Zeus was placed over the altar of burnt offerings, and Josephus reported that the emperor had swine sacrificed on that altar (*Antiquities* 12.5.4). It is unclear exactly how this reference to an incident from the distant past is supposed to function in Mark, chapter 13. The phrase could be used as a trope, a feature that has become standard within apocalyptic discourse. In other words, the phrase could simply have been a stock prediction of the sacrilege perpetrated by forces opposed to God's elect immediately prior to the *eschaton*. On the other hand, for those who see Mark, chapter 13, as a "prediction after the event" (*vaticinium ex eventu*), the phrase could refer to a specific incident, the attempt by the Roman emperor Caligula in 40 CE to erect a statue of himself in the Temple. Caligula was assassinated before these plans could be carried out, thus making this interpretation somewhat dubious. Others take the phrase as a reference to the antichrist, the figure in Christian apocalyptic literature who stands opposed to Christ in the culminating events of the eschatological drama.

Some commentators see the references to Judea and the hills outside Jerusalem as direct references to the siege of Jerusalem under Titus (70 CE), giving the material a Palestinian setting, while others emphasize the mutual "handing over" of parents and children to the authorities for execution (13:9–13) as support for the traditional Roman setting, as such actions reflect the conditions in Rome in the mid 60s under Nero. However one may make sense of the historical referents in chapter 13, they nonetheless function in Mark as the appropriate capstone to Jesus' ministry and the transition to his arrest and execution.

The Passion of Jesus (Mark 14:1—15:47)

Mark inaugurates his account of the passion by intercalating the plot to kill Jesus (14:1–2, 10–11) and the anointing at Bethany (14:3–9).

The reader knows that the plot against Jesus will succeed and that the oil used at Bethany signifies the preparation of Jesus' body for suffering (prior to combat or competition a person often received anointing) and burial (anointing was part of the processes of honoring and preserving a corpse). These developments subsequently lead the reader to Mark's brief account of the Last Supper (14:17–25), where Jesus predicts his betrayal and Peter's failure, and provides his disciples with the interpretation of his death: the shedding of his blood will establish a new covenant that will bind "the many" into one body.[30] The actions of this meal are highly ritualized, but the meal cannot be the Passover Seder Jesus would then have been tried and executed on Passover—highly unlikely in first-century Jerusalem.[31] Readers ought to interpret the Last Supper in the context of Passover, to be sure, but the meal itself functions much more like the table fellowship Jesus practiced throughout his ministry. Given his anticipated execution, Jesus' actions at the meal thus become highly symbolic.

With the scene in the garden of Gethsemane (14:26–52), the disciples once again fail to heed Jesus' instruction, specifically by failing to keep vigil and pray. Moreover, when the mob comes for Jesus, "those who left everything to follow Jesus have now left everything to get away from him."[32] Even Simon Peter follows "at a distance" (14:54) and denies Jesus in the end, as Jesus predicted he would. The subsequent Jewish and Roman trials parallel each other, with false witnesses and abusive onlookers. Yet the Jewish trial focuses on Jesus' actions in the Temple (not questions of Torah observance) and the question of Jesus' relationship to God ("Are you the Messiah, the son of the Blessed One?" [14:61]). The Sanhedrin trial concludes when the high priest, presumably Caiaphas though he remains unnamed in Mark, pronounces a verdict. Pilate, on the other hand, is much less resolute, and more interested in Jesus' relationship to the empire ("Are you the king of the Jews?" [15:2]). The fact that Pilate is far less convinced of Jesus' guilt than is the high priest suggests the manner in which Jesus distanced himself from the political-revolutionary ideas commonly associated with the title *Messiah* at that time. Yet for Mark, the real issue is the authority and identity of Jesus and the manner in which the Sanhedrin, Pilate, and the crowds reject that authority and instead mock Jesus, spit on him, and hand him over for execution.

On the way to Golgotha, the place of execution outside the city walls, a passerby, Simon of Cyrene, is pressed into service to help Jesus carry the cross; in so doing he becomes a model for Christian discipleship at a point in the narrative when all of Jesus' disciples have fled. The crucifixion scene itself then unfolds around three time markers: the third, sixth, and ninth hours. At the third hour (approximately 9 a.m.), the crowds,

chief priests, and scribes mock Jesus. Even those who were also being crucified with Jesus join in the mocking, thus making the rejection of Jesus utterly complete and dramatically fulfilling Jesus' earlier predictions about his rejection and suffering. The women who ministered to him in Galilee can only watch passively from a distance. At the sixth hour (approximately noon), the words of the prophet Amos are fulfilled in the darkening of the sun at midday (Amos 8:9). During the ninth hour (approximately 3 p.m.), Jesus utters his only words from the cross, a quotation from Psalms 22:2: "My God, my God, why have you abandoned me?" The cry stands a long way from the words of intimacy Jesus uttered in Gethsemane, at the beginning of the passion narrative, where he called God, "Abba, Father" (Mark 14:36). In this way, Mark powerfully highlights the sense of Jesus' complete abandonment, left by all who were close to him.

His abandonment continues after his death, for he is buried, not by his followers, but by a pious member of the Sanhedrin, Joseph of Arimathea. But at the very moment of his death, the vindication of Jesus begins to unfold. The veil that separates the holy place in the Temple is torn, thus depriving the Temple of its sanctity and vindicating Jesus' condemnation of the Temple. At the same time, as the Gentile Roman guard who has watched these events unfold utters the truth about Jesus: "Truly this man was the Son of God!" (15:39).

The Resurrection of Jesus and the Ending of Mark

The ending of Mark has long been a point of contention among New Testament scholars. The best manuscripts of Mark end at 16:8, with later manuscripts offering several alternate endings. These alternate endings are universally recognized as scribal additions that reflect the tendency to harmonize the Synoptic Gospels, characteristic of the Matthean tradition, though the so-called longer ending (Mark 16:9–20) also includes the Ascension of Jesus, a uniquely Lukan passage (Luke 24:51). Most scholars believe that Mark intended his Gospel to conclude at verse 8 with the women fleeing in fear and disobeying the young man's command to "go and tell his [Jesus'] disciples and Peter" of the Resurrection. This ending seems to reflect a certain consistency in Mark where the disciples often display fear and fail to follow through on Jesus' directives. Such an ending, rather than leaving the proclamation of the Resurrection in doubt, serves as an admonition to the Markan community about faith and courage in the midst of persecution and trials. After all, the opening of Mark suggested that this was "the beginning of the gospel of Jesus Christ," and that "beginning" concludes in 16:7 with the implicit command to announce Jesus' Resurrection. From Mark's perspective, the gospel still waits to be enacted in the lives of those who would follow Jesus, even amid their fears and failings.[33] At the end of the day, the spreading of the gospel, its triumph in a world torn apart by sin and violence, rests with God, who overcomes the failures of human beings.

TEXTUAL CRITICISM AND THE ENDING OF MARK

There is no autographed copy of any book in the New Testament. The oldest surviving portion of any part of the New Testament is a papyrus fragment (P52) of the Gospel of John dating to around the middle of the second century CE. The translations that most Christians use are based on a compilation of a number of manuscripts and represent the best guesses modern scholars can make about what the original text said. Such a compilation is termed a "critical text," one that reflects the best judgment (recall that the Greek word *kritikos* is related to "judgment") of scholars on the issue. While this critical text represents a great service to those who read the Bible, the results of modern scholarship are often indecisive at best. Many important questions concerning the text of the Gospels cannot be conclusively resolved, and it remains incumbent upon the exegete to make sound judgments regarding textual issues.

There are many manuscripts of the Bible, but they may be classified into three basic categories:

Papyri: The earliest copies of the New Testament were made on pieces of papyrus. Papyrus was relatively abundant and inexpensive compared to more durable materials like leather or parchment. While papyrus was well suited as a writing surface, it tends to decay quickly, leaving us few papyrus copies of the New Testament.

Uncials: The best preserved copies of the New Testament come from the late classical period (the fourth to tenth centuries). These manuscripts are called the "great uncial codices" (*uncial* is Latin, meaning "inch," i.e., the size of the letters; *codex*, meaning "book"). Uncials are of great importance for determining the best text of the New Testament. These formal documents were prepared on parchment (scraped sheepskin), which was much more durable than papyrus.

Cursives: In the ninth century, a cursive style of writing emerged, making the copying of manuscripts much easier and quicker. These "minuscule," or "cursive," manuscripts became abundant in the Middle Ages. At one time scholars uncritically assumed these were the best manuscripts

continued

TEXTUAL CRITICISM AND THE ENDING OF MARK *continued*

because they were the most abundant and were in substantial agreement with one another. These manuscripts became the basis of what is commonly called "the Byzantine Majority text" (M). This text type was employed by earliest printed editions of the Greek New Testament: Cardinal Ximenes's *Complutensian Polyglot Bible* (1514) and the edition of Erasmus (1516), later to become known as the *Textus Receptus*. In the West, the various churches of the Reformation embraced the Byzantine Majority Greek text as they returned to the original languages and produced a number of Bible translations based upon it, while the Roman Catholic Church maintained that the official text of the Bible, both Old and New Testaments, was that of Jerome's Latin translation, called the Vulgate (since Latin was the "vulgar" or common language of the people at the time Jerome made his translation).

The Development of Textual Criticism as an Art and a Science

The age of archeological discovery began in the nineteenth century. Scientists uncovered many new manuscripts and papyri that challenged the text of Erasmus and the other reformers. Constantine von Tischendorf discovered an early uncial, now known as Codex Siniaticus, in the monastery of Saint Catherine on Mount Sinai in 1844. This discovery began the quest for the original text of the New Testament, a discipline called "textual criticism." One of the basic tasks of textual criticism is to discern the possible relationships that exist between different manuscripts. How does one decide which reading is closer to the original? There are several schools of thought on the issue of textual criticism, but a general consensus has emerged over time. Below are listed some criteria for making judgments about the text of the New Testament. These criteria, among many others, have helped both Roman Catholic and Protestant Christians

come to a consensus and helped to generate a common critical text published by the United Bible Society (also Nestle-Aland).

External Criteria

- a reading that is found in multiple families or types of manuscripts is generally to be preferred
- a reading is suspect when it is found in different places in different manuscripts

Internal Criteria

- *lectio brevior potior*—"the shorter reading is the stronger"
- *lectio difficilior potior*—"the more difficult reading is the stronger"
- a reading that reflects harmonization with (assimilation to) other Gospels is suspect
- a reading that reflects an improvement in style is suspect
- the style, vocabulary, or theology of a reading is suspect when it is at odds with the rest of the text; it is preferred when it is in harmony with the rest of the text

The Ending of Mark

The manuscript evidence suggests that Mark's Gospel ends at verse 8. Two of the best uncial manuscripts and several of the early Christian writers who quote Mark end the Gospel at verse 8, while only the latest cursive manuscripts include 16:9–17. Only the latest uncial manuscripts and a few Ethiopic and other translations include the so-called shorter ending. Thus most scholars feel that external evidence supports the ending of Mark's Gospel at 16:8. Internal evidence also supports this conclusion:

- *lectio brevior potior*—"the shorter reading is the stronger"

  The ending at 16:8 is the shorter reading.

TEXTUAL CRITICISM AND THE ENDING OF MARK *continued*

- *lectio difficilior potior*—"the more difficult reading is the stronger"

  The ending at 16:8 fails to provide a "tidy" ending for Mark's narrative and sets him apart from the other evangelists.

- a reading that reflects harmonization with (assimilation to) other Gospels is suspect

  The longer endings to Mark reflect assimilation to Matthew and Luke.

The other endings of Mark, however, are quite interesting and influential even if they are not original to Mark's Gospel. In fact, the signs that are supposed to accompany believers, which include expelling demons, speaking in tongues, drinking poison, and handling snakes (16:17–18), have influenced the development of some pentecostal churches in the southern United States. This is particularly true of the practice of snake handling. The Church of God of Prophecy (an offshoot of the Church of God in Cleveland, Tennessee) is one of the largest denominations to practice snake handling in worship. Though outlawed in most places, snake handling and drinking poison are still practiced in congregations and independent churches in Appalachia as regular signs of Christian belief.[34]

Conclusion

The Gospel of Mark can seem anything but "good news" to many readers—even the Resurrection account in chapter 16 seems to be robbed of its brightness and optimism. Yet Mark is "the beginning of the good news of Jesus Christ." For Mark and the earliest Christians, the news is truly good as fear and trembling give way to the proclamation of God's work in Christ. In the lives of those who would follow Christ, the joy and brightness of the Resurrection shines, but the beginning of that joy is in the truth of Jesus, of his rejection and the rejection and suffering of those who follow him in faith.

This brief and representative overview of Mark supplies the reader with a framework for understanding the creative energy and theological insight of the author standing behind the Gospel. Moreover, the picture of Jesus that Mark presents is startling and provocative. Jesus emerges as a sign to be embraced or contradicted, accepted or rejected. The pace of Mark and the neat manner in which the first half and second half of the narrative move convey an invitation to confront the truth about Jesus and the cost of discipleship (i.e., to embrace the cross). Mark's Gospel suggests that just as for the blind man in Mark, chapter 8, discipleship will involve more than one moment of conversion or insight.

| QUESTIONS FOR UNDERSTANDING

1. Describe the "lived context" of Mark's Gospel. When was it written, and what were the circumstances faced by those for whom the Gospel was written?

2. Describe the Christology of Mark. What titles or themes are developed in Mark's portrayal of Jesus?

3. How does Mark portray the disciple? Discuss two examples from the Gospel.

4. What is intercalation? Discuss three examples of intercalation in Mark.

5. How does Mark's Gospel change after Simon Peter's confession in Mark, chapter 8?

6. What is the "desolating abomination" in Mark, chapter 13?

| QUESTIONS FOR REFLECTION

1. Many scholars suggest that the historical context within which a text is written (in this case, the Gospel of Mark) should be minimized in favor of the text itself and the world of the reader. In your opinion, how has the discussion of "lived context" both helped and hampered your reading of the text?

2. Although psychological readings of ancient texts are fraught with difficulty, Mark seems to invite such analysis, or at least some speculation. How would you describe the psychology of the author and the intended audience of the Gospel of Mark? What do you make of the author's emphasis on the failure of the disciples, as well as the tension around Jesus and the stark terms used by Jesus to frame the demands of discipleship in Mark chapters 8–10?

3. Scholars continue to debate whether the Gospel of Mark originally ended at 16:8. Look at three commentaries on Mark and summarize the case for and against Mark 16:8 as the original ending. With which position do you agree? Why?

| FOR FURTHER READING

Boring, M. Eugene. *Mark: A Commentary*. The New Testament Library. Louisville: Westminster John Knox, 2006.

Hooker, Morna D. *The Gospel According to Mark*. Black's New Testament Commentary. London: Black, 1991.

Moloney, Francis J. *Mark: Storyteller, Interpreter, Evangelist*. Peabody, MA: Herdrickson, 2004.

| ENDNOTES

1. Brendan Byrne, SJ, *A Costly Freedom: A Theological Reading of Mark's Gospel* (Collegeville, MN: Liturgical, 2008), x.

2. Eusebius, *Ecclesiastical History*, 3.39.15. See also 2.15.2, where Eusebius cites Clement of Alexandria and his lost work, *Hypostases*, Book 6.

3. See, for example, Joel Marcus, "Mark: Interpreter of Paul," *New Testament Studies* 46 (2000): 473–487.

4. Irenaeus, *Against Heresies*, 3.1.

5. Perhaps the most prominent proponent of the traditional associations with Rome and the aftermath of Nero's persecution is Martin Hengel. See *Studies in the Gospel of Mark* (Philadelphia: Fortress, 1985). For a more recent reading of Mark from the perspective of Rome, see Brian J. Incigneri, *The Gospel to the Romans: The Setting and Rhetoric of Mark's Gospel*, Biblical Interpretation 65 (Leiden: Brill, 2003).

6. For example, see Francis J. Moloney, *The Gospel of Mark: A Commentary* (Peabody, MA: Hendrickson, 2002), 11–15.

7. Francis J. Moloney, *Mark: Storyteller, Interpreter, Evangelist* (Peabody, MA: Hendrickson, 2004), 11.

8. Karl Ludwig Schmidt, *Der Rahmen de Geschichte Jesu* [*The Framework of the Historical Jesus*] (Berlin: Trowitzisch, 1919), 281. See also Martin Dibelius, *Die Formgeschichte des Evangeliums* [*The Form Criticism of the Gospels*] (Tübingen: J. C. B. Mohr, 1919). Prior to Schmidt, scholars such as Kenneth Lachmann and Julius Holtzmann shared a similar view concerning Mark.

9. Ched Myers, *Binding the Strong Man: A Political Reading of Mark's Story of Jesus* (Maryknoll, NY: Orbis, 1988), 120–121. The narrative elements are borrowed from the structuralism of A. J. Greimas, especially his *On Meaning: Selected Writings in Semiotic Theory*, Theory and History of Literature (St. Paul: University of Minnesota Press, 1987).

10. Bonnie B. Thurston, *The Spiritual Landscape of Mark* (Collegeville, MN: Liturgical, 2008).

11. Byrne, *A Costly Freedom*, 16–19.

12. William Wrede, *Das Messiagehemnis in den Evangelien* [*The Messianic Secret*] (Tübingen: Vandenhoeck and Ruprecht, 1901).

13. M. Eugene Boring, *Mark: A Commentary*, The New Testament Library (Louisville: Westminster John Knox, 2006), 30–32.

14. Readers should note that Scripture quotations in the ancient world were often tenuous, for several reasons. First, written copies of Scripture were not generally available, and Scripture was often memorized by hearing it in the context of communal prayer and worship. Second, Scripture was often taken from texts or translations (Septuagint, Targumim, etc.) that do not correspond to the text used by modern readers. For these reasons and others, readers should not be too surprised to find some irregularities in Scripture citations, even in the Bible itself. To consider these irregularities "errors," however, applies a standard of judgment not applicable to the ancient texts or the realities within which these texts were understood and learned.

15. Joachim Jeremias, *New Testament Theology* (New York: Scribner's, 1971).

16. See Joseph A. Fitzmyer, SJ, *Essays on the Semitic Background of the New Testament*, Biblical Resource Series, Combined Edition (Grand Rapids, MI: Eerdmans, 1997).

17. Vincent Taylor, *The Gospel According to Mark* (London: Macmillan, 1952), 296–297.

18. See Rudolf Bultmann, *History of the Synoptic Tradition* (Oxford: Blackwell, 1963), 214, regarding "the magic word."

19. Mention of "anointing the sick" is curious. Jesus is never depicted as anointing the sick, but it appears to be a practice from the very early church (see James 5:14).

20. The Catacombs of San Callisto in Rome provide but one example.

21. See Dale C. Allison Jr., *The Luminous Dusk: Finding God in the Deep, Still Places* (Grand Rapids, MI: Eerdmans, 2006), 105. Thanks to my colleague Patricia Sharbaugh for giving me this reference.

22. Ranjini Wickramarante Rebera, "The Syrophoenecian Woman: A South Asian Feminist Perspective," in *A Feminist Companion to Mark*, ed. Amy Jill Levine (Sheffield: Sheffield Academic Press, 2001), 101–110.

23. See the commentaries on Mark by Rawlinson and Klostermann, both of whom point to parallels in the Hellenistic account of Alcetas of Halice's vision of the god Asclepius, where the god touched Alcetas's eyes and he could only make out "the trees in the Temple precincts." See Wilhelm Dettinberger, *Sylloge Inscriptionum Graecarum*, third edition, 3:1168.

24. Taylor, *Mark*, 379–380.

25. Byrne, *A Costly Freedom*, 143.

26. Ibid., 152.

27. Taylor, *Mark*, 408–410.

28. Morna Hooker, *The Gospel According to Mark*, Black's New Testament Commentary (Peabody, MA: Hendrickson, 1991), 233.

29. Byrne, *A Costly Freedom*, 198–200.

30. The Greek expression *hyper pollōn* in Mark 14:24 literally means "for many," but it is an idiomatic expression meaning "for all." The translation of this phrase in the new English translation of the Eucharistic Prayer in the Roman Missal as "for many" has caused some controversy.

31. For a discussion of the timing of the Last Supper, see John P. Meier, *A Marginal Jew: Rethinking the Historical Jesus*, vol. 1, *The Roots of the Problem and the Person* (New York: Doubleday, 1991), 386–401.

32. Raymond E. Brown, *An Introduction to the New Testament*, ABRL (New York: Doubleday, 1997), 146.

33. See Hooker, *Mark*, 394.

34. Ralph Hood Jr., and W. Paul Williamson, *Them That Believe: The Power and Meaning of the Christian Serpent-Handling Tradition* (Berkeley, CA: University of California Press, 2008).

CHAPTER 5

THE GOSPEL ACCORDING TO MATTHEW

Introduction: Historical and Theological Background

Matthew provides readers with perhaps the most familiar account of the gospel. Although Matthew uses more than 80 percent of Mark's Gospel in his narrative, Matthew edits, supplements, and reorganizes that material to make it his own. Even the most casual reader can easily draw out Mark and Matthew's contrasting styles, particularly Matthew's more didactic portrait of Jesus and his stronger and more explicit emphasis on Old Testament images and themes. In this initial section of the chapter on Matthew, an analysis of the historical or lived context of Matthew's Gospel will provide a context for a brief overview of how Matthew structures his account and the theological themes he develops.

Authorship and Lived Context

As is the case for each of the Gospels, the earliest discussions regarding the origins of Matthew appear in writings of the second-century writer Papias, preserved for us only in a quotation in the writings of the fourth-century historian, Eusebius. In that work, Eusebius relates a report from Papias, who wrote the following: "Matthew compiled the sayings [of Jesus] in the Hebrew language [he probably means Aramaic], and everyone translated them as well as he could."[1]

The claim that Matthew wrote in Aramaic (or Hebrew) does not seem to apply to the text as it exists today, which is clearly not a Greek translation of an Aramaic original. Whatever document Papias was describing, it was not the canonical Gospel of Matthew.

Over the past two centuries, several alternative theories about the origins of Matthew's Gospel have emerged. One theory, offered by the noted Swedish Lutheran scholar Krister Stendahl, states that the Gospel is the product of a school of scribes. For Stendahl, Matthew 13:52 ("Every scribe who has been instructed in the kingdom of heaven is like the head of a household who brings from his storeroom both the new and the old") describes the school and its method in composing the Gospel: reading the story of Jesus through the lens of the Jewish Scriptures.[2] Some scholars even suggest that Matthew is offering an alternative to the scribal tradition that was then being established among the Pharisees at Jamnia following the destruction of Jerusalem in 70 CE.

Several important developments took place in the decades following the failure of the first Jewish Revolt that resulted in the destruction of Jerusalem and the Temple in 70 CE (see also chapter 1). With the loss of the Temple, central to the Jewish worldview for centuries, Judaism began to articulate a new self-understanding, focusing anew on covenantal fidelity in a way that transcended the confines of the Temple service. The group uniquely suited for this task was the rabbis, essentially the heirs of the Pharisees, who had for centuries been extending covenantal concerns about purity to include almost every aspect of daily living. The Pharisees had also developed a body of traditions having to do with Torah observance, sometimes called the Oral Torah (distinct from the first five books of the Bible, the written Torah). These developments help account for the greater adaptability of Pharisaic Judaism—in contrast to the Sadducees and the Essenes, for whom Judaism without the Temple was virtually inconceivable.

After the destruction of Jerusalem, a group of rabbinic scholars, led by Yohanan ben Zakkai, established themselves at Jamnia (a city located west and north of Jerusalem) and began to exercise an increasingly normative function within the wider Jewish community. Over the next two centuries the work of the rabbis would be collected into the Mishnah, which would serve as the fundamental codification of Oral Torah within Judaism. The Talmuds of Palestine and Babylon would later supplement this collection of texts (*talmûd* means "teaching" in Aramaic and refers to the collection of rabbinic commentary on the Torah and the Mishnah).

The specifics of these theological and historical developments go beyond the lived context for Matthew, but in the first century, rabbinic Judaism became increasingly dominant, while the other Jewish groups—including the Sadducees, the Essenes, and the followers of Jesus—became equally marginal. While scholars continue to debate exactly how and when Judaism and Christianity eventually became two separate religions, it is widely accepted that after the Temple was destroyed in 70 CE, Jewish Christians faced important challenges to their identity amid the claims of emerging normative Judaism as expressed by the rabbis. Matthew contains widespread evidence of this development. For example, Matthew regularly identifies the Pharisees, often coupled with the scribes, as Jesus' opponents (e.g., 5:20; 9:11, 9:34; 12:2; 23:2–3; 27:62), and Jesus calls the members of these groups "hypocrites," "blind guides," and "blind fools" (23:1–39). Moreover, references to "their" synagogues (4:23; 9:35) and "their" scribes (7:29) suggest that Matthew's community saw itself as separate from that of the rabbis. All of this material, along with Matthew's distinctive theological motifs, paint a picture of a Christian community engaged in a bitter dispute with an emerging normative Judaism.

CURSING THE CHRISTIANS?

The study of Matthew's Gospel highlights the issue of the relationship between the early Jewish Christian community and the form of Judaism that began to emerge following the destruction of the Temple in 70 CE. A problem for historians of this period is the paucity of sources available. The Mishnah, the late-second-century collection of rabbinic commentary on the Torah, provides ample material on rabbinic Judaism from the first two centuries of the Common Era. That material, however, spans a long period during which many developments unfolded rapidly, making it difficult to determine exactly which material might be relevant for understanding

continued

CURSING THE CHRISTIANS? *continued*

Jewish faith and practice prior to the destruction of the Temple, and what might pertain to Judaism post 70 CE.

The so-called Eighteen Benedictions offered at the end of the synagogue service provide interesting and controversial material for their reconstruction of the relationship between early Judaism and early Christianity.[3] The Eighteen Benedictions are mentioned (but not specified) in the Mishnah, but the Babylonian Talmud (compiled several centuries after the Mishnah) states that the rabbis at Jamnia devised the benedictions, therefore dating the benedictions to the latter part of the first century.[4] Among these benedictions was the *birkat ha-minim* (Hebrew for "blessing [i.e., "cursing"] of the heretics"), which was originally devised during the time of the destruction of the Temple and focused primarily on the Jews who had acted as "informants" (*malšinim*) against their coreligionists.[5] In the Middle Ages, this benediction also seemed to be directed against Jewish converts to Christianity who acted against the Jewish community. In general, the *birkat ha-minim* became a way of excluding heretics or schismatics (*ha-minim*) from the synagogue service, and cursing them was meant to make it impossible for them to maintain their presence in the service. After all, what person would participate in a service in which they were forced to curse themselves? Moreover, the person who uttered the *birkat ha-minim* was the leader of the synagogue service, and as such, his orthodoxy had to be impeccable. For this reason, the Talmud demands that anyone who makes a mistake in reciting the *birkat ha-minim* should be replaced.

In one version of the *birkat ha-minim* discovered in a storage room for discarded sacred manuscripts in an ancient Cairo synagogue, a line is devoted specifically to the Christians, and many scholars trace this form of the *birkat ha-minim* to an early Palestinian setting. The text reads as follows:

> For the renegades let there be no hope, and may the arrogant kingdom soon be rooted out in our days, and the Nazarenes and the *minim* perish as in a moment and be blotted out from the book of life and with the righteous may they not be inscribed. Blessed art thou, O Lord, who humbles the arrogant.[6]

Some scholars see this cursing as evidence of heated polemics between Jewish Christians and early rabbinic Judaism in the first century.[7] This conclusion receives some support from references by church fathers like Justin Martyr (see, e.g., *Dialogue with Trypho*, 96) to the cursing of Christians in synagogue services in their day.

The precise reconstruction of the *birkat ha-minim* in the first century and its historical relevance to Matthew's Gospel remain elusive.[8] It is clear, however, that in the first centuries of the Christian era the relationship between early Christians and early Jews was fraught with tension. Invectives, often bordering on the violent and outrageous, were a common feature in internecine disputes at the time, and not limited to the relationship between Jews and Christians. In fact, within the broad umbrella of rabbinic Judaism, heated argument was enshrined as a virtue, as evidenced by the many arguments about the Torah recorded in both the Mishnah and the Talmud. The use of harsh invectives is also found in the Qumran material (e.g., the "Wicked Priest" and the "Teacher of Righteousness" in 1QpHab; see also 4QMMT). The more outrageous statements in the New Testament writings—and in early Jewish sources—should be tempered with this knowledge.

Matthew's emphasis on a mission to the Gentiles helps to signal the fact that Matthew's community was composed of both Jewish Christians and Gentile Christians. For many scholars, the precise location of Matthew's community remains elusive, but a location like Antioch in Syria, which Acts tells us had a mixed community, is plausible. Given the themes developed in Matthew (i.e., its obvious polemics with an early expression of normative rabbinic Judaism) and its dependence on Mark, most scholars suggest that the Gospel emerged late in the first century, perhaps between 80 and 90 CE.

The Structure and Flow of the Gospel

Early in Christian antiquity, commentators on Matthew's Gospel recognized five distinct blocks of material in which Jesus offers extended discourses with formulaic conclusions. These discourses are marked off from the material that follows with various phrases that signal the conclusion of the discourse. For example:

- "When Jesus finished these words, the crowds were astonished at his teaching" (7:28).
- "When Jesus finished giving these commands to his twelve disciples, he went away from that place to teach and to preach in their towns" (11:1).
- "When Jesus finished these parables, he went away from there" (13:53).
- "When Jesus finished these words, he left Galilee and went to the district of Judea across the Jordan" (19:1).
- "When Jesus finished all these words, he said to his disciples . . . "(26:1).

The structure of Matthew tends to revolve around these discourses, with the infancy narrative and the passion forming bookends to the narratives and discourses in the middle. Some have suggested that by building his Gospel around these five discourses Matthew deliberately evokes the five books of the Pentateuch (the five books of the Torah), but most contemporary scholars are skeptical about such claims.[9] Yet, any account of the structure and flow of the Gospel must center on the five discourses and make sense of the narrative material interspersed between them. The following outline represents the basic structure of Matthew:

1. Prologue (1:1—2:23)
2. Proclamation of the Kingdom and Gathering of Israel (3:1—7:29)

   a. Narrative: John the Baptist and Calling the Disciples (3:1—4:25)

   b. **Discourse One:** Sermon on the Mount (5:1—7:29)

3. Ministry in Galilee (8:1—10:42)

   a. Narrative: Healings and Exorcisms (8:1—9:38)

   b. **Discourse Two:** Missionary Discourse (10:1–42)

4. Opposition to Jesus (11:1—13:52)

   a. Narrative: Disbelief and Disputes (11:1—12:50)

   b. **Discourse Three:** Kingdom Parables (13:1–52)

5. Christology and the Church (13:53—18:35)

   a. Narrative: Healing, Feeding, Controversy, and Confession (13:53—17:27)

   b. **Discourse Four:** Church Order (18:1–35)

6. Jerusalem (19:1—25:46)

   a. Narrative: Judgment, Temple, and Clash with Authorities (19:1—23:39)

   b. **Discourse Five:** Eschatological Discourse (24:1—25:46)

7. The Passion and Resurrection (26:1—28:20)

One challenge faced by interpreters who adopt the above outline concerns the relationship between the narrative material and each of the discourses that follow. The reading of Matthew offered below attempts to make these connections where possible.

Theological Themes

Readers will inevitably compare Matthew and Mark. The similarities are striking, given that Matthew incorporates more than 80 percent of Mark into his Gospel. Yet for all the similarities many obvious differences persist in their respective theologies. These differences can be attributed to the distinct lived contexts for each Gospel. For Mark, the emphasis fell on suffering and the failure of the disciples, while Matthew appears to be intent on demonstrating that Jesus is the fulfillment of Old Testament expectations, a figure who calls the Christian community to fulfill the covenant in a more radical way.

After the infancy narrative in chapters 1 and 2, Matthew generally follows Mark's outline, especially after chapter 13, though the five pivotal discourses contain most of the material Matthew has added to Mark, whether from Q or from Matthew's own source. In addition to the discourse material, however, we find two important trends in Matthew: his more positive portrayal of the disciples of Jesus and his more negative portrayal of Jesus' Jewish opponents. Note, for example, that in response to the explanation of the parable of the Sower and the Seed, Mark portrays the disciples as failing to understand (Mark 4:13) while Matthew portrays the disciples as understanding perfectly (Matthew 13:16, 51).

Additionally, in response to Peter's declaration that Jesus is the Christ, Jesus praises Peter in Matthew 16:17–19 and identifies him as the "rock" on which Christ would build the church; this material is strikingly absent from Mark, chapter 8. The embarrassing episode in which James and John request places of honor in the kingdom (Mark 10:35–40) is softened in Matthew, where their mother makes the request (Matthew 20:21–23).

For Matthew, the Christian way, the way of the gospel, requires the practice and cultivation of virtue or righteousness. As such, Matthew emphasizes the necessity of putting Jesus' instruction into practice. For example, in Matthew, Jesus frequently uses the images of "bearing fruit" (see Matthew 7:15–20; 12:33–37; 13:8, 24–30). Matthew connects discipleship with action, and the disciples prove adept in this regard: Jesus tells them, "Your light must shine before others, that they may see your good deeds and glorify your heavenly Father" (Matthew 5:16). Matthew's emphasis here resonates with the historical setting mentioned above: the practice of righteousness formed the centerpiece of the rabbinic tradition and also of Matthew's, as they both sought to demonstrate the authenticity of their community as God's people.

In his effort to associate Jesus more closely with the story of Israel, Matthew frequently uses Old Testament allusions and mentions Old Testament characters with great frequency. For example, he explicitly mentions David seventeen times, Moses seven times, and Elijah nine times. Matthew also subtly plays with the identification of Jesus and Moses, especially in the infancy narrative and the Sermon on the Mount. In addition to references to biblical characters, Matthew cites the Old Testament more than sixty times, frequently as part of explicit fulfillment formulas (e.g., "Then was fulfilled what had been said through Jeremiah the prophet" [Matthew 2:17]). Jesus himself refers to the prophets in response to questions or events that unfold in his ministry (see, e.g., Matthew 5:17; 15:7–9; 26:56).

The struggle that was then taking place between Jewish Christians and those Jewish leaders who were beginning to reform Judaism following the destruction of the Temple in 70 CE informs Matthew's theology and his understanding of Jesus. For Matthew's community, Jesus provides the key to understanding and living the faith: Jesus is the supreme and definitive teacher of a higher form of righteousness, which surpasses that practiced by the "scribes and Pharisees." He is portrayed as the definitive teacher of the Mosaic Law, even a new Moses (notice that Jesus' birth is accompanied by great danger from a murderous king and a miraculous escape, paralleling the birth of Moses in Exodus, chapter 1). At the start of his ministry, Jesus delivers a radical interpretation of the Mosaic Law from a mountaintop—the Sermon on the Mount (5:1—7:29)—in which he calls upon the disciples to practice this higher righteousness.

Matthew also effectively uses christological titles. Like Mark, Matthew uses the title *Son of God* at significant points in his narrative. For example, the disciples confess that Jesus is the Son of God (16:16) and worship him as the Son of God (14:33) at key moments. At Jesus' trial, the hour of decision and testing, the religious leaders of Israel condemn Jesus for saying that he is the Son of God and thereby bring condemnation on themselves (26:63–64; cf. 21:33–46; 27:41–43). Second, Matthew employs the title *son of David* ten times, in addition to Jesus' preferred self-designation, Son of Man. These statements, combined with the details in Matthew's narrative, depict Jesus as the one whom God has promised, the fulfillment of Israel's story, the anointed one sent to bring salvation to Israel and the world.

Matthew's christological concerns are complemented by his focus on the Christian church. For Matthew, the Christian church is the new people of God, and as such, it inherits the role ascribed to Israel. The church also practices a higher form of righteousness and is thus able to be a light to the Gentiles (Isaiah 49:6) and fulfill Israel's eschatological vocations. Yet this emphasis on righteousness is also tempered by the expectation that those who cannot or will not practice this righteousness will constantly beset the Christian community, and thus Matthew places a premium on forgiveness as a distinctively Christian practice. Matthew also emphasizes the role of God as the ultimate judge of human actions and character, versus the faulty judgments of human beings (6:12–15; 18:21–35). The Christian church, therefore, is the new people of God, but a people defined by a diversity of righteousness. The judgment of the rabbis, which has called into question the identity of Jewish Christians in Matthew's community, now finds its counterpart in the Christian expectation that human beings cannot judge righteousness adequately, they can only practice it.

The issues of Christian identity and the diversity of the Christian community in Matthew point to a final distinctive theme of the Gospel, namely the importance of the mission to the Gentiles. It is this last theme, the inclusion of the Gentiles in the Christian church, which Matthew anticipates at several key points: the adoration of the magi (2:1–12), the healing of the centurion's servant (8:5–13), and the sending of the disciples "to make disciples of all nations" (28:16–20). While Matthew portrays Jesus as having come "to the lost sheep of the house of Israel"(10:6), the rejection of Jesus by those in authority paves the way for the Gentiles to respond favorably to the gospel and to be included in the new people of God, a people composed of both Jews and Gentiles. Moreover, the rejection of Jesus by the authorities sets the stage for the destruction of Jerusalem and Matthew's chilling account of its justification in the execution of Jesus, as the assembly cries out: "His blood be upon us and upon our children'" (27:25).

Matthew's Account of the Gospel

Matthew develops his theological themes through his unique source material and his subtle reworking of Markan material. His portrayal of Jesus as the Davidic messiah, a new Moses, and the fulfillment of the covenant permeates the narrative. As Matthew's account of the good news unfolds, the five great discourses help to shape the overall proclamation and to reinforce Matthean themes.

Prologue: A Theological Overture (Matthew 1:1—2:23)

In contemporary theater and opera, audiences are well aware of the overture and its function: It orients the audience to the material that follows, it sets the mood, and it develops themes that will be revisited throughout the performance. The first two chapters of Matthew's Gospel function like a theological overture and signal all the major themes developed in the narrative that follows. Of course, the historicity of the infancy narrative often comes into question, and it was not long ago that biblical scholars in Roman Catholic circles found themselves under scrutiny for raising historical questions about this material.

The late Myles Bourke famously articulated the following thesis about the genre of Matthew's infancy narrative. He argued: "That the author of such a work might have introduced it by a *midrash* of deep theological insight, in which

---

MIDRASHIM

The interpretation of Scripture within early rabbinic Judaism often took the form of what came to be called *midrash*, a Hebrew word meaning "to seek." The term tends to reflect the allegorizing interpretations so prevalent in the Hellenistic world, yet one can find early examples of midrashim in the Old Testament itself centuries prior to the rise of Hellenistic influences in Judaism (see Ezekiel, chapter 16, for an early example of midrashic interpretation). In late Second Temple Judaism, midrashim became more common, as examples from Sirach (chapters 44–50) and Wisdom (chapters 16–19) demonstrate. In the New Testament, Hebrews, chapter 11, stands out as an example of a midrash. Paul also uses midrashim in his letters, as in his adaptation of the Genesis story of Sarah and Hagar (Galatians, chapter 4). Paul's interpretation of Abraham in Romans, chapter 4, is another example of a midrash.

Midrashic interpretations always look to maximize the interpretive value of a text and therefore employ bold imagination. Midrashim are not concerned with the author's intention or even with the literal level of the text. The point is always to draw lessons for the present from the sacred texts of the past. In the rabbinic tradition, two types of midrashim were developed: those pertaining to legal texts (halakah) and those related to narrative (haggadah).

Matthew employs midrashim in several places in his Gospel account. A large part of the infancy narrative in Matthew, chapters 1–2, is a midrash on several Old Testament texts, including Numbers 24:17, Hosea 11:1, Jeremiah 31:15, and Judges 13:5. Each of these Old Testament passages is subjected to imaginative expansions in the narrative, expansions that move away from the literal meaning of the text as connections to the story of Jesus are developed.

Jesus appears as the true Israel and the new Moses, (thus containing the themes of the entire Gospel), and in which the historical element is very slight seems to be a thoroughly probable hypothesis."[10] While such a statement may not appear to contemporary interpreters to be particularly remarkable, at the time (half a century ago), it caused much controversy. Today, biblical scholars almost universally agree that Matthew's infancy narrative, while perhaps containing certain historical elements worthy of note, is not primarily concerned with transmitting historical details of Jesus' birth. Rather, the story functions primarily as a way of signaling the identity of Jesus in relation to the story of Israel.

Matthew begins with a genealogical list (*toledot* in Hebrew) that recounts the ancestry of Jesus from Abraham through the Babylonian exile and finally to Jesus' birth. The list includes the names of David and his descendants, the kings of Judah (note the famous names such as Solomon, Hezekiah, and Josiah). The author contends that the list from Abraham to David, from David to the exile, and from the exile to Jesus contains fourteen generations in each segment. This claim is not entirely accurate (the generations from the exile to Jesus number thirteen), but the number fourteen has more than literal significance. First, it is a play on the name of David, as the numerical values of the Hebrew characters in the name add up to fourteen:

David —דוד ([ד=4] + [ו=6] + [ד=4] = 14)

Some scholars suggest, however, that the number fourteen is significant because it is a multiple of seven, the perfect number in the ancient world. The point of the numerical aspects of the genealogy serves to indicate the timeliness of Jesus' birth: he is a descendant of David, the long-awaited king, who was to come at the appointed time, a time appointed by God.

Matthew's genealogy follows the family tree by recounting the father of each child, but at four places in the list, Matthew includes the names of women: Tamar, Rahab, Ruth, and Bathsheba. Each of these women forms an important link in the story of Israel and the ancestry of David, yet none of them appear to be Israelites. Moreover, the women enter into the ancestral lineage in unconventional ways. Tamar (Matthew 1:3) was a neglected widow who seduced Judah, the father of her dead husband(s) (Genesis, chapter 38). Rahab (Matthew 1:5), a prostitute in Jericho and a Gentile, survived the holy war and the corresponding slaughter that followed because she cooperated with a pair of Israelite spies sent to reconnoiter the city (Joshua 2:14; 6:22–25). The story of Ruth (Matthew 1:5), another Gentile, includes a journey to the hometown of her deceased husband, Bethlehem, in the company of her mother-in-law, where she seduces a new husband, Boaz (Ruth, chapter 3). Finally, the story of David's rape of Bathsheba and murder of her husband is well known (2 Samuel, chapter 11). Matthew's inclusion of these women tends to suggest the controversial context of Jesus' birth was nothing new in the story of Israel, and Gentiles had long figured into the story of Israel and even had a role in the birth of Israel's messiah.

The story of Jesus' birth in Matthew focuses more on Joseph than on Mary, portraying him as a "righteous" man. As the beneficiary of divine revelation in a dream, Matthew models Joseph after his namesake in Genesis, the interpreter of dreams for the pharaoh. The birth of the child unfolds as the fulfillment of Isaiah 7:14. The Isaiah passage originally referred to the birth of the son of Ahaz, Hezekiah, and served as a sign that God would defend the kingdom of Judah against Israel (the northern kingdom) and its ally Syria during the Syro-Ephraimite War around the year 734 BCE. The passage reads as follows:

> In the days of Ahaz, king of Judah, son of Jotham, son of Uzziah, Rezin, king of Aram, and Pekah, king of Israel, son of Remaliah, went up to attack

Jerusalem, but they were not able to conquer it. When word came to the house of David that Aram was encamped in Ephraim, the heart of the king and the heart of the people trembled, as the trees of the forest tremble in the wind. Then the Lord said to Isaiah: Go out to meet Ahaz, . . . and say to him: Take care you remain tranquil and do not fear; let not your courage fail before these two stumps of smoldering brands [the blazing anger of Rezin and the Arameans, and of the son of Remaliah]. . . .

> Thus says the Lord:
> This shall not stand, it shall not be!
>
> .   .   .   .
>
> But within sixty years and five,
> Ephraim shall be crushed, no longer
>   a nation.
> Unless your faith is firm
> you shall not be firm!

Again the Lord spoke to Ahaz: Ask for a sign from the Lord, your God; let it be deep as the nether world, or high as the sky! But Ahaz answered, "I will not ask! I will not tempt the Lord!" [. . .] Therefore the Lord himself will give you this sign: the virgin shall be with child, and bear a son, and shall name him Immanuel. He shall be living on curds and honey by the time he learns to reject the bad and choose the good. For before the child learns to reject the bad and choose the good, the land of those two kings whom you dread shall be deserted. (Isaiah 7:1–16)

The Hebrew word translated as "virgin" in verse 14 ('almah) refers to a young woman who has reached puberty and is thus available for marriage in the ancient world. The Septuagint, the Greek translation of the Old Testament used by the early Christians and by Greek-speaking Jews, translates the word as *parthenos*, a woman who has not had sexual intercourse. Thus, the Greek word is more limiting, more restrictive, than the Hebrew word. Only in the Christian tradition does the Isaiah passage come to refer to the birth of the messiah, and it is clear from Matthew's editorial activity and his use of the verse that its ultimate meaning is revealed in relation to the birth of Jesus, regardless of its original meaning in Isaiah. Matthew thus provides readers with a powerful and bold example of a Christian "rereading" of an Old Testament passage, a rereading that moves the importance of the passage beyond the intention of the original author and the author's historical context.

The righteousness of Joseph is mirrored by the Gentile magi, astrologers from the East (the term *magos* usually referred to a member of an aristocratic caste of astrologers from Persia). As Gentile astrologers, the *magoi* have no recourse to the Scriptures of Israel and cannot know of the Messiah's birth. Yet, attentive to the stars, the natural means by which the heavens communicate to human beings, the magi leave everything to find the child and worship him. The astrologers and Joseph also act as foils to Herod the Great in Matthew's portrayal (i.e., they are portrayed in such a way as to highlight the contrast between themselves and Herod). Although Herod is an ethnarch, the Roman title given to Herod (literally "ruler of a people," i.e., the Jewish people), he has no knowledge of the child's birth, but instead has to consult his scribes. When his scribes present the facts to him, instead of going to worship and welcome the child, he plots to kill him. In many ways, Matthew plays with the story of Moses' birth and implicitly likens Jesus to Moses and similarly compares Herod to the Egyptian pharaoh. Like the murderous pharaoh, Herod ruthlessly exterminates any threat to his rule, and like Moses, Jesus is spirited away only to be called out of Egypt to Israel and the place Jesus will call home, Nazareth. It is out of Nazareth that Jesus will emerge as his ministry begins to unfold in chapter 3.

Proclamation of the Kingdom and the In-Gathering of Israel (Matthew 3:1—7:29)

Following the infancy narrative, Matthew generally follows his Markan source material throughout up to 4:25. The first part of this section provides the familiar narrative of John the Baptist and the baptism of Jesus. However, Matthew makes some subtle but important changes to the Markan text. The particularly harsh treatment that the Pharisees and Sadducees receive in Matthew 3:7–12 demonstrates the heightened tension between the early Christian community and emerging normative Judaism. Additionally, prior to the baptism scene, Matthew takes a moment to clarify the relationship of Jesus and John the Baptist by having John object to Jesus' request for baptism. The notion that Jesus' baptism will "fulfill all righteousness" (3:15) is enigmatic, but it is also in keeping with Matthew's concern to portray Jesus and his disciples as "righteous" Jews.

The story of Jesus' temptation, an episode shared by Luke and therefore attributable to the Q source, has a much briefer Markan parallel, an instance of "Mark-Q overlap." In Matthew's account of the temptation scene, the basic Markan material has been supplemented by Q material that includes a threefold exchange between Jesus and Satan. The number three in the biblical world was significant, often signifying completeness. The Q material seems to indicate that although the scenes of temptation in the wilderness have their own dramatic quality, the temptations themselves seem to reflect the conviction that Jesus endured these sorts of tests or temptations throughout his life. The power of Jesus, a power he will begin to manifest publicly in the next chapter, gives Jesus the capacity to manipulate those he encounters so that they might be coerced into responding positively to his message. Using that power for coercion

instead of invitation is the great temptation. After all, turning stone into bread to feed the basic human needs of the crowds he will encounter, or dazzling the crowds at the Temple, will surely secure their allegiance (4:3, 5–6). If these avenues fail, why not make use of imperial power to enforce a positive response? Satan knows full well, it seems, that such coercion stands opposite the dynamic of invitation and response characteristic of God's dealings with Israel. The proclamation and ministry of Jesus evoke conversion and faith as the proper, indeed the redemptive, response to God's reign. After Jesus rejects the diabolical temptations, he sets about gathering Israel to receive the message of God's reign. At this point, Matthew returns to the Markan material and carries the reader forward to the first great discourse of the Gospel, the Sermon on the Mount.

Some have suggested that the scene in which Jesus delivers this first of five discourses in Matthew is laden with Moses typology. While typological concerns are probably part of Matthew's presentation, caution is advised. Rather than simply providing a profile of Jesus as a new Moses, Matthew portrays Jesus as the supreme teacher of "righteousness," a portrait that is only intelligible in light of the Torah and Prophets.

The discourse begins with the Beatitudes (5:1–12), which sets the stage for and establishes the eschatological nature of the instructions found throughout the sermon (5:1—7:29). The Beatitudes are an example of a well-established genre of wisdom literature in which a group is identified as enjoying blessing or happiness (the Greek word *makarioi* that begins each of the eight beatitudes means "happy"). In Matthew, the state of blessing foreshadows an eschatological future when the blessed or happy one will enjoy some additional reward. These Beatitudes are Q material, shared with Luke, who seems to have preserved them in a form closer to the original. A comparison with Luke's version is informative (see sidebar on facing page): Matthew has generally "spiritualized" the Beatitudes, for example by changing "Blessed are the poor" to "Blessed are the poor in spirit," "hungry" to "hunger and thirst for righteousness," as well as by adding beatitudes on meekness, mercy, cleanliness of heart, and peacemaking. The addition of "clean of heart" is indicative of Matthew's concerns and can serve as an example of the general direction of Matthew's editorial activity. The phrase is borrowed from the Psalms of the Old Testament and refers to undivided obedience toward God. The heart, here and elsewhere in Scripture, is not primarily or exclusively associated with emotion or affect; rather, it is the locus of will, thought, and to a lesser extent, feeling. In Psalm 24:4, a song recited upon entrance into the Jerusalem Temple, only the "clean of hand and pure of heart," that is, those whose purity is comprehensive, inward and outward, may enter the house of God. By including phrases such as "clean of heart" in the Beatitudes, Matthew signals his intention to portray Jesus as the teacher of a higher righteousness that is nonetheless in concert with the demands of the Torah and the Temple.

The six antitheses (5:21–48) provide the Sermon on the Mount with some of its most memorable and jarring examples of the higher righteousness emphasized in Matthew. Matthew provides the reader with a succinct and provocative account of Jesus' approach to the Torah (5:17–20) and its fulfillment in the practices of righteousness rooted in the demands of love (see 23:23) prior to setting forth the great antitheses. In the antitheses Jesus assumes the role of definitive interpreter of Torah by stating some principle from Torah and then radicalizing or extending that principle. Matthew has designed these antitheses to illustrate the teaching of Jesus and the antitheses are by no means exhaustive of that teaching on Torah; rather, they epitomize, for Matthew, Jesus' real concern for

Torah observance. In particular, Jesus appears to drive at the heart of the commandments, not content to allow mere prohibitions to satisfy the demands of covenantal fidelity. The series brings into sharp focus the requirements of the higher or surpassing "righteousness" (5:20) that Matthew's Jesus demands and culminates in the admonition to follow the example of God (5:45) by cultivating love in dealings with others.

The antithesis on anger (5:21–26) aptly illustrates the dynamics evident in each of the six antitheses. In this example, Jesus radicalizes the prohibition of murder in Exodus 20:13 by demanding that the one who grows angry with his "brother" or who uses insults (*raqa* appears in the text and is the Aramaic equivalent of "blockhead") will be subject to both human judgment (i.e., from the Sanhedrin) and divine judgment (i.e., the fires of Gehenna). Moreover, the notion of grievances in this antithesis provides a fascinating example of the dynamics behind Matthew's concern for the Christian community. Readers should note that in Matthew, Jesus does not instruct those who *have* a grievance against their neighbor; rather, Jesus counsels those *against whom* their neighbor has a grievance. In other words, the one suspected of having done wrong should seek out the one who has been injured and strive for reconciliation. The series of antitheses go on to include teachings on adultery, divorce, oaths, retaliation, and love of enemies, and they help to spell out more specifically the general instruction on Torah observance Jesus has given in 5:17–20.

The material following the antitheses includes teachings on the pillars of Jewish piety: almsgiving, prayer, and fasting where Jesus pleads for a simple and transparent practice in each of these areas. He counsels his followers to adopt simplicity in these acts and cautions them against ostentatious displays designed to impress onlookers (6:1). Of course, the most famous example of Jesus' reform here is the reform of prayer. Interestingly, Jesus begins his instruction

THE BEATITUDES IN MATTHEW AND Q (LUKE)

Most scholars believe that Luke tends to preserve the more original form of the Q material and Matthew adds to or adopts it. So when comparing Matthew and Luke on a common passage, Matthew generally is seen as the redactor or editor of the passage.

MATTHEW 5:3–12	LUKE 6:20–26
Blessed are the poor in spirit, for theirs is the kingdom of heaven.	Blessed are you who are poor, for the kingdom of God is yours.
Blessed are they who mourn, for they will be comforted.	Blessed are you who are now hungry, for you will be satisfied.
Blessed are the meek, for they will inherit the land.	Blessed are you who are now weeping, for you will laugh.
Blessed are they who hunger and thirst for righteousness, for they will be satisfied.	Blessed are you when people hate you, and when they exclude and insult you, and denounce your name as evil on account of the Son of Man.
Blessed are the merciful, for they will be shown mercy.	Rejoice and leap for joy on that day! Behold, your reward will be great in heaven. For their ancestors treated the prophets in the same way.
Blessed are the clean of heart, for they will see God.	But woe to you who are rich, for you have received your consolation.
Blessed are the peacemakers, for they will be called children of God.	But woe to you who are filled now, for you will be hungry.
Blessed are they who are persecuted for the sake of righteousness, for theirs is the kingdom of heaven.	Woe to you who laugh now, for you will grieve and weep.
Blessed are you when they insult you and persecute you and utter every kind of evil against you [falsely] because of me. Rejoice and be glad, for your reward will be great in heaven. Thus they persecuted the prophets who were before you.	Woe to you when all speak well of you, for their ancestors treated the false prophets in this way.

not by referencing Pharisaic prayer, as one might expect given the polemical nature of much that has already been said in the sermon; rather, he holds up Gentile prayer as a negative example. Gentile prayer appears to be the attempt to manipulate or persuade a deity not otherwise disposed to act. In his teaching on prayer, Jesus reverses that assumption: God already knows what is needed (6:8), so the goal or purpose of prayer is thereby nuanced.

SCRIPTURE IN DETAIL: THE LORD'S PRAYER (MATTHEW 6:9–13)

The Lord's Prayer stands as one of those fascinating passages where there is a convergence of stage-one and stage-three material (see chapter 3, SB 1: "The Development of the Gospel Tradition"). As many scholars have noted, and the late Joachim Jeremias made famous, addressing God with the Aramaic vocative *abba* ("Father") remains one of the few areas upon which most historical Jesus scholars can agree. Jesus in fact characteristically called God his father. The simplicity of the prayer's opening address, "Our Father," stands in remarkable continuity with the characteristic prayer of Jesus of Nazareth. At the same time, the prayer stands as a powerful example of Matthew's theology. In fact, as Matthew's Gospel became dominant in the early church, so too did his wording of the Lord's Prayer (Luke also includes a version of this prayer), so much so that early church manuals like the first-century *Didache* include Matthew's form of the Lord's Prayer as a standard feature of early Christian celebrations of the Eucharist and as part of daily prayer (see also Cyril of Jerusalem's *Catechetical Orations* from the fourth century). While the prayer itself is often assumed to be a simple prayer of praise and petition, a closer examination highlights some important features.

The placement of the prayer in the Sermon on the Mount, the first great discourse in Matthew, is significant. The sermon itself, delivered from the mountaintop, stands as an interpretation of Israel's covenant and supplies the recently gathered disciples with sound instruction on the higher form of righteousness that they must embrace as Jesus' disciples. The sermon presupposes the reader's familiarity with the Torah and with Jewish mores and customs, particularly the hope for the in-breaking of God's reign and the end of the age. The simplicity of the sermon, the higher form of righteousness, and the urgency of the eschatological future pervade the sermon and the prayer.

The simplicity of the prayer can be illustrated by looking at the prayer's structure. Three sets of petitions structure the prayer following the opening address.

1. Address: "Our Father in heaven"
2. Three "you" petitions

    a. May your name be hallowed

    b. May your kingdom come

    c. May your will be done

3. Two "we" petitions

    a. Give us today the bread of tomorrow

    b. Forgive us as we forgive others

4. Concluding petition

    a. Do not lead us into temptation

    b. Deliver us from the evil one

God's role as Israel's father and as the father of the Davidic king was well established in the

continued

THE LORD'S PRAYER *continued*

Old Testament narrative (e.g., Isaiah 63:16; Jeremiah 31:20; Psalms 2:7). The address is characteristic of Jesus' intimacy with God. God is Father, and as Paul states in both Romans 8:15 and Galatians 4:5–6, in baptism, Christians are given the status of adopted children and can call out to God, "Abba." The address stands as a Christian reflection on the practice of Jesus and as a testament to the theology of the early Christian community. The traditional translation, "Our Father who art in heaven," is cumbersome, archaic, and awkward. The Greek construction (poorly translated by William Tyndale, who was followed by the translators of the King James Version) probably ought to be rendered as "Our heavenly Father."

The first set of petitions is directed to God in the second person. In Matthew, there are three such "you" petitions, yet they all stand together as a petition for the arrival of God's reign on earth. In early Jewish prayers like the Qadesh and even as far back as Ezekiel 38:23, one can find references to the "hallowing" of God's name. In other words, because God's name is profaned, and his word is ignored on earth, God and humanity stand far apart. With the advent of God's reign comes the doing of the divine will and the hallowing of God's name. Notice the continuity between the heavenly realm and the earthly realm in the petition: God's will is to be accomplished on earth the same way it is accomplished in heaven. So too, in the penultimate section of the prayer, are sins forgiven: as we forgive those indebted to us, so shall we be forgiven by God.

The two "we" petitions collectively ask for the arrival of God's reign and reflect the need for forgiveness as constitutive of that reign. A critical interpretation (*crux interpretum*) in this part of the prayer is the adjective that is translated by Martin Luther as *taglisch* or "daily" (*epiousion*). The Vulgate (Latin) translation reads *supersubstantialis* (sometimes awkwardly rendered in English as "supersubstantial"), but Jerome admits that the Hebrew or Aramaic substratum of the prayer included the word *machar*, meaning "tomorrow." Most scholars contend that this "tomorrow" reflects the great tomorrow or the eschatological tomorrow. In other words, rather than a plea for daily sustenance, the petition, once again, seeks the immediate arrival of the *eschaton*, the advent of God's reign. In light of that reign, the forgiveness of God will be mirrored on earth as it is in heaven, or the manner in which we are forgiven is directly related to our practice of forgiving one another. The expression in Greek "forgive us our debts" (*aphes hēmin ta opheilēmata hēmōn*) reflects a thoroughly Hebrew idiom (see, e.g., Deuteronomy 15:1–2 where the Hebrew word for debt [*chob*] is used for "offense").

Interestingly, the verb in the second clause of the second petition, "as we forgive," has been rendered as past, present, and future in various manuscripts and commentaries in the early church. Some commentators suggest that such a range of variants can only be accounted for by a "timeless Aramaic participle," which would have been something like "as we also habitually forgive."[11] Notice once again how the habitual practice of the believing community is to mirror what occurs in heaven.

The concluding petition asks for deliverance from temptation and the evil one. Both petitions help to signal the eschatological nature of the prayer: the trials and temptations, as well as the work of the evil one, characterize the dangers of the end of the age. For Matthew, the prayer stands out not only for its simplicity but also as a characteristically Christian prayer insofar as it actively petitions for the end of the age.

An interesting textual note on the Lord's Prayer concerns the doxology (i.e., "For Thine is the kingdom, the power . . ." KJV). The

THE LORD'S PRAYER *continued*

doxology formed part of the liturgy of ancient Christians (see, e.g., *The Didache* and the *Apostolic Constitutions*) and found its way into late manuscripts that make up the Byzantine Majority text on which many of the early Protestant versions were based (the doxology was absent from Jerome's Vulgate). From there it was incorporated into the Anglican Book of Common Prayer during the reign of Elizabeth I, where it exerted a decisive influence in the English-speaking Protestant community. The doxology, though acknowledged as a scribal addition to Matthew, is still customarily used in Protestant circles when the Lord's Prayer is recited, and Roman Catholics introduced the doxology into the Liturgy of the Eucharist as both an ecumenical gesture to other Christians (including the Orthodox, who had used a form of the doxology in their liturgy for centuries), and in an attempt to recover ancient Christian liturgical practices following the reforms of Vatican II.

The Sermon on the Mount concludes with a series of sayings on discipleship and the struggle to live the higher righteousness demanded of disciples. In the end, the sermon is punctuated by a characteristic summons to "bear fruit" (7:15–20) and a corresponding caution against those who call out "Lord" but do not do the will of the Father, that is, those who fail to put the gospel into action (7:21–23). Both episodes point to recurring themes in Matthew regarding the performance of a higher righteousness, as does the final analogy of two houses (7:24–27), in which Jesus calls the disciples to put his words into action. While few would suggest that these admonitions are in conflict with Paul's emphasis on faith over and against Torah observance, Matthew's portrayal of Christian moral exhortation seeks to mitigate any notion of Christian faith that does not value practicing Jesus' teaching. But the New Testament itself provides evidence that controversy and misunderstanding surrounding these issues bedeviled the early Christian community, and one need look no further than the writings of Paul, Matthew's Gospel, and the Letters of John and James for examples.[12]

Ministry in and around Galilee (Matthew 8:1—10:42)

Following the Sermon on the Mount, Matthew rejoins the Markan narrative for a fast-paced collection of healings and exorcisms (8:1—9:38)—not, however, without modification. One can easily see the Markan parallels at this point. The story of Jesus in Mark really begins with a collection of miracle stories, while Matthew has taken Mark's collection of miracles and moved it after the Sermon on the Mount. Several of the miracles in this section of Matthew, however, are not found in Mark, including the healing of the centurion's servant in 8:5–13, which seems to be another example of Matthew's characteristic concern for the mission to the Gentiles. Many commentators think that the series of ten miracles is meant to evoke the image of Moses and the ten plagues in Egypt, yet one might rightly question the narrative consistency on this position given that the miracles *follow* the lengthy Torah–Sinai-centered discourse in Matthew chapters 5–8.

The miracles in this section appear to be grouped into three sets, or clusters, with narrative bridges or transitions in between.[13] In the first triad of healings (8:1–15), two Markan narratives are supplemented by the Q story of the centurion and his servant. In all three healings, Jesus reverses the clean and unclean distinction common within first-century Palestinian Judaism, a distinction in which one becomes unclean by touching a leper or some other person or thing that is unclean. But when Jesus touches the leper (8:3), instead of the leper's uncleanness being transmitted to Jesus, quite the reverse happens; Jesus' touch makes the leper clean. (In some instances, faith in Jesus obviates the need for physical contact—as in the case of the centurion's servant.) In some ways, Jesus takes on the burden of the unclean, thereby enacting the role of Isaiah's Suffering Servant (Isaiah 53:4). Material from Q informs the next set of healing stories about the demands of discipleship (8:18–22), where burying the dead, normally a pious practice of immense importance in rabbinic Judaism, is superseded by the demands of discipleship.[14]

The second triad of miracles (8:23—9:8), taken from Mark, involves questions about the identity and power of Jesus. The calming of the storm depicts the authority of Jesus over the powers of nature; the exorcism of the Gadarene demoniac includes the demon identifying Jesus as the Son of God; and the curing of the paralytic raises questions about the authority of Jesus to forgive sins. The final triad is preceded by teaching material on disciples and discipleship (9:9–17). This, in turn, leads into another set of healings (9:18–34).

The story of the harvest and laborers (9:35–38) provides a bridge from the narrative material to the missionary discourse (10:1–42). This second discourse, combining Markan and Q material, centers on the demands as well as the consequences (persecution) of preaching the gospel. While one can recognize the sources for the material presented here, one can also recognize Matthew's strong editorial hand. Matthew makes subtle changes to the Markan material,

like calling the twelve disciples *apostles*. This term from the early church designated those sent by Christ, and thereby identifies this sending of the disciples with their postresurrectional sending (28:16–20). This small change rounds out some of the other changes Matthew makes that help to connect the persecutions faced by the disciples prior to and following the Resurrection. A clear example of this telescoping of the two eras is evident in that Matthew incorporates material from Mark's eschatological discourse (Mark 13:9–13) into this missionary sermon as Jesus warns of the fate of disciples who will preach the gospel in the future (Matthew 10:17–22). Matthew concludes the discourse with reassurances of divine aid amid persecution and suffering (10:26–31). Matthew also emphasizes acceptance of Jesus as the criterion for eschatological judgment. As the one who has sent the disciples, Jesus stands as the ultimate authority behind the disciples, thus guaranteeing divine power and protection during the time in between the sending and judgment.

Opposition to Jesus (Matthew 11:2—13:52)

Although one would classify the next section of the Gospel (11:1—12:50) as narrative for the purpose of understanding its function in relation to the major discourse that follows it (chapter 13), the material developed here actually includes relatively little narrative, consisting instead of mostly either didactic material or controversy stories about the identity and authority of Jesus. For example, the controversy about John the Baptist and the woes that follow (11:2–24) serves as an indictment of the Pharisees for their refusal to respond properly to John's baptism and his call to repentance.

A passage from Q (11:25–30) begins the next section in Matthew where Jesus provides encouragement to the disciples. Jesus implores his followers to come to him, and promises to give them rest (11:28), striking a tone not prominent, if not altogether absent, from Mark's portrayal of discipleship. Matthew articulates a high Christology based on themes found in the wisdom tradition, making explicit Jesus' authority and identity as the Father's Son, or God's Wisdom sent into the world.[15] Elements of wisdom Christology help to bolster Matthew's overall christological concern, namely to proclaim the story of Jesus as Israel's story by deeply connecting and identifying Torah (through which God's wisdom dwells with Israel; see, e.g., Sirach 24:1–31) and Jesus. Following a block of Markan material in 12:1–14, Matthew complements the Christology in this section with additional material from Isaiah, added to a brief summary of Jesus' healings. The addition of Old Testament quotations to Markan or Q material is a common redactional or editorial element in Matthew, and the quote from Isaiah helps once again to make explicit the christological emphasis of the Gospel. The series of controversies that follow (mostly borrowed from Mark) serve to illustrate the growing opposition to Jesus; Jesus solemnly warns those who refuse to believe.

The third discourse in Matthew, and what some might consider the centerpiece of his Gospel, builds upon the narrative material that focused on the rejection of Jesus by the religious authorities. The parables discourse (13:1–52) incorporates the Markan parable of the Sower and its explanation, but adds seven parables either from Q or from Matthew's own source. Collectively the parables illustrate various dynamics of faith and discipleship within the Christian community and may be divided into three parts.[16] Each of the three components includes one to three parables, an explanation of the parables in general, and an interpretation of a specific parable.

In the first section of the discourse (13:1–23), Matthew imports the parable of the Sower and its interpretive material from Mark. Yet Matthew

adds some of his own material here, most notably the explicit citation of Isaiah 6:9–10. Matthew's inclusion of the Isaiah passage helps to sharpen the sense that the problem with the reception of the parables rests not with their obscurity, but rather with those who refuse to hear and refuse to be converted by the parable's prompting. Matthew thus makes more explicit what Mark had left somewhat implicit in his account.

In the second block of material in the parables discourse (13:24–43), distinctive Matthean themes become more pronounced. For example, the image of the weeds among the wheat, as well as the call for patience in the face of evil, offer stark illustrations. The method of dealing with the weeds (sifting them out at harvest) is not, on a practical level, the best course of action, and presumably Matthew's audience was well aware of this fact. Farmers need to deal with weeds as early as possible in order to mitigate their pernicious effects. Parables often contain something strange and arresting, and this counterintuitive way of dealing with weeds provides a fine example of such strangeness. For Matthew, only God's eschatological judgment can properly distinguish the weeds from the wheat—the power of God can do what human beings cannot.

Perhaps the most interesting parable in Matthew is also one of the briefest: the parable of the Yeast (13:33). Comprising only a single verse, the parable strangely utilizes the image of yeast, a common and almost always negative symbol in Scripture. Leaven was an impurity to be excluded at the Passover feast and excluded from any offering in the Temple. By the first century it had come to symbolize evil or sin, and even Paul uses it in that manner (see, e.g., 1 Corinthians 5:6–7; Galatians 5:9). Matthew's use of the image to illustrate the kingdom of heaven (i.e., kingdom of God) thus proves startling to say the least. In the parable, Jesus likens the kingdom to the yeast or leaven a woman mixes or "hides" (*enekrypsen*) in "three measures" (*saton*) of wheat flour. Elsewhere in the Gospel, Jesus has spoken of the kingdom as "hidden," available only to those willing to risk conversion to find it (e.g., 10:26; 11:5; 13:35). Additionally, commentators often associated the measures of flour with the three cakes made by Sarah for the Lord (the three angels) in Genesis 18:6, or that which was offered to God in the sanctuary (see Judges 6:19 and 1 Samuel 1:24); or the abundance associated with the *eschaton*. The brief parable thus takes what has been considered unclean or impure and makes it a mark, a sign, or an epiphany of messianic abundance in the kingdom.[17]

The third part of the parables discourse (13:44–52) begins with two images of the discovery of the kingdom and the great investment one makes upon its discovery. In the parables, the hearer is asked to compare the total investment and the complete joy one has when one comes upon wealth. The wealth of the kingdom dwarfs the treasure and the pearl, and the disciple knows full well the rewards brought by the kingdom. The image of a catch of fish (13:47–48) revisits the parable of the Weeds among the Wheat, and recalls the need to wait for the final judgment to separate the good and the bad.

The sermon concludes by emphasizing that the listeners understand all that Jesus has taught, which stands in sharp contrast to Mark's portrayal of the disciple's failure to understand Jesus'

teaching at almost every turn. Some consider 13:52 to be a summation of the Matthean community, defined by a new scribal activity in which Jesus' new interpretation of Mosaic tradition becomes the means by which that (old) tradition is brought forward, preserved and expanded. As such it is the "pen portrait" or autobiographical statement of the evangelist as well as a description of the ideal disciple.[18]

Christology and the Church (Matthew 13:54—18:35)

The series of narratives in 13:54–17:27 follows the basic sequence of Mark chapters 6–8, yet with some important additions and modifications. One of the most interesting Matthean additions in this section is the episode with Peter, inserted into the account of Jesus walking on water (Matthew 14:22–36), in which Peter attempts but fails to walk on the water with Jesus. In this segment, as at several other points in the Gospel, Matthew draws attention to Peter as a leader of the disciples. The failure of Peter's faith in this episode signals the weakness of the disciples and foreshadows Peter's failure during the passion. The confession of Peter plays a pivotal role in Matthew (16:16), as it did in Mark, but Matthew adds some special material to the Markan account.

PASSAGE IN FOCUS: THE COMMISSIONING OF PETER (MATTHEW 16:13–20) AND ECCLESIOLOGY

Perhaps no single biblical passage has had a more controversial impact on Roman Catholic ecclesiology than the commissioning of Peter in Matthew 16:13–20. This passage has supplied the basic proof text for the primacy of Peter as ordained by Jesus himself, and its influence can

hardly be overestimated. This text from Matthew was used to support the universal jurisdiction and supreme authority of Peter's successors as the bishops of Rome, the popes. The passage,

continued

THE COMMISSIONING OF PETER AND ECCLESIOLOGY *continued*

however, has become subject to competing interpretations among some Catholic and Protestant interpreters.

The story comes from Mark 8:27–30. Matthew preserves many elements from Mark in the first four verses of the episode (16:13–16). For example, Jesus and his disciples are traveling in the region of Caesarea Philippi when Jesus asks the disciples, "Who do people say that the Son of Man is?" The disciples relate a variety of opinions that are held by the crowds (e.g., Jesus is one of the Old Testament prophets, perhaps Elijah, or even John the Baptist). When Jesus turns to the disciples for their response, Simon Peter boldly proclaims, "You are the Messiah," and Matthew adds "the Son of the living God." The next three verses (16:17–19) pose interesting issues for the exegete of Matthew's Gospel.

Interpreters generally agree on the interpretation of verse 17 where Jesus blesses Simon Peter because "flesh and blood has not revealed this to you, but my heavenly Father." Here, Matthew contrasts "flesh and blood" with God in heaven. God is eternal and unlimited, and only through the gift of God's revelation—the gift of faith—can one acknowledge the identity of Jesus as Simon Peter has just done. Verses 18 and 19, however, provide the occasion for significant discrepancies in interpretation, discrepancies that can have their origins in confessional commitments, both Catholic and Protestant.

In verses 18 and 19 Jesus declares, "And so I say to you, you are Peter [*petros*], and upon this rock [*petra*] I will build my church, and the gates of the netherworld shall not prevail against it. I will give you the keys to the kingdom of heaven. Whatever you bind on earth shall be bound in heaven; and whatever you loose on earth shall be loosed in heaven." *Petra* is the Greek word for *rock*, and it is feminine. To call a man *petra* would not make sense, so the name *Petros*, or Peter, is simply a stylistic accommodation that Simon is

male, and it reflects the Aramaic word for rock, *kepha* (or *Cephas*, as it is rendered elsewhere in the New Testament; see, e.g., Galatians 1:18). Peter, or his statement of faith, is to be the rock on which the church is built. Some Protestant scholars, however, insist that in this passage Jesus is contrasting the two words: *petros*, a small stone, with *petra*, bedrock. For some Protestant scholars, "this rock" refers to the words of Jesus that follow in verse 19 where "the keys to the kingdom of heaven" are understood as the words of Christ.[19] In this context, Jesus is insisting that the church is to be built on the words of Christ, the bedrock, for the words of Jesus alone have the power to bind and to loose.

Verse 19 presents additional issues regarding the ecclesiology of Matthew and, as such, the development of ecclesiology and church practices in many different Christian churches. The so-called power of binding and loosing, whether understood as a power restricted to Simon Peter or extended more generally to the church, demands a careful look at the words in verse 19. The central issue involves a Greek construction called a periphrastic future perfect. The first verb in this periphrastic construct, *estai* ["will be"], is in the future tense and the second verb, *dedemenon* ["already bound"], is a participle in the perfect tense. Simply put, the construction should perhaps be translated as, "what you declare bound on earth *will have been bound [estai dedemenon]* in heaven, etc." In other words, Peter cannot simply command heaven to bind or loose; rather, heaven commands the church on earth so that the power of binding and loosing reflects the conformity between the judgments of heaven and the judgments of the church on earth. Readers should recall the discussion of the Lord's Prayer earlier in this chapter. The basic dynamics of the prayer call for a conformity between heaven and earth, and this is the promise made about binding and loosing.

The rest of the narrative material largely follows the Markan account except for the inclusion of the question of the Temple tax (17:24–27). This episode appears to be a Matthean addition that once again addresses the concern to depict Jesus and the disciples as practitioners of righteous acts.

The fourth of Matthew's five great discourses deals with life in the Christian community, and for this reason it is often called the church order discourse (18:1–35). The discourse has three parts: the first develops the character of the community as it relates to the weakest and the most vulnerable (18:1–14); the second outlines a rather detailed and somewhat arduous procedure for reconciliation among grieved members of the Christian community (18:15–20); and the third offers a parable on teaching limitless forgiveness (18:21–35).

In the first part of the discourse, Jesus offers his disciples a paradigm for understanding the nature of the church and the exercise of authority therein: "Unless you turn and become like children, you will not enter the kingdom of heaven" (Matthew 18:3). One must recall that children were not to be seen and certainly not heard in the ancient world; children were really "nonpeople" and not the center of family life as they are in contemporary culture. Not only must one become like a child, one must also receive the "little ones" and guard them from sin. Avoiding scandal and avoiding sin (18:6) should be top priority for those who seek to be great in the kingdom (the Greek verb *skandalizō* means "to cause one to sin," and appears alongside the noun *skandalon*, or "stumbling block," throughout this section). However, the provocative exhortation that Jesus offers here ought to give pause. As in other exhortations to seize upon the kingdom's arrival (e.g., the parables of the Pearl of Great Price and the Hidden Treasure), Jesus tells his disciples that nothing should keep them from the kingdom—not even parts of their own bodies. But when is a hand, an eye, or any other body part actually the cause of sin? Does one's hand or one's eye cause sin? Rather, Jesus employs hyperbole here as a summons to conversion and faith. If it were only as "easy" as cutting off one's hand, sin would never reign in the world. But as it is, sin abides because of the refusal to become like a child, to trust in the power of God in Christ, to be converted. This trust and openness is far more demanding and difficult.

Matthew uses the parable of the Lost Sheep (18:10–14), from the Q source, as an example of the care the pastors of the Christian community must have for "the little ones." The passage serves as a bridge to the prescriptive material that follows (see Luke 15:1–7 for a very different use of this parable). In 18:15–20, Jesus offers a strangely precise procedure for dealing with discord and sin in the Christian community with the notable feature of the role played by the entire community in the process of reconciliation. In fact, it is the entire church that "binds" and "loosens" in this case. Another interesting and somewhat opaque aspect of the instruction occurs in verse 17, where Jesus encourages the church to treat one who will not heed the admonitions of the community as they would treat "a Gentile or a tax collector." On the one hand, Jesus may be invoking the traditional treatment of Gentiles and tax collectors in the Jewish community, where such individuals were avoided in public and excluded from worship. On the other hand, Jesus has regularly had fellowship with Gentiles, tax collectors, and sinners, and has encouraged his disciples to do the same. As such, the instruction would then be to have the church emulate the practice of Jesus and extend fellowship and friendship even in the midst of disagreement (see 8:5–13; 9:9–13; 15:21–28). Rounding out this section is a unique and memorable saying on the power of the church: "For where two or three are gathered together in my name, there am I in the midst of them" (18:20).

The discourse closes with the parable of the Unforgiving Servant (18:21–35), a passage unique to Matthew's Gospel. The parable is introduced by a question from Simon Peter concerning the number of times a disciple must forgive. Jesus insists on superabundant forgiveness: the number "seventy-seven" implies limitless forgiveness that reflects God's own practice of mercy (18:22). The parable then unfolds as an illustration of the way the Christian community is to reflect the loving mercy of God.

The parable is carefully constructed around three scenes. In the first scene (18:23–27), a king calls in a loan he has made to one of his servants. The servant is probably responsible for parlaying the king's money so as to make a profit for himself as well as for the king—a dangerous but profitable business. The huge sum of money involved (ten thousand talents or sixty million denarii; one denarius being equal to a day's wage) indicates the sort of work for which the servant was responsible. Unable to produce the money the king demanded, the man and his family were to be sold into slavery and all of their property sold, as was the custom, in order to pay off the debt. Some suggest that the king was merely proving a point to the servant and was only seeking to gain the servant's attention and submission—which does, in fact, happen. As the servant begs and pleads for time to pay off the debt, the king goes one better and forgives the debt entirely. As is typical of many parables, the behavior of the king is so entirely strange—no one would forgive such a huge debt—that it causes the hearer to pause and ponder. The king's extravagant forgiveness throws the second scene into bold relief: the servant's selfish and cruel behavior toward his own debtors is all the more reprehensible given the comparatively paltry sum owed (18:28–30). In the final scene (18:31–35), the king exacts revenge. In a chilling reminder of divine judgment, the king vents his anger (the wrath or anger of God is a common theme in apocalyptic literature) and hands over the unjust servant to torturers. The parable sums up the discourse on church order by once again calling on the church to treat one another as God has treated them (18:35), to make God's heavenly reign a reality on earth (see 6:9–15).

Jerusalem (Matthew 19:1—25:46)

The narrative portion (19:1—23:39) prior to the final, eschatological discourse depicts Jesus traveling to Jerusalem by way of the eastern shore of the Jordan River so as to avoid passing through Samaritan towns, as was the custom among pious Jews at the time. The narrative begins (19:1–12) with a reprisal of Mark's teaching on divorce, but Matthew incorporates some curious additions into the Markan material. In Matthew, Jesus prohibits divorce "except in the case of *porneia*" (19:9, author's translation). The word *porneia* has become a source of controversy. Generally it refers to sexual immorality, so the passage could simply be saying that divorce is permissible when a spouse has committed adultery. The use of the word *porneia*, however, sometimes had a more restricted meaning in early Christian circles, where it can refer to marriage within forbidden bloodlines. Such marriages were common enough among many Romans and Greeks, but were offensive and unlawful to Jews. In this case, could the exception to the general prohibition on divorce imply that those who had contracted such marriages were free (or even required) to divorce the spouse once they entered the Christian church (see Acts 15:20; 1 Corinthians 5:1)?

Another interesting addition to the teaching on divorce is the reference to those who have "become eunuchs" for the kingdom of heaven (19:12, a servant who has been castrated. Eunuchs were then given privileged access to the domestic life of important families, for castration ensured that no sexual improprieties could occur between the servant and the female family members. It is not clear if this statement about becoming eunuchs reflects the occasional hyperbole or exaggeration characteristic of Matthew's portrayal of Jesus' preaching (e.g., "If your hand . . . causes you to sin, cut it off"), or whether this reflects the practice of celibacy of some segment of Matthew's community. Celibacy was rare in first-century Judaism, but it was practiced by groups with strong apocalyptic outlooks (e.g., the Essenes at Qumran), and it may be the case that both men and women made the choice to remain unmarried (especially widows) in order to devote themselves to the mission of the church (see Acts 9:39; 1 Timothy 5:3–16).[20]

The teaching on discipleship and possessions (19:16–30) precedes Matthew's great parable of the Workers in the Vineyard (20:1–16). In Isaiah, chapter 5, the vineyard is a metaphor for Jerusalem, and Matthew plays with that association. The parable is framed by similar statements in 19:30 and 20:16, asserting that "the last" will be first and "the first" will be last, thus emphasizing the dynamics of eschatological reversal. The reversal has perhaps less to do with the order of who is paid first in the parable than with the generalized reversal of expectation and value: assumptions about what constitutes love and justice on earth will be radically challenged in the kingdom of heaven. (The envious workers question the justice of the landowner). In a slavishly literal translation, the landowner's response might be rendered, "Your evil eye is because I am good?" The NAB appropriately translates "evil eye" as "envious," reflecting the notion that the eye tends to be the locus of intent and will. The evil eye is, however, also an ancient phenomenon with destructive power. In ancient times, people assumed that the eye emitted a light that enabled one to see, and looking with evil intent, envy, or lust could result in physical harm (see the teaching on adultery in 5:28, where the look was already an act of adultery; see also 6:22–23). In 20:15, the juxtaposition of the evil eye and the good landowner is deliberate on Matthew's part and serves to highlight the goodness of God and the manner in which human beings often fail to receive and appropriately reflect God's goodness in their lives.

As Matthew continues his narrative, he supplements or modifies Markan material in a variety of ways. Noted earlier in this chapter is Matthew's modification of the Markan story about the request of James and John to sit at Jesus' right and left to make the two disciples look better (20:20–28). In Matthew, the disciples' mother, not the disciples, makes the request. Additionally, Jesus' entry into Jerusalem (21:1–9) includes an explicit citation of Zechariah 9:9 wherein the author depicts Jesus as a parody of the conquering hero entering a vanquished city.[21] In the cleansing of the Temple, Matthew adds the children's reprise to the cry of the crowds upon Jesus' entry into Jerusalem: "Hosanna (i.e., "save us") to the son of David" (21:15–16). These changes highlight the animosity between the religious authorities and Jesus, especially in light of his claims to authority as God's Messiah, as the climax of the Gospel unfolds.

In the midst of the growing animosity and heated invectives involved in Jesus' dispute with the religious authorities, Matthew introduces three parables that reflect Matthew's certainty regarding the reasons for Jerusalem's destruction in 70 CE. These parables, of the Two Sons, the Tenants, and the Wedding Feast, highlight the culpability of the religious leaders and claim their rejection of Jesus as the cause of the destruction (21:28—22:14).

Perhaps the most damning of the three parables is that of the Wedding Feast (22:1–14). As one can see by reading the parallel account in Luke, the original Q passage emphasized the laxity and carelessness of the initial guests, who presumably do not really understand the importance of the invitation. Their refusal is unfortunate, and they are left out of the festivities as the marginalized find pride of place in the generous man's great feast (Luke 14:15–24). Matthew, on the other hand, changes the passage in several respects in order to highlight the eschatological dimensions of the parable. First, by making the feast a royal wedding feast for the king's son, Matthew has already tied in the christological themes he has developed throughout the Gospel. Moreover, the image of the wedding feast serves to highlight the eschatological dimensions of the passage. The culpability of the initial invitees becomes apparent in the violent way the king's messengers are treated: the parable now becomes an allegory about the destruction of Jerusalem rather than a story about invitation and response.

Additionally, the final verses of the parable highlight two distinctive features of Matthew's Gospel. First, notice that both the good and the bad are invited to the wedding feast, but the king subsequently identifies the bad person when he sees the man who lacks appropriate attire. On a literal level, wedding guests in first-century Palestine were expected to dress appropriately for a wedding feast as a sign of respect for the hosts and for the couple. But in this allegorized parable, the lack of a wedding garment represents the absence of righteous deeds or righteous practices. Such a guest is thus cast out, using Matthew's typical language of "darkness" and "grinding of teeth," both of which signify suffering, anger, remorse, and exclusion (for "grinding of teeth," see Matthew 8:12; 13:42, 50; 24:51; 25:30; and for "outer darkness," see Matthew 8:12 and 25:30).

In the comparison of the Matthean and Lukan accounts that appears on page 141, the major points at which Matthew's version differs from that of Luke (and Q?) are placed in bold type.

The animosity between Jesus and the religious authorities spills out in scenes of conflict with Jesus, especially in Matthew's unique additions to the Markan account of the conflict with the scribes and Pharisees (23:1–36). Of particular importance is the manner in which Matthew utilizes the word hypocrite (*hypokritēs*) throughout. In Greek, this word means "actor"; the hypocrite is not simply someone who says one thing and does another. Rather, the hypocrite plays one role for public consumption, but in private, takes off his mask and plays another (see Paul's use of the term in Galatians 2:11–14). For Matthew, this insincerity is the centerpiece of Jesus' invectives against the scribes and Pharisees. The structure of the denunciation centers on seven uses of the phrase "Woe to you!" followed by condemnation for various offenses, most of which involve a contrast between the exterior and the interior. The scribes and Pharisees are concerned with the exterior observance of piety while their interior is corrupt, and this incongruity is the basis for the charge of hypocrisy or lack of authenticity. The invectives end alarmingly with reference to the murder of the prophets and the crucifixion of those whom God has sent as guides (23:34–36). The transition to the final discourse, however, offers a softer tone as Jesus laments the destruction of Jerusalem (23:37–39).

In Matthew's final major discourse (24:1—25:46), he reprises much of the material from Mark, chapter 13, but with significant additions, including several important parables. Jesus no longer directs his instruction to the crowds or to his opponents; rather, this instruction is for his disciples. It begins with the "signs" of Mark, chapter 13, and proceeds to the lesson of the fig tree (24:32–35). But perhaps most characteristic of Matthew is the unique material on the example of vigilance provided by the story of Noah. For Matthew, the disciples, like Noah, must be prepared for the coming of the Son of Man, or else they will be swept away with the people of this world (24:36–44). The rhetorical device of pairs ("two women will be grinding at the mill; one will be taken, and one will be left" [24:41]) sets up the contrasting destinies developed in the judgment scene in 25:31–46.

MATTHEW 22:2–14	LUKE 14:16–24
The kingdom of heaven may be likened to **a king who gave a wedding feast for his son.** He dispatched his servants to summon the invited guests to the feast, but they refused to come. A second time he sent other servants, saying, "Tell those invited: 'Behold, I have prepared my banquet, my calves and fattened cattle are killed, and everything is ready; come to the feast.'" Some ignored the invitation and went away, one to his farm, another to his business. **The rest laid hold of his servants, mistreated them, and killed them. The king was enraged and sent his troops, destroyed those murderers, and burned their city. Then he said to his servants, "The feast is ready, but those who were invited were not worthy to come.** Go out, therefore, into the main roads and invite to the feast whomever you find." The servants went out into the streets and gathered all they found, **bad and good alike, and the hall was filled with guests.** **But when the king came in to meet the guests he saw a man there not dressed in a wedding garment. He said to him, "My friend, how is it that you came in here without a wedding garment?" But he was reduced to silence. Then the king said to his attendants, "Bind his hands and feet, and cast him into the darkness outside, where there will be wailing and grinding of teeth." Many are invited, but few are chosen.**	A man gave a great dinner to which he invited many. When the time for the dinner came, he dispatched his servant to say to those invited, "Come, everything is now ready." But one by one, they all began to excuse themselves. The first said to him, "I have purchased a field and must go to examine it; I ask you, consider me excused." And another said, "I have purchased five yoke of oxen and am on my way to evaluate them; I ask you, consider me excused." And another said, "I have just married a woman, and therefore I cannot come." The servant went and reported this to his master. Then the master of the house in a rage commanded his servant, "Go out quickly into the streets and alleys of the town and bring in here the poor and the crippled, the blind and the lame." The servant reported, "Sir, your orders have been carried out and still there is room." The master then ordered the servant, "Go out to the highways and hedgerows and make people come in that my home may be filled. For, I tell you, none of those men who were invited will taste my dinner."

Three parables of preparation (including the parables of the Servants, the Ten Virgins, and the Talents) set the stage for the coup de grâce of the eschatological discourse, the judgment scene [25:31–46]. While this scence may not be a parable, the image nonetheless has parabolic force since it is meant to provoke a variety of responses among those who hear it and thereby are led to conversion and faith.

The judgment scene is perhaps, next to the Sermon on the Mount, the most celebrated passage in Matthew. In this section, the metaphors of king and shepherd are mixed with the title *Son of Man*, pointing to Matthew's creative work in bringing together material from Jesus' sayings, parables, and the allegory of the last judgment.[22] The image of sheep and goats evokes a familiar scene in first-century Palestine, yet there is some disagreement among scholars about the practice of separating the sheep and the goats at night after a day spent grazing together. The sheep are more valuable for their meat, wool, and skin. The goats are comparatively less valuable and require special care at night since they are less equipped to deal with the cold.[23] In the judgment scene, the Son of Man sits before all the nations (i.e., the Gentiles) and separates the sheep and the goats, giving the sheep the place of honor (i.e., the right-hand side) while the goats are dishonored by their place on the left. The sheep and goats are then judged on the basis of their having received or rejected "the least," referring to the Christian missionaries Jesus has been describing for several chapters. The criteria for judging the Christian community are their vigilance and righteous deeds, as has been presented through the collection of three parables prior to this parable of judgment.[24]

The Passion and Resurrection (Matthew 26:1—28:20)

Matthew's account of the passion generally follows Mark but also includes some stunning additions. Rather than treat these changes piecemeal, it would be best to group these changes under three distinct themes. First, a series of changes Matthew makes to highlight or expand the culpability of the religious authorities and even the people of Jerusalem, not only for the death of Jesus but for bringing upon themselves the destruction of Jerusalem. Second, a series of changes made by Matthew serve an apologetic goal, namely, to defend the notion of a suffering and risen messiah in light of Jewish expectations. Third, Matthew makes changes to signal the importance of the church in his theology and a corresponding improvement in the depiction of the disciples.

AN ALTERNATIVE EXEGESIS: THE PARABLE OF THE TALENTS IN MATTHEW 25:14–30

In his exegesis of the parable of the Talents, sociologist Michael Budde reverses the apparent meaning of the text within its Matthean context.[25] As part of Budde's critique of the manner in which capitalism has seeped into the fabric of Christian thought and practice in the United States, he sees the parable as an opportunity to radically challenge capitalist assumptions about the compatibility of capitalism and Christianity.

In a more traditional reading of the parable, the master of the estate is God, and the admirable servants are the ones who made a profit for their master. The one who failed to make a profit is thus the negative example. Budde readily admits, "that's how we should read the parable," but in a playful twist he suggests that if one changes the identification of the characters a bit to bring the parable in line with the actual dynamics of wealth creation in first-century Palestine, then a decidedly different interpretation begins to emerge. From this perspective, the master of the estate is Satan instead of God. The parable then takes a dramatic turn. The master "reaps where he does not sow and gathers where he did not reap," indicating that the wealth he has accumulated has actually come at the expense of the poor and the vulnerable. Moreover, the incredible rate of return secured by two of the master's servants appears to have come at the expense of others through exorbitant interest rates or by seizing collateral on the loan; how else can one explain doubling an investment?

The disobedient or lazy servant, whom Budde now identifies as Jesus himself, is no longer seen as lacking ambition or as timid; rather, this servant takes a stand against the exploitation of the vulnerable. In other words, Jesus is the one who is prepared to suffer unjust punishment at the hands of satanic forces rather than create wealth for his master at the expense of the vulnerable. In the end, Budde uses this rereading of the parable to reinforce his contention that God is not a capitalist.

As for the first point, Matthew makes several key additions and changes to expand the culpability of the religious authorities. First, Matthew names the high priest (Caiaphas), thus placing blame squarely on specific figures in Jerusalem, and he puts the initial interrogation of Jesus in the house of Caiaphas, a violation of the rules for holding any kind of trial in first-century Palestine (26:57–68). Moreover, when the trial scene moves to Pilate, Matthew provides a far more sympathetic picture of the Roman governor. Pilate pleads with the crowd to choose Jesus over Barabbas, but when the crowd starts to become unruly, Pilate accedes to their demands (27:11–26). In the meantime, he is warned by his wife to have nothing to do with the death of Jesus (27:19), and so Pilate symbolically washes his hands, declaring himself innocent of the blood that is about to be spilled (27:24). The response of the people is disturbing, as they cry out in unison, "His blood be upon us and upon our children" (27:25). This verse helped contribute to a troubling legacy of Christian anti-Semitism, even though such attitudes were far from the mind or the intention of Matthew.

Matthew also has specific apologetic goals in mind in his construction of the passion and Resurrection narratives. The sharp attacks from the opponents of Matthew's community no doubt inspired some important editorial activity, particularly the details added to the account of Jesus' death (27:51–56): earthquakes and the resurrection of the dead mark the moment of Jesus' death. In his *Epistle to the Trallians*, the early church father Ignatius of Antioch (c. 110 CE) wrote that those in heaven, on earth, and under the earth (cf. Philippians 2:10–11) were witnesses to the suffering and death of Jesus. The darkening of the sky (heaven), the earthquake (on earth), and the raising of the dead (under the earth) thus correspond to the death of Jesus.[26] Moreover, these signs were customarily associated with the *eschaton* and the judgment of God. In early Christian circles, the claim that Jesus was the Messiah promised by God would have met with skepticism from those familiar with the general parameters of Jewish apocalyptic thought. After all, the death and resurrection of an individual had no currency in such a worldview. N. T. Wright makes this point straightforwardly: as a matter of deep concern on the part of early Christians, the resurrection of an individual sounds like good news for that individual, but it is not entirely clear how this would be good news for anyone else.[27] The apocalyptic signs accompanying the death of Jesus function as a theological statement by Matthew that the cross represents a decisive eschatological act by God (whether or not the signs might also reflect a historical tradition that Matthew is reporting). The earthquake, the resurrection of the saints (i.e., "holy ones"), as well as other signs evoke apocalyptic passages from a variety of sources, such as Isaiah 26:19, Daniel 12:2, and *1 Enoch* 93:6.

Matthew's apologetic motives are also apparent in his treatment of the burial of Jesus. Only in Matthew do we find an elaborate subplot involving allegations of body snatching (27:62—28:15). In an effort to defend the Christian claims of Resurrection against Matthew's opponents, we find the strange request from the Jewish authorities for Roman permission to set guards at the tomb of Jesus. With the Resurrection of Jesus, the earthquake, and the angelic appearance, the guards become spellbound and faint as though dead. When they report the events, like Judas, they are paid off for their cooperation and silence (28:11–15).

In the third cluster of themes in Matthew's account of the passion, we find perhaps his most distinctive material. In his concern to develop a theology of the Christian community, Matthew has consistently softened Mark's negative portrayal of the disciples. While the disciples are still less than ideal and less than consistent, they nonetheless receive a more generous portrayal in Matthew than in Mark, in part due to Matthew's sense that the Christian community as a whole is suffering from a negative characterization at the hands of its opponents within the sphere of the emerging rabbinic tradition. As in Mark, the anointing scene in 26:6–13 offers the anonymous female disciple as a foil to those who plot against Jesus, including Judas. The woman, not a sinful figure as in Luke, prophetically and piously anoints Jesus' body in preparation for burial. Barbara Reid suggests that the woman may also be interpreted as preparing Jesus for his mission as "anointed one," that is, as priest, prophet, and king, as he moves toward these roles in his passion and Resurrection.[28] Although Judas betrays Jesus and subsequently chooses death rather than the difficult road of repentance, he nonetheless provides an important negative example. The two Marys find the tomb empty (28:1–10), and although they are amazed, they nonetheless fulfill the angel's command and the command of Jesus to tell the disciples. In the end, unlike Mark's harsh and demanding conclusion, Matthew supplies a reassurance for the believer: Jesus appears in Galilee and gives the disciples a mandate that they will be empowered to fulfill: "I am with you always, until the end of the age" (28:20).

Conclusion

Matthew's Gospel stands out in relation to the other Synoptics for several reasons. First, Matthew has consistently emphasized the congruence between Jesus and the hopes and prophecies of the Old Testament. At every turn, Matthew drops in allusions, supplies a fulfillment passage, or develops a typology that will help his audience to see Jesus as the fulfillment of God's covenantal promises to Israel. Second, Matthew has slowed the pace of the Markan narrative by including special didactic material that rounds out his distinctive portrayal of Jesus as the teacher of a higher righteousness through a more radical obedience to the covenant. This leads to another Matthean distinction: Jesus has the authority to offer this radical vision of the covenant because of his identity, God-with-us (Emmanuel). Finally, Matthew places a distinctive emphasis on the church as the new people of God, the new Israel. Matthew's community is not a replacement for an abandoned people; rather, Matthew's community *is* Israel; they are Jews who have come to welcome Gentiles through a realization of prophetic texts like Isaiah 2:2–3, which highlight their eschatological vocation.

| QUESTIONS FOR UNDERSTANDING

1. Describe the lived context of Matthew's Gospel. When was it written, and what were the circumstances faced by those for whom the Gospel was composed?

2. Describe the Christology of Matthew. What devices does the author use to develop this Christology?

3. How does the infancy narrative serve as a theological overture to the rest of the Gospel?

4. List and briefly describe the content of the five major discourses in Matthew.

5. Why is the parables discourse in Matthew, chapter 13, considered central to Matthew's presentation of the Gospel? What themes are developed in that chapter that help to anchor Matthew's account of the Gospel?

6. Discuss at least three ways Matthew changes Mark's account of the passion and death of Jesus.

| QUESTIONS FOR REFLECTION

1. Do you think the Gospel of Matthew is anti-Semitic or anti-Jewish? Is there a difference between anti-Semitism and anti-Judaism? What passages support your opinion?

2. Matthew places significant emphasis on the church in his Gospel, particularly on its character as an assembly of both the righteous and the wicked. What passages from the Gospel help to support this view?

3. Matthew makes extensive use of Old Testament quotations in an effort to demonstrate that Jesus' life and ministry are the fulfillment of various prophecies. Yet some of the texts that Matthew cites appear to be interpreted outside the original context of the passage. For example, the use of Isaiah 7:14 in the infancy narrative moves well beyond the original context for Isaiah's oracle. Does it strike you as legitimate to interpret a passage out of context in this way? In other words, can a passage mean something different than what the original author intended it to mean? Are there any limits? Explain.

| FOR FURTHER READING

Allison, Dale, and W. D. Davies. *Matthew: A Shorter Commentary*. International Critical Commentary. London: T and T Clark, 2005.

Reid, Barbara E. *The Gospel according to Matthew*. New Collegeville Bible Commentary. Collegeville, MN: Liturgical, 2005.

Senior, Donald. *The Gospel According to Matthew*. Interpreting Biblical Texts. Nashville, TN: Abingdon, 1997.

| ENDNOTES

1. Eusebius, *Ecclesiastical History*, 3.39.16.

2. See Krister Stendahl, *The School of St. Matthew and Its Use of the Old Testament*, second edition (Philadelphia: Fortress, 1968).

3. W. D. Davies and Dale Allison, *A Critical Exegetical Commentary on the Gospel According to Matthew*, ICC (Edinburgh: T and T Clark, 1995), 1:136.

4. *Berakhot*, 28b–29a.

5. See David Flusser, "4QMMT and the Benediction against the *Minim*," in *Judaism of the Second Temple Period*, vol. 1, *Qumran and Apocalypticism* (Grand Rapids, MI: Eerdmans, 2007), 84–94.

6. Quoted in C. K. Barrett, ed., *The New Testament Background*, rev. ed. (San Francisco: Collins, 1989), 211.

7. E.g., see Philip S. Alexander, " 'The Parting of the Ways' from the Perspective of Rabbinic Judaism," in *Jews and Christians: The Parting of the Ways, A.D. 70–135*, ed. James D. G. Dunn (Grand Rapids, MI: Eerdmans, 1999), 1–26.

8. See P. W. van der Horst, "The *Birkat ha-minim* in Recent Research," *The Expository Times* 105 (1994): 363–368.

9. For the classic position on Matthew as a new Pentateuch, see Benjamin W. Bacon, *Studies in Matthew* (London: Constable, 1930), 145–261.

10. Myles M. Bourke, "The Literary Genus of Matthew 1–2," *Catholic Biblical Quarterly* 22/2 (1960): 160–175, at 175.

11. E.g., see A. H. McNeile, *The Gospel According to Matthew* (London: Macmillan, 1952), 81.

12. Neither in the Letter of James nor in Matthew is there any real tension with Paul, for whom the issue was Torah observance as a prerequisite for Christian fellowship. For both Matthew and James, among whom there is no evidence of contact or shared sources, the issue is the life of discipleship modeled after the demands of the covenant as expressed in Torah and the Prophets. E.g., see Peter Davids, *The Epistle of James: A Commentary on the Greek Text*, NIGTC (Grand Rapids, MI: Eerdmans, 1982), 47–51.

13. Brendan Byrne, *Lifting the Burden: Reading Matthew's Gospel in the Church Today* (Collegeville, MN: Liturgical, 2004), 73–84.

14. See, e.g., *Berakhot*, 3.

15. On the Wisdom images in this passage see Sirach 51:23–30.

16. Davies and Allison, *Matthew*, 2:370–372.

17. For a wonderful reading of this parable see Robert W. Funk, "Beyond Criticism in Quest of Literacy: The Parable of the Leaven," *Interpretation* 25 (1971): 149–170.

18. Benedict T. Viviano, OP, "The Gospel According to Matthew," in *The New Jerome Biblical Commentary*, ed. R. E. Brown, J. A. Fitzmyer, and R. E. Murphy (Englewood Cliffs, NJ: Prentice Hall: 1990), 657.

19. See, e.g., Robert H. Gundry, *Matthew: A Commentary on His Handbook for a Mixed Church under Persecution*, second edition (Grand Rapids, MI: Eerdmans, 1994), 328–337.

20. On celibacy at Qumran, see Geza Vermes, *The Dead Sea Scrolls in English* (New York: Penguin, 1987), 16–18, though dissenting opinions abound. On the widows in the early Christian community, see Barbara E. Reid, OP, *The Gospel According to Matthew*, New Collegeville Bible Commentary (Collegeville, MN: Liturgical, 2005), 98.

21. See Reid, *Matthew*, 105.

22. For a discussion of the pastiche this story represents see John A. T. Robinson, "The 'Parable' of the Sheep and the Goats," in *Twelve New Testament Studies* (London: SCM, 1962), 76–93.

23. Although some scholars dispute this assertion (e.g., see Reid, *Matthew*, 126–127), others side with the analysis of Joachim Jeremias (e.g., see Daniel J. Harrington, SJ, *The Gospel of Matthew*, SP [Collegeville, MN: Liturgical, 1991], 356). See Joachim Jeremias, *The Parables of Jesus* (Philadelphia: Westminster, 1971), 206. On the history of interpretation of this passage, see S. W. Gray, *The Least of My Bothers: Matthew 25:31–46; A History of Interpretation*, SBLDS (Atlanta, GA: Scholars, 1989).

24. Donald Senior, CP, *The Gospel According to Matthew*, IBT (Nashville, TN: Abingdon, 1997), 163–164.

25. For what follows see Michael L. Budde, "God Is Not a Capitalist," in *God Is Not: Religious, Nice, "One of Us," an American, a Capitalist*, ed. D. Brent Latham (Grand Rapids, MI: Brazos, 2004), 77–95, at 90–92.

26. See Raymond E. Brown, SS, *The Death of the Messiah*, ABRL (New York: Doubleday, 1994), 2:1120–1121.

27. See N. T. Wright, *The Resurrection of the Son of God* (Minneapolis: Fortress, 2003), 200–206 and 688–689.

28. See Reid, *Matthew*, 128–129.

CHAPTER 6

THE GOSPEL ACCORDING TO LUKE

Introduction: Historical and Theological Background

Luke's Gospel forms the first part of a two-part work that includes the Acts of the Apostles; the two works are collectively known as Luke-Acts, and they comprise approximately one quarter of the entire New Testament canon. Luke's two-volume proclamation stands apart from Mark and Matthew, though it still has much in common with both. Luke incorporates only about 60 to 65 percent of Mark into his narrative (compared to roughly 80 percent for Matthew), and about two hundred and twenty verses from Q. These two sources, Mark and Q, comprise about half of Luke, with the rest of the material coming from Luke or sources unique to him, resulting in a Gospel that is at once traditional but also unique. Luke's theological voice is both distinctive and dominant, standing apart from the other canonical Gospels and occupying the rest of the New Testament canon.

Authorship and Lived Context

While scholars generally believe that a single author composed this massive two-volume work, the question of that author's identity has troubled scholars in modern times. Since the early centuries of the Christian era, the author of the Third Gospel has been identified as Luke, the physician and one-time companion of the Apostle Paul (see Colossians 4:14; 2 Timothy 4:11; Philemon, verse 24). The identification of the author with this elusive figure from the Pauline corpus, however, presents at least two significant difficulties. First, if the author of the Third Gospel was the companion of Paul, it seems odd that the author should fail to reproduce any of the basic characteristics of Pauline theology. Theological themes like justification, cultic or sacrificial interpretations of Jesus' death, and important Pauline vocabulary like fellowship (*koinōnia*) are all but absent in Luke-Acts. Surely the influence of a prolific, powerful, and influential figure such as Paul should find its way into Luke's massive and carefully constructed corpus. But in fact, Mark's Gospel, particularly his theology of the cross, appears to resonate with Pauline theology better than Luke's. The second difficulty involves the so-called we sections in the Acts of the Apostles, passages that many have cited as evidence of the author's participation in the events of Acts (see Acts 16:10–17; 20:5–15; 21:1–18; 27:1–28:16). Scholars disagree on whether these sporadic passages indicate the historical recollections of the author or are the product of some rhetorical device.

Several factors assist in dating Luke's Gospel. On the one hand, Luke appears to depend on Mark as a source, and this Gospel also seems to presuppose the siege of Jerusalem, given the vividness of the narration in Luke 21:20–24. These two factors suggest a date after about 70 CE. On the other hand, Luke does not seem to know of the localized persecutions inaugurated by the Roman emperor Domitian in parts of Asia in the 90s CE, and Acts seems to be known to Clement of Rome, who was writing at the end of the first or in the beginning of the second century. For these reasons and others, biblical scholars generally agree that the Gospel of Luke was probably composed between 80 and 90 CE.

Locating the Christian community and the historical situation behind Luke-Acts has proven elusive, but any proposed location must take into account the predominantly Gentile makeup of Luke's audience (Luke seems preoccupied with the place of the Gentiles in the economy of salvation). Perhaps Achaia, the first-century term for what is modern-day Greece, is the best candidate, but certainly not the only one (some would suggest Syria or the regions around modern-day Turkey). Made up of mainly Gentiles, Luke's primary audience would have been faced with a number of issues, but no major crises of the scope and intensity one sees in Mark, Matthew, and John. The community seems to be wrestling with issues of inclusion within a still largely Jewish movement, or at least a movement that still sees itself as largely Jewish. This Gospel portrays Jesus as the Jewish messiah, but a messiah who has come for the salvation of all, including in a special way Greek or Hellenistic Gentiles. The universality of salvation plays a major role in this Gospel.

Theological Themes

It appears that some of the main theological issues confronting Luke are apologetic. He seeks to defend Christian faith to those in the Greco-Roman world who might find the Christian movement threatening or irrelevant. Luke's Gentile audience appears to be concerned with at least two important questions. First, what is the connection between a Jewish messiah and the salvation of Gentiles? In other words, how can a religious figure from a tradition distrustful of outsiders (at least since the time of Ezra—see, e.g., Ezra 9:1–4 and Nehemiah 13:1–3) be the way of salvation for the people previously regarded as a threat? Second, the destruction of Jerusalem and the fact that most Jews had not embraced Jesus both suggest that God has abandoned the people of Israel and forgotten the covenant. Naturally the question would arise: How can this God be trusted if the covenant can be dissolved?

As a response to the first question, Luke's Gospel offers assurance in the form of a Christology in which Jesus identifies with the outsider, the neglected, and the weak. Of course, this identification strongly echoes and perhaps amplifies the other portraits of Christ in the New Testament, but nowhere else does this identification with the marginalized find more consistent articulation than in Luke, where the poor and marginalized become the focus of Jesus' proclamation of the kingdom. Throughout the Gospel of Luke, one finds Jesus demonstrating God's special care and concern for the poor and the marginalized (Luke and LXX use the Greek word *ptōchoi* to translate the Hebrew word *'anāwim*, which means "poor" and served as a focal point in the messages of the prophets in Israel; see, e.g., Isaiah 51:21–23; Jeremiah 15:10–21; Zephaniah 2:3; 3:12). They wait on God, and it is the poor through whom God shows mercy, forgiveness, and salvation to the world. In fact, the theme of eschatological reversal and the corresponding invitation for the Christian community to identify with marginalized people plays a central role in Luke. With the advent of the kingdom, the mighty will be dispossessed and the weak gifted; the hungry will be filled and the rich sent away empty (Luke 1:46–55). For Luke, like Matthew and Mark, the kingdom is understood as a future event, and the eschatological reversals (i.e., those who weep now will laugh in the eschatological future) are to be anticipated in the life of believers at present with the offer of salvation. In other words, while the definitive reversal awaits future consummation, the *ptōchoi* anticipate that reversal in their present lives, a point we will return to in this chapter.

The place of women in Luke's account of Jesus' ministry provides an interesting and important aspect of Luke's theology of the poor and marginalized. More than the other Synoptic Gospels, Luke emphasizes the role of women in the early Christian community and in the activity of Jesus, even explicitly naming those women who supported Jesus and the Twelve (8:1–3). Even the casual reader will pick up several other examples: Luke's portrayal of Mary, the mother of Jesus, stands out against both Mark and Matthew's versions. This feature of Luke's Gospel reflects more accurately the practice of Jesus as an egalitarian Jew who subverted many of the social and religious practices of first-century Palestinian Judaism. Moreover, Luke develops the theme of God's unmeasured hospitality, a practice of unfathomable welcoming for those who were on the margins. This theme is particularly evident in uniquely Lukan passages like the Good Samaritan, the Prodigal Son, the celebration of the Last Supper, and the Emmaus story.

In response to the question of whether God has abandoned his covenant with Israel, Luke assures his audience by emphasizing the continuity of the new covenant Jesus announces and the covenant between Yahweh and the people of Israel. This continuity seems slightly out of place if Luke's audience is primarily Gentiles, but continuity with the Old Testament is essential for Luke's overall argument: God is faithful to the covenant. Luke unfolds the story of Jesus in an "orderly" way (Luke 1:3) and demonstrates that the events of Jesus' life and ministry are not haphazard, but part of Yahweh's plan of salvation that has been unfolding in history and foretold in Scripture. Luke often refers to the Jewish Scriptures both directly and indirectly to demonstrate that events in Jesus' life (1) are "necessary" (the Greek word for necessary, *dei*, is a favorite word of Luke's), (2) are in line with the story

FIVE GREAT PRAYERS IN LUKE

Prayer punctuates Luke's presentation of the Gospel. At key moments in the narrative, socially marginalized characters (e.g., Simeon, Zechariah, or Mary) play central roles in the story of salvation, and as their role unfolds, they offer spontaneous prayers of joy. Although two of the prayers come from angels, the angels address marginalized figures like the shepherds or Mary. Five of these prayers have been preserved in the prayer life or liturgy of the Christian church.

TRADITIONAL TITLE	PASSAGE IN LUKE	COMMON TITLE	CONTEMPORARY USE
Ave Maria	1:42–45	Hail Mary	Rosary
Magnificat	1:46–55	The Canticle of Mary	Vespers or Evening Prayer
Benedictus	1:68–79	The Canticle of Zechariah	Lauds or Morning Prayer
Gloria	2:14	Gloria	Eucharistic Liturgy
Nunc Dimittis	2:29–32	(N/A)	Compline or Night Prayer

of Israel (see, e.g., Luke 7:11–17 where Jesus raises the dead in a story that strongly parallels a story about Elijah in 1 Kings 17:17–24), and (3) fulfill what has been written in the Scriptures (Luke 4:16–30). Although the emphasis on covenantal fidelity might seem paradoxical in a Gentile context, Jesus' fulfillment of the Old Testament yields a picture of Yahweh as faithful, thus overcoming hesitation regarding the credibility of the Gospel for Gentiles. Luke portrays Jesus as the Jewish messiah, the fulfillment of the Old Testament, but also as the universal savior. In fact, the universality of Jesus' saving work provides the basis of Luke's two-volume text, for Acts narrates the proclamation of the gospel to the ends of the earth.

SACRIFICE AND THE SAVING WORK OF CHRIST

The authors of the New Testament provide readers with a range of images and ideas that control various attempts to understand the meaning of Christ's death (more than can be presented here). They make use of various symbols and narratives at the heart of Jewish life, and no single approach is canonized. Yet the ritual of sacrifice associated with the expiation of sin on the Day of Atonement (in Hebrew, Yom Kippur) provides New Testament authors with much of their language for understanding the saving work of Jesus. In particular, Leviticus, chapter 16, describes the ritual in which the high priest had to orchestrate a number of acts to regularly remove the sins of the people of Israel. The ritual centered on blood and expulsion.[1]

First, the high priest offered a bull and a goat as sacrifices before entering the most sacred place on Earth: the holy of holies. This was the inner sanctuary of the Temple in Jerusalem, and it was where, prior to the Babylonian exile, the ark of the covenant had been kept. Here the high priest was to apply the blood of the sacrificed animals on the *kapporet* (the covering of the ark itself, where God was enthroned). Blood was a sacred substance because it contained the power of life and death. It had the power to destroy as well as to cleanse or sanctify, power that properly belonged to God alone. As such, it was dangerous for humans to handle blood. In this context, blood had the force to cleanse the sanctuary of impurities. After cleansing the holy of holies and then the altar outside the holy of holies with the blood, the high priest was presented a live goat: the scapegoat (see Leviticus 16:20–22). This goat symbolically received the sins of the people from the high priest. The goat was then driven out of the community and into the desert, where it would die. Thus, the sins of the community were carried away by the scapegoat while community impurities were eradicated by the blood offering.

Some New Testament authors draw from, or perhaps combine, these rituals as they explore the religious significance of Christ's death. Yet New Testament soteriology is not limited to sacrificial metaphors. In fact, Paul does not confine his soteriology to sacrificial language. Among several other images, Paul uses an economic or social metaphor when he employs the terms *redemption* or *ransom* (*apolutrōsis*) to express the believer's freedom from sin as a release from slavery (e.g., Romans 3:24; 1 Corinthians 1:30). Within this metaphor, a ransom was the price paid to free or to redeem a slave from bondage. For the early Christians, this became an apt metaphor for the experience of salvation—in Christ they were redeemed from slavery to sin. Luke moves away from the cultic approach to the saving work of Christ, particularly since his audience, Hellenistic Gentiles, seems to be less connected to the worldview of first-century Palestinian Judaism.

The soteriology or salvation story offered by Luke also presents an interesting and important alternative to the rest of the New Testament, in which salvation tends to revolve around the death of Jesus and a future reward of heaven. For Luke, Jesus makes the offer of salvation here and now, and makes a point of saying that salvation is available "today" (e.g., 2:11; 4:21; 19:9; 23:43). This anticipated reception of salvation colors Luke's outlook and his presentation of Jesus and the early church in Acts. Moreover, Luke avoids connecting the salvation Jesus offers with the blood shed on the cross. In fact, Luke avoids the language of "ransom" found in Mark (e.g., Mark 10:45), the image of the sacrificial lamb (e.g., John 1:29–35), or the interpretation of Jesus' death "for the forgiveness of sins" (Matthew 26:28).

Rather, for Luke, the life and ministry, the teaching and example, the fellowship of Jesus and his very presence, provide access to salvation and make it available now through the response of conversion and faith. Certainly, for Luke as well as for the rest of the New Testament, the death of Jesus is the climactic event, and it plays a decisive role in Christian accounts of salvation. But Luke sidesteps the cultic approaches underwritten to a greater and lesser extent by other New Testament authors to provide a soteriology emphasizing the redemptive significance of Jesus' entire life and ministry, one which stresses repentance, conversion, and self-denial.[2] For Luke, the transformation of the believer (or the failure to transform) grounds an account of Jesus' saving work.

The Structure and Flow of the Gospel

Unlike the other Synoptic Gospels, Luke begins with a classical prologue that imitates the high literary style of ancient Greek writers (1:1–4). The prologue purports to offer a reliable account of "the events that have been fulfilled among

A GENERALIZED OVERVIEW OF LUKE'S USE OF HIS SOURCES

MARK	THE ORDER OF LUKE'S GOSPEL	INTERPOLATIONS (Q & L)
	Luke 1:1—2:52	Interpolation (L)
Mark 1:1–15	Luke 3:1–22	
	Luke 3:23—4:30	Interpolation (Q and L)
Mark 1:21–39	Luke 4:31–44	
	Luke 5:1–11	Interpolation (Q and L)
Mark 1:40—3:19	Luke 5:12—6:19	
	Luke 6:20—8:3	Interpolation (Q and L)
Mark 4:1—6:44	Luke 8:4—9:17	
Mark 8:27—9:40	Luke 9:18–50	
	Luke 9:51—18:14	Interpolation (Q and L)
Mark 10:13–52	Luke 18:15–43	
	Luke 19:1–27	Interpolation (Q and L)
Mark 11:1—13:32	Luke 19:28—21:33	
Mark 14:1—16:8	Luke 22:1—24:12	
	Luke 24:13–53	Interpolation (L)

us," one that is based on "eyewitness" testimony. Luke addresses the work to a certain Theophilus; whether this is the author's patron or simply a literary device (*Theophilus* means "friend of God" in Greek) remains unclear.

The narrative begins in 1:5—2:52 with parallel accounts of the birth of John the Baptist and Jesus, whom Luke uniquely portrays as relatives. Both births are accompanied by wondrous events, and they provide the occasions for the two most poignant prayers in the New Testament: the songs of Mary (1:46–55) and Zechariah (1:68–79). A transitional section (3:1–4:13) sets up Luke's portrayal of Jesus' ministry. In this section, one finds a genealogy of Jesus in which he is portrayed as the child of Adam and a descendent of the Davidic line. Luke's genealogy, however, is quite different from Matthew's (cf. Matthew 1:1–17). Luke presents the history of God's saving work as distinct moments or periods that unfold in history: the story of Jesus, to which the genealogy provides the transition, can only begin after the Baptist has been arrested (Luke 3:18–20), just as the story of the Holy Spirit and the inauguration of the church in the Acts of the Apostles can only begin with the departure of Jesus (Acts 1:6–14; 2:1–47).

The next section incorporates a significant amount of Markan material on the ministry of Jesus in Galilee (4:14—9:50), though Luke does leave out Mark 6:45—8:26, a move scholars have termed the Great Omission. This omission precedes what is often called either the Great Interpolation (i.e., a large section added to the material Luke took from Mark) or the travel narrative (9:51—19:27). Here Luke presents a wide range of material within the broad context of Jesus' journey from Galilee to Jerusalem. In this central section of Luke, most of the material is not taken from Mark; rather, it includes an abundance of Q passages, perhaps preserved in a more original form than in Matthew, as well as material from Luke's own special source (L) or

his own creative energies, including some notable passages like the story of the Good Samaritan (10:29–37) and two of the parables of loss (15:1–32). This travel narrative builds tension and suspense as Jesus approaches Jerusalem and the climax of the story. Jesus predicts his coming passion and strongly admonishes the disciples to bear witness to him (e.g., 12:8–12).

Luke rejoins Mark's narrative (with minor additions and transpositions) via the arrival of Jesus in Jerusalem and the elders' rejection of Jesus (19:28—21:38). The story of Jesus' passion (22:1—23:56) is punctuated with Luke's special concern to portray the innocence of Jesus. Not only does Herod Antipas (the King of Galilee) find him innocent (23:6–12), Pilate goes so far as to declare Jesus' innocence three times (23:13–25). The final section of Luke recounts the Resurrection and the appearances of Jesus (24:1–53). While Luke borrows from various sources, he includes much original material as well. For example, Jesus appears to the disciples in Jerusalem (not in Galilee), and Luke includes the powerful story of the disciples on the road to Emmaus (24:13–35). The narrative ends with another uniquely Lukan scene in which Jesus blesses his disciples, tells them to proclaim the Gospel to all the nations, and then ascends into the heavens. This ending provides a key point of transition to volume 2 of Luke's Gospel: the Acts of the Apostles and the story of the church in the power of the spirit.

Luke's Account of the Gospel

Luke is the most literary of the four canonical evangelists, and his use of Greek far surpasses any other writer in the New Testament. The prologue marks Luke's account of the Gospel as a literary document in the tradition of the ancient Greek histories or biographies.[3] Luke's use of the Greek word *diēgēsi*, meaning narrative(s) in 1:1 ("Since many have undertaken to compile a narrative of the events that have been fulfilled among us") signals his intention to provide a chronologically connected account. Moreover, he contends that his narrative relies on the testimony of "eyewitnesses" and ministers of the word. The testimony of these two groups provides the basis for Luke's claim to write an "orderly" account of the events of Jesus' life and ministry (1:3). This account is aimed to give Luke's benefactor Theophilus,

John the Baptist	Event	Jesus
1:5–7	Introduction of Parents	1:26–27
1:8–23	Annunciation	1:28–33
1:24–25	Mother's Response	1:38–56
1:57–58	The Birth	2:1–20
1:59–66	Circumcision and Naming	2:21–24
1:67–79	Prophetic Response	2:25–38
1:80	Growth of the Child	2:39–52

the figure to whom the account is addressed, an assurance (*asphaleia*) that is perhaps both historical (in the sense that it provides an account of past events) as well as rhetorical—the assurance of Christ's saving work. Throughout the Gospel, Luke provides a vivid narration that depends on the basic Markan account, yet Luke offers significant changes in focus and pace to fit his own narrative style and his own theological agenda.

The Infancy Narrative: A Theological Overture (Luke 1:5—2:52)

The royal genealogy of Jesus provided at the outset of Matthew's Gospel finds no real parallel in Luke. Luke does include an elaborate infancy narrative that shares several key details with Matthew (e.g., Jesus' birth in Bethlehem, born to Mary and Joseph, from the family of David, conceived through the power of the holy Spirit").[4] But Luke's account differs markedly in other ways, as evidenced by a comparison of the genealogy of Matthew and Luke. Luke's genealogy of Jesus (3:23–38), following the conclusion of the

infancy narrative, highlights his comparatively insignificant and marginal ancestry, particularly in the context of King David's line. Luke introduces Jesus as the son of nonroyal figures in the Davidic household, and traces Jesus' lineage all the way back to Adam, the ancestor of all humanity. The universalism of Jesus' genealogy aptly punctuates the portrait of Christ offered in Luke's first two chapters, where a theological overture unfolds in the parallel accounts of the birth of John the Baptist and Jesus.

As Raymond Brown points out, the entire birth narrative forms a diptych or an open book with two sides: John the Baptist and Jesus.[5] In the birth story of the Baptist, Luke introduces the first of a number of important characters marked by poverty and sanctity and who patiently await the advent of God's kingdom. Elizabeth and Zechariah, the parents of John the Baptist, embody the characteristics of the ancient heroes of Israel: they are of a priestly family, though they are not from the chief priests or the aristocratic families, and they are aged and without children. Echoing the plight of such figures as Abraham and Sarah (see Genesis, chapter 18), Elizabeth and Zechariah receive the blessing of an annunciation of the birth of a remarkable child from the angel Gabriel, an Old Testament figure who provides messages forecasting the messianic age (see Daniel 8:16–26; 9:21–27).[6] Zechariah is struck mute until the naming of the child, ostensibly for doubting the word of the angel. Gabriel then visits Mary, and a similar series of events unfold with the annunciation of the birth of Jesus; however, the manner in which this birth is to take place demands some attention.

In Matthew, Jesus' conception is simply attributed to the work of divine power after the fact: Joseph is informed in a dream of the manner in which Mary has become pregnant ("she was found with child of the holy Spirit" [Matthew 1:18]). In Luke, however, the dialog takes place between the young woman Mary and the angel Gabriel. When Mary asks how, as a virgin, she will come to bear the child the angel describes, the angel says, "The power of the Most High will overshadow you" (1:35). The verb *overshadow* (*episkiazō*) is found in LXX Exodus 40:35, where it signifies Yahweh's presence and power in the tabernacle as the Hebrews wandered in the desert (see also Psalms 91:4). In other words, the power of God's presence will overshadow Mary, but not as a "divine marriage;" rather, the power-presence-glory of God will bring about the conception of the child. Note that there is no intimation of the sex act here in Luke, in contrast to many parallels in the ancient world (e.g., the Olympians and other deities who impregnate women through sex). Rather, God's powerful presence will bring about the birth of the child.[7]

Mary's pregnancy and visit to her relative Elizabeth provide the literary context for the confirmation of the relationship between the two births and the careers of Jesus and John the Baptist. For Luke, the coordinated births and ministries of these two figures reinforce the historical periodization he develops throughout his

Gospel and Acts: the work of salvation in history unfolds according to a strict, divinely mandated plan. Luke brings the first movement of the diptych to a high point with the great canticles of Mary and Zechariah. Both canticles connect the birth of these remarkable figures, Jesus and John, to the saving work God had begun in Israel.

The narratives of Jesus' birth in Luke and Matthew differ considerably. In Matthew, the aristocratic magi come bearing gifts of wealth, signifying, among many things, the royal status of the child. In Luke, as one can see in the first half of the infancy narrative, the lowliness of Jesus and his family is emphasized. Moreover, the opening of the birth narrative (2:1–7) provides an example of just how lowly Jesus' family is. Like the rest of the Roman world, the emperor and his governors forced them to travel away from the security of their home, compelling them to find lodging in the entrance and stable area of a family home. This clearly makes them vulnerable, though not really homeless as is often suggested. They are welcomed and shown hospitality in accordance with their social status as a relatively poor family. At the same time, the figures of imperial power have become unwitting pawns in God's plan of salvation. While significant historical problems are associated with the census mentioned in the text (e.g., Quirinius was governor at least ten years after the death of Herod, who is mentioned in 1:5 as king when Jesus is born) these details hardly matter for the portrait that Luke is rendering in the birth narrative. The angel of the Lord announces the birth of the child to shepherds, some of the lowest and poorest people in first-century Palestine (the job was sometimes given to women, children, or young men), who come to observe the child even as he rests in a feeding trough for animals.

Luke moves the narrative to the Temple in Jerusalem, where he portrays Mary and Joseph as pious and observant Jews, attending to the rituals of purification for the mother (see Leviticus

THE MAGNIFICAT (LUKE 1:46–55) AND THE SONG OF HANNAH (1 SAMUEL 2:1–10)

Most commentators recognize the roots of the canticles or hymns in Luke in various Old Testament texts. Although the Psalms, Genesis, and other passages in the intertestamental literature provide important parallels, the song of Hannah in 1 Samuel provides the basic framework and an interesting parallel to the Lukan narrative. For example, Hannah is without child but becomes pregnant after she finds favor with God. Her son, Samuel, will be the last of the great judges in Israel, and he will usher in the age of the monarchy. Although the material in Luke's canticle probably reflects the theology and the popular use of similar hymns in early Christian worship, the hymn nonetheless develops important Lukan themes, including what modern theologians call "the preferential option for the poor" and the theme of eschatological reversal.

LUKE 1:46–55 (MARY)		1 SAMUEL 2:1–10 (HANNAH)
My soul proclaims the greatness of the Lord; my spirit rejoices in God my savior.	Introductory Praise	My heart exults in the Lord, my horn is exalted in my God. I have swallowed up my enemies; I rejoice in my victory. There is no Holy One like the Lord; there is no Rock like our God.
For he has looked upon his handmaid's lowliness; behold, from now on will all ages call me blessed. The Mighty One has done great things for me, and holy is his name. His mercy is from age to age to those who fear him.	First Strophe	Speak boastfully no longer, nor let arrogance issue from your mouths. For an all-knowing God is the Lord, a God who judges deeds.
He has shown might with his arm, dispersed the arrogant of mind and heart. He has thrown down the rulers from their thrones but lifted up the lowly. The hungry he has filled with good things; the rich he has sent away empty.	Second Strophe	The bows of the mighty are broken, while the tottering gird on strength. The well-fed hire themselves out for bread, while the hungry batten on spoil. The barren wife bears seven sons, while the mother of many languishes. The Lord puts to death and gives life; he casts down to the nether world; he raises up again.

continued

THE MAGNIFICAT AND THE SONG OF HANNAH *continued*

LUKE 1:46–55 (MARY)		1 SAMUEL 2:1–10 (HANNAH)
	Second Strophe *continued*	The Lord makes poor and makes rich, he humbles, he also exalts. He raises the needy from the dust; from the ash heap he lifts up the poor, To seat them with nobles and make a glorious throne their heritage. He gives to the vower his vow, and blesses the sleep of the just. For the pillars of the earth are the Lord's, and he has set the world upon them. He will guard the footsteps of his faithful ones, but the wicked shall perish in the darkness. For not by strength does man prevail; the Lord's foes shall be shattered.
He has helped Israel his servant, remembering his mercy, according to his promise to our fathers, to Abraham and to his descendants forever.	Conclusion	The Most High in heaven thunders; the Lord judges the ends of the earth Now may he give strength to his king, and exalt the horn of his anointed!

12:2–8). However, Luke seems to have confused the ritual of purification (in which turtledoves are sacrificed; see Leviticus 12:2–8) with the redemption of the firstborn male (for whom five shekels are paid to a priest—see Exodus 13:2 and Numbers 3:47–48). As the rituals of purification, dedication, and circumcision are accomplished, the family runs into two interesting and prophetic figures, Simeon and Anna (Luke 2:25–38), both of whom represent the righteous and pious poor who wait patiently for God's reign. Simeon, whose Hebrew name in long form means "God has heard," offers words of foreboding for Mary, words that portend the divided reception Jesus will receive and the cost of discipleship that even Mary will bear. In Luke, we find the earliest portrayal of Mary as a model of discipleship. Additionally, Anna echoes the position of Simeon, since she has waited on God's anointed too. Anna rounds out Luke's depiction of the male and female pairs of pious and "upright" Palestinian Jews at the time of Jesus' birth: Elizabeth-Zechariah, Mary-Joseph, and now Anna-Simeon.

The story of the boy Jesus in the Temple (2:41–52) is unique in the New Testament, though the *Infancy Gospel of Thomas*, a non-canonical or apocryphal source, provides an interesting if late parallel to the biblical text. The genre attests to the tendency among early Christians to speculate about the powers of Jesus, on display so powerfully during his public ministry. In Luke, Jesus and his family fit the model for the pious and observant people of the land, reinforcing one of the many important themes Luke develops in the infancy narrative and throughout his Gospel.

Ministry in Galilee (Luke 3:1—9:50)

As Luke begins this first major section of his Gospel, he provides a secondary historical introduction focused on how the start of Jesus' ministry inaugurates a new age. Luke offers a multifaceted scheme with which to pinpoint the turning of the age: he identifies the reigning emperor, royal figures (i.e., the tetrarchs or minor client-kings of the region), governor, and high priest at the time that Jesus began his ministry (3:1–2). Luke reiterates his concern for history, avoiding any distinction between secular history and salvation history. It follows, then, that in this section Luke focuses his attention on defining the character of Jesus' mission through his instruction (especially the synagogue scene in chapter 4 and the Sermon on the Plain in chapter 6). Luke establishes Jesus' identity in relation to that mission through, among other things, presenting the miraculous works of Jesus (mostly taken from Mark).

At the outset of Jesus' Galilean ministry, one finds many familiar Markan passages, especially the series of exorcisms and healings in Luke 4:31–44. In 5:1–11, Luke has reordered the Markan narrative and placed the miraculous catch of fish, a story unique to Luke, alongside the healing

---

PASSAGE IN FOCUS: THE REJECTION OF JESUS AT NAZARETH (LUKE 4:16–30)

The scene in the Nazareth synagogue provides Luke with an episode that sets the tone for the entire ministry of Jesus, but especially for its Galilean phase. The basic scene in Luke 4:16–30 is taken from Mark, but Luke also adds substantially to Mark to bring the story in line with his portrayal of Christ (though some suggest that the parallels with Mark are so slight that the Lukan story must come from some other source). The passage unfolds in seven segments of uneven length.

I. Setting (4:16)

II. Reading the Isaiah Scroll (4:17–20)

III. Jesus' Pronouncement (4:21)

IV. Reaction I: Approval (4:22)

V. Jesus' Provocation (4:23–27)

VI. Reaction II: Hostility (4:28–29)

VII. Departure (4:30)

The entire episode revolves around the dual reaction of the synagogue assembly based on Jesus' reading of the material from Isaiah (4:18–19). While some see a schism motif present, the passage clearly develops the theme of Gentile outreach. Jesus arrives in his hometown and is welcomed in the synagogue by his neighbors; however, Jesus recognizes the superficiality of their welcome and provokes those who are initially well disposed to him.

continued

THE REJECTION OF JESUS AT NAZARETH *continued*

The initial movement in the passage presents Jesus as a pious Jew, coming to the synagogue in his hometown "according to his custom" (4:16). He takes the scroll as part of the service (all Jewish men were allowed to read in the synagogue service), and reads a passage from Isaiah—a conflation of LXX Isaiah 61:1–2 and 58:6, passages associated with the Jubilee (see Leviticus 25:8–17, 29–31) and with messianic expectation (particularly evident at Qumran, e.g., 1QH 18.14; see also 11QMelch 18 for an interesting parallel to the use of Isaiah 61:1 and 52:7). The Isaiah passage offers the practices associated with the Jubilee year as a paradigm for understanding the messianic age. As Jesus pronounces the fulfillment of the messianic prophecies in verse 21, the initial reaction of those present revolves around the interpretation (not just the translation) of the verb *martyreō* ("to give witness") with the dative *autō* ("to him"). Although the dative in Greek functions basically as the indirect object in a sentence, the dative can also carry a variety of additional meanings and nuances. One such meaning is called "the dative of advantage"; in other words, an over-translation of the passage might be something like: "they gave witness to his advantage." Additionally, the verb *thaumazō* ("to wonder") can express either admiration or opposition, but with the positive interpretation of the previous words, translators will render the word as "amazement" with the connotation of admiration. In the end, interpreters see the initial reaction of the onlookers as unambiguously positive.

Jesus' subsequent provocation seems remarkable at first glance, but the major themes of the Gospel having already been established (e.g., the offer of salvation to all), the provocation lays bare the resistance to Jesus' call to conversion and faith. The first part of the provocation has an interesting if elusive provenance. There are examples from early Jewish midrashim for the maxim, "Physician heal thyself" (*Genesis Rabbah* 23:4), but there are secular parallels as well, including Euripides (*Fragment* 1086). All of this material seems to be the result of Luke fleshing out the story in more vivid detail (perhaps using special source material) to fill out the Markan narrative of rejection (Mark 6:1—6). It becomes for Luke, however, the occasion to draw on the stories of Elijah and Elisha in 1 and 2 Kings.

Elijah and Elisha are figures often associated with messianic expectations, particularly Elijah. Both prophets come from the northern kingdom of Israel (the region of Galilee would have been part of that ancient kingdom) and had careers of healing, exorcism, and raising the dead. The ministry of Jesus strongly resonates with each of these prophets, particularly that they both extended the offer of God's grace beyond Israel. Indeed, this offer of grace beyond the covenant stood out as a sign of judgment against the infidelity of Israel. Similarly, Jesus contends that his own ministry, which calls for repentance and conversion, will meet with rejection among his own people, and the offer of salvation will thus be extended to the Gentiles. His remarks provoke a hostile response from those assembled, who resent being compared to the wicked Israelites at the time of Elijah and Elisha. The Jubilee, the time of favor, is contingent upon real repentance and faith; it comes at a cost. The refusal to accept that cost—the refusal to accept the demands of Jesus' proclamation—precipitates the murderous hostility of the crowd. The teaching of Jesus will meet with some success, but even more rejection. The rejection of his own townspeople causes Jesus to move on to strangers, and it foreshadows the inclusion of still more distant strangers (Samaritans and Gentiles) in Acts.

of Simon's mother-in-law. This provides a basis for the immediate response of the first disciples. Luke's concern to tell the story more effectively than Mark finds confirmation here. Next comes the healing of a leper (5:12–16), followed by a series of five controversies with the Pharisees (5:17—6:11), most of which are familiar from the Markan narrative (see Mark 2:1—3:6), yet at the end, the Herodians are omitted from the group plotting to kill Jesus, probably because such a reference would have been meaningless to Luke's readers.

In 6:12–49, the reader finds an account of the positive reception of Jesus' message. The selection of the Twelve and the subsequent series of healings precedes the Sermon on the Plain (6:20–49), Luke's parallel to Matthew's Sermon on the Mount. Here, the entire sermon is directed to all of Jesus' disciples, not just the Twelve. Yet, like Matthew, Luke's sermon covers a lot of ground. It begins with a series of benedictions or Beatitudes followed by four woes (6:20–26), which help to punctuate Jesus' message through a forecast of eschatological reversal. Unlike Matthew, Luke's benedictions pair what seem clashing or opposing ideas, further developing Luke's characteristic emphasis on eschatological reversal: those who are vulnerable will be made secure in God's plan of salvation. Generosity in relationships characterizes the material following the Beatitudes, with the command to "love your enemies" and to return blessings to those who utter curses (6:27–36). Moreover, the disciples are also called upon to imitate God's mercy in their dealings with one another and with those who are outside the community of believers (6:37–42). They are to understand that any limits or boundaries placed on mercy are imposed by human beings, not God.[8] The sermon concludes with an emphasis on integrity and consistency: word and deed, intention and action, must flow together in the life of the disciples; there is no patience for religious

grandstanding or ostentatious piety, but rather care, concern, mercy, and outreach mark the one who is good (6:43–49).

A series of Markan stories that recount healing, exorcism, and even a few parables provide the context for the initial response to Jesus' ministry and his identity. These responses span a considerable range from various characters in the narrative. The two miracle passages, the Q passage involving the cure of the centurion's slave (7:1–10, foreshadowing the Gentile mission), and the L passage of the widow of Nain's son (7:11–17), all connect Jesus to the careers of Elisha and Elijah (see the parallels in 2 Kings 5:1–27 and 1 Kings 17:7–24 respectively). The Old Testament figures of Elisha and Elijah, first evoked in chapter 4 in the synagogue in Galilee, now provide a typology, or model, which Luke proceeds to develop. Another compelling Lukan passage finds a penitent woman approach Jesus in the house of Simon the Pharisee. She is offered as a model of faith and penance in contrast to the thin hospitality of Simon (7:36–50). The passage, while enjoying a few similarities with the anointing at Bethany recounted in the other Gospels (see Matthew 26:6–13; Mark 14:3–9; John 12:1–8), is distinctly Lukan and highlights the themes of God's hospitality and generosity as well as Luke's soteriology of repentance and forgiveness.

At 8:4–56, following an interesting description of Jesus as an itinerant supported by the resources of various women (Luke 8:1–3), Luke rejoins the Markan narrative with a presentation of familiar material such as the parable of the Sower, the calming of the storm, and the Gerasene demoniac. The material functions in Luke similar to the way it functions in Mark: it highlights the power and identity of Jesus. The climactic scene in which Simon Peter identifies Jesus as the Messiah precedes the instruction on the necessity of Jesus' suffering and the suffering of the disciples (9:18–50). Yet, unlike both Mark and Matthew, Luke fails to recount Simon

Peter's protest or Jesus' rebuke. The teaching on suffering seems much less controversial for Luke, and his way of framing Jesus' injunction to "take up" the cross includes the word "daily" (9:23), thus spiritualizing the suffering of discipleship (though with a clear sense that martyrdom is also a likely outcome). Having used both Markan material and his own sources, Luke has firmly established the identity of Jesus and the content of Jesus' instruction. Luke has thus set the stage for the major interpolation of special material, which comprises the travel narrative and the central portion of Luke's Gospel.

The Travel Narrative (Luke 9:51—19:27)

The travel narrative in Luke represents a major departure from the Markan narrative and serves to indicate Luke's unique theological interests. Although many commentators have noted the importance of the travel narrative, Joel Green has identified at least five needs that this narrative satisfies for Luke:[9]

1. The travel narrative carries forward and further develops themes related to the coming of salvation to all peoples, themes articulated in the first two sections of the Gospel.

2. The expectation that Jesus will cause division (see Luke, chapters 2 and 4) is further confirmed and developed.

3. The division Jesus causes also foreshadows Luke's portrait of Jesus as one who will be rejected and suffer.

4. As the failures of the disciples become more apparent, so too does the need for instruction and formation.

5. Resonance with the Exodus narrative helps to identify more firmly the true family of Jesus (i.e., those who hear and put into practice his teaching). Like Moses, Jesus gives the

people instruction; some follow his teaching, while others reject it.

Even in the opening verse of the travel narrative, readers can find indicators of the purpose behind Luke's great interpolation; it begins with the acknowledgment that the time had arrived for Jesus to be "taken up," and therefore Jesus "resolutely determined" (literally "set his face") to journey to Jerusalem (9:51). The language of being "taken up" echoes the biblical and postbiblical traditions of the assumption of both Elijah and Moses, the two most important prophetic figures for understanding Jesus' ministry in Luke.[10] Both figures were remembered as having been assumed into the heavenly realm upon the completion of their prophetic missions, and both faced strong opposition to their work (see 2 Kings 2:11 and the pseudepigraphal *Assumption of Moses*). The Mosaic theme of journey and exodus finds a strong echo in Luke's travel narrative. Like the people of Israel in the journey from Egypt to the promised land, the disciples require a period of formation and instruction prior to Jesus' exodus to the Father. Moreover, Jesus' recognition that he faces strong opposition makes the journey to Jerusalem foreboding, since it anticipates the conflict and suffering that will unfold at the journey's end.

In the travel narrative, readers will find some of the most beloved and familiar passages in Luke's Gospel: the parable of the Good Samaritan (10:29–37), the parable of the Prodigal (or Lost) Son (15:11–32), and the parable of the Rich Man and Lazarus (16:19–31). These parables, like most of the travel narrative, highlight the Lukan theme of open and radical hospitality; the salvation God offers in the ministry of Christ transcends all human boundaries. The development of these themes in Jesus' ministry will provide the basis for much of the opposition Jesus faces, as readers have seen from the outset of Luke's narrative (see Luke 4:16–30).

ALTERNATIVE APPROACHES TO SCRIPTURE: AUGUSTINE AND THE GOOD SAMARITAN (LUKE 10:29–37)

One of the most beloved parables from Luke's Gospel is, in some sense, not really a parable at all. Rather, Rudolf Bultmann and other form critics contend that this story is actually an example story because the literary setting in which Jesus delivers it involves a response to a question from an expert in the Torah.[11] When Jesus identifies the greatest commandments as love of God and love of neighbor, his interlocutor inquires about the identity of one's neighbor. The story serves as Jesus' response: the neighbor is anyone in need regardless of circumstance or identity. The identity of the hero of Jesus' story helps drive home this point, for Samaritans and Jews were long-standing enemies who avoided one another as a matter of religious obligation. Virtually all contemporary scholars express these basic points, yet such unanimity reflects modern exegetical sensibilities. In the early Christian church and throughout the Middle Ages, allegorical interpretation dominated, and in the case of the Good Samaritan, the interpretation attributed to Augustine, in particular, held sway. Readers should note that Augustine inherited much of his interpretation from Ambrose, Cyril, and Origen, thus making it ancient, as early as the second century. Although many contemporary exegetes dismiss his approach as far-fetched, it also has its supporters as the kind of rich and instructive exegesis lacking today.[12]

For Augustine, the interpreter of Scripture requires faith to discern the spiritual sense of any passage, and in faith, the story of the Good Samaritan stands as an epitome of the economy of salvation. As an allegory, each element in the literal story (i.e., the story as it is narrated by Luke through the character Jesus) has a corresponding element within another story beyond or outside the literal story. For Augustine, the allegory falls out this way:[13]

LUKE'S NARRATIVE	ALLEGORICAL INTERPRETATION
The traveler	Adam (or humanity in general)
Jericho	The world (but also immortality)
Jerusalem	The heavenly city
The robbers	The devil and his angels
The wounds suffered at the hands of the robbers	The effects of sin
The Priest and the Levite	The Old Testament
The Samaritan	Jesus Christ
Oil and wine	Baptism and the other sacraments
The Samaritan's beast (animal)	The flesh of Christ
The inn	The church
The innkeeper	The apostle(s) (sometimes just Paul) or each Christian
Two denarii (silver coins)	Commandments: Love of God and love of neighbor
The Samaritan's return and settling of debts	The Parousia and judgment

continued

AUGUSTINE AND THE GOOD SAMARITAN *continued*

While this interpretation transgresses the limits of contemporary exegesis, many scholars think Augustine's interpretation bears a closer look. After all, Augustine's principles of interpretation emphasize two important points theologians recognize: (1) the end or goal of biblical interpretation must be practice, and (2) the author's intention is important but not absolute (*Christian Instruction*, 3.27.38). Augustine's approach to the story of the Good Samaritan emphasizes the manner in which the model of Christ provides Christians with the paradigm for imitation. Additionally, while Augustine's approach moves beyond the confines of historical-critical interpretation, it nonetheless provides a compelling testament to the power of the Gospel to sustain multiple meanings at the same time.

Chapter 13 includes some of the most intriguing and sophisticated passages in Luke. In 13:1–9, Jesus addresses the problem of evil: evil that is man-made, and evil that is arbitrary or random. In one case, the Roman governor Pontius Pilate had massacred a group of Galilean pilgrims, and Jesus questions those who would suggest that they were somehow more evil or culpable than those who were spared. The second example refers to the collapse of a tower in Siloam where eighteen people were killed. Such random events often act as a catalyst for religious sensibilities to run wild: people assumed that God must have been punishing them for their offenses. Jesus uses both events as warnings not to make judgments about others but to recognize that time is short and one must seize the moment and repent now. The theme of repentance permeates this part of the travel narrative with an emphasis on overcoming obstacles like wealth and other attachments. In other words, the difficulties one experiences in embracing repentance come not from God's demands but human attachments, as illustrated in the parables of the Narrow Door (13:22–30) and the Great Feast (14:15–24).

Luke utilizes the Q passage on the parable of the Lost Sheep as the first of three parables of loss in chapter 15. The three parables each play on something strange in the parabolic narrative (see C. H. Dodd's definition of a parable in chapter 2): What shepherd leaves the flock? Who would invite guests to celebrate the recovery of a lost coin? What father would throw a party to celebrate the return of a younger son who had only a short time earlier wished that his father were dead? The parables of the Lost Sheep and the Lost Coin are collected here to set off the story of the Lost Son and his brother. They highlight the threefold teaching on the incongruity between the limits of human forgiveness and God's unbounded forgiveness and hospitality.

Although the Christian church has traditionally named the third story "The Prodigal Son," that title does not really capture the heart of the parable, which centers more on the older brother and his relationship to his father. Brendan Byrne has suggested that the title "The Lost Son and Brother" better captures what is at stake in the passage.[14] As the story unfolds, the younger son asks for his "share" of his father's estate so that he can go out and live on his own. While such a request might serve as the prelude to a modern story about a young man's journey of self-discovery and independence, in the ancient world such a request was tantamount to telling your father that you wished he were dead. By asking for his share of his father's estate (the Greek word *bios* means "life" and property, reflecting the seriousness of the son's request), the younger son expressed that he felt burdened by being under the authority of both his father and his older brother. After irresponsible living impoverishes the younger son, he returns home. This return, however, is not occasioned by repentance or contrition; rather, it is because he is hungry (Luke 16:17–18). The father, a man of great honor and wealth, waits for his son's return and goes out to meet him. In the first-century Mediterranean world, a man of high honor and social standing would not "go out" to greet a son in the manner described. Yet, the father flouts all social custom and embraces his less than perfectly contrite son and honors him, much to the dismay of the older son.

The reaction of the older son then becomes the focus of the last part of the story. The older son's reaction links the text back into the narrative context of parable in which the scribes and Pharisees have raised questions about Jesus' association with public sinners (Luke 15:1–2), and these three parables of loss have been directed to them. The refusal of the older brother to celebrate the return of the younger son seems, on the face of it, a reasonable response. Yet, Luke's theme of unlimited hospitality raises the stakes here: (1) the inheritance both sons stand to gain is not theirs by right but by gift (see Numbers 27:8–11; 36:7–9); (2) the father's celebration of the younger son costs the older son nothing, and so his refusal to celebrate stands out as an indictment of the older son (and the scribes and Pharisees). [15] Recalling the profound giftedness of God's salvation then becomes central, and attitudes of entitlement and resentment stand out as fundamentally inappropriate.

Chapter 16 develops the theme of wealth and the dangers it represents for the possibility of conversion and salvation. Included in this section of the travel narrative are the fascinating example of the Dishonest Steward (Luke 16:1–13) and the story of Lazarus and the Rich Man (Luke 16:19–31). Both stories deal with the danger of wealth from different perspectives. In the story of the dishonest steward, the manager writes off his share of the debts his master's creditors owe. In so doing, he forsakes his own profit to secure the goodwill of his master's creditors upon his impending termination. The moral of the story centers on the creative manner in which the manager acts—securing his future in the face of the loss of transitory wealth. [16]

In the story of Lazarus, wealth becomes a blinding obstacle and creates division and impediments to God's universal offer of salvation and unbounded hospitality. In Luke, the crossing of boundaries stands out as a major theme connected to conversion and salvation, and the refusal of the rich man to cross the boundary of wealth that separates him from Lazarus proves to be the rich man's doom, providing a powerful summons to traverse boundaries while there is still time.

The end of the travel narrative focuses on the demands of discipleship and the ongoing challenge of Christian living. Although Luke provides many glimpses and moments of eschatological anticipation, he does not seem to expect an imminent *eschaton* and judgment. The instruction of Jesus to his disciples and to the crowds along the way to Jerusalem sets the stage for Jesus' confrontation with the authorities in the city. In the Roman trial before Pilate, the religious leaders of Jerusalem will accuse Jesus of "misleading" or "perverting" the people (*diastrephō*, 23:2), a charge which may be a play on the word for "conversion" throughout the Septuagint (*epistrephō*). Over the entire travel narrative, Jesus has spelled out the challenge conversion represents for the social and religious order. The travel narrative thus presents the core

SCRIPTURE IN DETAIL: LAZARUS AND DIVES (LUKE 16:19–31)

The structure of the parable of the Rich Man and Lazarus has captured the imagination of the western world for the better part of two millennia. The rich man and the poor Lazarus stand out as a chilling example of the consequences of human actions and how the theme of eschatological reversal, prevalent throughout Luke, really has teeth.

Most scholars point out that the passage in Luke has two subsections, with a break between verses 21 and 22. The scene in 16:19–21 unfolds around the house of Dives, where Lazarus is found outside, longing for the scraps from Dives's table but getting nothing. In verse 22, both men die and the reversal begins to unfold. In death, Dives longs for water to which Lazarus, resting in the bosom of Abraham, has access. A chasm separates the two men and prevents Lazarus from crossing over. It illustrates the tremendous consequences of attachment to wealth and the corresponding disregard for the poor and suffering.

A. Dives is blessed in this life (16:19)

   B. Lazarus suffers in this life (16:20–21)

   B[1]. Lazarus is blessed in the afterlife (16:22)

A[1]. Dives suffers in the afterlife (16:23–24)

Wim Weren argues, however, that the parable does not center on the reversal of fortunes; rather, movement governs the structure of the parable.[17] For Weren, the parable revolves around what he calls "gates" and "the gulf" ("door" and "chasm" in NAB, respectively). In the first half of the parable, Dives excludes Lazarus from the table, even though nothing prevents them from being together. The suffering of Lazarus may indeed find relief at the table of Dives, if only Dives would pass through the "gate" and invite Lazarus to share the bounty. In the second part of the parable, when both men have moved to the abode of the dead, a great gulf now separates the two. Abraham tells Dives that Lazarus is unable to pass over to the side where Dives is tormented. The second request from Dives reflects his despair at his own situation, but hope for his brothers who are still living. He asks Abraham to entrust Lazarus with another task, to instruct his brothers about his fate. Abraham denies Dives again, this time out of a sense of pessimism: Abraham claims that the prophets and Moses are enough for the living, even though Dives disagrees, pleading his case that if one was to return from the abode of the dead, then the living would believe.

The hearer of the parable is left with an open ending, and Weren suggests that several points are made in the story. First, the possibility of movement governs the first part of the parable (16:19–21). Dives and Lazarus can still cross the gated boundary between them. The fact that this gate is never crossed, that no one passes through to the other side, says a lot about Dives and the reality he created for Lazarus. Dives can cross, but he has no desire to do so. In death the situation is reversed. But now, in this reversal, an impassable gulf separates the two men (16:26); movement is desired but no longer possible. Dives suggests that if one were to cross from death into life, then this person would have the capacity to alert people, to warn them, and the warning would take the following form: do not make earth a "living hell"; instead, cross over, pass through the gate while it is still possible.

- Movement for Dives is possible but not pursued
- Movement from life to death for both men
- Movement for both is impossible though pursued by Dives
- Movement from death to life as a proposed solution; rejected as ineffective

continued

LAZARUS AND DIVES *continued*

The story ends with the skepticism of Abraham, but Luke's Christian audience understands that Jesus has crossed over; he has passed from death into life. Jesus' words, then, ought to carry the requisite credibility. Alas, those who did not listen to Moses and the prophets are not inclined to listen to Jesus. The parable, however, leaves the hearer wondering about the statement of Abraham, whether or not the gate will be crossed. The entire Gospel of Luke has focused on the necessity of outreach and identification with the poor and the marginalized, but does the command of Jesus enjoy the credibility Dives thinks it will have?

---

of his ministry as the grounds for Jesus' execution, thereby connecting Jesus' death to the non-sacrificial, non-cultic soteriology articulated in Luke, reinforcing Jesus' suffering as a necessity in terms of the outcome related to the refusal of many to embrace the demands of conversion. Yet, as in each of the Synoptic Gospels, time is short in the sense that the hour of deliverance is at hand for those who choose to respond in conversion and faith.

Jerusalem, Passion, and Resurrection (Luke 19:28—24:53)

Although the narrative rejoins its Markan source, Luke's account of the Jerusalem ministry of Jesus and the events surrounding the passion are grounded in the travel narrative and the themes articulated there. The offer of salvation, uniquely privileging those who are on the margins of society (and therefore uniquely enabled to receive and enact it with joy), provokes those in power. Those invested in the religious, political, and social status quo evince blindness and a hardness of heart that sets them in opposition to Christ and his ministry. Their hardness has already set the wheels in motion for Jesus' execution, but with his arrival in Jerusalem, the plans to destroy Jesus find the opportunity for fulfillment, and, paradoxically, the fulfillment of Jesus' saving vocation.

The eschatological discourse, which is common to all three Synoptic Gospels, is once again occasioned by the remarks of the disciples as they wonder at the splendor of the Jerusalem Temple. Yet, unlike the other evangelists, Luke situates the discourse in the Temple itself. Several features of the discourse are unique to Luke, including the following:

- persecution because of the name "Jesus" (21:12)

- promise of [divine] wisdom that cannot be contradicted by opposing testimony in court (21:13–15)

- confidence for believers: "not a hair on your head" will perish (21:18)

- Jerusalem will be surrounded, indicating the manner in which Jerusalem was destroyed in 70 CE (21:20)

- a long period of time presupposed between Jerusalem's destruction and the end (21:24)

In Luke's eschatological discourse, as in all apocalyptic literature, the reassurance and consolation of the contemporary community (i.e., Luke's audience in the late first century) provide the main purpose for the material. At the same time, many of the events narrated are after the event; the prophecy has already been vindicated in the events that have taken place between the time of Jesus and the writing of the Gospel. These events thus also provide a typology for the future day of judgment. In sum, the discourse reiterates the injunction to stay vigilant and to avoid attachments to the things of this world (21:34–36).

The passion narrative in Luke stands in a strange position in relation to Mark and Matthew on the one hand and John on the other. Luke clearly depends on Mark for the basic framework of his narrative, and he follows his source in most respects. Yet, at several points in the narrative, Luke moves away from his Markan source and seems to strike a resonant chord with the passion account in the Fourth Gospel. Here are a few items that differentiate Luke from Mark and align the former more with John's account of Jesus' passion (though not in the details):

- Jesus is in control; in freedom he hands himself over to his executioners
- Jesus heals the ear of one member of the cohort who comes to arrest him and offers forgiveness to one of the criminals
- An overwhelming love permeates Jesus in the passion account, and this love is at the heart of the soteriology presented throughout the rest of the narrative

As the passion unfolds, readers would do well to note the subtle but substantial differences in the Lukan account over and against Mark and Matthew.

THE WORDS OF INSTITUTION AT THE LAST SUPPER

MATTHEW 26: 26–28	MARK 14:22–24	LUKE 22:19–20	1 CORINTHIANS 11:23–25
While they were eating, Jesus took bread, said the blessing, broke it, and giving it to his disciples said, "Take and eat; this is my body." Then he took a cup, gave thanks, and gave it to them, saying, "Drink from it, all of you, for this is my blood of the covenant, which will be shed on behalf of many for the forgiveness of sins."	While they were eating, he took bread, said the blessing, broke it, and gave it to them, and said, "Take it; this is my body." Then he took a cup, gave thanks, and gave it to them, and they all drank from it. He said to them, "This is my blood of the covenant, which will be shed for many."	Then he took the bread, said the blessing, broke it, and gave it to them, saying, "This is my body, which will be given for you; do this in memory of me." And likewise the cup after they had eaten, saying, "This cup is the new covenant in my blood, which will be shed for you."	The Lord Jesus, on the night he was handed over, took bread, and, after he had given thanks, broke it and said, "This is my body that is for you. Do this in remembrance of me." In the same way also the cup, after supper, saying, "This cup is the new covenant in my blood. Do this, as often as you drink it, in remembrance of me."

In Luke, the Last Supper (22:7–38) is longer than in either Mark or Matthew. Luke's version emphasizes the earnest desire of Jesus to share this meal with his disciples, signifying not only the deep import of the moment in his ministry but also recapitulating both the fellowship he enjoys with his friends and the emphasis on hospitality so prevalent in his message. Luke adds a clause in 22:16 and 18 (see also Matthew 26:29), asserting that Jesus will not eat or drink again until he does so in the kingdom, and this addition enhances the eschatological tone of the entire meal.

Luke's account of the trial of Jesus is unique for several reasons. First, Luke goes out of his way to assert the political nature of the charges against Jesus. The political aspect is emphasized in the trial before the high priest, the inquest with Herod Antipas (the tetrarch of Galilee), and in the trial before Pilate. Luke also asserts the unanimous recognition of Jesus' innocence. In Luke's narration of the trials or inquests, the legal and historical questions surrounding the Gospel depictions of the proceedings involving Jesus are notorious among scholars of the New Testament. The major figures all seem to be impressed with Jesus' innocence (Pilate declares him innocent three times: 23:4, 14, 22), yet they nonetheless find no reason to release or exonerate him. The persistence of the chief priests, scribes, and the people (a three-tiered description representing all Israel) in compelling Pilate to crucify Jesus distinctively marks Luke's narrative.

Luke's account of the release of Barabbas stands out as a strange episode, particularly given that many ancient manuscripts omit 23:17 with its mention of the supposed festal custom of releasing a prisoner. If verse 17 is a scribal addition, attempting to assimilate or harmonize Luke with the other three Gospel accounts, then Luke would stand out as the only Gospel without the mention of this supposed custom (many scholars claim that there is no evidence for such a custom). Pilate's release of the insurrectionist and murderer, while crucifying the innocent Jesus, would then seem all the more bizarre and heinous.

The mockery of Jesus during his crucifixion comes to a climax when those who are crucified with him join in with onlookers in insulting Jesus. However, the two thieves who revile Jesus in both Matthew and Mark are divided in Luke, with one reviling Jesus and the other expressing penance (23:39–43). The story of the penitent thief in Luke's account of the crucifixion supplies yet another instance of Luke's emphasis on Jesus' outreach to those most vulnerable in society. After all, being nailed to a cross is perhaps the height of vulnerability. The penitent thief, who in the midst of almost universal mockery sees the truth of Jesus, receives the assurance that "today" he will find salvation and be with Christ in paradise (23:43).

The Resurrection narrative in Luke includes the intriguing episode of the two disciples on the road to the town of Emmaus just outside Jerusalem (24:13–35). This Lukan masterpiece recapitulates the themes developed throughout the Gospel.

- The opening exchange centers on the events that have taken place in and around Jerusalem (recall Luke's emphasis on history and the events that have unfolded through God's saving work).

- Readers learn that the Old Testament (i.e., the Scriptures) becomes the center of discussion among the three travelers, and that Jesus supplies the authoritative interpretation of the prophecies as they articulate the hopes of Israel in the context of the covenant.

- The culmination of the Emmaus episode involves open and even dangerous hospitality as the two disciples press the strange traveler to stay with them.

- Only when they engage in this open hospitality in the breaking of the bread (note the eucharistic imagery) is the truth of the situation fully manifested.

The Emmaus story, along with the vividness of narration and the plot tension it develops (i.e., the failure to recognize Jesus), brings together so many important themes in Luke that it stands on its own as a Gospel in miniature.

TEXTUAL CRITICISM IN LUKE'S PASSION NARRATIVE (LUKE 22:43–44 AND 23:34)

In Luke's passion narrative, readers encounter one of the most famous verses in the Gospel. Although there are several issues in the text of Luke's passion narrative, including questions about 23:17 and the Passover custom of releasing a prisoner, two passages in particular pose significant questions for textual critics and also hold significance for the Christian tradition.

First, in the Garden of Gethsemane, Jesus prays prior to his arrest. In Luke 22:43–44, readers find the following account: "And to strengthen him an angel from heaven appeared to him. He was in such agony and he prayed so fervently that his sweat became like drops of blood falling on the ground." The image of the angel comforting Jesus in his agony has inspired artists and writers in recent centuries, and it helps to round out a sympathetic and human portrait of Christ. Yet these verses are absent from some of the oldest copies of Luke: two papyrus manuscripts, P60 and P5, and some important uncial manuscripts (e.g., Codex Vaticanus [B], Codex Alexandrinus [A], and the "Freer Gospels" [W]). Its inclusion in other important manuscripts (e.g., Codex Sinaiticus [Д], Codex Bazae [D], and Codex Coridathianus [Θ]) complicates any judgment based solely on manuscript evidence. Although Joseph Fitzmyer cites the widespread evidence of its omission in the Lukan textual tradition, and the fact that these verses are unique in the Synoptic Gospels, as evidence against the originality of the verses, Joel Green and others suggest that the verses stand in remarkable continuity with Luke's theology and narrative propensities.[18] Among the arguments made in favor of the originality of the verses, three points appear with consistency: (1) the vocabulary is consistent with the rest of Luke's Gospel, (2) Luke emphasizes the role of angels in his narrative (see Luke, chapters 1 and 2), and (3) Luke often signals physical manifestations of various emotional or spiritual events (e.g., Luke 1:20; 3:22).

Another textual problem is found in the crucifixion scene in 23:34. In the moment of his crucifixion, Jesus cries out in prayer, "Father, forgive them, they know not what they do." The prayer has found a prominent place in the life of Christians and attests wonderfully to the demands of forgiveness even in the face of cruel injustice. Yet the verse is not an original part of Luke's Gospel. Rather it appears to have been added by a scribe centuries after the Gospel's composition. The evidence for this judgment rests in the manuscripts: a papyrus manuscript called P75, the oldest complete copy of Luke (c. 200 CE), omits the verse, as do all of the earliest uncial manuscripts (i.e., Codex Vaticanus [B], Codex Sinaiticus [Д], Codex Bazae [D], Codex Coridathianus [Θ]). It appears that the verse was added after the writing of the Gospel, yet it was included in many Old Latin copies and found its way into Jerome's Vulgate, through which it was subsequently regarded as canonical, inspired, and read in worship. For most contemporary scholars, the verse bears the hallmarks of Jesus' teaching and therefore merits consideration as the kind of thing Jesus would say. Yet the question remains: Can Christians canonize a scribal addition made centuries after the text was written? Are there any limits for such a practice?

The appearance of Jesus in Jerusalem, his greeting to the disciples ("Peace be with you," 24:36), and the request for food stand remarkably close to the Resurrection narrative found in John's Gospel, with its strong apologetic interests against proto-Gnostic or Docetist strains within the church that would deny any bodily incarnation or Resurrection.[19] The entire Resurrection sequence, including Luke's account of Jesus' ascension, gains its focus from its setting in Jerusalem, the key place of departure for the missionary disciples. They are to proclaim the Gospel next in Samaria and then to ends of the earth (Acts 1:6–12). For Luke, Galilee has already served its function and there is no need for the narrative to return there as it did for both Mark and Matthew; it was the place of departure and not a destination, like Jerusalem. The ascension sets the scene for the next stage in the drama of God's saving work: the outpouring of the Spirit and the work of the church.

Conclusion

Luke stands apart from Mark and Matthew and represents an important development in the gospel tradition. The soteriology he offers as well as the social vision he projects in Jesus' teaching indelibly mark his account of the gospel and the entire Christian tradition. For Luke, salvation awaits fulfillment in the eschatological future, but it is also available here and now through conversion and the practice of boundless hospitality. This hospitality subverts the established social and religious norms, but it does not threaten or abrogate the covenant between Yahweh and Israel; rather, the covenant finds its definitive articulation and fulfillment in Christ and opens the community of salvation beyond the boundaries that had been previously delineated. Luke insists that those who are aware of their own need for conversion and their own need to be welcomed, those whose only resource is God, are the ones in whom this salvation is realized most readily and most obviously. This dynamic provides the centerpiece of Jesus' life and practice and also functions as the catalyst for the religious and political opposition to Jesus. The focus on a "preferential option for the poor," as it has come to be known in modern theology, and the promise of eschatological reversal, make Luke's account of the Gospel politically provocative. Without advancing any particular political vision, it simultaneously disturbs the complacent and reassures those who are most vulnerable.

| QUESTIONS FOR UNDERSTANDING

1. What does *interpolation* mean in the context of Luke, and what is "the great interpolation"?

2. What are the two questions Luke's Gospel appears to address? Why are these questions so important for Luke's audience?

3. How does the infancy narrative in Luke differ from the infancy narrative in Matthew? What themes does Luke's infancy narrative develop?

4. Identify three distinctively Lukan episodes from the "travel narrative" and explain how each story exemplifies a distinctly Lukan theme.

5. List and describe two distinctive features of Luke's account of Jesus' passion.

6. How does the Emmaus story recapitulate the major themes in Luke's Gospel?

QUESTIONS FOR REFLECTION

1. Luke has become a favorite Gospel for contemporary theologians who practice what is known as liberation theology, and for those who advocate for the political dimensions of the gospel. Investigate liberation theology, and try to determine why Luke (more so than Matthew, Mark, or John) is more appealing to those who see the political dimension of the gospel as central?

2. Reread the sidebar on textual criticism in Luke's passion narrative. What is at stake in the practice of textual criticism? In other words, what is the value of determining what the original manuscripts of a given biblical book said? What if contemporary textual criticism determined that a beloved piece of Scripture was the result of a scribal interpolation? Might this make a difference in the canonical status of that text? Should it?

3. Read Matthew's account of the Sermon on the Mount (Matthew, chapters 5–8) and Luke's Sermon on the Plain (Luke, chapter 6) and identify three points of contrast between the two sermons. How do these points of contrast resonate with each of the respective Gospels? Which of the sermons presents a more demanding vision of Christian discipleship? Explain.

FOR FURTHER READING

Byrne, Brendan. *The Hospitality of God: A Reading of Luke's Gospel*. Collegeville, MN: Liturgical, 2000.

Fitzmyer, Joseph A. *The Gospel According to Luke*. Anchor Bible. 2 Vols. New York: Doubleday, 1981.

Green, Joel B. *The Gospel of Luke*, New International Commentary on the New Testament. Grand Rapids, MI: Eerdmans, 1997.

ENDNOTES

1. See Stephen Finlan, *Problems with Atonement* (Collegeville, MN: Liturgical, 2005), 11–38.

2. See, e.g., I. Howard Marshall, "Luke: As Theologian," in *Anchor Bible Dictionary*, ed. D. N. Freedman (New York: Doubleday, 1992), 4:403.

3. See Joseph A. Fitzmyer, SJ, *The Gospel According to Luke*, Anchor Bible (New York: Doubleday, 1981), 1:287–299 for a discussion of the details of Luke's prologue.

4. The NAB translation deliberately leaves the word "holy" in "holy Spirit" in lowercase in an effort to signal to readers that the doctrine of the full divinity and distinct status of the Spirit in Trinitarian theology did not find clear definition until the fourth century at the First Council of Constantinople in 381.

5. See Raymond E. Brown, SS, *The Birth of the Messiah*, 2d ed., ABRL (New York: Doubleday, 1993), 248–253.

6. Gabriel is also a prominent messenger in the apocalyptic Enoch literature.

7. See the classic study by Raymond E. Brown, SS, *The Virginal Conception and Bodily Resurrection of Jesus* (New York: Paulist, 1972), 62–63.

8. See Brendan Byrne, SJ, *The Hospitality of God: A Reading of Luke's Gospel* (Collegeville, MN: Liturgical, 2000), 66–67.

9. Joel B. Green, *The Gospel of Luke*, NICNT (Grand Rapids, MI: Eerdmans, 1997), 394–399.

10. Elijah's assumption in the fiery chariot is recorded in 2 Kings 2:1–12, while the assumption of Moses is recounted in postbiblical books like *The Assumption of Moses*.

11. Rudolf Bultmann, *History of the Synoptic Tradition* (Oxford: Blackwell, 1963), 177–178.

12. See Fitzmyer, *Luke*, 2:885, and Henri de Lubac, *Catholicism: Christ and the Common Destiny of Man* (San Francisco: Ignatius, 1988), 204–205.

13. Augustine develops different aspects of the passage in several works, including his sermons (particularly *Sermon* 171).

14. See Byrne, *Hospitality*, 128–132.

15. See Michael F. Patella, *The Gospel According to Luke*, NCBC (Collegeville, MN: Liturgical, 2005), 105–107.

16. See Fitzmyer, *Luke*, 1094–1102.

17. Wim Weren, *Windows on Jesus: Methods in Gospel Exegesis* (Harrisburg, PA: Trinity, 1999), 44–49.

18. See Fitzmyer, *Luke*, 1443–1444, and Green, *Luke*, 780.

19. Gnosticism and Docetism were two heresies, the former from the second century and the latter with roots in the late first century. The origins of both were deeply rooted in the early church. Both heresies demonized material reality while denying the reality of the incarnation and the bodily Resurrection.

CHAPTER 7

THE GOSPEL ACCORDING TO JOHN

Introduction: Historical and Theological Background

The Gospel of John, or the Fourth Gospel, bears witness to a unique tradition within the earliest Christian communities, and it stands in marked contrast to the Synoptic Gospels with its multilayered narrative and extensive use of symbolism. The latter feature troubled many, who believed that the Gospel concealed secret doctrines advanced by heretical groups (John became a favorite among early Gnostics), and the Fourth Gospel came under significant suspicion in some quarters in the early centuries of the Christian church. At the same time, however, the Fourth Gospel enjoyed popularity and prestige in most Christian circles owing to the perception that the author of the Gospel was a dear friend of Jesus: the enigmatic Beloved Disciple.

JOHN AND THE SYNOPTIC GOSPELS: A SELECTIVE COMPARISON

PASSAGE	SYNOPTICS	JOHN
Prologue on the *Logos* (John, chapter 1)		X
Birth of Jesus (Matthew, chapters 1–2; Luke, chapters 1–2)	X	
Association with John the Baptist (e.g., Mark 1:2–8; John 1:24–34)	X	X
Baptism of Jesus (e.g., Mark 1:9–11 pars. [i.e., parallel passages in the Synoptic Tradition])	X	
Wedding at Cana (John 2:1–12)		X
Controversies with religious leaders (e.g., Mark 3:1–6 pars.; John 5:10–18)	X	X

continued

JOHN AND THE SYNOPTIC GOSPELS *continued*

PASSAGE	SYNOPTICS	JOHN
Cleansing the Temple (e.g., Mark 11:15–17 pars.; John 2:13–22)	X	X
Call to repentance and renunciation of possessions (e.g., Mark 1:15; 10:17–22 pars.)	X	
Exorcisms (e.g., Mark 5:1–20 pars.)	X	
Parables (e.g., Mark 4:1–9 pars.)	X	
Concern for and interaction with women (Mark 5:25–34 pars.; John 4:1–42)	X	X
Nicodemus' story (John 3:1–21)		X
Transfiguration (e.g., Mark 9:2–8 pars.)	X	
Raising Lazarus (John 11:1–36)		X
Last Supper with the disciples (Mark 14:12–31 pars.; John 13:21–38)	X	X
Washing the feet of the disciples (John 13:1–20)		X
Mockery and crucifixion of Jesus (Mark 15:16–32 pars.; John 19:1–3, 17–22)	X	X
Doubting Thomas (John 20:24–29)		X

Authorship and Lived Context

Considerable debate accompanies any attempt to describe the author of the Fourth Gospel, particularly given the frequent appearance in the narrative of the enigmatic "disciple whom [Jesus] loved" (John 13:23; 19:26; 20:2; 21:7, 20). Generally, one may discern three schools of thought on the Beloved Disciple in the Fourth Gospel:

1. The disciple whom Jesus loved is a circumlocution for an actual historical person who was either the author of, or the authoritative source behind the Fourth Gospel.

2. The author of the Fourth Gospel has created the Beloved Disciple as a literary-theological construction that symbolically represents the ideal Christian disciple.

3. The Beloved Disciple is a historical person behind the Gospel account but also a figure that has taken on a literary identity and function in the context of the Fourth Gospel.

While the Christian tradition as early as Irenaeus (second century) identified the Beloved Disciple as John, the son of Zebedee and a disciple of Jesus, contemporary scholars have raised other possibilities, including Lazarus (John 11:3) and Mary of Magdala.[1] Increasingly, however, scholars have recognized the theological-literary function of the Beloved Disciple and have generally refrained from proclaiming the identity of the historical figure behind the literary construct. Instead, the anonymity of the disciple functions as an invitation to the reader or hearer of the Gospel to self-identify with that ideal disciple. Whatever one's conclusions, one must recognize the difference between the Beloved Disciple as the inspiration behind the Gospel and the actual author(s) and editor(s) of the Fourth Gospel, for like the Synoptic Gospels, the Gospel of John evidently incorporates a variety of sources, and the final form of the Gospel was shaped by an editorial hand distinct from the author.

THE BELOVED DISCIPLE IN THE FOURTH GOSPEL

- The Beloved Disciple reclines on Jesus' chest at the Last Supper (John 13:23)
- The Beloved Disciple acts as intermediary between Peter and Jesus (John 13:24–25)
- The Beloved Disciple ushers Peter into the court of the high priest (John 18:15–16)
- The Beloved Disciple is given care of Jesus' mother (John 19:26–27)
- The Beloved Disciple testifies to the blood and water flowing from Jesus' side (John 19:34–35)
- The Beloved Disciple outruns Peter to the empty tomb and believes in the Resurrection (John 20:4–8)
- The Beloved Disciple is singled out to "remain" after the departure of Jesus, when Peter asks the resurrected Christ, "Lord, what about him?" (John 21:21–23)
- The Beloved Disciple provides the testimony behind the Fourth Gospel (John 21:24)

Although the Beloved Disciple is an endearing figure in Christian thought, one cannot help but notice the harsher side of the Fourth Gospel as well, particularly in its portrayal of Jesus' opponents: "the Jews." Readers of the Fourth Gospel have sometimes mistakenly interpreted the apparently anti-Jewish rhetoric to indicate that somehow Jesus or the early church was hostile toward all Jews. This interpretation fails to recognize that Jesus, his early followers, and a substantial portion of the early Christian community would have self-identified as Jews. Recent scholarship has established that first-century Judaism was extremely diverse and that the Gospel portrayal of Jesus' interaction with various groups within Judaism varies considerably: it is sometimes positive, sometimes tense or negative. Rather than representing the situation that existed in Jesus' time, scholars suggest that the Fourth Gospel reflects a state of turmoil or contention between Jewish Christians and non-Christian Jews at the time when the Gospel was written, turmoil that probably involved some Jewish Christians being expelled from local synagogues (somewhat similar to the situation behind Matthew's Gospel). Most scholars therefore date the Fourth Gospel to 90–100 CE, for a variety of reasons, not least of which is the growing division between Jews and Jewish Christians.

The evangelist's theological emphasis on the decisive importance of Jesus' relationship to the Father and the Gospel's correspondingly high Christology both seem to suggest that issues other than the tensions within Judaism were critical influences driving the Fourth Gospel. Some scholars have viewed John's emphasis on

THE JEWS (HOI IOUDAIOI) IN JOHN

Modern Christian anti-Semitism has its roots in perceived anti-Judaism in the pages of the New Testament in texts like Matthew 27:25 ("His blood be upon us and upon our children"), certain passages from Paul regarding his so-called Judaizing opponents, and the Gospel of John's peculiar use of *hoi Ioudaioi* (i.e., "the Jews"). The word *Ioudaios* occurs far more frequently in John than in the other Gospels (seventy-one times in the Fourth Gospel), yet its use varies considerably. John often employs the plural form (*hoi Ioudaioi*) neutrally and generically simply to identify those people, including Jesus and his followers, who share the covenant life expressed through obedience to the Torah and worship in the Temple. Additionally, John uses *hoi Ioudaioi* to identify a subgroup that opposes Jesus and his followers.

In the first sense, John consistently identifies Jesus and his disciples as part of this group. For example, Jesus and his disciples attend synagogue services and make pilgrimages to Jerusalem on the three great pilgrimage feasts in the first century, Passover, Dedication, and Booths. Moreover, in several episodes, like the story of the Samaritan woman, Jesus self-identifies as a Jew (John 4:9) and declares, "salvation is from the Jews" (John 4:22). Additionally, John makes use of the expression *hoi Ioudaioi* to identify Jews in a neutral sense when he employs expressions like "the Passover of the Jews" (John 2:13; 11:55) or "the Jewish burial custom" (John 19:40). In the Lazarus story (John 11:45), he describes those who come to console the sisters as *polloi . . . ek tōn Ioudaiōn* (i.e., "many of the Jews").

"The Jews" also designates a subgroup in opposition to Jesus and his disciples and often represents some aspect of officials from Jerusalem. The expression occurs in John 1:19 in just this sense: an embassy from Jerusalem inquires about John the Baptist and his ministry. Additionally, in John 20:19 the disciples hide in Jerusalem "for fear of the Jews." Of course, the disciples are themselves *hoi Ioudaioi* in the sense described in the previous paragraph, but the verse identifies a subgroup hostile to Jesus and his disciples. In John, chapters 7 and 8, readers find an interesting shift in the identification of Jesus' opponents; at one point John identifies them as "the chief priests and Pharisees" (7:45—8:20) while later in the same section he identifies them as "the Jews" (8:22) and tells them that their father is the devil (8:44). In his account of the trial of Jesus, John identifies those who sought the execution of Jesus as "the Jews," but in all of this conflicting data, it is perhaps best to understand the referent of *hoi Ioudaioi* as designating those religious authorities (probably mostly Sadducees and Herodians) opposed to Jesus.

As in the case of Matthew, John composed his account of the Gospel at the end of the first century and uses the term *hoi Ioudaioi* to address the contemporary audience and not to represent the times of Jesus. In other words, how John describes "the Jews" has more to do with what John and his fellow Christians were experiencing than with historical recollections about the life and ministry of Jesus. Like Matthew's community, John's community has been expelled from the synagogue and has undertaken a new identity in relationship to the emergence of normative Judaism at the close of the first century. In this context, *hoi Ioudaioi* becomes a vehicle for identifying the "other," the majority of first-century Jews who did not accept the message of Jesus and who now excluded Jewish Christians on the basis of their "otherness."

the identity of Jesus and a corresponding high Christology as evidence that the Fourth Gospel was possibly battling a growing cult of emperor worship in Asia Minor (the emperor Domitian probably instituted persecutions in this area at the end of the first century). This theory, however, has fallen into disfavor in recent years because it tended to reduce John's Christology to a mere defensive strategy rather than seeing it as a positive statement of faith. These theories about intra-Jewish tensions and emperor worship, however, do not resolve the issue of the location of the evangelist or his community. The traditional argument for the Greek city of Ephesus on the west coast of modern Turkey is plausible, though this location was popularized by the mistaken identification of the author of John's Gospel with the author of Revelation, who was exiled on the island of Patmos off the coast from Ephesus (Revelation 1:9).

Raymond Brown famously traced a hypothetical history of the community behind the Fourth Gospel and the Johannine letters as it passed through four distinct stages.[2] The first stage of the community's history involves a circle of ex-disciples of the Baptist, among whom is the enigmatic Beloved Disciple, whom Brown contends was not one of the Twelve. The Beloved Disciple links the community with the life and ministry of Jesus. In the second stage of the community's history, Samaritans and members of other anti-Temple groups begin to enter the community and exert significant influence. As the community starts to change so does its Christology. A relatively low Christology, characteristic of the early years following the life and ministry of Jesus gives way to a high Christology that emphasizes an identification of Jesus and God through the use of Wisdom or *Logos* Christology and devices like the emphatic "I AM" (*egō eimi*) statements. At this time, the community begins to compose the Fourth Gospel, which articulates an account of the Gospel distinct from other Christian communities, particularly the Christology exemplified by the Jerusalem church under the leadership of James.

In a third stage of the community's history, when the Johannine letters are written, Brown characterizes the community as increasingly insular and suffering from internal division. The letters outline the basic lines of demarcation within the community as at least two factions compete with one another to rightly interpret the tradition as it is embodied in the Fourth Gospel. On the one hand, a more conservative group begins moving in the direction of the other Christian communities and embedding their Christology and their ethics in history. This group, mostly responsible for the letters, attacks their opponents for certain tendencies today identified as proto-Gnostic: de-historicizing the gospel, and downplaying the concrete ethical obligations associated with a life of Christian discipleship. Finally, Brown sees a fourth stage in the community's history, as the warring factions are subsumed into two groups. The more conservative group is assimilated into the larger "orthodox" church (see the letters of Ignatius of Antioch, written within two decades or so of the Fourth Gospel). The other group becomes part of the Gnostic movement that begins to flourish in the early second century. Brown (as well as others) attributes the popularity of the Fourth Gospel among the Gnostics to this assimilation.

Theological Themes

As signaled in the previous section, readers of the Fourth Gospel cannot help but notice the powerful use of language (irony, misunderstanding, symbolism) and the heavy emphasis on the identity of Jesus as the one in whom God is definitely revealed. The evangelist emphasizes the intimacy between and even the identification of Jesus and God, his Father, and nowhere is this intimacy more apparent than in the opening verses of the Gospel. The hymn to the divine Word (*Logos* in Greek) in John, chapter 1, draws on the wisdom tradition that had emerged in a robust form shortly before the time of Jesus. In this tradition, at once thoroughly Jewish but also heavily influenced by Greek thought, God created and sustained the world through the Word or Wisdom. For example, the first story of creation in Genesis celebrates the creative power of God's word, and in other Old Testament texts God's word continually carries out God's will (Isaiah 55:10–11), and God's wisdom dwells with Israel as the Torah (Sirach 6:37; 24:22–23).

The hymn, and indeed the entire Fourth Gospel, identifies Jesus as the Word incarnate. In comparison to the Christology found in the Synoptic Gospels, the Christology of the Fourth Gospel gives Jesus divine status prior to his life on earth (1:1). This high Christology is further reflected in the so-called I AM statements (e.g., 8:24, 28, 58). The use of the first-person personal pronoun is rare in New Testament Greek. These I AM statements evoke the image of Yahweh in the burning bush scene found in Exodus 3:14, especially in those cases where there is no predicate (John 8:58; 13:19). With these emphatic statements Jesus, in a sense, identifies himself with Yahweh and thereby accentuates the authority behind all he says and does, even to the extent of prefixing teachings with an emphatic double *amen*, an Aramaic word that means "it is so" (John 1:51; used twenty-five times in John).

The Fourth Gospel depicts Jesus as the fulfillment or perfection of all things related to the covenant. This theme remains controversial even today, because fulfillment in John sometimes seems to include the replacement of Jewish institutions. One might well reason that if the evangelist intends to bring to fullness the central features of Judaism, then his portrayal of Jesus could mean that Judaism has thereby been made irrelevant. An example of this theme is Jesus' replacement of the heavenly manna associated with Passover. In John, chapter 6, Jesus insists that he is the true bread come down from heaven, not the manna the Israelites ate in the desert. Similarly, Jesus offers himself as the new temple in 2:19–22 and 4:20–24. Contemporary exegetes work diligently to provide an adequate interpretation of the fulfillment theme in John so that the institutions of the covenant continue to retain their significance in John even as they find their perfection in Jesus.[3] Roman Catholic readers should note Catholic Church documents on the enduring significance of God's covenant with Israel and the importance of this enduring significance when reading and interpreting Scripture.[4]

The theology of the Fourth Gospel emphasizes a provocative sacramental perspective. Of course, the term *sacrament*, much less an elaborate sacramental theology, did not exist per se in the first century. The Fourth Gospel, however, does develop the meaning of baptism and the Eucharist in the person of Christ at several key points in the narrative. For example, as was noted above, the Fourth Gospel has no narrative of the institution of the Eucharist. Rather, the meaning of the Eucharist is developed without reference to a command of Christ: (i.e., there is no instance in which Jesus says, "Take and eat; this is my body"). Yet the Fourth Gospel presents the reader with a rich understanding of the Eucharist, particularly in the Bread of Life Discourse (6:22–71) where Jesus identifies himself as "the bread that came down from heaven" (6:41). The acknowledgment of Jesus as the heavenly bread brings with it certain moral demands that are dramatically illustrated in the foot-washing at the Last Supper and clarified by Jesus' new commandment that accompanies the act: "love one another" (John 13:34). The only explicit reference to the Eucharist is the morsel of bread that Jesus gives to Judas during the meal. The meaning of the Eucharist (and, in this instance, both baptism and the apostolic authority in the

THREE CONVERSATIONS WITH WOMEN IN JOHN

The first chapter in this text briefly discussed the complex situation of women in the society of first-century Palestine. Early Jewish literature contains a number of negative characterizations of women. Take, for example, the oft-cited Mishnaic description of a woman as a "pitcher full of filth with its mouth full of blood, yet all run after her" (*Shabbat* 152a). Moreover, women were often considered intellectually inferior and not worthy of instruction in the Torah: "It is better that the words of the Law be burned, than that they should be given to a woman" (*Numbers Rabbah* 9.204). Throughout the New Testament, however, one finds numerous examples of women taking on significant roles, exercising responsibility and influence in the ministry of Jesus and in the early Christian community. In John, Jesus subverts negative social and religious stereotypes by engaging in significant interaction with three women: the Samaritan woman at the well, Martha of Bethany, and Mary of Magdala. Each of these women responds to Jesus with courage, understanding, and faith.[5]

The Samaritan Woman

In the story of the Samaritan woman, Jesus crosses both social and religious barriers (4:4–42) in his public conversation with a nonrelative and a Samaritan. The surprise of the Samaritan woman is indicative of the scene's provocative nature, and the shock of the disciples upon their return further accentuates the dramatic nature of Jesus' action. Yet the response of the woman to Jesus' teaching, the fact that she leaves her water jars and goes to tell the townspeople the news of Jesus, indicates that she acts like the other disciples who earlier had left everything to follow Jesus. The Samaritan woman then becomes a model of missionary (apostolic) activity. Moreover, John contrasts the role of the Samaritan women in relation to Nicodemus in the previous chapter. Whereas the Samaritan woman responds immediately and publically to Jesus, Nicodemus is hesitant and clandestine in his response.[6]

Martha, Sister of Lazarus

In the Lazarus episode, John portrays Martha and Mary, the sisters of Lazarus, as women of deep faith in Christ with whom Jesus has a unique relationship (Lazarus, Martha, and Mary, along with the Beloved Disciple, are described as "loved" by Jesus). The sisters have confidence in Christ, but they assumed, as Martha explicitly states, that Lazarus can only rise on the last day (John 11:24). Jesus, however, provokes Martha to recognize that her hope for resurrection is being realized in Christ, as he emphatically pronounces: "I am the resurrection and the life" (11:25). Martha's response (11:27) parallels that of Simon Peter in the synoptic tradition.[7] The early church recognized this parallel, and a tradition about her significance in the early church grew in the first centuries of the Christian era.

Mary of Magdala

John's Gospel reaches its climax in the Resurrection narrative, where the identity of Jesus finds full articulation. John presents Mary of Magdala as the decisive figure in this narrative. She arrives at the tomb of Jesus "while it was still dark" early Sunday morning and discovers the tomb empty. When she tells Simon Peter and the Beloved Disciple of her discovery (20:2), they investigate her claim. Shortly thereafter Mary encounters the risen Christ, and he instructs her to deliver the news of his Resurrection to the disciples; she complies, thus becoming "the apostle to the apostles" (Hippolytus, *Commentary on The Song of Songs* 25.6). Raymond Brown suggests that John portrays Mary Magdalene as holding a place within the tradition about women disciples analogous to that of Peter among the male disciples, that is, commissioned to proclaim the good news of Jesus' Resurrection.[8]

early church) rests in the faithful response to Jesus and the practice of loving service. It is through love that Christ abides in the believer and the believer abides in Christ.

Theologically, John's Gospel has many unique features but also significant overlap with the synoptic tradition. Certainly, Jesus calls for the response of faith and gathers disciples around him. Jesus commands his disciples to practice love of one another, to serve one another, and to forsake attachments, even attachments to this life and this world. And although in John one does not find the same emphasis on the poor and the marginalized one finds in Luke, for example, Jesus still holds women in high esteem among his disciples, and he does so in a remarkably countercultural way.

Structure and Flow

The structure of the Fourth Gospel is fairly simple. There are two main parts of the account: the Book of Signs (1:19—12:50) and the Book of Glory (13:1—20:31), with a prologue (1:1–18) and an epilogue (21:1–25) rounding out the material. In the prologue, readers find a hymn to the *Logos* or the Word. This hymn is most likely not an original composition by the author of the Fourth Gospel; rather, because the flow of the hymn itself is interrupted with editorial comments from the author or editor, it appears to be a piece of the early Christian liturgical tradition that has been incorporated into the text.

The multilayered narrative of the first major section, the Book of Signs (1:19–12:50), revolves around a series of seven signs, though many

---

A GENERAL OUTLINE OF JOHN

I. The Prologue (1:1–18)

II. The Book of Signs (1:19—12:50)

   A. Seven Days of Revelation (1:19—2:11)

   B. Replacement and Reaction (2:12—4:54)

   C. Sabbath, Passover, Booths, and Dedication (5:1—10:42)

   D. Lazarus (11:1—12:50)

III. The Book of Glory (13:1—20:31)

   A. The Last Supper and Discourse (13:1—17:26)

   B. The Passion (18:1—19:42)

   C. Resurrection and Sending of the Spirit (20:1–31)

IV. Epilogue (21:1–25)

---

scholars debate whether the actual number of signs is intentional. The signs reflect many of the same types of works found in the synoptic tradition (healing of the official's son, feeding the five thousand, walking on water), but they appear to be sourced in a uniquely Johannine tradition. In the Fourth Gospel, Jesus reveals and glorifies God through the signs, unlike the Synoptics where Jesus battles the powers of Satan in the world through exorcisms and healings. As in the Synoptics, these signs cause bystanders to react in one of several ways: some reject the signs and Jesus, while others accept Jesus because of the signs; some see God revealed in the signs, and some believe without signs. The Book of Signs does not simply revolve around these wondrous deeds; rather, it contains a variety of important material, including provocative encounters with individuals (e.g., Nicodemus, the Samaritan, Martha and Mary, and Lazarus). In addition to the striking narratives in the Book of Signs there are also important and highly symbolic

THE SEVEN SIGNS IN JOHN

1. The wedding at Cana (2:1–12)
2. Healing the royal official's son at Cana (4:46–54)
3. Healing of the sick man at Bethesda (5:1–9)
4. Multiplication of the loaves (6:1–15)
5. Walking on the water (6:16–21)
6. The man born blind (9:1–41)
7. The raising of Lazarus (11:1–44)

discourses that Jesus offers in conjunction with Jewish holy days: the Sabbath and the discourse on the authority of the Son (5:19–30); Passover and Jesus' discourse of the Bread of Life (6:22–59); the Feast of Tabernacles or Booths (7:1–13) and Jesus' discourse on the Light of the World (8:12–20).

Some scholars suggest that any reading of the Book of Signs should also include an account of the geographical movements of Jesus and how they reinforce the theological interests of the author, most especially the conviction that Jesus comes from "beyond."[9] The Book of Signs contains three cycles in which Jesus moves from a place "beyond" to another location, and eventually to Jerusalem (5:1; 7:10; 12:1). The first section (1:19–3:21) starts with a geographical marker, "This happened in Bethany across the Jordan, where John was baptizing" (1:28), and moves to Cana (2:1), Capernaum (2:12), and Jerusalem for the Passover (2:13). The theological significance of these movements revolves around Jesus coming from a place "beyond" and echoes throughout the Book of Signs. Obviously, the primary "beyond" is the Father, or heaven, the ultimate origin and destiny of Jesus. In the first section of the Book of Signs (1:19—3:21) Jesus instructs Nicodemus, "No one has gone up to heaven except the one who

has come down from heaven, the Son of Man" (3:13), and "God did not send his Son into the world to condemn the world, but that the world might be saved through him. . . . And this is the verdict, that the light came into the world, but people preferred darkness to light, because their works were evil" (3:17, 19).

The "hour" spoken of in the initial sign at Cana (2:4) refers to the moment of the Son's glorification in his death and Resurrection or exaltation. These are the events around which the Book of Glory revolves. In Mark, Jesus is handed over to be victimized by the Roman authorities and the crowds, but in the Fourth Gospel, the "hour" is appointed by God as the moment of his glorification, and Jesus is in full control of events. In John, chapters 13–18, the reader encounters a lengthy description of Jesus' last meal with his disciples, yet one does not find a formal account of Jesus, instituting the Eucharist there. Instead this passage includes the ceremony of foot-washing (13:1–20) and a lengthy sermon, often called the Farewell Discourse (13:31—16:33). In this passage, Jesus instructs his disciples to fulfill the commandment of love and promises them persecution. In the midst of their persecution they will be consoled by "another Advocate" (14:16). The Greek word for *advocate* (*paraklētos*) has a wide range of meanings, including "counselor," or "one who consoles." Jesus understands his own role as that of *paraklētos*, and the promise of "another" *paraklētos* indicates, among other things, Jesus' love for his disciples and for the world.

Throughout the passion, Jesus stands in control of all events, and even at the moment of his death on the cross, Jesus does not cry out in agony but serenely hands over his spirit to his Father. The symbolism of blood and water flowing from Jesus' side at his death (19:31–37) is often interpreted, particularly by Catholic scholars, as a reference to the sacraments of the Eucharist and baptism, the sources of life for the church. For many scholars this symbolism, along with Jesus' discourse on the Bread of Life, dramatically compensate for the lack of a narrative of eucharistic institution. The Book of Glory closes with the Resurrection of Jesus and his appearance to Mary Magdalene and the others. The epilogue in John, chapter 21, consists of an entire chapter added late in the editorial process, which narrates the rehabilitation of Peter and more material on the Beloved Disciple.

John's Account of the Gospel

John's account of the gospel and portrait of Jesus is not at odds with the synoptic tradition; it simply moves in a distinct orbit. Throughout the narrative, John portrays Jesus in control as he majestically travels through the countryside and Jerusalem. Jesus regularly indicates that his Father has given to him a task and a destiny. The narrative flows, as mentioned above, through the signs or miracles that reveal the glory of God in Christ, eliciting a level of faith from some and provoking opposition among the religious leaders. With the ultimate sign, the raising of Lazarus, the opposition is set and the hour of glorification is at hand. The second half of the Gospel centers on the instruction of Jesus to the disciples concerning the new commandment and the promise that he will abide with them even beyond his hour of glory. Throughout the narrative, the in-breaking of the kingdom of God is not at issue; rather, the issue is the identity of Jesus as sent from God, as God himself, and as the fulfillment of the Temple and the Torah. The author uses several devices to highlight these themes.

The Prologue (John 1:1–18)

The prologue to John's Gospel, which appears to be derived from an early Christian tradition, functions as a theological overture much the same way the infancy narratives function in Matthew and Luke. All the major theological themes of the Gospel are articulated in the prologue, particularly revelation, faith and unbelief, and light and darkness. Of the many scholars who have wrestled with the prologue's structure, Francis Moloney has articulated an eminently simple and helpful arrangement:[10]

1. The Word becomes the light of the world (1:1–5)
2. The incarnation of the Word (1:6–14)
3. "The only Son, God, who is at the Father's side, has revealed him" (1:15–18)

The prologue's first section highlights the themes of revelation and its connection to Christology. The first verse of the Gospel represents one of the most poignant and somewhat controversial texts in the early Christian tradition. A literal translation from the Greek reads:

1a In the beginning was the Word,

1b and the Word was with God,

1c and the Word was God.

This NAB translation remains perfectly accurate and idiomatically correct, but it does obscure the fact that, in Greek, "God" has a definite article in the second line (i.e., "the God") but not in the third. As early as the second century, the verse began to provoke exegetes to see a significant differentiation between the Word and "the" God. Although the Word is God, the word is also "with [the] God." Some early Christian writers like Origen saw not just a distinction but a differentiation between God ("the God") and the Word: the Word was understood as God, but somehow inferior or subordinate to the Father.[11]

Although Origen and others read too much into the verse, he does pick up on the central christological issue that began to emerge more pointedly at the end of the first and the beginning of the second century: What was the precise relationship between the Word or the Son and the Father ("the God")?

To make sense of the issues at stake here, it may help to recall some points from the discussion in an earlier chapter on the development of Christology in the New Testament. The prologue in John develops the insights of the Jewish wisdom tradition, which had long been wrestling with the problem of connecting the transcendent God with the vagaries of human history. The wisdom tradition emphasized the Wisdom of God as the means by which God creates and interacts with the world. The divine Word or Wisdom thus provided a means for understanding the convergence of the divine and the human in Israel's story. One important feature of Jewish wisdom traditions includes its tendency to personify Wisdom, particularly by associating the wisdom of God and the word of God. Both expressions—wisdom and word—signify the active presence of God in the world. This divine presence creates, communicates, sustains, and guides Israel. The personification of God's Word or Wisdom is apparent in texts like Psalms 33:6 and Isaiah 55:10–11.

The second section of the prologue identifies the Word as God's self-communication in the world, an idea that anchors much of the Fourth Gospel, as the theme of revelation and sonship provide the solution to the problem of sin and evil in John. In other words, the identity of Jesus in relation to the Father, the intimacy Jesus enjoys, is not attributable to a special grace or favor from God; rather, Jesus is the preexistent Word through whom all things were created. This intimacy with the Father distinguishes sonship as developed in John from the adoptive sonship of Israel or Israel's king in the Old Testament. Yet this intimacy with the Father is offered to those who have faith, who come to believe in his name; these "he gave power to become children of God" (John 1:12).

In 1:14, readers find an important verse that employs two verbs to describe the incarnation of the divine Word. Whereas in verse 1 John describes the preexistent Word and its relationship to God using the Greek verb *eimi* ("to be"), when he describes the incarnation of the Word, or the unfolding of God's plan of salvation on earth in verse 14, he employs the Greek verb *ginomai* ("to become"): "the Word *became* flesh." As the Word took on flesh (the Greek word *sarx* can encompass everything from mere meat and bones to all that it means to be human), it entered into human history and therefore "became" history. The prologue thus signals an important insight that later Christian theology will develop extensively, namely the distinction between "being" and "becoming." This distinction will facilitate greater discipline when discussing God as God exists ("is") in eternity and how human beings experience the unfolding of God's self-disclosure in history (in Trinitarian theology this distinction is articulated in the terms immanent Trinity and economic Trinity).

The second verb in 1:14 also alludes to the story of Israel: "The Word became flesh and made his dwelling among us." The Greek verb *skēnoō* ("to make a dwelling" or "to pitch a tent") relates to the word used in LXX Exodus 25:8–9 to describe the tabernacle, the tent of dwelling in which the ark of the covenant was housed (*skēnē*). Moreover, in prophetic literature, the verb is used to describe the hope or expectation that God will dwell with Israel again (see, e.g., LXX Zechariah 2:10, *kataskēnoō*). Some see in this verse a signal for a Temple theme in John. As Jesus is the incarnate Word, pitching his tent or making his dwelling with Israel, Jesus actually replaces the Temple in Jerusalem.[12]

The prologue also introduces the theme of faith (also knowledge, sight, and understanding); the world's lack of faith colors the reception of the Word in the world. When the Word comes to "his own" (1:11), he is not received, but those who do receive him, he empowers to become children of God. In the contest between faith and unbelief, light is the origin of sight, belief, and understanding. The opposite pole, darkness, represents evil, lack of understanding, and unbelief. These binaries made the Fourth Gospel susceptible to Gnostic interpretations and helped to cast doubt on its character in the second century. Yet the symbolism of the Fourth Gospel also helps to account for its power. The Light of the World, the Life of the World, the Creator and sustainer of the world has entered into the world in a profound way; the repercussions of receiving him or failing to receive him could not be more momentous.

The final section of the prologue reiterates the theme of revelation, but in a way that focuses on two, as it were, competing foci of revelation: John the Baptist and the Torah. The prologue gives explicit testimony of the Baptist, reiterated following the prologue (1:15), in which the Baptist identifies his role as a forerunner. With reference to the Torah, the prologue states that grace and truth are made manifest, made present, in Christ, and this manifestation is a gift. In the episode where Jesus encounters the Samaritan woman (John, chapter 4), Jesus identifies himself as a gift from God. Within first-century Judaism, the Torah was often called "the gift," much as it is described here (1:16–17). The perfection or fulfillment of the Torah thus occurs through the incarnate Word, Christ. Since human knowledge, the human capacity, is not sufficient to apprehend or image God, even as God's Wisdom has dwelt with Israel as the Torah, God's plan of salvation unfolds to the point of God's direct entry into the world, for the Son is always turned toward and directs others to the Father (1:18).

The Book of Signs (John 1:19—12:50)

The first part of the Book of Signs unfolds as seven days of revelation culminating in the first of the great signs in John: the miracle at Cana (2:1–11). John 1:19–28 is a synoptic-like account of John the Baptist's testimony. The author, however, pays special attention to John the Baptist's denial that he is the messiah or even Elijah (contradicting the affirmation of Jesus in the synoptic tradition). In 1:29, John the Baptist boldly identifies Jesus as "the Lamb of God, who takes away the sin of the world." "Lamb of God" can have at least three different but interrelated meanings:

- The sacrificial Passover lamb (Exodus 12:21–28)

- The apocalyptic lamb that overcomes evil (see *Testament of Joseph* 29:8)

- The Suffering Servant (Isaiah, chapter 53)

On the second day, John the Baptist, not the narrator, describes the vision of the Spirit descending on Jesus "like a dove" (1:32). The definitive character of John the Baptist's testimony removes the ambiguities inherent in the synoptic accounts of his testimony and subsequent doubts. Many scholars have suggested that this aspect of the Fourth Gospel reflects the tension in the early Christian community surrounding the continued existence of a community devoted to John the Baptist. The narrative here, then, owes itself primarily to the apologetic concerns of the Christian community.

The third day of the narrative begins in John 1:35, where Jesus once again passes by John the Baptist, who then points to Jesus and again calls out, "Behold, the Lamb of God" (1:36). The two disciples standing with John the Baptist, one of whom is the anonymous (Beloved) Disciple, immediately abandon John to follow Jesus. The

SEVEN DAYS OF REVELATION (JOHN 1:19—2:11)

The first section of the Book of Signs unfolds over seven days (suggesting a new creation) and culminates with the revelation to the disciples who came to believe in Jesus as the Messiah.[13]

Day one (1:19–28)

Day two (1:29–34)

Day three (1:35–42)

Day four (1:43–51)

"On the third day" (2:1–11)

The days climax in the story of the first sign at the wedding in Cana that begins to reveal Christ's "glory" (2:11). Francis Moloney sees parallels between the language used around the wedding scene and the description of the giving of the Law at Sinai (LXX Exodus 19:16). In the Exodus passage, and particularly in the early rabbinic interpretations of that material (see the *Mekilta on Exodus*), the glory of Yahweh is revealed to Moses and Israel "on the third day." Prior to this revelation, there are four days of remote preparation. For Moloney, the theme of the giving of the Torah at Sinai, which is Yahweh's Word, or Wisdom dwelling with Israel (see Sirach 24:1–31) and the associated revelation of Yahweh's glory, bind the material in John 1:19–2:11.

strong association between Jesus and the followers of John the Baptist in the Fourth Gospel has prompted John Meier and others to suggest that Jesus' early followers were drawn from among the followers of John the Baptist. On the fourth day (1:43), Jesus encounters Philip and Nathanael and calls them to join the band of disciples.

The theme of replacement emerges in the first of Jesus' seven signs in the Fourth Gospel: the miracle at the wedding at Cana (2:1–11). The wedding scene has eschatological dimensions, which are developed in a variety of ways throughout the Gospel. As a guest at the wedding, Jesus, the eschatological bridegroom, seems oddly out of place. The host family or those responsible for the planning would have been deeply shamed about the wine running out during a wedding celebration meant to last a week. Jesus' act of supplying wine can thus be taken as a face-saving gesture for the benefit of the embarrassed host. Yet the generosity of the action represents perhaps the most superficial aspect of the action in the context of John's Gospel. The eschatological dimensions of the wedding, Jesus' odd position as guest, and the lack of sufficient wine for the celebration, combine to move the focus of the episode from the wedding feast to the person of Jesus. The mention of six stone water jars for ritual purification provides Jesus with the opportunity to dramatically demonstrate the inadequacy of purification rituals and to signify the messianic abundance made present in him, as the number six also carries symbolic significance as an indicator of imperfection— as opposed to seven, a perfect number in the ancient world.

The exchange between Jesus and his mother strikes many readers, especially Catholics with a devotion to Mary, as disturbing (2:3–5). The relationship between the two seems strange and dismissive, yet the exchange between Mary and her son reflects basic themes in John. The "hour" of Jesus is the hour of his glory: his crucifixion and Resurrection. The relationship between Jesus and his mother will come to its fulfillment at the hour of Jesus' glory. Jesus' apparent dismissal of his mother at Cana needs to be read against the backdrop of the Fourth Gospel's approach to Mary as a symbol of the new community—the church—and not simply an individual in the story of Jesus' life. Mary's role as the mother of the new community, signified by Jesus in calling her "woman," echoes the role of Eve in Genesis, chapter 2, where Eve is also called "woman." What modern readers might see as a dismissal of Mary in verses 3–5 actually stands as a recognition of her special role. At the "hour" of Jesus' glorification, he will once again address her as "woman" in an act of tenderness, when the new community is born. This first sign in John thus points to the ultimate sign of Jesus' glorification and the sending of the Spirit that will birth the new community, which the mother of Jesus symbolizes (see John 19:25–27).

A comparison between the synoptic account of the cleansing of the Temple and the account of the same incident in the Fourth Gospel is telling (2:13–25). In the synoptic tradition, the Temple cleansing takes place during the climactic week in Jerusalem at the end of Jesus' life. Yet in the Fourth Gospel, Jesus travels regularly to Jerusalem for the major pilgrimage feasts (at least three times in John), and the Temple incident occurs early in Jesus' career. The placement of the Temple cleansing at the outset of Jesus' ministry accomplishes several things for the evangelist's portrayal of Jesus. First, by placing it here the evangelist preserves the majesty of Jesus' entry and final days in Jerusalem, leaving the tumult and the accusations about the Temple out of the arrest and trial of Jesus. Furthermore, the evangelist adeptly juxtaposes the Temple action with the other replacement episodes, thereby creating a cumulative effect early in the Book of Signs in which Jesus is presented not as an opponent of Jewish rituals and institutions, but as their fulfillment and ultimate goal. Another difference with the Synoptic accounts is that John cites Psalm 69:9 and Zechariah 14:21 in describing the event, whereas the Synoptics cite Jeremiah.

The misunderstanding that unfolds in 2:18–22 is typical of John. When "the Jews" respond to Jesus' actions in the Temple by asking for a sign that will confirm Jesus' authority for this provocation, Jesus responds with the sign of his Resurrection: "Destroy this temple and in three days I will raise it up" (2:19). The opponents of Jesus misunderstand him, thinking he refers to the Temple complex that Herod the Great had expanded during his reign. The Temple of stone will not be raised in three days, but rather the temple of Jesus' body, for that is the true dwelling of God with his people.

With the Nicodemus episode (3:1–36), the evangelist continues to explore the replacement theme—in this case the replacement of the traditional teachers of Judaism and the replacement of natural birth into the chosen people with birth in the Spirit. Nicodemus comes to Jesus at night, presumably out of fear, signifying his lack of understanding or real faith. While Nicodemus admirably demonstrates a willingness to believe, he has not arrived at an authentic or true faith. His affirmation that Jesus is a "teacher who has come from God" (3:2) falls well short of the mark established in the first verse of the Gospel; although Nicodemus is a "teacher of Israel" (3:10), he fails to comprehend. Nicodemus's misunderstanding of the Greek word *anōthen*, which can mean either "from above" or "again," animates the entire scene.

Christians have, for centuries, read this passage without realizing that the fourth evangelist here supplies readers with one of the clearest feminine images of God in the New Testament.[14] The literalism of Nicodemus regarding reentering the maternal womb allows the evangelist to draw attention to the fact that the image of birthing is precisely the image Jesus seeks to evoke by using such language. Especially in the Fourth Gospel, Christians are "children of God" (John 1:12), born of the Spirit, their mother. Entry into the people of God comes through birth in the Spirit from above, not through natural generation. Moreover, the people of God are not instructed by human beings like Nicodemus, a teacher of Israel. Rather, the Spirit instructs the people of God, who are born in truth, and the work of the Spirit is made manifest in the lives of those who believe.

The second sign at Cana (4:46–54) brings the first part of the Book of Signs to a close. The passage echoes the synoptic account of the healing of the centurion's servant (see Matthew 8:5–13 and Luke 7:1–10), where Jesus commends the

PASSAGE IN DETAIL: THE SAMARITAN WOMAN AT THE WELL (JOHN 4:1–42)

Often it is important to note the literary structure of a biblical passage, or pericope. The story of the Samaritan woman is structured as a chiasm.[15] In this structure the elements in the first part of the passage mirror elements in the second part. The two parts enclose a central element (D), which is the key to interpreting the passage.[16]

A. Jesus travels through Samaria on his return from Jerusalem (4:1–6)

  B. Jesus asks Samaritan woman for water; dialogue on water (4:7–15)

    C. Woman told to go and bring her husband (4:16–18)

      D. Dialogue on true worship (4:19–26)

    C[1]. Woman goes and brings the villagers (4:27–30)

  B[1]. Disciples ask Jesus to eat; dialogue on food (4:31–38)

A[1]. Jesus resumes his journey to Galilee (4:39–45)

Two important pieces of background help in interpreting this complex passage. First, the interpreter must acknowledge the animosity between first-century Palestinian Jews and the Samaritans. Their mutual antipathy stemmed from an event that unfolded in the decades following the Babylonian exile when the Samaritans opposed the rebuilding of the Jerusalem Temple (c. 515 BCE) and tried to dissuade Persian authorities from funding the project since, in the Samaritan mind, Mount Gerazim was home to the cult of Yahweh (see Ezra 4:1–24; relations were

further strained by the destruction of the Samaritan sanctuary on Mount Gerazim by the Jewish leader John Hyrcanus in 128 BCE). Second, the patriarch Jacob (also known by the name Israel; see Genesis 32:23–32) was the eponymous ancestor of Israel's twelve tribes. For the reader, the name of Jacob recalls a time when the nation was united, and there was no division between kingdoms or between Jews and Samaritans. Early tradition identified Jacob as the source of miraculous waters that well up from the ground at Sychar. An ancient Targum (an Aramaic translation, gloss, and commentary on the Old Testament) exemplifies this tradition.

> When our father Jacob raised the stone from above the mouth of the well, the well overflowed and came up to its mouth, and was overflowing for twenty years—all the days that he dwelt in Haran (*Targum Neofiti* to Genesis 29:10).

The gift of Jacob's water provides a type of the eternal water Jesus makes available: the Spirit (see, e.g., Isaiah 44:3; Ezekiel 36:25–27; Joel 3:1).[17] The use of the Greek word *hallomai* in John 4:14 signals the gift of the Spirit, since it is used to uniquely express God's gift of the Spirit in the Septuagint. Yet one must also reckon with the image in Ezekiel of water flowing from the restored Temple (Ezekiel 47:1–12). The image in Ezekiel helped to entrench a mythology about the Temple resting above the great abyss of

continued

THE SAMARITAN WOMAN AT THE WELL *continued*

creation (Genesis 1:2) or the rivers of Eden (Psalms 46:4; 74:13–15).[18] Moreover, the narrative also plays on the connection between the gift of the Spirit and the gift of the Torah, making the discussion about true worship transcend mere ritual or sanctuary but encompassing the truth of a way of life expressed in authentic Torah observance.

The theme of authentic worship, made available in Jesus, acts as the backdrop for the awkward exchange between Jesus and the woman concerning her "husband" (John 4:16–18). The prophetic traditions of the northern kingdom, exemplified in Hosea in particular, connect the worship of foreign deities (especially Ba'al) to adultery. The word *ba'al* can be the proper name of the chief Canaanite deity, or it can mean both "lord" and "husband" in Aramaic; that ambiguity seems to underlie Jesus' remarks concerning the woman's "husband." Jesus thus raises a question about the legitimacy of the worship of the Samaritans. The sexual inappropriateness of the Samaritan woman (e.g., she is alone at the well in the middle of the day, she speaks to an unknown man, she is living with a man who is not her husband) symbolizes the inauthentic worship of the Samaritans. Conversely, the sexual-romantic-nuptial tension between Jesus and the woman identifies Jesus as the real bridegroom—the true husband—the true Lord and true worship.[19]

---

faith of the Gentile and laments the incredulity of his own people. In the Johannine passage, Jesus is approached by a "royal official," about whom we know nothing more. From the synoptic parallel, one might assume that the figure is a Gentile, but that is far from certain. What stands out in the episode is the faith displayed by the royal official and the manner in which that faith produces faith throughout his household. This growth in authentic faith provides a contrast to the faith exhibited by those around Jesus: the royal official believes the word of Jesus (John 4:50).

The second half of the Book of Signs moves from an exploration of the reactions to Jesus from various constituencies to a presentation of Jesus as the fulfillment and perfection of four feasts in first-century Judaism: the Sabbath, Passover, Tabernacles, and Dedication. In John, chapter 5, Jesus, the new Moses, replaces the Sabbath ordinance as he encounters the paralyzed man at the pool of Bethesda on the Sabbath. Some late manuscripts add 5:3b–4 here, which describe an angel who would disturb the waters of this ancient pool (the Sheep pool) so that the first person to touch the waters would be healed. These verses helped to explain the situation, but they are obviously late additions to the text, added by scribes who sought to clarify the ambiguity of the man's situation. The actual healing has Jesus bypass the rituals around the pool, evoking the scene with the paralytic in Mark 2:11. The synoptic-like passage is followed by an exchange, characteristic of this section of the Fourth Gospel, in which the authority and identity of Jesus come under question from Jesus' opponents (John 5:16). The response of Jesus (5:19–30) demonstrates the christological emphasis of the present section; Jesus has authority from the Father, the authority of life and judgment. Throughout these verses, Jesus speaks without interruption or prompting.

The Passover feast provides the essential theological background to the so-called Bread of Life discourse in 6:1–71. Throughout the discourse, readers are asked to recall the identification of the Torah and manna, particularly in the rabbinic tradition. The manna of the desert and the manna of the Torah find their fulfillment, their end, in the person of Jesus. As such the Fourth Gospel has Jesus self-identify as the true bread from heaven, not in contrast to the Torah but as its fulfillment, that to which Torah is directed.

A play on the word *apolumi* occurs in John 6:12 ("be wasted") and 6:27 ("perishes"). In the former, in the context of the feeding story, Jesus commands the disciples to gather the leftovers so that nothing might perish or be wasted. In the latter instance, he instructs his disciples not to labor "for food that perishes but for the food that endures for eternal life, which the Son of Man will give you." In Jewish tradition, there was a vocation to work or labor to respond to the demands of the Law. Also in Jewish tradition, the manna given in the desert was no longer needed once Israel entered the promised land; it was replaced by the nourishment given by the Torah. Now, in a provocative blend of realized and future eschatology, Jesus presents himself as the fulfillment of the Torah, and this identification supplies the basis for the authoritative teaching Jesus has articulated throughout the Gospel.

In John 6:41–51, the opposition begins to articulate itself once again, this time by raising questions about the origins or parentage of Jesus. The questions from Jesus' opponents are offered on the most banal level (essentially, "Who is your father?"), while the response of Jesus directs the reader back to the prologue and the heavenly origin of the Word. Moreover, in John 6:52–58, the opposition objects to Jesus' reference to eating and drinking. There are obvious references to the Christian celebration of the Eucharist, and most would suggest that this material takes the place of the words of institution offered in the synoptic tradition but omitted in the Johannine tradition. But the evangelist presents a multilayered approach to

the identification of Jesus as the Bread of Life, including his instruction and his promise to abide with his disciples. In other words, Jesus' declaration "I am the bread of life" should not be read as a simple vindication of the Roman Catholic doctrine of transubstantiation. Rather, the person of Jesus, his teaching, his communion with the Father—all help to fill out the different ways Jesus is the Bread of Life in John, chapter 6.

Jesus' provocative remarks elicit a twofold response from Jesus' disciples (6:60–71). As the disciples return, many of them find it impossible to accept Jesus' assertions, but Jesus continues to challenge them. He suggests that they may be looking for further evidence to support his claim to be the definitive revelation of God: "What if you were to see the Son of Man ascending to where he was before?" (6:62). Jesus' question brings forward all that he has previously said about the Son of Man, who has come from heaven (3:13), yet Jesus now promises an Enoch- or Elijah-like ascent to heaven from earth. These disciples have already witnessed the signs of Jesus (i.e., the multiplication of loaves and fish in 6:5–15 and the walking on water in 6:16–21) and have heard the sayings on the bread of life, yet they still refuse to acknowledge the presence of God in Christ. The evangelist signals to the reader that true disciples come to faith not by their own devices, but by means of the Father's revelation of the Son (6:64–65).

When Jesus asks the Twelve if they, too, wish to leave him, Simon Peter affirms the faith of the group by asking Jesus, "Master, to whom shall we go? You have the words of eternal life" (6:68). The Father has drawn the Twelve to Jesus, and they recognize the truth of his words, the words that have caused the others to abandon the fellowship of the disciples. In some ways, this confession of Simon Peter functions similarly to his confession in the synoptic tradition.

Jesus' response to this confession of faith turns to the frailty of that faith by announcing the presence of a betrayer in their midst. Even among those who are most intimate with Jesus and who profess faith in his identity and origins, there is a betrayer who will hand him over to his enemies. The shadow of Jesus' betrayal and his violent death stretches across much of the Passover narrative (e.g., John 6:12, 15, 27, 51), and it emerges again here at its end, pointing to the ultimate replacement of the Passover in Jesus' death.

As the Book of Signs turns to the Feast of Tabernacles (chapters 7–10), the reader will need some background about the basic purpose and rituals associated with the feast. The only available sources on the first-century celebration of this feast come from the rabbinic literature collected in the Mishnah. There we discover that Tabernacles is an autumn harvest festival, and like Passover, it is a time of thanksgiving connected to the narrative of Israel wandering in the desert. Three rituals of thanksgiving structure the observance of Tabernacles (in Hebrew, *Sukkoth*): the water ceremony, the ceremony of light, and the rite of facing the Temple. Each of these ceremonies helps to highlight some of the themes developed in John, chapters 7–10.

- *The water ceremony.* On the morning of each of the seven days of the Feast of Tabernacles, a procession led by priests and singing Levites, accompanied by a crowd of people, went down to the pool of Siloam to gather water in a golden container. Accompanied by the crowds and blasts of the *shofar* (the ram's horn used in Temple worship), the procession returned to the Temple area through the water gate, and then circled the altar accompanied by the singing of psalms. A priest then poured the water and wine into vessels on the altar so that they would overflow onto the altar as a libation. According to the prophet Zechariah (14:12–16),

enemies will make war against Jerusalem, but will be destroyed by a plague; thereafter, all the surviving nations will go up to Jerusalem for the Feast of Tabernacles. Drought will accompany those who refuse to participate. Later tradition draws out the theme of bread as a gift in the Exodus and as a messianic gift (see *Ecclesiastes Rabbah* 1:8). The connection between messianic expectation and the gifts of water and bread helps to illuminate Jesus' self-identification as the Bread of Life and as water in this part of the Gospel.

- *The ceremony of light.* Four candle stands, or menorahs, were set up in the center of the court of the women in the Temple during the Feast of Tabernacles. On each night during the celebration, people danced under the lights, while the Levites sang psalms. The use of light to illuminate a large outdoor venue must have been an awe-inspiring sight in the ancient world. Once again, Zechariah provides a connection with this aspect of Tabernacles and messianic hopes. "On that day there shall no longer be cold or frost. There shall be one continuous day, known to the Lord, not day and night, for in the evening time there shall be light" (Zechariah 14:6–7).

- *The rite of facing the Temple.* Just before dawn on each of the seven days of the Feast of Tabernacles, the priests of the Temple went to the east gate of the Temple mount and faced away from the Temple toward the Mount of Olives. The Mishnah tells us that at the moment of sunrise they turned their backs upon the sun and faced the sanctuary of the Temple, reciting, "Our fathers when they were in this place turned with their backs toward the Temple of the Lord and their faces toward the east, and they worshipped the sun toward the east (see Ezekiel 8:16); but as for us, our eyes are turned toward the Lord" (*Sukkah* 5:4). This ceremony recognized Yahweh as the one true God to whom all worship was directed.

The association of the Feast of Tabernacles with the *eschaton* and the appearance of the Messiah in Zechariah play a large part in the disputes between Jesus and his various interlocutors at this point in the Fourth Gospel.

So much of what unfolds in John chapters 7–10 centers on the identity and authority of Jesus; Jesus is nothing less than the incarnate Word of God, but the opposition continues to find Jesus' claims to authority threatening and troublesome. In response to the suspicions of his opponents, Jesus calls all those who thirst to find in him and in the Spirit whom he will send "rivers of living water" (John 7:38). Jesus' provocation causes further division and tumult in the crowds, with Jesus intervening once again in John 8:12 to proclaim that he is "the light of the world." In both proclamations, Jesus inserts himself into the rituals of the feast. Claiming divine origin and an identification with the Father, Jesus calls for the response of faith. He asserts, "When you lift up the Son of Man, then you will realize that I AM" (8:28–29). Jesus also promises to make known the glory of the Father to all who believe (8:54–58).

PASSAGE IN DETAIL: THE WOMAN CAUGHT IN ADULTERY (JOHN 7:53—8:11)

The story of the woman caught in adultery (John 7:53—8:11) presents the interpreter with a variety of issues, not the least of which is the question of whether it was originally part of John's Gospel. No Greek manuscript of the Gospel contains the story until the early Middle Ages,[20] and early Latin manuscripts include the story in various places: some in chapter 8, some as an addendum at the end of the Gospel, and some even in Luke's Gospel. In sum, the story appears to be a piece of tradition that did not have a home in the early manuscripts. Well-meaning scribes inserted the story where it seemed most appropriate. But in that case, why insert it into John's Gospel and why in chapter 8? A closer reading of the passage may help answer these questions.

The story illustrates an important aspect of Jesus' ministry, namely his attitude toward the interplay between the significance of the Mosaic Law (what the rabbis would call *halakah*) and the principle of mercy and forgiveness at the heart of Jesus' ministry. In the story, the Pharisees apprehend a woman caught in the act of adultery and present her to Jesus as a test case (one may fairly wonder what happened to her partner), asking whether they should stone her as the Torah seems to require. As the Pharisees present the woman, the narrator describes Jesus as writing with his finger on the ground. Jesus stops writing, stands, and invites anyone who is without sin to cast a stone at the woman. He then bends down to write with his finger on the ground a second time. John Paul Heil has rightly pointed to this act of writing as the decisive element in the passage.[21] While some early Christian writers like Jerome suggested that Jesus wrote down the personal sins of those who had accused the woman, the text offers no evidence for this interpretation—in fact, the text offers no indication of what Jesus wrote, only that he wrote and wrote twice.

For Heil, this act of writing with the finger recalls the story of Mount Sinai and Yahweh's

continued

THE WOMAN CAUGHT IN ADULTERY *continued*

inscribing the letters of the commandments with his own finger (Exodus 31:18; Deuteronomy 9:10; 10:2). Jesus' enigmatic action recalls that the tablets had to be rewritten because Moses smashed the original set in anger when he descended the mountain and found the people of Israel in a drunken orgy of worship around the golden calf. For Heil, the story of the woman caught in adultery centers on the covenantal mercy of God, mercy made available through and present in the person of Jesus. The story boldly contrasts the failure of the Pharisees to grasp God's offer of mercy and the authoritative voice of Jesus. The Torah and the Prophets testify to the mercy, or covenantal faithfulness (*chesed*) of Yahweh, that despite Israel's sin, disobedience, and failure, God gave them another chance. When Jesus writes with his finger on the ground, and particularly when he writes the second time, Jesus reminds his interlocutors of their own story. Jesus challenges those who would use the commandments to target the woman while neglecting the narrative that tells the powerful story of God's love, mercy, and fidelity (*chesed*).

The most compelling reason for inserting this story in the Fourth Gospel is its high Christology. Specifically, the story identifies the finger of Jesus with the finger of God at Sinai. This identification of Jesus and the God of Israel remains one of the most consistent features of the Wisdom-*Logos* Christology of the Fourth Gospel, and the story of the woman caught in adultery appropriately highlights just such a Christology.

But why here, why situate this passage at the beginning of chapter 8? The passage awkwardly interrupts the ongoing debates in chapters 7 and 8. Yet the material in this section of John unfolds during the Feast of Tabernacles, or Booths, when the Jewish people celebrated the time of wandering in the wilderness. As such, a debate about the Torah and its application is appropriate here. Moreover, the boastful comments about the Torah made by the religious leaders in chapter 7 help to highlight the irony of Jesus' simple teaching in the story of the adulteress. Also Jesus' continued insistence that he does not judge (8:15) resonates with the drama of this story—and renders ironic the claim of the Sanhedrin that only the mob, "which does not know the law," follows Jesus (7:49). In 8:21–59, the evangelist continues to develop his portrayal of Jesus as the one in whom full divine power of judgment resides, providing a powerful echo of the theme articulated in the adulteress passage.[22]

The final episode in this section of the Book of Signs unfolds around the Feast of Dedication (Hanukkah) where God consecrates Jesus in place of the Temple altar (10:36). As in the previous feasts, the identity of Jesus in relationship to the Father remains central, and implicit in the material are references to Jesus as the Light of the World and the connection to the theme of light in the Feast of Dedication. The account of the man who was born blind serves as a bridge between the Feasts of Tabernacles and Dedication, since both celebrations emphasize the power of light in darkness. As Jesus continues to proclaim himself as the "light of the world," the light that comes to the blind man stands out for its symbolic value. This penultimate sign in the first part of the Gospel highlights the suffering of the man born blind but also exposes the vanity of the religious authorities and counters the accusation that the man suffers blindness as a consequence of sin, either his own or that of his parents.

The theme of light developed in chapters 8 and 9 culminates in the story of Lazarus (11:1–10), the seventh and final sign in the first half of John. The evangelist ties the Lazarus episode with earlier material in at least two ways. First, the evangelist characterizes the encounter with the blind man and with Lazarus as opportunities for the revelation of God's glory (9:3; 11:4). Second, the healing of the blind man and the raising of Lazarus provide the occasion for the Jewish authorities to ground their opposition to Jesus (chapter 10; 11:8). The raising of Lazarus also forms an *inclusio* with the first miracle in the series (the wedding at Cana) insofar as both stories reveal the "glory" of God (2:11; 11:4). This climactic sign recapitulates major theological themes at the heart of the first half of the Gospel: Jesus is the Life and the Light of the World (5:19–30; 8:12–20).

Martha and Mary, sisters of Lazarus, send for Jesus (11:3). Their request for Jesus to intervene echoes the request of Jesus' mother at the wedding of Cana (2:3) insofar as it does not demand a particular course of action on Jesus' part. In response to their request, Jesus declares that the Son of God will be glorified through this illness and thereby the glory of God himself will be manifested. The close connection between Jesus and the Father, clearly presented in John, chapters 8–10, is evident here as well.

In 11:17–27, the scene moves to Bethany and the home of Lazarus, Martha, and Mary. When Jesus arrives, he discovers that Lazarus has been in the tomb for four days, and the corpse has begun to decay (hence the stench discussed in 11:39). Each of the previous healings in the Gospel has been in response to those in desperate need: the son of the royal official (4:49), the paralytic (5:5), and the blind man (9:1). The story of Lazarus thus represents the climactic moment in the string of healings performed by Jesus—but now he seems to be too late to save Lazarus. The faith of Martha is on display in her interaction with Jesus, whom she confesses is the Messiah, Son of God, and the One coming into the world (11:27). Francis

Moloney controversially suggests that even here Martha's faith remains imperfect, however, since she does not echo the words of Jesus ("resurrection" and "life") but instead employs expressions used by others in the Gospel who have had their faith corrected by Jesus, such as the Samaritan woman (4:25, 29) and Nathanael (John 1:49).[23] In contrast, Jesus declares that he is the resurrection and the life (Martha only hopes for resurrection on the last day); in other words, Jesus reveals that he is the source of resurrection and of life itself.

The healing of Lazarus is rich in the immediacy of humanity and has larger implications. Jesus' encounter with Mary and the weeping relatives and friends as he goes to the tomb of Lazarus prompts an emotional response from Jesus: "Jesus wept" (11:35). In the raising of Lazarus, Jesus demonstrates his obedience to the Father; the will of the Father and that of the Son coincide perfectly. He calls for Lazarus and orders him to be loosed from the bonds of burial clothes, symbolizing the biblical themes of exodus, freedom, and victory over sin and death.

The transition from the Lazarus scene to the Book of Glory unfolds in John 11:55–57 with the mention of Passover. The theme of Jesus' death is introduced in the anointing scene, where John has Mary, the sister of Martha and Lazarus, anoint Jesus in a sign of preparation for Jesus' death and burial (12:1–11). The protest of Judas that the expensive oil used in the anointing could have been sold and the money given to the poor stands out as one of the few instances in which the Fourth Gospel explicitly mentions concern for the poor. The contrast between Mary and Judas, already described as the one who will betray Jesus (6:71; 12:4), could not be more apparent. Mary understands the utterly unique significance of Jesus' impending death and the revelation of God's glory while Judas plays the hypocrite, feigning concern for the poor and missing the cosmic importance of Jesus' death. The presence of Lazarus at the anointing of Jesus (12:1–8) helps to further emphasize the identity of Jesus as "the resurrection and the life;" the way to the Father. Enthusiasm over the raising of Lazarus occasions the Palm Sunday scene (12:9–36) and culminates the themes of life and light in this section of the Gospel.

The Book of Glory and the Epilogue (John 13:1—21:25)

The Book of Glory begins with a section that includes the Last Supper, yet without any presentation of the institution of the Eucharist (chapter 13), and concludes with Jesus' Last Discourse (chapters 14–17). In this discourse, the author adopts the literary genre of a "testament," something much in vogue at the end of the first century.[24] Yet, the challenge for readers of the Fourth Gospel centers on the organization and interrelationship of the material in John, chapters 13–17. Moloney offers a chiastic outline that helps shed light on this issue.[25]

An Outline of John, Chapters 13–17

A. John 13:1–38

Jesus makes known God's perfect love (foot-washing) and glorifies God. The disciples are sent and are to image the love of the Father and the Son in their love for one another.

B. John 14:1–31

Jesus instructs the disciples on his departure and on their responsibility. They are promised the Paraclete, who will unite them with the love of the Father and the Son.

C. John 15:1–11

Unity and fruitfulness are the gifts of the disciples' communion with Jesus and with the Father.

D. John 15:12–17

The disciples are to love as they have been loved by Christ.

C¹. John 15:18—16:3

Rejection, hatred, and persecution will come from those who oppose Jesus and his disciples.

B¹. John 16:4–33

Jesus instructs his disciples on his departure. They are promised the assistance of the Paraclete.

A¹. John 17:1–26

Jesus makes known God's perfect love and glorifies God. The disciples are sent and are to image the love of the Father and the Son in their love for one another.

Moloney's outline helps to weave together the elliptical material and to make sense of some of the apparent repetition here. Perhaps most importantly, the chiastic outline helps to direct the narrative forward, to the passion, Resurrection, and the conclusion to the Gospel, where believers are mandated to carry the demands of discipleship into the world.

The Last Supper in John does not resemble the synoptic account except for a few details, such as the mention of Judas and his departure during the meal. The Johannine scene instead puts the symbolic action of foot-washing in the center of the narrative. From a sociological perspective, the act of foot-washing demonstrates the abasement of Jesus and therefore God in his loving service to the world by portraying Jesus as performing a service that even slaves were not usually required to perform.[26] Yet this rather thin interpretation ignores the real focus of the narrative, a focus brought out forcefully in Sandra Schneiders' powerful reading of the passage.[27]

Schneiders offers a threefold typology of service to get beyond a superficial reading of the text. In the first model, service is an obligation imposed on one party. The obligation arises out of an inequality between the parties and subtly reinforces that inequality by imposing the obligation of service. In the second model, the one who gives service does so freely, but the service still emerges from the inequality between the server and the one being served. That is, the server has something, a capacity that the one who is being served does not have; the server freely uses that capacity for the benefit of the other. Like the first model, service emerges from the inequality between the parties and actually reinforces that inequality. Only when service emerges out of friendship does the service escape the perverting dynamics of power and inequality, and it is precisely within this context that Jesus enacts the ritual of foot-washing. In authentic friendship, the good of the other is also one's own good, so that there is no obligation or condescension. A little later, during the meal, Jesus will call the disciples "friends," not servants (15:12–17), and this provides the real context for Jesus' action. The entire act of the incarnation, life, death, and Resurrection is not the act of a master on behalf of an unworthy slave, but the act of a friend. In all of these actions, Jesus acts to abolish the inequality between himself and his disciples. In the act of foot-washing, Jesus ritually enacts all that his journey has epitomized in the intimacy of their relationship, an intimacy with profound implications. And Simon Peter's protest about the foot-washing ought to be understood in light of these implications.

The narrative indicates that Simon Peter realizes, at some deep level, that by doing this act of foot-washing and transcending the barrier between God and humanity through friendship, Christ is abolishing all forms of domination. As the leader of the disciples, Peter's own model for leadership and service must then undergo a conversion, and it is precisely that conversion that Peter resists in the narrative. The desire of the disciples to dominate one another is well founded in the Gospel tradition (e.g., Matthew 20:20–28; Mark 9:38–41; Luke 22:24–27). In the act of foot-washing, Jesus calls into existence a community of friends for whom power and dominance give way to mutual service. "By the foot-washing Jesus has transcended and transformed the only ontologically based inequality between human beings, that between himself and us."[28] This act thus provides the symbolic basis for the instruction and the prayer that follow in John, chapters 14–17, with its emphasis on the relationship between the Father, Jesus, and the disciples, as well as the theme of communion and abiding developed in images like the vine and the branches in John, chapter 15.

The second major part of the Book of Glory centers on the passion of Jesus (18:1—19:42) and brings together the major themes of the entire Gospel. As Jesus goes to the garden and his betrayal and arrest unfold, readers will notice some striking dissimilarities to the synoptic tradition. First, Jesus experiences no anguish over his impending death. In fact, he is resolutely in control of all the events unfolding around him, and it is all for the glory of the Father. Second, his interrogations by the high priest and by Pilate do not include mention of Jesus' action in the Temple; rather, the inquest centers on Jesus' disciples and his teaching. Interestingly, Jesus' response concerning his teaching asks his accusers to question the disciples about what he has taught, certainly a nod in the direction of the demands of discipleship and the necessity of providing witness to the teaching of Jesus and to his identity.

In both the interrogation before the high priest and the interrogation before Pilate, interesting scene shifts help contribute to the unfolding drama. In the interrogation before the high priest (18:13–27), the parallel story of Peter's denial unfolds. In a series of alternations between the scene of Jesus' interrogation inside and the scene of Peter's interrogation outside, the affirmations of Jesus stand in contrast to Peter's weak denials: Jesus' resolute and emphatic "I AM" statements versus Peter's emphatic denials, "I am not." Similarly, in the interrogation before Pilate, Pilate moves back and forth, in and out of the praetorium (i.e., the Fortress Antonia where Pilate performed administrative duties when he was in Jerusalem) to speak with Jesus and then to speak with the crowd. The crowd outside the fortress represents "the world" that has chosen not to believe, and the court of the praetorium where Jesus stands is the spiritual world. Pilate is thus caught between the two worlds as he struggles to decide the fate of Jesus, a task in which he is utterly uninterested and that he is ill equipped to undertake. His lack of interest is manifested in his plea that the Sanhedrin authorities take and judge Jesus for themselves. That he is ill equipped for the task is demonstrated by his question, "What is truth?" (18:38). But the reader knows, Truth is staring him in the face (see 14:6).[29] In the end, Pilate identifies himself as a "friend" of Caesar, the king of this world, rather than as a "friend" of Jesus (i.e., a disciple of Jesus, see the comments on John, chapter 13, above). He releases Barabbas to the crowd while handing Jesus over for crucifixion.

In John's account of the crucifixion, Jesus is always portrayed as in control of the events unfolding around him. For example, there is no Simon of Cyrene to help carry the cross, and there is no anguished cry from the cross as in the synoptic accounts. Rather, Jesus controls his destiny, and those around him, including the two thieves, do not revile Jesus. While the trials or interrogations were accompanied by abusive speech and action, the crucifixion is remarkably

CASTING LOTS AND THE SEAMLESS GARMENT (JOHN 19:23–24)

In all four canonical Gospels, one finds the episode of the soldiers casting lots for the clothes of the condemned man, Jesus. Historians tell us that such a practice would not have been unusual since pillaging was a basic form of remuneration for soldiers up until modern times. The soldiers were often entitled to the personal property of the condemned man, and because the distribution of that property might cause conflict, games of chance would logically provide a means for addressing any discrepancies. At the same time, casting lots for the garments also acts to fulfill what is written in Psalm 22:19, a powerful and important passage for understanding all four Gospel accounts of Jesus' crucifixion.

Only in John do readers find the mention of a "seamless tunic." Readers of the Fourth Gospel ought to note at least two symbolic dimensions of the tunic: it represents the garment of the high priest, and it represents the unity of the church. Scholars often cite the account of the Jewish historian Josephus, in which he describes the high priest's garment as "not composed of two pieces" (Antiquities 3.7.4). This aspect of the garment may be intended to identify Jesus as the new (messianic) high priest, thus rounding out the portrayal of Jesus as the royal messiah, pronounced in the charges inscribed above his head. Moreover, the crucifixion of Jesus "at noon" (in Greek "at the sixth hour") on the day of preparation for the Passover is the same time at which the Passover lambs were slaughtered for the evening meal (see Exodus 12:6).[30] The tunic is often seen as a symbol of the unity of the church over and against the schism that has defined the Johannine community: the schism with the synagogue. Both symbolic dimensions of the tunic find support in the writings of the early fathers, and both merit attention from contemporary interpreters, though neither can be definitively ascribed to the intention of the evangelist.

serene. The complaints of the chief priests (19:21) are not directed at Jesus, but involve the *titulus* of charges that Pilate places over the head of Jesus. This *titulus* reads, "Jesus of Nazareth, King of the Jews" in Latin, Greek, and Hebrew, a (relatively) universal declaration of Jesus' identity.

Two events at the crucifixion of Jesus epitomize the evangelist's theological interest: the "giving" of Jesus' mother to the Beloved Disciple (19:26–27), and the blood and water flowing from the side of the crucified Jesus (19:31–37). In the first scene, unlike in the Synoptic Gospels where women from Galilee are mentioned as being near the cross after the death of Jesus, John has the women interacting with Jesus while he is still alive. Additionally, the evangelist mentions the mother of Jesus and the Beloved Disciple. As he brings the two into a mother-son relationship in 19:26–27, Jesus constitutes the Johannine community that is his mother and his brothers.

Following the gesture with the hyssop and sponge, Jesus serenely hands over his spirit to his Father (19:30). As the soldiers break the legs of the others who were crucified with Jesus (breaking the condemned men's legs would prevent them from holding themselves up to breathe, thus speeding their death without making it any less torturous), they discover that Jesus has already died. To ensure that he is dead, a soldier lances the side of Jesus, and blood and water pour out. The symbolism here is distinctly Johannine and connects to other episodes earlier in the Gospel, particularly the Samaritan woman (John, chapter 4), Nicodemus (John, chapter 3), and Jesus' promised gift of "living waters" (7:37–39). While the image may represent baptism and Eucharist, it fundamentally evokes the connection between the Spirit (water) and the life (blood) poured out from Christ to constitute the community of believers.

The Resurrection scene in the Fourth Gospel stands out against the synoptic accounts. In John, chapter 20, Jesus appears only in Jerusalem, and four scenes provide models of the variety of possible faith responses to the Resurrection. Sandra Schneiders offers a provocative and compelling reading of the finding of the empty tomb, one that revolves around Simon Peter and the Beloved Disciple's discovery of the "face veil" in John 20:1–10 (in the NAB the face veil is is called "the cloth that had covered his head").[31] She concurs with most commentators on two basic points: (1) the passage centers on the Beloved Disciple and the statement in 20:8b, "He saw and believed," and (2) the arrival of the Beloved Disciple at the empty tomb prior to Simon Peter indicates the evangelist's affirmation of the spiritual superiority of the former over Simon Peter. Schneiders argues that the discovery of the face veil functions as a sign that leads the Beloved Disciple to faith, while Simon Peter still awaits the encounter with the risen Christ to come to faith. Schneiders argues that a close examination of word choice in Exodus and John suggests the "face veil" in John be interpreted in light of the face veil that covered Moses' face after his encounter with Yahweh on Sinai had made his skin radiant (Exodus 34:33–35). Moses used the veil to converse with the Israelites but removed it when he went to speak with God. The veil thus symbolized a kind of mediation. In addition, Paul uses the Exodus story of Moses' veil to symbolize the barrier between God and his people, a barrier that Christ has removed: "All of us, gazing with unveiled face on the glory of the Lord, are being transformed into the same image from glory to glory" (2 Corinthians 3:7–18). For Schneiders, the setting aside of the veil in John (it is folded and left to the side unlike the other linens in the tomb) refers to the setting aside of the veil of Christ's flesh so that the glory of God might be seen in Christ.

The Resurrection stories of the closed room and of Thomas's subsequent experience of the risen Christ stand together as a single narrative. The Thomas scene functions on many levels, but there is certainly an apologetic dimension to

Thomas's probing the nail marks in the hands of Jesus. The same apologetic motif is evident in Jesus' eating breakfast with his disciples in Galilee in the epilogue (21:1–14), namely the concern to affirm the corporeality of Jesus even in his risen state. The antimaterialist sentiments of some strands of early Christian thought (i.e., Docetism and incipient Gnosticism) would have tried to find evidence for other doctrines in the Resurrection narrative, but John consistently reinforces the union of the divine Word and the created world (see John 1:14).

AN ALTERNATIVE APPROACH TO SCRIPTURE: TRAUMA THEORY AND JESUS' PROMISE TO REMAIN

Shelly Rambo has recently offered a provocative reading of Jesus' promise to remain with his disciples in light of trauma theory.[32] The word translated as "remain" or "abide" has an important theological function in the Fourth Gospel. In the image of the vine and the branches (15:1–17), in particular, Jesus reinforces a soteriology and even an ecclesiology centered on a participation in and a fellowship with God in Christ. For Rambo, trauma theory, with its emphasis on rupture in history, memory, relationship, and identity that creates a silent or speechless situation, provides a way of rethinking the emphasis on "remaining" in the closing scenes of the Fourth Gospel as Jesus speaks to his disciples following the Resurrection.

Both the death of Jesus and the subsequent death of the Beloved Disciple mark the Johannine community as traumatized. The events of the past, their relationships with Jesus and the Beloved Disciple, and their self-understanding, are all at risk. The question of Jesus and the Spirit abiding with the disciples makes the Gospel a type of "survival literature," on which the French philosopher and literary critic Jacques Derrida wrote extensively.[33] Derrida's notion of "living on" after death becomes important for understanding the function of the Fourth Gospel. By interpreting the closing scene in John as survival literature, Rambo uses Derrida to overcome the triumphalism often attached to the Resurrection, particularly through the literary trope of "haunting." Certainly, for the author of the Fourth Gospel, ghosts and "haunting" represent the exact opposite of what the evangelist seeks to affirm in the account of Jesus' Resurrection: the evangelist affirms the corporeal character of the risen Christ, against Docetist belief.

Yet the lived context of the historical author and that of the contemporary reader stand worlds apart. Contemporary literary theory has recently privileged haunting as a way of rethinking death and the manner in which death can exceed its boundaries—and this is certainly one dimension of the Resurrection narrative in Scripture. In the narrative of the Resurrection, Jesus announces the abiding, the remaining, of the Beloved Disciple after the departure of Jesus and the death of other disciples, including Peter (21:20–25). The task of the Beloved Disciple is to abide in the Spirit as he hands on the text. In the Spirit, the voice of both Paracletes (Jesus and the Spirit) beckons the reader to engage in the work that is to be accomplished. In the handing over of the text, the possibility of abiding, of connecting beyond death, finds realization in meaningful speech that overcomes the traumatic loss of Jesus and the Beloved Disciple. The anonymity of the Beloved Disciple, the surviving one, opens a space for the possibility of the reader giving his or her own name to that anonymous disciple, enacting what must be done in the wake of the trauma experienced by the community.

The original ending of John appears to come in 20:30–31, where there is a final confirmation of the nature of the Gospel and its relationship to the events narrated. But there is a curious supplement or epilogue in chapter 21 that appears to have been appended to the Gospel at a later date. The material in the epilogue includes a symbolic catch of fish that represents the missionary activity of the Christian community, but the narrative centers on the rehabilitation of Peter and his relationship to the Beloved Disciple. As for the former, the epilogue records a powerful encounter between Jesus and Peter, in which Peter is afforded the opportunity to reaffirm and recommit himself to the work of the gospel. Three times Christ asks Simon Peter if he loves Jesus more than the other disciples, and each time Simon Peter responds in the affirmative. The threefold questioning and commission to feed or tend the sheep of the Christian community, drawing on the image of the Good Shepherd in 10:1–18, mirrors the threefold denial made by Peter while Jesus was being interrogated. Although many commentators since the time of Origen in the third century have tried to explain why John employs two different words for "love" in this episode (*phileō* and *agapaō*), most modern scholars think that there is no difference in the meaning of the two words.[34] The material in 21:18–23 seems strange to many readers inasmuch as it bears witness to a rivalry between Peter and the Beloved Disciple. Jesus informs Peter of the certainty of Peter's martyrdom (a well-known fact to John's readers, since Peter was executed around 64 CE). Peter somewhat awkwardly replies, "What about him?" That is, what will be the fate of the Beloved Disciple? Jesus does not answer this question except to admonish Peter that, in the end, the fate of the Beloved Disciple is not Peter's concern.

Conclusion

The Fourth Gospel stands apart from the synoptic tradition and provides a distinctive account of the gospel. John amplifies the christological insights of the wider Christian tradition, but sets the church on course to articulate fully an understanding of Jesus that moves beyond the early images and models. The apocalyptic eschatology so apparent in some parts of Mark and Matthew gives way to a more realized eschatology, one that sees the culmination of human history in the advent of Jesus and the offer of salvation (similar to what one finds in Luke). Although the community behind the Gospel has suffered a schism with the larger Jewish community and subsequently will experience a schism within its own ranks, the Gospel nonetheless presents an account of the abiding and uniting presence of Christ in the life of the believing community. It is this conviction concerning the abiding presence of the believing community in the Son and the Son's abiding presence in the Father that drives the entire Gospel and makes the Fourth Gospel such a profound christological and ecclesiological statement.

| QUESTIONS FOR UNDERSTANDING

1. List and describe the three ways contemporary scholars understand the identity or function of the Beloved Disciple.

2. Describe each of the four stages of development Raymond Brown believes defined the community behind the Fourth Gospel.

3. Citing three examples from the text of the Gospel, describe the Christology of the Fourth Gospel.

4. Pick two stories from the Book of Signs and describe the manner in which the theme of replacement is developed in them.

5. Describe the significance of the Feast of Tabernacles for understanding the material in John, chapters 7–10.

6. List and describe two ways the account of Jesus' crucifixion in John differs from the portrayal found in the Synoptic Gospels.

| QUESTIONS FOR REFLECTION

1. Why is Jesus' rebuke of Simon Peter at the Last Supper in John, chapter 13, so pivotal for understanding the significance of the foot-washing, according to Schneiders? Based on Schneiders's reading, what are the implications of this passage for leadership in the Christian church?

2. The final sidebar on trauma theory and Jesus' promise to remain or abide with his disciples uses the notion of haunting made popular in the writing of Derrida and others. In your opinion, is the notion of haunting a good or a bad, an adequate or inadequate way of speaking about Jesus abiding with his disciples and the church? Explain.

3. In your opinion, given the demands and the sensibilities of contemporary culture, is the Gospel of John a more effective, powerful, or persuasive account of the Gospel than the synoptic accounts, or vice versa? Explain.

| FOR FURTHER READING

Brown, Raymond E. *The Community of the Beloved Disciple*. New York: Paulist, 1979.

Moloney, Francis J. *The Gospel of John*. Sacra Pagina. Collegeville, MN: Liturgical, 1998.

Schneiders, Sandra M. *Written That You May Believe: Encountering Jesus in the Fourth Gospel*. Revised edition. New York: Herder, 2003.

| ENDNOTES

1. See Sandra M. Schneiders, "'Because of the Woman's Testimony . . .': Reexamining the Issue of Authorship in the Fourth Gospel," *New Testament Studies* 44 (1998): 513–535. For a complete discussion of many of these issues, see Raymond E. Brown, *An Introduction to the Gospel of John*, ABRL (New York: Doubleday, 2003).

2. See Raymond E. Brown, SS, *The Community of the Beloved Disciple* (New York: Paulist, 1979).

3. See Francis J. Moloney, *Signs and Shadows: Reading John 5–12* (Minneapolis, MN: Fortress, 1996).

4. See, e.g., Pontifical Biblical Commission, "The Jewish People and Their Sacred Scriptures in the Christian Bible," *http://www.vatican.va/roman_curia congregations /cfaith/pcb_documents/rc_con_cfaith_doc_20020212_ popolo-ebraico_en.html.* (accessed 12/28/2010).

5. See Karen Heidebrecht Thiessen,"Jesus and Women in the Gospel of John," *Direction* 19 (1990): 52–64,

and Sandra M. Schneiders, "Women in the Fourth Gospel," in *Written That You May Believe: Encountering Jesus in the Fourth Gospel*, rev. ed. (New York: Herder, 2003), 93–114.

6. See Ben Witherington, *Women in the Ministry of Jesus: A Study of Jesus' Attitudes to Women and Their Roles as Reflected in His Earthly Life*, SNTSMS 51 (Cambridge: Cambridge University Press, 1984), 57.

7. For a fuller discussion of the Martha tradition in John, see Allie M. Ernst, *Martha from the Margins: The Authority of Martha in the Early Christian Tradition* (Leiden: Brill, 2009), particularly 23–68.

8. Brown, *Community of the Beloved Disciple*, 43.

9. See René Kieffer, "L'Espace et le temps dans l'évangile de Jean," *New Testament Studies* 31 (1985): 395–409.

10. Francis J. Moloney, SDB, *The Gospel of John*, SP (Collegeville, MN: Liturgical, 1998), 35–41.

11. Origen, *Commentary on John* 2.2.

12. See, e.g., Paul M. Hoskins, *Jesus as the Fulfillment of the Temple in John's Gospel*, PBM (Carlisle: Paternoster, 2006).

13. Moloney, *John*, 48–63.

14. Sandra M. Schneiders, "Born Anew," *Theology Today* 44, no. 2 (1987): 189–196.

15. Many different outlines of the passage and even many different chiastic outlines have been proposed in addition to the one offered here.

16. The outline is taken from Fredric Manns, *L'Evangile de Jean à la lumière du Judaïsme*, SBFA 33 (Jerusalem: Franciscan, 1991), 124–127, as adapted in Mary Coloe, *God Dwells with Us: Temple Symbolism in the Fourth Gospel* (Collegeville, MN: Liturgical, 2001), 86–87.

17. On the word *gift* in John, chapter 4, and its significance in the Targumim on Jacob's well, see Jerome H. Neyrey, SJ, *The Gospel of John in Cultural and Rhetorical Perspective* (Grand Rapids, MI: Eerdmans, 2009), 108–111.

18. On the Temple mythology, see Margaret Barker, *The Gate of Heaven: History and Symbolism of the Temple in Jerusalem* (London: SPCK, 1991), 18. One might exercise caution here given the author's provocative thesis regarding the Temple and Jesus, a thesis that has not as yet achieved consensus.

19. On the sexual improprieties of the woman, see Jerome Neyrey, SJ, "What's Wrong with this Picture," *Biblical Theology Bulletin* 24 (1994): 77–91.

20. The story is found in Greek and Latin in the Western manuscript known as Codex Bezae (D) from the fifth century.

21. John Paul Heil, "The Story of Jesus and the Adulteress (John 7:53—8:11) Reconsidered," *Biblica* 72 (1991): 182–191.

22. On the portrayal of Jesus as judge in John, chapter 8, see Jerome H. Neyrey, "Jesus the Judge: Forensic Process in John 8:21–59," *Biblica* 68 (1987): 509–541.

23. Moloney, *John*, 339. He acknowledges that this is a somewhat "maverick" interpretation, but one I think is supported by the text.

24. The genre has the speaker announce his or her imminent departure, recall the deeds or accomplishments of his or her life, and command those to whom the discourse is addressed to continue the work at hand. The testaments of Jacob (Genesis, chapter 49), Moses (Deuteronomy, chapter 33), and David (1 Chronicles chapters 28–29) stand out as examples. Moreover, the first century witnessed a proliferation of this genre, and major works like the *Testaments of the Twelve Patriarchs* serve as a reminder of the influence the genre had in the first century.

25. Moloney, *John*, 478.

26. See Raymond E. Brown, SS, *The Gospel According to John*, 2 vols. AB (Garden City, NJ: Doubleday, 1966, 1970), 2:564.

27. See Sandra M. Schneiders, "A Community of Friends (John 13:1–20)," in *Written That You May Believe*, 184–201.

28. Ibid., 195.

29. Scott M. Lewis, *The Gospel According to John and the Johannine Letters*, NCBC (Collegeville, MN: Liturgical, 2005), 91.

30. The custom at the time of Jesus as described in the rabbinic sources was to slaughter the lambs in the Temple on the day of preparation, and the great number that had to be slaughtered demanded that the priests interpret Exodus 12:6 (the Hebrew text specifies the time as "half-way between the sunsets,"—i.e., noon). See Raymond E. Brown, *The Death of the Messiah*, 2 vols., ABRL (New York: Doubleday, 1994), 847 no. 47.

31. See Sandra M. Schneiders, "Seeing and Believing in the Glorified Jesus (John 20:1–10)," in *Written That You May Believe*, 202–210.

32. See Shelly Rambo, *Spirit and Trauma: A Theology of Remaining* (Westminster: John Knox, 2010), and "Haunted by the Gospel: Theology, Trauma, and Literary Theory in the Twenty-First Century," *Publication of the Modern Language Association* 124/4 (2010): 936–941.

33. Jacques Derrida, "Living On: Border Lines," in *Deconstruction and Criticism* (New York: Seabury, 1979), 75–176.

34. Brown, *John*, 2:1102–1103.

A

anawim This Hebrew word means "the poor" and designates those who wait on God's mercy and action in the Old Testament. Luke's Gospel appears to develop the theme of God's care for the "poor one" or the *anawim* (*ptōchoi* in Greek).

anti-Semitism The denigration or hatred of all things Jewish, especially the Jewish people, has troubled the Christian tradition for centuries. The word *Semite* refers to the descendants of Shem, one of Noah's three sons in Genesis 10:21–31, and refers to a wide sociolinguistic group. Customarily, though, the term *Semite* has been applied exclusively to the Jewish people. In the Christian era, many interpretations of Jesus' teachings have resulted in a negative portrayal of Judaism and have provided a foundation for modern anti-Semitism.

antitheses In the Sermon on the Mount in Matthew's Gospel, Jesus promises that he has come not to abolish the Torah but to fulfill it. He proceeds then to offer a radicalization of Torah observance and morality in general when he contrasts a saying in Scripture with a higher demand for his disciples (see Matthew 5:21–48).

apocalyptic eschatology (apocalyptic theology) This theology emerged within Judaism in the centuries around the time of Jesus and is characterized by an anticipation of God's decisive act in human history to bring about the destruction of evil and the vindication of the righteous. It is termed apocalyptic because it involves the communication of a revelation (*apocalypsis* in Greek), usually highly symbolic, through an intermediary about the end or culmination of human history (*eschaton*). This theology, designed to comfort those suffering persecution, included the idea of a final cosmic battle, the resurrection of the dead, and judgment of the wicked.

Aramaic This Semitic language emerged and spread through the successive Assyrian, Babylonian, and Persian empires, and it came to dominate the region around Palestine even in the first century. Aramaic appears to be the language of Jesus and the earliest disciples. Traces of Aramaic can be found throughout the New Testament.

B

Babylonian exile Following the capture and destruction of Jerusalem by the Babylonians under the leadership of Nebuchadnezzar in 587 BCE, the Babylonians took a significant portion of the region's people into forced exile hundreds of miles away in Babylon. During that time, the exiles longed to return to Jerusalem and to restore their kingdom. The exile came to an end around 539 BCE when the Persian king Cyrus ("the Great") conquered Babylon and allowed the Jews to return home and to rebuild the Temple.

Beloved Disciple This anonymous character in the Fourth Gospel is simply called "the disciple whom [Jesus] loved" (John 13:23; 19:26; 20:2; 21:7, 20). The identity of this character is often debated, and scholars have outlined three basic positions: (1) The Beloved Disciple is a circumlocution for an actual historical person who was either the author of, or the authoritative source behind, the Fourth Gospel (though not John, one of the Twelve); (2) The Beloved Disciple is a literary-theological construction that symbolically represents the ideal Christian disciple; (3) The Beloved Disciple represents both the historical person behind the Gospel but is also a figure that has taken on a literary identity and function in the context of the Fourth Gospel (i.e., a combination of options 1 and 2).

birkat ha-minim As early as the first century, the cursing of the traitors or heretics formed part of the synagogue service and the leader of the service was required to utter these curses. Originally directed against those who cooperated with civil authorities against their fellow Jews, some forms of the curses seem to be directed at Christians. Some have suggested that these curses formed an aspect of the conflict between Jews and Christians in the first century.

Bultmann, Rudolf (1884–1976) Bultmann was a prominent twentieth-century theologian who denied the importance of historical Jesus research. For Bultmann, the proclamation of the risen Christ—the kerygma—provides Christians with the basis of their faith as it calls them to faith as an existential decision in response to God's gift of grace.

C

canon/canonization In Greek, a *kanōn* was a reed used as a measuring stick, but the term has come to be used analogously to that which is normative. The word *canon* usually refers to the collection of texts regarded as sacred, and in the the Christian church the Bible is the canon or norm for faith.

chesed This Hebrew word has a wide range of meanings, but it includes love, mercy, and fidelity. The *chesed* of God "endures forever" (see Psalm 136), and it forms the heart of the covenant between God and the people of Israel.

chiasm The Greek letter chi (X) is a perfect mirror of itself, and the term *chiasm* has come to describe the structure of a text. In this structure, elements within the narrative sandwich or envelop a central item to which the reader's attention is drawn.

Christ (Messiah) The Greek word *christos* translates the Hebrew word *messiah*, which means "anointed one." The title evoked the hope in Israel that God would raise up a descendant of David (and perhaps even a new high priest) to restore the nation and usher in the final age. The title *Christ* was applied to Jesus early in the Christian tradition.

christological moment A scene in the Gospel stories that the evangelists used to express and crystallize their understanding of Jesus—an understanding that was the product of the Resurrection. The scene, rather than a recollection of an event from Jesus' life, is a vehicle for the expression of a postresurrectional Christology.

Christology The disciplined investigation into how Christians have identified and articulated the religious significance of Jesus is called Christology.

codex Refers to the most ancient form of book. It was devised by Christian scribes as the format for the Bible, replacing the scroll format that had long been in use.

D

Dead Sea Scrolls In 1947 shepherds discovered a group of caves near a place called Qumran that contained dozens of scrolls with biblical and nonbiblical texts from the Jewish sect known as the Essenes. The scrolls became important for helping scholars understand Jewish theology in the first century and for supplying some of the oldest copies of biblical books.

Dei verbum (Dogmatic Constitution on Divine Revelation)   Promulgated at the end of the Second Vatican Council (1965), this document set forth Catholic teaching on divine revelation and included an account of Scripture and its interpretation. The document vindicated the historical-critical method as a necessary tool for understanding Scripture.

demythologizing   Term used by Bultmann and his followers to describe the process of deconstructing or "peeling back" the elements of a first-century Jewish (apocalyptic) worldview that are no longer applicable or meaningful today. The process of demythologizing yields a contemporary existential interpretation of the gospel.

Deuteronomist/Deuteronomistic history   The Deuteronomistic tradition is one of the four or more traditions that make up the Torah, or first five books of the Bible (Genesis to Deuteronomy). Emerging in the northern kingdom of Israel in the eighth century BCE, the Deuteronomistic tradition was carried to the southern kingdom of Judah following the destruction of Samaria in 722 BCE. It became the basis for Josiah's religious reforms prior to the destruction of Jerusalem in 587 BCE, where the king attempted to unify the system of worship around the Jerusalem Temple and install a uniform code of covenantal conduct as well. The Deuteronomistic history is the account of Israel's history that runs through Joshua, Judges, 1 and 2 Samuel, and 1 and 2 Kings. The basic outlook of this theology was that Yahweh would grant long life and prosperity to those who were righteous and faithful while the wicked would be destroyed.

Diaspora   Following the Babylonian exile (c. 587 BCE–532 BCE), Jews began to live permanently outside the land of Israel (they were "dispersed" beyond Israel). Egypt, Babylonia, Greece, and even Rome become major centers of Jewish life over the centuries before Christ.

Divino afflante spiritu ("Inspired by the Divine Spirit")   This encyclical letter was published by Pope Pius XII in 1943 and signaled a major shift in church teaching on the Bible. Critical methods were now officially endorsed by the Catholic Church's teaching office.

Docetism   The Greek verb *dokeō* means "to seem," and Docetism was an early Christian heresy that claimed that Jesus only seemed to be human. Several New Testament texts appear to be directed against Docetist Christologies, including the Resurrection appearances in Luke and John where Jesus eats with his disciples, and the prologue of John's Gospel where verse 14 ("The Word became flesh and made his dwelling among us") seems to be directed against Docetic or early Gnostic interpretations of Christ.

E

Enoch (first book of)   This book emerged during the intertestamental period (i.e., between the close of the Old Testament and the first Christian writings) and is an example of Jewish apocalyptic eschatology. It is attributed to the biblical figure Enoch, who was said to have been assumed into heaven (see Genesis 4:17–18). The book was widely known in early Christian circles, and it is particularly important for understanding the origins and meaning of "the Son of Man" figure.

eschaton   *Eschaton* means "end" or "culmination," and it refers to the end or culmination of human history. Several different forms of eschatology are found in Scripture, including prophetic, realized, and apocalyptic.

Essenes   One of the so-called sects within first-century Judaism. It is commonly thought that this group was responsible for the Dead Sea Scrolls found in a series of caves near Qumran. These scrolls contain a number of biblical books as well as biblical commentaries. But perhaps the most important documents from the Dead Sea are the sectarian documents that reflect the worldview and theology of the Essenes themselves. This group was generally composed of those who believed that the Temple in Jerusalem and the priests who operated it were corrupt, and they awaited God's visitation when he would judge the Temple and its priesthood.

exegesis   The Greek word *exegeō* means "to draw out." Exegesis refers to the discipline of interpreting or drawing meaning out of a text. The opposite of exegesis is eisegesis or "putting meaning into a text" (i.e., giving an interpretation or meaning to a text that the text does not support).

F

Fideism   The Latin word *fides* means "faith," and Fideism refers to an outlook in which all that human beings can know comes through faith since human reason is so corrupted by sin. Characteristic of many forms of Christianity during the Enlightenment, Fideism tends to vilify human reason in favor of an appeal to faith and revealed truth.

form criticism   In the early twentieth century, biblical scholars began to turn their attention to the prehistory of biblical material in its original form, usually as an oral text. It was often assumed by form critics that these forms were borrowed from ancient nonbiblical literature and that biblical passages retained these specific forms and patterns. Additionally, form criticism was often concerned with ascertaining the provenance and historicity of a biblical passage. Some important form critics include Rudolf Bultmann and Martin Dibelius.

G

Gehenna   Often translated as "hell" in modern New Testament translations, *Gehenna* is the Greek transliteration of the Hebrew *ge-hinnom*, or "Valley of Hinnom" (or *ge ben-hinnom*, "Valley of the son of Hinnom"). Located outside the southwest walls of Jerusalem, this valley became the site where residents of Jerusalem reportedly offered children as sacrifices to Molech, a deity commonly associated with the Phoenicians in the years prior to the Babylonian exile (see, e.g., Jeremiah 7:30–34). In the Gospels, Jesus uses the word to name a place of punishment in the afterlife.

Gnostics/Gnosticism   A complex dualist religious movement (related to Docetism) that emerged in the second century CE. Gnostics denied the goodness of the material world and emphasized that "knowledge" (the Greek word for knowledge is *gnōsis*) of one's true nature as spirit can bring about liberation from the "prison" of the material world.

H

historical-critical interpretation and method   This term covers a wide range of disciplines, but it is generally concerned with discerning the world behind the text. The historical-critical method seeks to determine the connection between biblical material and both the history of the events it narrates and the context in which the author(s) worked. This approach has come under criticism for its tendency to limit or narrow the meaning of biblical texts.

honor (shame) The ancient world (and many contemporary cultures) determined the status of a person within a social system based on how that person was understood and valued by others. Relationships in an honor-shame culture were dyadic; identity came through relationship to others. Factors outside one's control (e.g., age, gender, health, and wealth) allowed one to accrue honor and, conversely, to lose it through shame.

I

"I AM" Throughout the Fourth Gospel, Jesus emphatically declares "I AM," often with no predicate (e.g., John 8:58; 13:19). Most scholars believe that these emphatic "I AM" statements are meant to evoke the divine name (Yahweh) from Exodus 3:14 where God declares that "I AM."

infancy narratives This genre of literature is common in the ancient world. Important figures in history often had the story of their lives prefaced by a tale of remarkable birth. Two of the Gospels (Matthew and Luke) include infancy narratives and contain some material of historical significance and other material that is primarily a reflection of postresurrectional Christology.

intercalation A literary device prominent in Mark's Gospel that involves the embedding of one story within another so that the stories are mutually interpretative.

Israel Although the word can refer to one of the patriarchs in Genesis (i.e., Jacob), or the historical kingdom composed of the ten northern tribes of Hebrews (922 BCE–722 BCE), or the land promised to the patriarch Abraham (see Genesis, chapter 15), Israel most often refers to the people of God. Israel are those people who are in covenant with the God of Abraham and who live in obedience to the Torah.

J

Jamnia A town west northwest of Jerusalem, it became the center for the reformation of Judaism following the destruction of Jerusalem in 70 CE. Under the leadership of Yohanan ben Zakkai, rabbis began to exert influence and bring about a normative expression of Judaism, and some scholars believe that this development left its mark on both the Gospel of Matthew and John's Gospel.

K

kerygma Literally means "proclamation." It refers to the faith proclamation of the earliest disciples of Jesus and it also served to call others to faith.

kingdom of God The central symbol in the message of Jesus, the kingdom (reign or empire) of God was a tensive symbol (i.e., a symbol that creates tension between the "now" and the "not yet") that evokes the experience of God reigning as king in the world. In the context of Jesus' ministry, the kingdom was proclaimed and inaugurated through the words and deeds of Jesus (e.g., parables and miracles) and stood as the solution to the problem of evil and the fulfillment of human longing. Its arrival is realized at once in the acceptance of Jesus' call to conversion and faith, but its full arrival awaits some decisive moment in the future.

L

logos (word) Means "word," "reason," "speech." In late Second Temple Judaism (around 100 BCE), the *logos* emerged as an important aspect of God and became personified as Wisdom. The Fourth Gospel begins with a hymn to the *Logos* and the incarnation of the *Logos* in Jesus.

Lord   At the close of the Old Testament period, the divine name, yhwh, was never pronounced (except by the high priest on Yom Kippur—the Day of Atonement). Instead *adonai* (the Hebrew equivalent of "Lord") was pronounced. For Paul, the title *kurios* (1) meant a way of referring to the glorified risen Christ; (2) expressed that this figure was due the same worship and honor as yhwh; (3) referred to the Christ of the Parousia (second coming) and only gradually came to be applied to earlier phases of Christ's existence; (4) implied that Jesus is something more than human; and (5) expressed Jesus' dominion over people.

M

Maccabean revolt   The Maccabees were a Jewish family who, in the second century BCE, led a revolt against the Greek Seleucid kingdom that controlled Jerusalem and had outlawed Jewish religious practice. During this period, many Jews suffered torture and death because they would not violate the commandments of Yahweh (2 Maccabees 6:18—7:42). Their deaths were seen as "sacrifices" for the sins of Israel from current and past generations (2 Maccabees 6:27–29). The Maccabees defeated the Seleucids with the help of Rome, and this relationship would set the course for Israel's history over the next two centuries.

Messiah   (see Christ)

messianic secret   First identified by William Wrede in the late nineteenth century, this prominent feature of Mark's Gospel has Jesus instructing many followers not to disclose his identity as the Messiah to anyone. Such secrecy was explained by Wrede as an apologetic device used by early Christians to explain away that during Jesus' lifetime, no one claimed that he was the Christ, but only

after his Resurrection. For Wrede, the messianic secret explains away this problem by suggesting that although everyone knew that Jesus was the Messiah, they simply followed Jesus' instructions not to reveal his identity until after the Resurrection.

metanoia   Often translated as "conversion," and it designates the appropriate response to Jesus' proclamation of the nearness of the kingdom of God.

midrash (pl. midrashim)   A distinctively Jewish style of writing popularized among the Pharisees, midrashim flourished throughout the first millennium CE. It is a homiletic or sermon-like exposition of a biblical text that usually attempts to answer questions not directly answered in the biblical text. For example, the apocryphal book of *Jubilees* is a midrash on Genesis and Exodus.

minor agreements   Among the three Synoptic Gospels (Mark, Matthew, and Luke), there are passages in which Matthew and Luke appear to have made the same minor editorial changes to Mark. These agreements over and against Mark seem to compromise the "two-source" hypothesis insofar as the premise of the hypothesis sees Matthew and Luke working independently of one another.

miracle   Derived from the Latin *miraculum*, which means "something to be wondered at." The New Testament uses Greek words like *dunamis* (power) and *ergon* (work) or *sēmeion* (sign) rather than miracle. Best understood as symbolic acts whereby Jesus proclaimed the kingdom of God, they may also be viewed as dramatic parables in action in which Jesus confirmed the faith of the recipient and challenged onlookers to be converted and accept the advent of the kingdom of God.

Mishnah   According to tradition, considered a collection of "Oral Torah" handed down from

Moses at Mount Sinai, but Mishnah is actually a collection of rabbinic teachings on the application of Torah from the first centuries of the Common Era that was compiled around 220 CE by Judah ha-Nashi ("the Prince"). Some of the material may reflect the attitudes of the rabbis around the time of Jesus, though this is unclear, and it remains an important source for understanding early Judaism.

modernist controversy In the early twentieth century, the Catholic Church identified certain tendencies in modern scientific thought that were considered antithetical to church teaching. These tendencies were lumped together under the title "modernism" and condemned in Pope Pius X's 1907 encyclical *Pascendi dominici gregis* ("On the Doctrines of the Modernists"). The modernist controversy brought modern biblical study into question for a half-century afterward in Roman Catholic circles.

myth The Greek word *mythos* has a wide range of meanings, but came to be used in a technical sense by several biblical scholars, especially in the work of David F. Strauss and Rudolph Bultmann. For these two New Testament scholars, myth refers to the symbolic narrative within which the message of Jesus and the early church is articulated. For both Strauss and Bultmann, the interpreter of the New Testament must get behind the myth to discover the truth behind the biblical material. Few contemporary scholars continue to share this understanding of myth.

N

Nero (died 68 CE) This Roman emperor was the last of Julius Ceasar's line to rule Rome. He is believed to have burned the city of Rome and then blamed and persecuted the Christian community for the fire. These persecutions, some believe, form the immediate context for the writing of Mark's Gospel.

P

parable The Greek word *parabolē* means comparison. A parable is a provocative story or image that teases or plays with the hearers' imagination and expectations. In so doing, the parable begins to force hearers to reconsider their position and their worldview. As such, Jesus' parables were an important tool in his proclamation of the kingdom.

paraclete The Greek word for *paraklētos* has a wide range of meanings: "advocate," "counselor," or "one who consoles." In the Fourth Gospel, Jesus understands his own role as that of *paraklētos*, and he promises the disciples "another" *paraklētos* after his departure. This promise serves, among other things, as a sign of Jesus' love for his disciples and for the world.

Parousia This Greek word means "visitation" and refers to the "second coming of Christ," at which time the dead will be raised and judged, and evil will be defeated. The *parousia* oriented one of the earliest patterns of New Testament Christology in which Jesus would become the Messiah in the fullest sense only upon his return.

Passover One of the great pilgrimage feasts in the first century, Passover celebrated the Exodus from Egypt. The killing and eating of the Passover Lamb and the commemoration of the Exodus were staples of the celebration that occurred on the fifteenth of the Hebrew month of Nisan.

patronage A social, political, and economic system in which the wealthy became the benefactors of those with limited financial or political resources. Benefactors, or patrons, did not receive payment for their deeds, but those who benefitted from the work of the patron (clients), were expected to show loyalty and gratitude.

Pharisees This sect within first-century Palestinian Judaism emerged during the second century BCE as opponents of those who wanted to find some accommodation with Greek and Roman cultural forces that had emerged in Palestine in the Maccabean period (their name means "separate ones"). The Pharisees "democratized" Judaism by making purity a goal not just for the priests who served in the Temple but for all the people of Israel. The Pharisees often argued with one another over the appropriate interpretation of the Mosaic Law. Jesus seems to fit in with this group in some ways. Both Jesus and the Pharisees were laypeople, and they were addressed as "teacher" or "rabbi." Both Jesus and the Pharisees sought to instill in the people of Israel a sense of righteousness and complete dedication to God.

Plato (Platonism) A Greek philosopher who lived in the fourth century BCE and whose philosophy remained widely influential for centuries after his death. Platonism refers to the system of thought attributed to him. Characteristic of his thought was an emphasis on the distinction between the "concrete" world and the ideal world of "forms" (see, e.g., Plato's *Republic*, Book 7).

prefect Roman administrators of Judea were called prefects (*praefecti*) until around 40 CE. Rome had taken over direct rule of Judea (the region around Jerusalem) when Archeleus, the son of Herod the Great proved to be inept as a tetrarch.

preferential option for the poor This phase has become characteristic of Roman Catholic social thought in recent decades, but it also expresses a common theme in the biblical material, particularly in the Old Testament prophets and in the Gospel of Luke. The Bible portrays God as having a unique relationship to those who wait on God's mercy and God's action (the *anawim*) and as acting on behalf of the poor and oppressed.

Q

Q The letter Q stands for the German word *quelle*, meaning "source." It refers to the hypothetical sayings source shared by Matthew and Luke in the composition of their respective Gospels. Q contains such passages as the Lord's Prayer, the Beatitudes, and the parable of the Great Feast.

R

ransom The Greek word *apolutrosis* is usually translated as ransom or redemption. It is a commercial term reflecting the buying of a slave's freedom. It is used frequently by Paul and throughout the New Testament to describe the saving work of Christ's death.

Rationalism In the eighteenth century, many had accepted the autonomy of reason over and against religious faith. Rationalism argued that the only things that are real, true, and good are what can be affirmed through scientific reason. A corollary to this was that faith had nothing to offer an account of the world or of God.

S

Sadducees Another sect within first-century Palestinian Judaism. The name *Sadducee* is derived from the name of King David's great high priest Zadok (2 Samuel 8:17). From the late second century BCE this group, largely comprised of priests, controlled the Temple, the Sanhedrin, and were the primary link with the Roman government in the region. While not as popular as the Pharisees, the Sadducees were highly influential and pragmatic.

Samaritans   Samaria had been the name of the capital city of the northern kingdom of Israel prior to its destruction by the Assyrians in 722 BCE. In the centuries that followed the destruction of Samaria and the depopulation of the area, a heterodox form of Judaism emerged that challenged the religious authorities in Jerusalem. Following the Babylonian exile, Samaritans contested the rebuilding of the Temple in Jerusalem by saying that God was to be worshiped on Mount Gerazim. Animosity grew between Jerusalem and the Samaritans so that in the first century, the region around Samaria was often avoided by pious Jews, and Samaritans were considered enemies.

Sanhedrin   In the first century, the Sanhedrin was that body of Jewish leaders, under the leadership of the high priest, who administered the Temple and oversaw the application of Torah in and around Jerusalem.

Schweitzer, Albert (1875–1965)   A musician, medical doctor, and theologian, Schweitzer won the 1952 Nobel Peace Prize for his work as a medical missionary in Africa. He is famous for bringing the idiosyncrasies and self-serving tendencies of the old quest for the historical Jesus under scrutiny. He ultimately put an end to the quest when he insisted that the historical Jesus was a first-century Jewish apocalyptic preacher who will forever remain alien to modern sensibilities.

Second Temple Judaism   The Temple in Jerusalem was rebuilt around 515 BCE, and this inaugurated a distinctive period in Israel's history and its religious outlook. The rituals of the Temple became more central, and Israel began to increasingly set itself apart from outsiders in an effort to retain purity and holiness. The Second Temple period lasted until the Temple's destruction by the Romans in 70 CE.

Septuagint (LXX)   This is the Greek translation of the Old Testament made by Greek-speaking Jews and subsequently by early Greek-speaking Christians. The Septuagint contains more books than the Palestinian canon in part because when it was being created no one had firmly delineated the limits of the canon.

Shema   The traditional Jewish prayer found in Deuteronomy 6:4–8, affirming the oneness of God and the duty of Jews to worship the one God, Yahweh. It was recited daily by Jews for centuries.

signs   In the Fourth Gospel, Jesus reveals and glorifies God through a series of signs that appear on the surface to resemble the miracles of the Synoptic Gospels. The signs in John cause bystanders to react in one of several ways: some reject the signs and do not come to faith in Jesus, while others accept Jesus because of the signs. Yet, in John, signs also reveal God's (or the Son's) glory. Moreover, the Fourth Gospel praises those who "see" God's glory and who come to faith without signs.

Son of God   This prominent christological role and title is found throughout the New Testament. As a role it refers to angels and any individual or group of individuals who have a special intimacy with God and a special mission. It became an important way for early Christians to express their faith in Christ and his intimacy with God. The Fourth Gospel (i.e., John) and other early Christians go further by describing Jesus as "the only begotten son of the Father," thus stressing the uniqueness of Jesus' relationship to God.

Son of Man   This figure from Jewish apocalyptic literature appears in Daniel, chapter 7, and in the nonbiblical book *1 Enoch*. He is closely associated with God and acts as God's eschatological judge. Jesus regularly identified himself as the Son of Man, particularly when speaking about his own suffering (see, e.g., Mark).

soteriology The Greek word *sōtēr* means "savior." The theological discipline of soteriology is the exploration of how Christ's life, death, and Resurrection bring about salvation. In the New Testament, economic metaphors (e.g., "ransom") and cultic metaphors (e.g., "expiation" or "sacrifice") tend to be the dominant soteriologies.

source criticism In this approach to the Bible, scholars are concerned with the origins or sources used by the biblical authors in composing their text. The Synoptic Problem of discerning source material for the Gospels of Matthew, Mark, and Luke, for example, is fundamentally an issue of source criticism.

Stoicism This Greek philosophical school exerted significant influence on early Christianity, particularly through its use of the term *logos* and through its rhetorical style and its approach to morality.

Suffering Servant An enigmatic figure in Isaiah that modern biblical scholarship has designated the "Suffering Servant" (Isaiah 42:1–7; 49:1–7; 50:4–9; 52:13—53:12). Often thought to be a collective figure (i.e., one that represents a group of people), the Suffering Servant is usually interpreted as Israel or the righteous in Israel. Through the suffering of the Servant, the covenant with Yahweh will be renewed. The Suffering Servant thus became an important image in Jesus' ministry and in the early Christian community for understanding the meaning of Jesus' own suffering.

Synoptic Problem The three Synoptic Gospels (Matthew, Mark, and Luke) contain similar, and even verbatim, material. Yet the Gospels also differ significantly. Put in simplest terms, the Synoptic Problem refers to the problem of understanding how to account for both the similarities and the differences among these three Gospels while acknowledging that the verbatim material and the similarities make it likely that there is a literary relationship among the three (i.e., their similarities and differences cannot be attributed to the vagaries of "oral tradition" or "faulty memories" but must include the use of common documents).

T

Tabernacles, Feast of One of the great pilgrimage feasts of first-century Judaism, the feast of Tabernacles (or Booths; *Succoth* in Hebrew) commemorated Israel's time of wandering in the desert between the reception of the commandments at Mount Sinai and the entry in the land of Canaan. In Zechariah, chapter 14, the feast becomes associated with messianic and eschatological hopes, for John's Gospel, particularly in chapters 7–10, where the themes of light and water are developed.

Temple Although Israelites constructed many temples in honor of Yahweh, the Temple in Jerusalem held special significance since its construction by Solomon. It housed the ark of the covenant and helped to centralize the worship of Yahweh in Judah after the return from the Babylonian exile and the rebuilding of the Temple in 515 BCE. As the unique locus of God's presence with Israel (God's presence centered in the holy of holies in the Temple), the Temple in Jerusalem was the site of the great pilgrimage feasts, and it was the only place of sacrifice for the Palestinian Jews of the first century.

third quest (the) The quest for the historical Jesus has passed through three distinct phases. The first quest (the old quest) unfolded in the nineteenth century. The new quest centered on the students of Rudolf Bultmann and their attempts to recover the historical Jesus. Since 1985, some scholars have discerned a shift in the quest for the historical Jesus, one in which the question of sources, criteria (or indices), the Jewishness of Jesus, and the miracle tradition all play a more prominent role. The term *third quest* was first offered by N. T. Wright.

toledot Means "begettings" and refers to a literary device common to many parts of the Old Testament in which narratives are connected to one another through these lists of "begettings" that record and connect the descendants of various protagonists in the narrative.

Torah The Hebrew word *torah* means "instruction" and refers to the first five books of the Bible (also called the Law of Moses, or the Pentateuch). The observance of Torah was a central concern for the Jews of the first century.

travel narrative In Luke's Gospel there is a block of material from 9:51—19:57 that breaks up the Markan narrative. In this block of material, Jesus is traveling to Jerusalem and hence it is called "the travel narrative." The narrative is made up of both Q material and Luke's own special material, and it represents a summation of many of Luke's major themes.

Twelve (the) Although the Gospels will sometimes use the expression "the twelve disciples," or "the twelve apostles," most historians agree that Jesus selected and designated a group known simply as "the Twelve" to symbolize a new eschatological Israel constituted through Jesus' ministry.

typology This approach to biblical interpretation maintains that texts, personalities, and events of the Old Testament prefigure or point to events in the life of Christ and the early Christian community. For example, Matthew's Gospel depicts Jesus as a type of Moses.

V

vaticinium ex eventu Literally "a prophecy from [or after] the event," this was a common feature in apocalyptic literature. Modern scholars suggest that such "prophecies" were not attempts to deceive or swindle a gullible public; rather, they simply reflected the belief that God was in ultimate control of history and that everything associated with the *eschaton* would unfold exactly according to God's plan. New Testament scholars sometimes characterize Luke 21:20–24 as a rewriting of Mark 13:14–19 and as a *vaticinium ex eventu*.

W

wisdom tradition One of the movements within Judaism that contributed greatly to the development of Christology. The wisdom tradition is embodied in the Psalms, Proverbs, and Job. The wisdom tradition emphasized, among other things, the nearness of God in the practical, everyday world. In Second Temple Judaism, the wisdom tradition began to emphasize the personification of God's wisdom and the communication of that wisdom as God's word—the *logos*. This approach led to a New Testament Christology borrowed heavily from the wisdom tradition of Israel.

Y

Yahweh (yhwh) The name of God given to Moses in Exodus 3:14, and it is often translated as "I AM." It is usually written without any vowels out of reverence (pious Jews in Jesus' day would not pronounce the divine name), and contemporary translations of the Bible often render it as LORD. In scholarly circles it is often used to differentiate the God of Israel from other conceptions of God.

Index